# Advancements in Model–Driven Architecture in Software Engineering

Yassine Rhazali
*Moulay Ismail University of Meknes, Morocco*

A volume in the Advances in Systems Analysis,
Software Engineering, and High Performance
Computing (ASASEHPC) Book Series

Published in the United States of America by
IGI Global
Engineering Science Reference (an imprint of IGI Global)
701 E. Chocolate Avenue
Hershey PA, USA 17033
Tel: 717-533-8845
Fax:  717-533-8661
E-mail: cust@igi-global.com
Web site: http://www.igi-global.com

Library of Congress Cataloging-in-Publication Data

Names: Rhazali, Yassine, 1989- editor.
Title: Advancements in model-driven architecture in software engineering /
    Yassine Rhazali, editor.
Description: Hershey, PA : Engineering Science Reference, an imprint of IGI
    Global, [2020] | Includes bibliographical references and index. |
    Summary: "This book prepares readers to exercise modeling and model
    transformation and covers state-of-the-art research and developments on
    various approaches for methodologies and platforms of model-driven
    architecture, applications and software development of model-driven
    architecture, modeling languages, and modeling tools"-- Provided by
    publisher.
Identifiers: LCCN 2019057490 (print) | LCCN 2019057491 (ebook) | ISBN
    9781799836612 (hardcover) | ISBN 9781799836629 (paperback) | ISBN
    9781799836636 (ebook)
Subjects: LCSH: Software engineering. | Model-driven software architecture.
Classification: LCC QA76.758 .A3686 2020  (print) | LCC QA76.758  (ebook) |
    DDC 005.1--dc23
LC record available at https://lccn.loc.gov/2019057490
LC ebook record available at https://lccn.loc.gov/2019057491

This book is published in the IGI Global book series Advances in Systems Analysis, Software Engineering, and High Performance Computing (ASASEHPC) (ISSN: 2327-3453; eISSN: 2327-3461)

British Cataloguing in Publication Data
A Cataloguing in Publication record for this book is available from the British Library.

For electronic access to this publication, please contact: eresources@igi-global.com.

# Advances in Systems Analysis, Software Engineering, and High Performance Computing (ASASEHPC) Book Series

Vijayan Sugumaran
Oakland University, USA

ISSN:2327-3453
EISSN:2327-3461

## MISSION

The theory and practice of computing applications and distributed systems has emerged as one of the key areas of research driving innovations in business, engineering, and science. The fields of software engineering, systems analysis, and high performance computing offer a wide range of applications and solutions in solving computational problems for any modern organization.

The **Advances in Systems Analysis, Software Engineering, and High Performance Computing (ASASEHPC) Book Series** brings together research in the areas of distributed computing, systems and software engineering, high performance computing, and service science. This collection of publications is useful for academics, researchers, and practitioners seeking the latest practices and knowledge in this field.

## COVERAGE

- Virtual Data Systems
- Distributed Cloud Computing
- Metadata and Semantic Web
- Storage Systems
- Engineering Environments
- Computer Graphics
- Enterprise Information Systems
- Performance Modelling
- Software Engineering
- Human-Computer Interaction

IGI Global is currently accepting manuscripts for publication within this series. To submit a proposal for a volume in this series, please contact our Acquisition Editors at Acquisitions@igi-global.com or visit: http://www.igi-global.com/publish/.

# Titles in this Series

*For a list of additional titles in this series, please visit:*
http://www.igi-global.com/book-series/advances-systems-analysis-software-engineering/73689

*Balancing Agile and Disciplined Engineering and Management Approaches for IT Services and Softwar Products*
Manuel Mora (Universidad Autónoma de Aguascalientes, Mexico) Jorge Marx Gómez (University of Oldenburg, Germany) Rory V. O'Connor (Dublin City University, Ireland) and Alena Buchalcevová (University of Economics, Prague, Czech Republic)
Engineering Science Reference • © 2021 • 354pp • H/C (ISBN: 9781799841654) • US $225.00

*Urban Spatial Data Handling and Computing*
Mainak Bandyopadhyay (DIT University-Dehradun, India) and Varun Singh (MNNIT-Allahabad, India)
Engineering Science Reference • © 2020 • 300pp • H/C (ISBN: 9781799801221) • US $245.00

*FPGA Algorithms and Applications for the Internet of Things*
Preeti Sharma (Bansal College of Engineering, Mandideep, India) and Rajit Nair (Jagran Lakecity University, Bhopal, India)
Engineering Science Reference • © 2020 • 257pp • H/C (ISBN: 9781522598060) • US $215.00

*Advancements in Instrumentation and Control in Applied System Applications*
Srijan Bhattacharya (RCC Institute of Information Technology, India)
Engineering Science Reference • © 2020 • 298pp • H/C (ISBN: 9781799825845) • US $225.00

*Cloud Computing Applications and Techniques for E-Commerce*
Saikat Gochhait (Symbiosis Institute of Digital and Telecom Management, Symbiosis International University, India) David Tawei Shou (University of Taipei, Taiwan) and Sabiha Fazalbhoy (Symbiosis Centre for Management Studies, Symbiosis International University, India)
Engineering Science Reference • © 2020 • 185pp • H/C (ISBN: 9781799812944) • US $215.00

*Soft Computing Methods for System Dependability*
Mohamed Arezki Mellal (M'Hamed Bougara University, Algeria)
Engineering Science Reference • © 2020 • 293pp • H/C (ISBN: 9781799817185) • US $225.00

*Grammatical and Syntactical Approaches in Architecture Emerging Research and Opportunities*
Ju Hyun Lee (University of New South Wales, Australia) and Michael J. Ostwald (University of New South Wales, Australia)
Engineering Science Reference • © 2020 • 351pp • H/C (ISBN: 9781799816980) • US $195.00

701 East Chocolate Avenue, Hershey, PA 17033, USA
Tel: 717-533-8845 x100 • Fax: 717-533-8661
E-Mail: cust@igi-global.com • www.igi-global.com

# Editorial Advisory Board

# Table of Contents

# Detailed Table of Contents

**Chapter 1**
Umple: An Executable UML-Based Technology for Agile Model-Driven Development .................... 1
>    *Timothy Lethbridge, University of Ottawa, Canada*
>    *Abdulaziz Algablan, University of Ottawa, Canada*

Umple is a technology designed to provide the benefits of model-driven engineering in a usable way. It is a textual modeling language, allowing agile developers to quickly incorporate state machines, associations, and many other modeling features into their codebase, with comprehensive code generation for multiple target languages. This significantly reduces the amount of code developers have to write. At the same time, Umple's always-on diagram generation and analysis allows quick understanding of model-driven projects and discovery of their defects. The chapter demonstrates the benefits of textual modeling languages and discusses multiple ways that Umple can help bring modeling to the agile development community, including its support for product-line engineering. Umple is in use worldwide, with the online version hosting over 200,000 user sessions a year.

**Chapter 2**
An Automatic Generation of Domain Ontologies Based on an MDA Approach to Support Big
Data Analytics........................................................................................................................................ 26
>    *Naziha Laaz, MISC Laboratory, Faculty of Sciences, Ibn Tofail University, Kenitra, Morocco*
>    *Karzan Wakil, Research Center, Sulaimani Polytechnic University, Sulaimani, Iraq*
>    *Sara Gotti, MISC Laboratory, Faculty of Sciences, Ibn Tofail University, Kenitra, Morocco*
>    *Zineb Gotti, MISC Laboratory, Faculty of Sciences, Ibn Tofail University, Kenitra, Morocco*
>    *Samir Mbarki, MISC Laboratory, Faculty of Science, Ibn Tofail University, Kenitra,*
>        *Morocco*

This chapter proposes a new methodology for the automatic generation of domain ontologies to support big data analytics. This method ensures the recommendations of the MDA approach by transforming UML class diagrams to domain ontologies in PSM level through ODM, which is an OMG standard for ontology modeling. In this work, the authors have focused on the model-driven architecture approach as the best solution for representing and generating ontology artifacts in an intuitive way using the UML graphical syntax. The creation of domain ontologies will form the basis for application developers to target business professional context; however, the future of big data will depend on the use of technologies to model ontologies. With that said, this work supports the combination of ontologies and big data approaches as the most efficient way to store, extract, and analyze data. It is shown using the theoretical approach and concrete results obtained after applying the proposed process to an e-learning domain ontology.

## Chapter 3

*Vladislavs Nazaruks, Riga Technical University, Latvia*
*Jānis Osis, Riga Technical University, Latvia*

Knowledge can be represented in different formats. At present, knowledge representation as ontologies is the mainstream, while much less is heard about frames. In order to understand the state-of-the art of knowledge frames application, the authors overviewed recent research work in IEEE Xplore Digital Library, SpringerLink, ScienceDirect, and ACM Digital Library from 2000 till 2020. The overview touched such aspects as knowledge acquisition techniques, constituent parts of frames, the actual state of technologies used, capabilities of frames integration with other formats, and limitations. The results showed that native limitations of knowledge frames lead to creation of hybrid knowledge bases. However, hybrid systems also have known issues in performance and inconsistency of knowledge due to a conflict between paradigms. Moreover, a large part of technologies mentioned is not supported nowadays. The results can be useful for researchers who investigate whether to use knowledge frames for managing knowledge.

## Chapter 4

*Ambra Molesini, Università di Bologna, Italy*
*Enrico Denti, Università di Bologna, Italy*
*Andrea Omicini, Università di Bologna, Italy*

Since most complex software systems are intrinsically multi-paradigm, their engineering is a challenging issue. Multi-paradigm modeling (MPM) aims at facing the challenge by providing concepts and tools promoting the integration of models, abstractions, technologies, and methods originating from diverse computational paradigms. In this chapter, the authors survey the main MPM approaches in the literature, evaluate their strengths and weaknesses, and compare them according to three main criteria—namely, (1) the software development process, (2) the adoption of meta-model techniques, (3) the availability of adequate supporting tools. Furthermore, the authors explore the adoption of other promising approaches for the engineering of multi-paradigm systems, such as multi-agent systems (MAS) and systems of systems (SoS), and discuss the role of situational process engineering (SPE) in the composition of multi-paradigm software processes.

## Chapter 5
*Guillermo López, Instituto Tecnológico de Aragon, Spain*
*Laura García-Borgoñón, Instituto Tecnológico de Aragon, Spain*
*Sira Vega, Universidad Politecnica de Madrid, Spain*
*Maria J. Escalona, University of Seville, Spain*
*Natalia Juristo, Universidad Politecnica de Madrid, Spain*

Controlled experiments are commonly used to evaluate software methods, processes, and tools. Literature presents that the validation of software engineering research results in industrial settings is a powerful way to obtain feedback about its value. However, to implicate industry and practitioners in experiments is not an easy task, and, even when a company is committed, frequently the number of practitioners involved is not enough to execute and validate the experiment. This chapter presents a guide of best practices that can be used in order to get a high number of participants that can validate research results from the industry. These practices are oriented to create an attractive environment for companies to conclude that the participation in a research experiment can be interesting for them. In order to illustrate them, the chapter also introduces the authors' experiences when running an experiment about early testing at the University of Seville, where they followed these guidelines to successfully enhance the participation of 76 practitioners from 32 different software companies.

## Chapter 6
*Imane Essebaa, Computer Science Laboratory of Mohammedia, Hassan 2 University of
    Casablanca, Morocco*
*Salima Chantit, Hassan 2 University of Casablanca, Morocco*
*Mohammed Ramdani, Computer Science Laboratory of Mohammedia, Hassan 2 University
    of Casablanca, Morocco*

Agile methods (AM) and model-driven engineering (MDE) are two principal domains of software development. AM proposes best practices in information programming, while MDE focuses on technical part of software development. Both of these domains are in the way of improvement and evolution in order to facilitate the development of IT projects. However, these areas evolve separately despite the great number of researches that focus on improving development project' techniques. Thus, in this chapter the authors present an overview of their approach "Scrum with MoDAr-WA", that aims to improve Scrum Agile methodology by combining two variants of MDE: model-driven architecture and mode-based testing with the V development lifecycle used to deal with sprint development in Scrum methodology. Then they present a comparison study between the standard Scrum process and Scrum with MoDAr-WA approach in order to highlight the authors' contribution to improve agile methodologies.

## Chapter 7
*Adra Hammoud, Ibn Tofail University, Morocco*
*Mohamed Lahmer, Moulay Ismail University, Morocco*
*Samir Mbarki, Ibn Tofail University, Morocco*
*Fatima Sifou, Mohamed V University, Morocco*

Software-defined networking is changing the way we design and manage networks. This prominent paradigm based on the separation of control and management plane is highly heterogeneous with different devices from various technologies and leads to an incredible growing of materials. As SDN expands in size of devices and complexity, it faces greater administrative and management challenges. The paradigm of MDA was introduced using NETCONF/YANG as a way to model in order to deal with these management challenges and soften the development of SDN applications. The researchers joined the MDA and its related concepts as model-driven engineering to SDN to implement a platform called model-driven networking increasing the level of abstraction on development. This chapter presents a comprehensive survey of the research relating to MDN paradigm. It starts by introducing the basic concepts of SDN. Next, it presents the concepts related to MDA, and the YANG which is a modeling language. Last, it highlights the studies introducing the MDN paradigm and its benefits in SDN applications.

## Chapter 8

*Samia Nasiri, ENSAM, Moulay Ismail University of Meknes, Morocco*
*Yassine Rhazali, ISIC Research Team of ESTM, LMMI Laboratory of ENSAM, Moulay Ismail University of Meknes, Morocco*
*Mohammed Lahmer, ISIC Research Team of ESTM, LMMI Laboratory of ENSAM, Moulay Ismail University of Meknes, Morocco*

Model-driven architecture (MDA) is an alternative approach of software engineering that allows an automatic transformation from business process model to code model. In MDA there are two transformation kinds: transformation from computing independent model (CIM) to platform independent model (PIM) and transformation from PIM to platform specific model (PSM). In this chapter, the authors based on CIM to PIM transformation. This transformation is done by developing a platform that generates class diagram, presented in XMI file, from specifications that are presented in user stories, which are written in natural language (English). They used a natural language processing (NLP) tool named "Stanford Core NLP" for extracting of the object-oriented design elements. The approach was validated by focusing on two case studies: firstly, comparing the results with the results other researchers; and secondly, comparing the results with the results obtained manually. The benefits of the approach are aligned with agile methods goals.

## Chapter 9

*Zineb Gotti, MISC Laboratory, Morocco*
*Samir Mbarki, MISC Laboratory, Morocco*
*Sara Gotti, MISC Laboratory, Morocco*
*Naziha Laaz, MISC Laboratory, Morocco*

Currently, the main objective of all programmers and designers is to render interactive systems usable and effective. So, users can complete their tasks and achieve their goals. To ensure that, programmers and designers require good understanding of system characteristics and functionality. This work focused on an approach to automate the process of extracting the system information. The approach is based on the

ADM initiative as the best solution for system's evolution. The OMG ADM Task Force defines a set of standards to facilitate that, like Knowledge Discovery Metamodel, captures design knowledge needed for the construction of future user interfaces. Actually, KDM allows abstract structural and semantical aspect representation. However, no support exists for expressing behavior of system content, interaction, user control, and activities of the front-end applications. The authors hope to alleviate this lack by extending KDM model to fulfill the needs of complete abstract model construction.

## Chapter 10
*El Mustapha MELOUK, MISC Laboratory, EST Kenitra, Ibn Tofail University, Morocco*
*Yassine Rhazali, ISIC Research Team of ESTM, LMMI Laboratory of ENSAM, Moulay Ismail University, Meknes*
*Youssef Hadi, MISC laboratory, Morocco & EST Kenitra, Morocco & Ibn Tofail University, Morocco*

The main key in MDA is the model's transformation. There are two transformation kinds into MDA: CIM to PIM and PIM to PSM. Most researchers focused on transformation from PIM to PSM because there are several points in common between these two levels. But transforming CIM to PIM is rarely discussed in research subjects because they are two different levels. This chapter presents a methodology to master model transformation from CIM to PIM up to PSM respecting MDA. The methodology is founded on creating a good CIM level, through well-chosen rules, to facilitate transformation to the PIM level. However, the authors establish a rich PIM level, respecting the three classic modeling views: functional, dynamic, and static. The method conforms to MDA by considering the business dimension in the CIM level, through BPMN which is the OMG standard for modeling business process. Nevertheless, they used UML models into the PIM level because UML is recommended by MDA in this level. Then, they use IFML the OMG standard for representing web interface model in PSM level.

## Chapter 11
*Nourchène Elleuch Ben Ayed, Higher Colleges of Technology, UAE*
*Wiem Khlif, University of Sfax, Tunisia*
*Hanêne Ben-Abdellah, Higher Colleges of Technology, UAE*

The necessity of aligning an enterprise's information system (IS) model to its business process (BP) model is incontestable to the consistent analysis of the business performance. However, the main difficulty of establishing/maintaining BP-IS model alignment stems from the dissimilarities in the knowledge of the information system developers and the business process experts. To overcome these limits, the authors propose a model-driven architecture compliant methodology that helps software analysts to build an IS analysis model aligned to a given BP model. The proposed methodology allows mastering transformation from computation independent model to platform independent model. The CIM level expresses the BP, which is modelled through the standard BPMN and, at the PIM level represents the aligned IS model, which is generated as use case diagram, system sequence diagrams, and class diagram. CIM to PIM transformation accounts for the BP structural and semantic perspectives to generate an aligned IS model that respects the best-practice granularity level and the quality of UML diagrams.

## Chapter 12

A Disciplined Method to Generate UML2 Communication Diagrams Automatically From the
Business Value Model.................................................................................................................... 218

*Nassim Kharmoum, Faculty of Sciences, Mohammed V University in Rabat, Morocco*
*Sara Retal, Faculty of Sciences, Mohammed V University in Rabat, Morocco*
*Yassine Rhazali, ISIC Research Team of ESTM, LMMI Laboratory of ENSAM, Moulay*
    *Ismail University of Meknes, Morocco*
*Soumia Ziti, Faculty of Sciences, Mohammed V University in Rabat, Morocco*
*Fouzia Omary, Faculty of Sciences, Mohammed V University in Rabat, Morocco*

One of the most crucial objectives of enterprises is bridging the gap between its businesses and information systems. In this vein, many approaches have emerged among them: the Model-Driven Architecture (MDA). This approach is an initiative of the Object Management Group (OMG) and considers the model as the central entity in the software systems development process offering many techniques allowing transformation between models. In addition, the OMG introduces for the MDA three abstraction levels, namely Computation Independent Model (CIM), Platform Independent Model (PIM), and Platform-Specific Model (PSM). This contribution proposes a disciplined method that ensures an automatic alignment between businesses and information system models at CIM and PIM levels. The source model consists of E3value model, which is the Business Value model, whereas, the generated model represents UML2 Communication diagrams, that are the UML's behavior and interaction models. The transformation is achieved automatically using meta-models and ATLAS Transformation Language and proved to be effective.

## Chapter 13

SERIES: A Software Risk Estimator Tool Support for Requirement Risk Assessment .................... 238

*Chetna Gupta, Jaypee Institute of Information Technology, India*
*Priyanka Chandani, Jaypee Institute of Information Technology, India*

Requirement defects are one of the major sources of failure in any software development process, and the main objective of this chapter is to make requirement analysis phase exhaustive by estimating risk at requirement level by analyzing requirement defect and requirement inter-relationships as early as possible to using domain modeling to inhibit them from being incorporated in design and implementation. To achieve this objective, this chapter proposes a tool to assist software developers in assessing risk at requirement level. The proposed tool, software risk estimator, SERIES in short, helps in early identification of potential risk where preventive actions can be undertaken to mitigate risk and corrective actions to avoid project failure in collaborative manner. The entire process has been supported by a software case study. The results of the proposed work are promising and will help software engineers in ensuring that all business requirements are captured correctly with clear vision and scope.

# Foreword

The field of software engineering has known since its appearance a continuous evolution and a great variety of technique. So we find symbolic languages, structured programming, functional programming, abstract machines, database management system, object-oriented programming, design patterns, web service, component programming, etc.

Modeling, which is presented as a key element in software engineering, has undergone an evolution similar to software techniques. UML, BPMN, SoaML, IFML, and other OMG standards offer a perfect architecture for software modeling.

Model-driven engineering is an approach that uses these models to estimate, simulate, communicate and produce. This book will present theoretical and practical cases of the MDE approach.

To date, a reference book was missing, allowing the computer scientist to understand and implement the latest technologies in model-directed engineering, so that MDE is no longer for specialists.

Combining latest theoretical research from university professors with practical research from professional industry researchers and a valuable educational approach, this book represents perfect reference of MDE approach.

*Youssef Hade*
*Higher School of Technology, Ibn Tofail University, Morocco*

**Youssef Hadi** *received his PhD degree from Mohammed V University, Faculty of sciences Rabat, Morocco in 2008. Currently, he is vice-director of the Higher School of Technology at Ibn Tofail University, Kenitra, Morocco. He is a research director, and responsible of many Masters Formations sections at the same university. He is a vice-director of the MISC Laboratory and a leadership of research's teams on Software engineering and model driven engineering. He has valuable contributions and publications in those topics of research.*

# Preface

Software engineering refers to all methods, techniques and tools used to produce software. The main objective of software engineering is to minimize cost, minimize time, minimize risk and produce quality software. Basically stages of software life cycle include analysis stage consisting specifications described in informal human language, then design stage ensured by using design models, afterwards source code resulting from development stage.

So software engineering is closely related with model engineering. Even now the MDE (model driven engineering) approach has been declared as an alternative method of software engineering based massively on models into different levels of software life cycle, which allows MDE automate the passages between this levels, what limit intervention of computer scientist in software life cycle. Indeed, MDE first level is CIM (Computation Independent Model) describes business process in formal model represented by the analysis stage in software engineering. However, MDE second level is PIM (Platform Independent Model) that represent design stage in software engineering. PSM (Platform Specific Model) is the third level in MDE that describes code model represented in software engineering by development stage. In MDE all steps are represented by models, even specifications and code. Transformations between the different levels in MDE begin with CIM to PIM transformation allowing build automatically PIM models from CIM models. Then, PIM to PSM transformation ensured by adding automatically technical information related to target platform in PIM models. Indeed, basically MDE allows recovering source code from specifications in a semi-automatic way.

Today MDE is the best practice in software engineering. Thereby, MDE ensure all software engineering goals, indeed, minimizes cost, minimizes time, minimizes risk and produces quality software, by automating the passages between software engineering levels and limiting computer scientist intervention in software life cycle.

The book is structured as follows, the first chapter demonstrates the benefits of textual modeling languages, and discusses multiple ways that Umple can help bring modeling to the agile development community, including its support for product-line engineering. The second chapter proposes a new methodology for the automatic generation of domain ontologies to support big data analytics, this method ensures the recommendations of the MDA approach by transforming UML class diagrams to domain ontologies in PSM level through ODM which is an OMG standard for ontology modeling. The third chapter touches such aspects as knowledge acquisition techniques, constituent parts of frames, the actual state of technologies used, capabilities of frames integration with other formats, and limitations, the results showed that native limitations of knowledge frames lead to creation of hybrid knowledge bases, however, hybrid systems also have known issues in performance and inconsistency of knowledge due to a conflict between paradigms, moreover, a large part of technologies mentioned is not supported nowadays, the results can be useful for researchers who investigate whether to use knowledge frames for managing knowledge. In the fourth chapter the authors survey the main MPM approaches in the literature, evaluate their strengths and weaknesses, and compare them according to three main criteria—namely, (i) the software development process, (ii) the adoption of meta-model techniques, (iii) the availability of adequate supporting tools, furthermore, the authors explore the adoption of other promising approaches for the engineering of multi-paradigm systems, such as Multi-Agent Systems (MAS) and Systems of Systems (SoS), and discuss the role of Situational Process Engineering (SPE) in the composition of multi-paradigm software processes. The fifth chapter presents a guide of best practices that can be used in order to get a high number of participants that can validate research results from the industry, these practices are oriented to create an attractive environment for companies to conclude that the participation in a research experiment can be interesting for them, in order to illustrate them, the chapter also introduces our experiences when running an experiment about early testing at the University of Seville, where the authors followed these guidelines to successfully enhance the participation of 76 practitioners from 32 different software companies. In the sixth chapter the authors present an overview of their approach "Scrum with MoDAr-WA", that aims to improve Scrum Agile methodology by combining two variants of MDE; Model Driven Architecture and Mode-Based testing with the V development lifecycle used to deal with sprint development in Scrum methodology, then, they present a comparison study between the standard Scrum process and Scrum with MoDAr-WA approach, in order to highlight the authors' contribution to improve agile methodologies. The seventh chapter in this book presents a comprehensive survey of the research relating to MDN paradigm, the authors start by introducing the basic concepts of SDN, next, present the concepts related to MDA, and the YANG which is a modeling language, last, they highlight the studies introducing the MDN paradigm and its benefits in SDN applications. The eighth chapter covers CIM to PIM transformation, this transformation is done by developing a platform that generates class diagram, presented in XMI file, from specifications that are presented in user stories, which are written in natural language (English), the authors used a natural language processing (NLP) tool named "Stanford Core NLP" for extracting of the object-oriented design elements. The ninth chapter focuses on an approach to automate the process of extracting the system information, the approach is based on the ADM initiative as the best solution for system's evolution. The tenth chapter presents a methodology to master model transformation from CIM to PIM up to PSM respecting MDA, this methodology is founded on creating a good CIM level, through well- chosen rules, to facilitate transformation to the PIM level up to PSM. The eleventh chapter proposes a Model-Driven Architecture compliant methodology that helps software analysts to build an IS analysis model aligned to a given BP model, the proposed methodology allows mastering transformation from Computation Independent Model to Platform Independent Model. The twelfth chapter proposes a disciplined method that ensures an automatic alignment between businesses and information system models at CIM and PIM levels, the source model consists of E3value model, which is the Business Value model, whereas, the generated model represents UML2 Communication diagrams, that are the UML's behavior and interaction models, the transformation is achieved automatically using meta-models and ATLAS Transformation Language and proved to be effective. The thirteenth chapter proposes a tool to assist software developers in assessing risk at requirement level, the proposed tool, SoftwarE Risk Estimator, SERIES in short, helps in early identification of potential risk where preventive actions can be undertaken to mitigate risk and corrective actions to avoid project failure in collaborative manner.

The objective of this book is to discuss the current approaches and techniques with illustrations and examples to clearly show the theory and practice of model driven engineering. It will be a crossroads of precious ideas into model driven engineering and will cover all of the major aspects and current trends of modeling. Moreover, it will be a perfect reference book for courses on model driven engineering. The material presented in this book will prepare readers for exercising modeling and model transformation in a better manner. This book intends to bring together state-of-the-art research and development on various approaches for methodologies and platforms of MDE, applications and software development of MDE, modeling languages and modeling tools.

# Acknowledgment

Many people have contributed greatly to this book on *Advancements in Model-Driven Architecture in Software Engineering*. I would like to acknowledge all of them for their valuable help and generous ideas in improving the quality of this book. With my feelings of gratitude, I would like to introduce them in turn. The first mention is the authors and reviewers of each chapter of this book. Without their outstanding expertise, constructive reviews and devoted effort, this comprehensive book would become something without contents. The second mention is the IGI Global staff, development editor and her team for their constant encouragement, continuous assistance and untiring support. Without their technical support, this book would not be completed. The third mention is my family for being the source of continuous love, unconditional support and prayers not only for this work, but throughout my life. Especially I dedicated this book to parents: Halima Haimed (my educator), Bouchaib (my chief), to brother and sisters: Simohamed (my chief), Ouafaa (my teacher), Bouchra (my chief), Saloua (my radiologist), Kaoutar (my engineer) and to my wife Ilham Bounakhla. The third mention is my colleagues for their support: Khalid Janati, Mounir Azzab and Khalil Moumen.

*Yassine Rhazali*
*Moulay Ismail University of Meknes, Morocco*
*March 10, 2020*

# Chapter 1
# Umple:
## An Executable UML-Based Technology for Agile Model-Driven Development

**Timothy Lethbridge**
https://orcid.org/0000-0001-9410-2056
*University of Ottawa, Canada*

**Abdulaziz Algablan**
https://orcid.org/0000-0001-5839-7782
*University of Ottawa, Canada*

## ABSTRACT

*Umple is a technology designed to provide the benefits of model-driven engineering in a usable way. It is a textual modeling language, allowing agile developers to quickly incorporate state machines, associations, and many other modeling features into their codebase, with comprehensive code generation for multiple target languages. This significantly reduces the amount of code developers have to write. At the same time, Umple's always-on diagram generation and analysis allows quick understanding of model-driven projects and discovery of their defects. The chapter demonstrates the benefits of textual modeling languages and discusses multiple ways that Umple can help bring modeling to the agile development community, including its support for product-line engineering. Umple is in use worldwide, with the online version hosting over 200,000 user sessions a year.*

## INTRODUCTION

When software engineers refer to *models,* they generally are referring to abstract representations of some part of a software system. Since the late 1990's UML has been the most widely usedlanguage to express such models, rendering them as several different types of diagrams, such as class diagrams and state machines.

Models are typically contrasted with *source code*, generally written in a textual programming language. Almost all software is currently written by humans is in the form of such source code, which is

DOI: 10.4018/978-1-7998-3661-2.ch001

the master formal description from which the system is built. By *formal*, we mean machine interpretable in this context.

The main contribution of the technology discussed in this chapter is a demonstration of how source-code based approaches and diagrammatic modeling approaches can be brought together as one, enabling greater adoption of model-based agile software engineering processes. Added benefits include improvements in separation of concerns, feature-based development, and product-line based development.

## Modeling Adoption Challenges

Petre(2013) showed that modeling in UML is not as widely practiced as its proponents might have expected. UML diagrams are commonly just drawn on whiteboards to help developers better understand what source code will be needed. UML diagrams, often created using a simple drawing tool, are reasonably common in documentation, but often become out of date. A key observation is that models are not widely used to generate code, except in certain niches such as some kinds of safety-critical software.

The grand vision of many modeling proponents is that models should *become* the master formal source of the system, or at least of parts of systems. Models can currently be used to verify or check designs for *planned* source code, with the source code then being handwritten. But comprehensive code generation seems the most reasonable path forward. Code generation avoids both duplication of development effort, and errors caused by incorrect human transformation of models into code.

Unfortunately, our own research (Agner, Lethbridge & Soares, 2019; Forward & Lethbridge, 2008) has shown that existing modeling tools have numerous weaknesses, particularly regarding code generation. Expensive, proprietary and complex tools are often able to generate reasonable code, but open source tools accessible to average developers tend to create only stubs or no code at all. A key goal for the work reported in this chapter was to create a highly usable tool that can do comprehensive and reliable code generation and build complete systems.

## Beneficial Properties of a Source-Code-Like Format

Creating a tool that manipulates models primarily in the form of diagrams will not, we realized, satisfy the vast majority of developers, even if such a tool was fantastic at code generation. Developers value many other properties of their textual source code:

1. **Compact and readable**: Source code tends to be compact, whereas diagrams consume a lot of space visually. By analogy, there was a fashion in the 1960's to create flowcharts, but good structured code was later found to take much less space and be as readable.
2. **Documentable**: Source code can be easily commented, with few constraints as to where the comments are placed, and without adding as much visual complexity as would be required on a diagram.
3. **Comparable and mergeable**: Versions of source code can be easily compared as *deltas* with widely used 'diff' tools; furthermore, version-control tools like Git store these deltas compactly, and allow easy merging of proposed changes. Code review tools allow reviewers to readily evaluate and comment on the precise changes being proposed in deltas. We explored this topic in earlier research (Badreddin, Lethbridge and Forward, 2014).

4. **Focusable**: Source code can be easily searched, with search results organized so as to focus onlists of relevant lines. Similarly, results of analysis (such as a compiler presenting errors and warnings), or the results of tests can be organized as lists of source code lines that need attention.

5. **Parsable and transformable**: Source code can be easily parsed, so third-party tools can be created with little effort to perform tasks such as transformation. This facilitates exchange among tools. Search-and-replace can be done easily to facilitate refactoring.

6. **Sophisticatedly editable**: Source code can be edited in any text editor, so useful features of text editors can be used (e.g. block collapsing), auto-indenting, and syntax assistance.

7. **Composableto specify variants**: Capabilities such as macros, file inclusion, and so on, can be layered onto textual forms easily.

Many of these properties of source code are particularly important for supporting the trend towards *agility*, the center of which is the ability to make frequent, small andproperly tested changes to systems. In particular, agility demands good version control and the ability comment on deltas (property 3); it demands ease of debugging through search, analysis and tool assistance (properties 4-6);it requires automatic testing, with test failures pointing to the right place (property 4); it requires easy refactoring (property 5); and it encourages lightweight in-code documentation (property 2).

Properties 3 and 7 also facilitate the ability to organize software into features (feature-oriented development) or variants in a product line (product line engineering).

The software engineering community has created textual languages such as XMI and other XML schemas to allow rendering of models as text for exchange. But only aspects of property 5 really apply to such languages. In particular, such formats are far from human readable(other than toy examples), and cannot be usefully edited by humans.

Table 1summarizes how the seven benefits of a textual format tend to be challenged or lacking when UML modeling is done diagrammatically with reliance on XMIto store and exchange the models. Later on, we will seethat Umple has done of the drawbacks.

*Table 1. Challenges faced by relying on models to be primarily conveyed as diagrams*

| Advantage of a Textual Form | Drawbacks of Reliance on Diagram Forms of Models |
|---|---|
| 1. Compact and readable | Diagrams are not compact; XMI is not human-readable |
| 2. Documentable | Comments are either hidden (requiring clicking/hovering to see them), or cause clutter if shown as 'callouts'. |
| 3. Comparable and Mergeable | This has been a challenging research problem, and tools are complex (Brunet et al, 2006; Bendix et al, 2008). Small changes to diagrams can lead to large changes in the saved XMI, meaning that ordinary text diffs do not work. |
| 4. Focusable | Search results or warning messages that point to places on a variety of diagrams can be unwieldy. |
| 5. Parsable and transformable | Tools require deeper semantic knowledge than required for textual formats. Also, XMI has long had problems with subtly incompatible versions of its schemas (Lundell, Lings, Persson &Mattsson, 2006). |
| 8. Sophisticatedly editable | Requires specific editors, so a market for many editors does not develop easily. |
| 9. Composable to create variants | This has been a challenging research problem for models (Jayaraman, Whittle, Elkhodary& Gomaa 2007). |

Despite Table 1, we do not mean to imply that diagrams are bad or to be avoided. They can help humans understand certain aspects of software much better than a textual format. As we will see in the next section, it is key to Umple that both text *and* diagram forms must exist simultaneously.

## Code-Diagram Duality and Mutual Benefit

Early in our research, we realized that the aboveproperties of textual languages are so compelling that textual 'code' is here to stay for the foreseeable future as a dominant way to represent mostsoftware.

But that certainly does not mean that diagrammatic models are irrelevant. Being able to see a diagram of how classes and their instances are organized (a class diagram), how a system behaves (a state diagram), or many other system views, isalsoextremely useful.

It became clear to us that some software engineering tasks are easier to do with diagrams and some are better done by working with a textual form. Reverse engineering tools can allow extraction of diagrams from arbitrary source, but such tools tend to break if the source code does not quite conform to expected conventions. Additionally, editing the diagram in order to update the source code – *round-trip engineering*(Medvidovic,Egyed& Rosenblum, 1999) – is a source of fragility. Engineers we have worked with report, "it just doesn't work in practice."

We became convinced therefore that what is needed is a modeling language that allows diagram and code forms to be simultaneously available, representing different views of the same model. We came to use the term *code-diagram duality* to describe this.

## Desired Characteristics of a Textual Modeling Technology

In 2007 we set out to design Umple as a language and accompanying toolset with the following characteristics:

- It has comprehensive and robust code generation for multiple languages.
- It has a simple-to-use readable textual representation of common UML constructs, that looks like what one expects in a good programming language.
- It preserves all the benefits of textual source code listed earlier. Indeed, it goes beyond UML in ways enabled by its textual form, such as allowing various ways to separate concerns textually (aspects, traits, mixins, and mixsets, all discussed later).
- Diagram *editing* is also available, enabling updating of the text without round trip engineering.
- It allows real-time diagram generation in several target languages so developers can see the code from the textual and diagram perspective at all times.
- It blends in with traditional code written in the same target languages, allowing parts of systems that cannot be represented using the modeling constructs to be incorporated parsimoniously in the same textual language. Such code is sometimes called 'action language' code.
- It is agnostic to the model driven software engineering approach being used, and can be used to represent models ranging from abstract technology-independent business models, all the way to concrete executable systems. This will be discussed more in the section on Model-Driven Engineering later.
- It allows comprehensive analysis of models, pointing out errors and warnings just like a programming language compiler.

- It free to use and open source (Github 2020a).

Umple, has been under development since 2007 and is now widely used, particularly in educational institutions, where it has been shown to help improve student grades (Lethbridge, Mussbacher, Forward & Badreddin, 2011), and has been found to be usable by students (Agner, Lethbridge & Soares, 2019). Umple's online server (UmpleOnline, 2020), which allows users to work with Umple in the cloud, receives over 200,000 user sessions, and over 2 million user interactions per year. Use of Umple on private computers (in Docker, in Eclipse and Visual Studio Code plugins, or on the command line) is not tracked, for privacy reasons.

## Other Approaches to Textual Modeling

Umple is certainly not the only textual modeling language. TextUML(Abstratt, 2020), USE (Gogola, Büttner, &Richters, 2007) and txtUML (Dévai, Kovács& An, 2014) are other examples of textual syntaxes for UML. Nor is Umple the only tool that enables executability of UML: Executable UML(Mellor &Balcer, 2002) is an example. Indeed, UML is not the only modeling language: SDL (Rockstrom&Saracco, 1982) has been around for over 35 years and has a textual form. Additionally, many 'formal methods' languages are textual and can be used for modeling parts of systems.Umple is the only current tool that combines all the above characteristics, or even most of them.

## Research Questions Addressed

The main research gap addressed by Umple is to a gain a fuller understanding of the benefits of textual vs. diagrammatic modeling and code-diagram duality, especially with regard to agility. We also want to build a technology that can scale, to build very large models with this technology (such as Umple itself) and to get it into widespread use in the open-source community.

By doing the above will we be able to delve deep into new modeling problems that emerge 'at scale'. Existing large-scale models tend to be hidden in proprietary technologies that are only minimally accessible to researchers.

In the coming section we give an outline of key Umple features, showing how Umple's textual representation aligns with UML diagrams, and goes beyond UML.

## OVERVIEW OF UMPLE

In this section we outline key features of Umple, along with some of the design rationale relating to agility, textual modeling and product-line or feature-based development.We give examples from a case study. Complete details of all Umple features can be found in the Umple user Manual (Umple, 2020a) and in the various papers cited in the following sections.

The user manual is a live document, with over 450 examples, all of which can be loaded into Umple-Online for analysis. The examples include cases that trigger all of the over 200 potential modeling problems that Umple's analysis engine can detect, along with their potential solutions.

Umple can be used in different environments: In addition to UmpleOnline, there are bindings for Microsoft Visual Studio and Eclipse, as well as the ability to use any text editor. A Docker image is also available, allowing offline use of UmpleOnline.

An Umple system is organized as a set of files with the .ump suffix. Within the files are various top-level entities (classes, associations, traits, state machines, mixsets and so on) all described later. Some elements can contain others (for example, a state machine has states, and a class has attributes and associations). An important feature of Umple is the *mixin*. If two top-level elements are repeated with the same name, then the contents of the top-level elements are 'mixed in' together to create a single top-level element. We will see examples of this later on.

## UML Class Diagram Support

## Classes

Classes are a core construct any object-oriented technology. Java, C++, PHP and other programming languages all support ways to declare classes that contain methods and instance variables (often called fields, and called attributes in UML), as well as generalizations (extends, or subclass relationships). Umple classes are declared in a very similar way as in other textual object-oriented languages.

The case study Umple code in the next section has three classes, starting on lines 7, 13 and 20.

Umple supports *interfaces*, but to simplify this chapter we will not discuss them.

## Traits

In addition to classes, Umple supports the notion of *traits* (Abdelzad & Lethbridge, 2015). A trait can be considered a class fragment, containing any elements that can be present in classes. One or more traits can be incorporated into a given class by a *copying* process, as opposed to inheritance. The concept of traits goes beyond UML and enables support for multiple inheritance, product-line development and feature-based development. For example, each trait incorporated into a class can serve as part of the implementation of a feature. Changing a trait could also be a way to create a variant product in product-line development.

Traits can be arranged in generalization hierarchies, and Umple performs extensive semantic analysis to ensure that traits are used to build classes in an error-free way.

The case study code below shows a trait starting at line 3. The trait is invoked using the *isA* keyword in the three classes, starting at lines 8, 14 and 21, ensuring that the classes all have the features that come with being devices. Generalization could have been used to achieve the same effect, but later on in the case study we will need to add a superclass to the SmartLight class; the use of traits helps avoid the complexity of multiple inheritance that would otherwise be required, and enables generation of code in languages that don't support multiple inheritance.

## Attributes

Umple attributes, just like in Java or C++, are specified using a type name followed by the attribute name. However, as in UML, Umple attributes are more than just variables. They are used to generate accessor methods (get and set methods), and are subject to constraints (discussed later).

Umple generates code to ensure that attributes are properly initialized in the constructor. If the developer does not want this initialization, they can switch it off with the stereotype *lazy*.

The case study code below shows attributes at lines 4, 15, 16 and 17. Note that line 4 has no specified type: In Umple,*String* is used as the default type.Badreddin, Forward and Lethbridge (2013a) and Forward (2010) give full details of Umple attributes.

## Generalization

Umple generalizations follow UML semanticsand are represented using the 'isA' keyword in the same way that traits are included in classes. Generalizations are translated into the different needed syntaxes of Java, PhP and C++ during code generation.There is an example of generalization later in the case study.

## Methods

Umple generates an API from each model with many methods generated from the modeling constructs (associations, attributes, etc.) present. Examples include methods to add a link to an association, or to set an attribute. Umple can generate a Javadoc-like set of webpages describing this API, with pointers back to the original Umple files.

The developer may also write *user-defined methods* to perform arbitrary actions; theseare written in Umple classes very much as they would be in the target language (Java, C++, Php etc.). The Umple compiler outputs them relatively unchanged when generating code. Umple does, however:

- Enable injection of preconditions into methods (see the section on constraints below)
- Enable injection of code into the start, end and labeled locations in methods (see the section on aspects below)
- Allow a method to have multiple bodies, one for each target language to be generated.

Methods can be included or excluded from being visible in class diagrams, by specifying an argument to the diagram generators.

Even in diagrammatic modeling approaches, the bodies of methods are written textually, so they are a natural fit for Umple's textual form.

## Associations

UML and Umple go further than popular programming languages and allows specification the key concept *association*. Associations describe the relationships (links) that will exist at run-time between instances of the associated classes. The case study code below shows associations on lines9, 10 and 22. When code is generated from this Umple sample, there will be methods to add and delete links of the associations, always maintaining referential integrity as in a database. Full details of Umple associations are described by Forward (2010) and Badreddin, Forward and Lethbridge (2013b).

## Mixsets

An additional feature of Umple shown in the sample code below is the *mixset*, as appears in lines 9 and 22. This builds on the notion of the mixin. A mixset block has a name and allows conditional modeling.The associations in lines 9 and 22 only appear if the 'basic' mixset is activated. The *use* statement in Line 1 performs this activation, but activation could also be performed by a build script passing the mixset name to the Umple compiler.

Multiple statements or groups of statements can be tagged with the same mixset label, to group them as a feature. Like traits, mixsets are yet another capability that takes advantage of Umple's textual programming-language-like form and goes beyond UML. Mixsets are discussed by Lethbridge and Algablan (2018).

## Case Study: Smart Light System

In order to explain various features of Umple, we present the following small case study, showing how it can be modeled in two steps using Umple's features.

A company is developing a smart light system. The hardware consists of a controller and various switches and lights connected by WiFi or Bluetooth. The user interface of the controller is a smartphone app; this is used to configure the system, and can be used in place of switches.

The system is to be developed in an agile manner, in a series of sprints. New versions will be released when each sprint is complete. Here we show two sprints only.

## Sprint 1: Basic Features

Each light has a serial number that is used to connect it to the system and a maximum lumens. All lights can have adjustable brightness between zero and 100%. Lights can be configured with a default percentage of the maximum brightness. A basic switch can be set to control a light. Switches also have a serial number.

## Sprint 2: Grouping and Modes

The second release of the case study system adds the ability for lights to have a name, and for switches to have dimmers. Lights can now be in named groups to allow several to be controlled as if they were a single light. A switch can be set to control a light or group.

An additional capability added in the second release is that the system can be set to random "away safety" mode, to simulate a residence being occupied, and "alarm" mode where all lights flash between maximum brightness and 75% brightness to alert others.

## Umple Model Code and Generated Outputs for Sprint 1 of the Case Study

The model code below might be put in a file called SmartLightV1.ump.We invite the readers to load this code and try it out; it is available as an example in UmpleOnline. The reader can try commenting out line 1 to see the associations at lines 9 and 22 disappear.

When processed by Umple, these 23 lines can be used to produce 765 lines of Java, as well as the diagrams shown in Figure 1 and Figure 2, and many other possible artifacts.

Figure 1 is a standard UML class diagram. Its 2-dimensional layout, with classes as nodes and associations as arcs, can greatly help the developer understand the system. UmpleOnline even allows editing of class diagrams, with edits instantly reflected in the textual code.But as we have been arguing, the textual notation below allows many complementary benefits: The text has comments, can be searched, errors can be easily highlighted, editing the text tends to be faster than editing a diagram, and git commits and merges work very well with it.

Figure 2 is a UML class diagram generated from the same code, but with the option to explicitly show traits, rather than merging them into the code. This illustrates how generating multiple diagrams (instantly) from a given textual source can be very useful.

```
1        use basic;
2
3        trait Device {
4          serialNumber;    // attribute; String by default
5          }
6
7        class SmartLightConsole {
8          isA Device;
9          mixset basic { 1 -- * SmartLight; }
10          1 -- * Switch;
11          }
12
13        class SmartLight {
14          isA Device;
15          Integer maxLumens;
16          Integer defaultBrightness; // value set to when simply 'on'
17          Integer currentBrightness;
18          }
19
20        class Switch {
21          isA Device;
22          mixset basic { * controller -- * SmartLight; }
23          }
```

## Umple Model Code for Sprint 2 of the Case Study

Below, we show relevant modeling code for Sprint 2 of the case study. We have added the following.

- New classes LightOrGroup (line 4), LightGroup (line 12), and DimmableSwitch (line 26).
- Generalizations (lines 9, 13 and 27).

*Figure 1. Class diagram of the basic version of the Smart Light system, as generated from the Umple code. The trait is invisible since its elements are folded into the classes.*

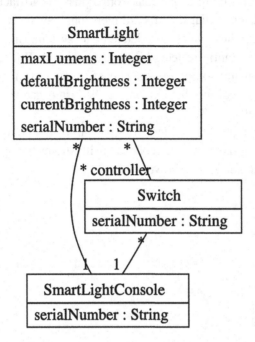

*Figure 2. Class diagram showing the trait explicitly.*

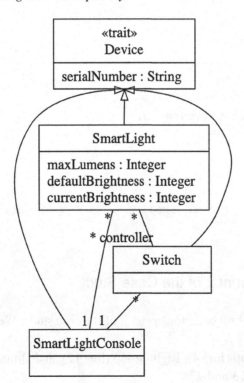

- Redefinitions of the associations from the original version, so that switches and the console are now connected to LightOrGroup. This is in the mixset starting in line 17, which is activated on line 1.
- Mixins adding extra functionality to classes SmartLight (line 8), SmartLightConsole (lines 17 and 31) and Switch (line 21), This ability to add new features to a class via mixins is a key feature of Umple, and is yet another way that Umple leverages its textual format.
- A state machine (lines 32-45), that will be explained in the next section.

The following code might be put in SmartLightV2.ump; when processed along with SmartLightV1. ump this generates 1299 lines of Java. Note that this case study shows one of many ways of organizing the source code. We have chosen to create a series of version-specific files. The system could instead be organized by class, or the two files could be merged.

```
1       use controlGroups;
2
3       // A named element that can be controlled as a unit, e.g.
4       'Living Room'
5       class LightOrGroup {
6         name;
7       }
8
9       class SmartLight {
10        isA LightOrGroup;
11      }
12
13      class LightGroup {
14        isA LightOrGroup;
15        0..1 -- * SmartLight;
16      }
17
18      mixset controlGroups {
19        class SmartLightConsole {
20          1 -- * LightOrGroup;
21        }
22        class Switch {
23          * controller -- * LightOrGroup;
24        }
25      }
26
27      class DimmableSwitch {
28        isA Switch;
29        Integer dimmerSetting;
30      }
31
```

```
32        class SmartLightConsole {
33          mode {
34            normal {
35              goAway -> awaySafety;
35              panicButton ->alarm;
37            }
38            awaySafety {
39              do {cycleLights();}
40              backHome -> normal;
41            }
42        alarm {
43              do {flashLights();}
44              panicButton -> Normal;
45            }
46          }
47        }
```

Figure 3 shows the class diagram generated from the above.

*Figure 3. Class diagram of the second version of the Smart Light system.*

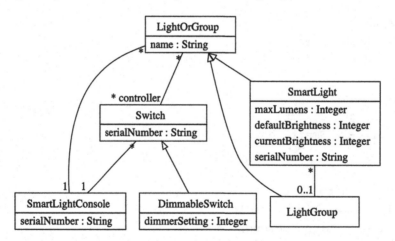

## UML State Machine Support

A state machine can be used to define the behavior of an entity such as an object, user interface, subsystem orentire system; Umple follows UML state machine semantics. The entity controlled by the state machine is said to be in a given *state*at each point in time; the initialization of the entity places it in a defined *start state*. When in a particular state,the entity has certain behaviour. This includes *actions* on entry and exit from the state, ongoing *activities* while in the state, and receptiveness to a certain set of *events* that can cause it to*transition* to another state (where it behaves differently). Constraints called *guards* can prevent this; guards are discussed more later in the section about constraints.

Although to save space we have not shown it in this chapter, states can be grouped hierarchically, allowing transitions to be defined that can take the entity from onestate or *superstate* (group of states) to another state or to the start state of another superstate. The states defined within a group are called *substates*.Several state machines operating concurrently can be defined for the same entity or within a superstate.

Umple allows developers to embedall the above state machine concepts in its textual form.

In the Umple case study given above, a state machine called 'mode' is defined starting at line 32. This has three states. The start state is 'normal' (line 33). When eventgoAway occurs (via a message call to a generated goAway() method from a button, perhaps on the user interface) the system changes to 'awaySafety' state (line 37). While in this state, the cycleLights() activity method is executed in a separate thread, which would be interrupted when the 'backHome' event is called. Similarly, if the user presses the panicButton, the system transitions to alarm state (line 41), which runs the flashLights() method in a thread until interrupted by a second press of the button.

The state machine diagram for this appears in Figure 4. As with Figures 1, 2 and 3, this diagram is kept in constant sync as the code is edited.

*Figure 4. State machine diagram of the second version of the Smart Light system.*

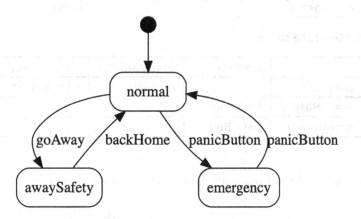

Like class diagrams, it is clear that state machines are naturally diagrammatic in nature, since they are two-dimensional. An Umple developer can constantly see the diagram change as they edit the textual code. The textual form provides all the advantages described earlier including compactness, document-ability, comparability, composability and editing in any tool.

Umple also provides additional outputs from state models, aside from standard state diagrams and generated code. Figure 5 shows the state tables, and Figure 6 shows a random sequence generated for the state machine. Both of these are ways of helping the developer understand whether or not their model is correct. Not shown here are the ability of Umple to generate formal method code to allow model checking in languages such as NuXmv (Adesina et al, 2018).All of these can be generated at any time from the model code.

## Some Other Umple Features That Benefit From a Textual Environment

This chapter does not have the space to cover all the features of Umple. However, the following are brief descriptions and examples of some of the additional features that derive synergies from being present in a textual modeling language, as opposed to a predominantly diagrammatic one.

*Figure 5. State tables generated by UmpleOnline from the state machinein the case study.*

**State-event table**

|  | backHome | goAway | panicButton |
|---|---|---|---|
| **normal** |  | awaySafety | emergency |
| **awaySafety** | normal |  |  |
| **emergency** |  |  | normal |

**State-state table**

|  | normal | awaySafety | emergency |
|---|---|---|---|
| **normal** |  | goAway | panicButton |
| **awaySafety** | backHome |  |  |
| **emergency** | panicButton |  |  |

*Figure 6. Randomly generated event sequence generated from the state machine in the case study.*

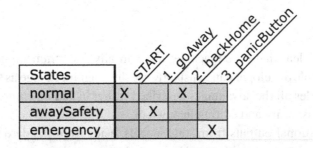

| States | START | 1. goAway | 2. backHome | 3. panicButton |
|---|---|---|---|---|
| normal | X |  | X |  |
| awaySafety |  | X |  |  |
| emergency |  |  |  | X |

| Event Number | Event | Next State |
|---|---|---|
| START | - | normal |
| 1 | goAway | awaySafety |
| 2 | backHome | normal |
| 3 | panicButton | emergency |

## Constraints

Umple has four types of constraints,three of which are derived from UML. Even in UML, which is otherwise diagrammatic, constraints are expressed textually.

- **Multiplicity of associations**. These specifying bounds on the number of links that can occur at run time. Several examples are given in the earlier code.
- **OCL-like constraints in classes**. Umple supports a subset of OCL to represent invariants, method preconditions and method postconditions; they are Boolean expressions written in square brackets.
- **Guards on state machine transitions**. These also appear in square brackets, and are syntactically the same as the OCL constraints that are used for method preconditions.
- **Various built-in stereotypes**. These are tags added to Umple elements to constrain the behavior of generated code. For example, the stereotype 'singleton' indicates that the generated code is to allow only one instance of a class to be created; the stereotype 'immutable' indicates that an attribute or entire class instance must not be allowed to be changed after instantiation.

The following simple mixin shows a use of constraints that could be added to the case study. This will limit the range of the attribute MaxLumens. We invite the reader to paste this into the example in UmpleOnline and generate code to see its effect.

```
class SmartLight { [maxLumens > 0] [maxLumens < 5000] }
```

## Aspects

An aspect contains a block of code (typically called *advice*) that can be injected into code according to the instructions found in a pattern (called a *pointcut*). Umple comes with an aspect capability that allows injection of code into both generatedand user-defined methods.For example, the following Java code would ensure adjustment of lights after a dimmer is set to a particular percentage:

```
class DimmableSwitch {
   after setDimmerSetting {
   for (aLight SmartLight: getSmartLights()) {
      aLight.setCurrentBrightness(dimmerSetting);
   }
   }
}
```

The reader is invited to paste this into the case study code in UmpleOnline to see its effect on the generated code.

Umple aspects have the ability to inject code *before* the start of any method matching a pattern, *after* methods (i.e. before all returns), and after any textual *label* found in the interior of matching methods. The latter capability allows construction of methods with capabilities that differ depending on which features are active.

## Filters

There are several situations when a user wants to query or *slice* part of a model. The full set of Umple files of a system represents the complete system. Umple's *filters* capability, which can be activated individually or in groups using mixsets, allows some of the following:

- **Specification of diagrams:** Some tools use a separate language to specify diagrams, but in Umple, filters select part of the model to be used for a diagram. Different filters are used to create separate diagrams, with activation of a mixset to cause display of the desired diagram. The multiple Umple metamodel diagrams (Umple 2020b) are generated this way.
- **Generation of part of the system:**It can be useful to split a system into two executables, each of which is specified by a filter.

The following mixin can be used to draw a diagram containingSmartLight, SmartLight Console, the association linking them, and any of theirsuperclasses. There are options, not shown here, to control the number of 'hops' from listed items (so as to add connected classes), as well as the types of arcs to be displayed.

```
filter { include SmartLight, SmartLightConsole;}
```

## Text Generation

Generation of textual output is needed in almost all application types. Examples include generating html or xml for webpages, code from compilers, messages to be transmitted to other systems, and so on.

Several languages have built-in capabilities for this, PHP being a well-known example where this capability is widely used to generate html. Umple has a text-generation capability that is integrated with the language in the same manner as PHP, but it has several unique features that distinguish it, such as being able use knowledge about associations or state machines and to synergistically work with all the other Umple features mentioned in this chapter.

Full details of text generation can be found in Husseini Orabi, Husseini Orabiand Lethbridge (2020). In brief, various kinds of nested blocks bracketed by << and >> can be specified to build templates. If the << is followed by ! then it indicates text to be output. If the << is followed by #, it indicates target language code used inside the template to computationally build output;this can call the Umple-generated API that refers to model elements. The 'emit' keyword is used to construct methods that use the templates.

The following example mixin would add in our case study a display() method to class SmartLightConsole that would show the name and brightness of each light.

```
class SmartLightConsole {
    rows <<!<<# for  (aLight: smartLights) {#>>
            <<=aLight.getName()>><<=aLight.getcurrentBright-
ness()>><<#}#>>!>>
  emit display()(rows);
}
```

## Synergies Among All the Above

We have described above many features of Umple that benefit from being rendered textually. These operate synergistically with each other, and facilitate agility as well as product-line development. Table 2 shows some of the characteristics of these features.

All of the features shown in column 1 of Table 2 benefit from the properties listed in Table 1 such as being documentable with code comments, focusable so warning messages can be displayed (as per the analysis described in the right column of Table 2), and composable using Traits.

In Table 2, Umple features marked ** are in UML as diagram elements. Those marked * are in UML textually. Those marked + are value-added textual features in Umple. Those marked & facilitate separation of concerns, such as for better modularity or feature-driven or product-line development.


## UMPLE AS A SYSTEM WRITTEN IN ITSELF

As a second case study in this chapter, we will discuss how Umple has been written in itself.

The Umple compiler and code generators are written completely in Umple, with embedded code in Java for the bodies of methods and state machine actions. As far as we are aware, Umple is the only modeling tool that can be said to be *self-hosted* or *boostrapped* in this manner. Umple was originally written in Java, with Jet for code emission and ANTLR for parsing. However, once the first version was in place, the compiler was *umplified* (Garzon et al, 2012), eliminating Jet and ANTLR. Umple has no dependencies on other technologies except Java and the previous version of Umple (needed for self-compilation).

The core compiler has 152 .ump files, comprising 69 KLOC of Umple, with additional code in several domain-specific languages. There are a total of 587 classes. Extensive use is made of mixins and aspects. Feature driven development is used to some extent, so the codebase is organized with a set of files per feature. Mixins for a class may appear in numerous files.

There are another 655 .ump files and 37KLOC in the various generators (Java, Php, C++, Ruby, various diagrams forms, SQL, unit test languages, etc.) that are organized and processed separately when building Umple. Extensive use is made of Umple's template generation capability.

The process used to develop Umple combines the best of both test-driven and model-driven techniques:There are over 300 test files, with 47 KLOC of tests, and over 5400 tests. These operate on over 99K lines of test data in over 1000 files. This does not include the compiler itself which serves as its own giant testcase as it has to be built and run on itself by every new version of the compiler. A new compiler version is not created unless 100% of the test cases pass.

It is fair to say that a system of Umple's size could not have been managed effectively if its model was rendered strictly as a set of diagrams. Most of the seven characteristics of textual forms we discussed earlier have helped Umple to be developed into a large and reliable system.

Umple's internal design is self-documenting: Various class diagrams are generated whenever a new version of the compiler is built. These can be seen online (Umple 2020a). Mixsets and filters are used to describe each diagram.

Umple's Javadoc plugin is used to keep Umple's documentation webpage up to date with respect to the Umple code. The result can be seen online (Umple 2020b).

*Table 2. Characteristics and effects of a subset of Umple features.*

| | Can Be Top Level | Can Be in Classes, Traits | Can Be Built in Pieces by | Diagram Effect | Effect on Generated API | Analysis Performed by Compiler Beyond Basic Syntactic Analysis |
|---|---|---|---|---|---|---|
| Class ** | Yes | | Trait, Mixin, Mixset | In default Class Diag. | Constructor and other methods | Extensive semantic analysis (e.g. avoiding circular inheritance) |
| Association ** | Yes | Yes | Aspect (for related behaviour) | In default Class Diag. | Methods to manipulate | Presence of referred elements, and extensive semantic analysis |
| Trait +& | Yes | | Mixin, Mixset | In special class Diag.; Default class Diag. merges elements into classes | API appears in classes that use it | Extensive semantic analysis such as required methods, relationships among traits |
| User Defined Method * | | Yes | Aspect | In class Diag. with option to show it or not | Output largely as is | (Syntactic analysis for signature only) |
| Mixin (repeated top-level element) +& | Yes | | | Diagram shows mixincontents all combined | Adds methods related to contents | |
| Mixset (set of similarly named mixins; a file is a special case) +& | Yes | Yes | Mixin | Class or state D. shows selected variant; Feature diagram | | Conformity to require statements, which impose rules on which mixsets can coexist |
| State Machine ** | Yes | Yes | Trait, Mixin, Mixset, Aspect | State Diag. | Adds events and other methods | Extensive semantic analysis (e.g. reachability) |
| Constraint * | | Yes | | | Modifies many methods | Presence of referenced elements, type conformity |
| Aspect +& | Yes | Yes | | | Modifies any selected methods | Presence of referenced elements |
| Filter +& | Yes | | Mixin | Diagram shows selected subset | | Presence of referenced elements |
| Text Generation Element + | | Yes | | | Generates emission methods | Presence of referenced elements |

Rigorous attention is paid to version control and code review. This would be more difficult if only diagrams were available of modeling elements. Pull requests are merged only when all tests pass, and a code review indicates there are no issues.

When a developer is modifying the compiler, the previous version of the compiler points out problems and localizes them to lines of Umple. Grep searches, IDE searches and failing testcases do the same, facilitating rapid correction of errors.

Refactoring has proved easy, due to the textual form of the language. Some unique refactoring techniques have been developed during the creation of Umple in itself, such as:

- **Extract mixin**: to pull out parts of a file to create a simpler file.

- **Separate pure model from methods**: Takes 'extract mixin' one step further by making the code for class diagrams stand out more clearly from the methods that operate on the various elements.

In addition to test-driven development, other agile techniques that are enforced include a product backlog: All changes are made in response to issues. Also, a continuous integration and release process is followed: Updates to the master version of Umple (which appears in UmpleOnline) occur whenever issues are closed, sometimes several times in a day.

Umple has been developed largely by students (PhD, masters and many 4th year capstone students). Yet its core compiler can run for months online without crashing. Infrequent crashes are rapidly solved with regressions of them prevented through test-driven development. This has only been possible due to

- The rigors imposed by the quality assurance processes (test-driven development, code review) we have discussed;
- Model-driven development, consisting of both the use of abstract modeling elements such as associations, and the presence of model diagrams generated from the text, to enable understanding the system;
- The benefits of the textual form (as per Table 1);
- Umple's value-added features such as the text-emission template capability andmixins to help organize the codebase;
- Extensive built-in model analysis that prevents many kinds of errors; and
- Complete code generation that both dramatically reduces errors that would appear if code were written by hand and also reduces code volume to about 10% of what would be required if the model code was written manually.

## UMPLE IN THE CONTEXT OF MODEL-DRIVEN ENGINEERING

One of the important features of model-driven software engineering is that models should not only represent various aspects of a system, such as the data (e.g. class diagrams) and behaviour (e.g. state diagrams), but that there also should be models at various levels of abstraction and platform commitment.

The OMG's Model Driven Architecture approach in particular (MeservyandFenstermacher, 2005), suggests that there should be several levels of modeling. MDA'smost abstract level is Computation Independent Models (CIMs), where modelers can definebusiness processes and general requirements before any commitment is made to design. MDA's next level is Platform Independent Models (PIMs);these incorporate design decisions (such as the specific data as represented in class diagrams)without commitment to particular frameworks, programming languages, databases, and so on. Finally, MDAincorporates Platform Specific Models (PSMs) that have the most concrete levels of detail.

MDA is centred on the development of*transformations* that allow generation of more concrete levels of modeling from more abstract levels. For example,Rhazali,Hadi, andMouloudi (2016) describe transformations from CIMs to PIMs; Rhazali et al (2020) describe transformations through all three levels, starting with business processes in BPMN and using transformations to ultimately produce concrete code.

There have been some attempts, such as that of Essebaa and Chantit (2018) to bring together agility and model-driven approaches, because both have the objective of enabling small, frequent and disciplined changes. Source-code-focused agile techniques do this by focusing on testing; MDA does this by focusing on automated transformation. For example, in MDA one might add a new use case to a CIM, derive new needed data from this in a corresponding PIM and from that generate a new PSM, and eventually new code. In a code-oriented agile approach one might write a user story in an issue, then write some new unit tests, then write the code in a small delta, finally committing tests and code together while referencing the issue.

A key feature of the Umple approach is that it is designed to be agnostic to any particular model-driven methodology, and can be used in a manner borrowing ideas from MDA, while also embracing code-oriented agile techniques. In particular, pure models (at the PIM level) can be maintained as artifacts that are separate from algorithmic code, as mentioned in our discussion of the *separate pure model from methods* refactoring above. Umple's ability to generate multiple targets, manage multiple target-language method bodies, and perform conditional modeling with mixsets facilitates the PIM-to-PSM and PSM-to-code transformations. Yet Umple's textual form facilitates creating small deltas containing model constructsalong with tests in the standard agile manner.

Umple does have a prototype capability for automated test generation and test-driven modeling. This is in preparation for release and will strengthen its integration of agility and model-driven development.

Umple currently does not manage some of the models found primarily at the CIM level, such as use cases, but such improvements are planned, as discussed in the section on future research directions, below.

## EVIDENCE FOR THE EFFECTIVENESS OF THE APPROACH

There are several lines of evidence supporting our proposition that the concepts embodied in Umple are an advance in the practice of software engineering:

- **A study of model comprehension**. Baddredin and Lethbridge (2012) conducted experiments comparing understandability of three versions of three systems: Each system had a UML diagram version, an Umple textual version and a Java version.Comprehension was measured by asking developers questions about the systems. The results showed that UML and Umple versions were equally understandable, and were considerably more understandable than the Java versions. Additional details can be found in Badreddin, Forward, and Lethbridge (2012).
- **A study of student grades**: Lethbridge, Mussbacher, Forward and Badreddin (2011) conducted a study with students in the classroom. Grades of 332 students prior to the introduction of Umple as the teaching tool were compared to those of 122 students after its introduction. Average grades increased by 9% on similar UML modeling questions. Surveys of the students also indicated they very much liked Umple's textual form, code-diagram duality and the code generation.
- **Surveys of tool use**: We conducted international surveys to study modeling tool use. The first survey was directed at 150 professors teaching software modeling with 32 modeling tools in 30 countries (Agner and Lethbridge, 2017). Umple was one of the few tools rated by the professors as being easy to use. The second survey (Agner, Lethbridge & Soares, 2019) covered 117 students in 7 countries.The students had used 14 tools, and20 of the students had used Umple. The tools were compared according to numerous criteria. Umple scored higher than any other tool in appreciation of its code generation, and also scored well in being easy to use and not being complex. Umple received relatively low scores for technical support, slowness of the website and buggi-

ness – problems which have all since been addressed. All other tools had low scores in a greater number of criteria than Umple did.

Additional evidence of Umple's usefulness can be seen in the uptake of UmpleOnline, which sees over 2 million transactions per year in over 200,000 user sessions.

Our first item of future work, as discussed in the next section, is to leverage the UmpleOnline platform to conduct additional experiments on the effectiveness of Umple, and textual modeling in general.

## FUTURE RESEARCH DIRECTIONS

We are planning several major future research directions for Umple.

The first is to add an integrated educational and experimental platform into UmpleOnline. This would allow experimenters or educators to present modeling problems to users and gather their answers as well as data about their experiences. There is a great need for more empirical studies of modeling and this platform should allow the Umple team to obtain help in this regard from its many thousands of users. In particular, we intend to create a mechanism that can be embedded in multiple tools, to allow comparison of Umple with competing tools such as Papyrus. This is described in Lethbridge (2019), and also in Umple issue 1490(Github 2020b)

The second direction is to add the ability to embed textual requirements languages into Umple, so that the link between CIM and PIM can be made. One idea is that Umple's strength at drawing diagrams from textual models would be further leveraged. Secondly, any Umple element would be taggable with an 'implements requirement' clause, adding traceability. These capabilities would synergistically combine with Umple's separation-of-concern mechanisms: For example, it would be possible to show the requirements for a particular feature or variant constructed from certain mixsets.

The third direction is to continue to expand Umple's modeling and code-generation capabilities as driven by customer demand. For example, where projects demand new generation targets (and the ability to embed methods from new languages), we will attempt to enablethem. There have been requests for Python, for example. Also, there have been requests for generation of example instance diagrams. There have also been requests to enable Umple to generate code that would work with sources of 'Big Data' corresponding to UML models.

## CONCLUSION

Textual modeling languages like Umple allow developers to use powerful modeling constructs, while also maintaining the numerous advantages of human-readable textual languages such as the ability to comment effectively, use textual toolchains and do effective version control.

Umple shares some features with other UML-based textual languages, such as having a syntax for associations and state machines. Some competing tools are also open source. However, Umple's key features that distinguish it from other modeling technology, including other textual modeling languages are:

- It transparently blends modeling constructs with code in multiple target languages, resulting in a single codebase.

- It generates comprehensive code sufficient for the development of diverse and complex systems, including of itself. It is the only modeling tool we are aware of that was developed in itself.
- It incorporates special features that only work effectively in textual languages to allow separation of concerns, feature-oriented development and product-line development such as mixins, mixsets, traits, text-emission templates and aspects.
- Its codebase can be organized in numerous ways, such as by class, by subsystem, by feature, and/or by separating pure model from user-defined methods.

Whether or not Umple becomes a major player in the commercial modeling market, we strongly suggest that other others developing modeling tools and languages should consider incorporating similar features.

Umple is also developed in a test-driven manner and has been hardened by widespread use in the education market.

The core lessons from our research and the success of Umple are:

- Modeling in UML can be successfully undertaken in a user-friendly, tool-agnostic way in order to build systems of all sizes. Research and experience shows that mainstream developers (other than those working in safety-critical domains) are reluctant to use UML except in an informal way because of weak or complicated tools. But Umple shows such limitations can be overcome.
- It is highly beneficial for a modeling language to have a human-readable textual form to make use of models simpler, to facilitate agility, and so that text-based tools and language features can be used. This does not preclude the simultaneous use of diagrams viewing and allowing editing of the same model: In fact, code and diagram forms of a model work synergistically with each other.

The next steps for Umple include 1) integrating the ability to use it to conduct modeling experiments; 2) incorporating requirements and other computation-independent modeling constructs, and 3) adding other customer-driven capabilities such as new transformation targets.

## ACKNOWLEDGMENT

The authors acknowledge the 60 students and other open source developers who have contributed to Umple and are listed in the Umple License file on Github.

This research was supported by the Natural Sciences and Engineering Research Council of Canada grant numbers 453224, 569913 and 634504.

## REFERENCES

Abdelzad, V., & Lethbridge, T. C. (2015). Promoting Traits into Model-Driven Development. *Software & Systems Modeling*, *16*(4), 997–1017. doi:10.100710270-015-0505-x

Abstratt. (2020). *TextUML*. Retrieved from http://abstratt.github.io/textuml/readme.html

Adesina, O., Lethbridge, T. C., Somé, S., Abdelzad, V., & Boaye Belle, A. (2018). Improving Formal Analysis of State Machines with Particular Emphasis on And-Cross Transitions. *Computer Languages, Systems & Structures*, *54*, 544–585. doi:10.1016/j.cl.2017.12.001

Agner, L. T. W., & Lethbridge, T. C. (2017). A Survey of Tool Use in Modeling Education. In *20th International Conference on Model Driven Engineering Languages and Systems* (MODELS) (pp. 303-311). IEEE. 10.1109/MODELS.2017.1

Agner, L. T. W., Lethbridge, T. C., & Soares, I. W. (2019). Student Experience with Software Modeling Tools. *Software & Systems Modeling*, *18*(5), 3025–3047. doi:10.100710270-018-00709-6

Badreddin, O., Forward, A., & Lethbridge, T. C. (2012). *Model Oriented Programming: An Empirical Study of Comprehension. In Conference of the Center for Advanced Studies on Collaborative Research.* IBM Corp and ACM.

Badreddin, O., Forward, A., & Lethbridge, T. C. (2013a). *Exploring a Model-Oriented and Executable Syntax for UML Attributes. In Software Engineering Research, Management and Applications.* Springer.

Badreddin, O., Forward, A., & Lethbridge, T. C. (2013b). *Improving Code Generation for Associations: Enforcing Multiplicity Constraints and Ensuring Referential Integrity. In Software Engineering Research, Management and Applications.* Springer.

Badreddin, O., & Lethbridge, T. C. (2012). Combining Experiments and Grounded Theory to Evaluate a Research Prototype: Lessons from the Umple Model-Oriented Programming Technology. In *First International Workshop on User Evaluation for Software Engineering Researchers* (USER) (pp. 1-4). IEEE. 10.1109/USER.2012.6226575

Badreddin, O., Lethbridge, T. C., & Forward, A. (2014). A Novel Approach to Versioning and Merging Model and Code Uniformly. In *2nd International Conference on Model-Driven Engineering and Software Development (MODELSWARD)*, (pp. 254-263). INSTICC and IEEE.

Bendix, L., & Emanuelsson, P. (2008). Diff and Merge Support for Model Based Development. In *International workshop on Comparison and Versioning of Software Models (CVSM '08)* (pp. 31–34). ACM. 10.1145/1370152.1370161

Brunet, G., Chechik, M., Easterbrook, S., Nejati, S., Niu, N., & Sabetzadeh, M. (2006). A Manifesto for Model Merging. In *International Workshop on Global Integrated Model Management (GaMMa '06)* (pp. 5-12), ACM.

Dévai, G., Kovács, G. F., & An, A. (2014). Textual, Executable, Translatable UML. OCL@ MoDELS, 3-12.

Essebaa, I., & Chantit, S. (2018). Model Driven Architecture and Agile Methodologies: Reflexion and discussion of their combination. In *Federated Conference on Computer Science and Information Systems* (FedCSIS) (pp. 939-948). IEEE. 10.15439/2018F358

Forward, A. (2010). *The Convergence of Modeling and Programming: Facilitating the Representation of Attributes and Associations in the Umple Model-Oriented Programming Language* (Doctoral Dissertation). University of Ottawa, Canada.

Forward, A., & Lethbridge, T. C. (2008). Problems and Opportunities for Model-Centric Versus Code-Centric Software Development: A Survey of Software Professionals. In *International Workshop on Models in Software Engineering*, (pp. 27-32). ACM. 10.1145/1370731.1370738

Garzon, M., & Lethbridge, T. C. (2012).Exploring how to Develop Transformations and Tools for Automated Umplification. In *Working Conference on Reverse Engineering (WCRE)*, (pp. 491-494). IEEE. 10.1109/WCRE.2012.58

Github. (2020a). *Umple*. Retrieved from http://code.umple.org

Github. (2020b). *UmpleOnline Module to Allow Running Experiments*. Retrieved from https://github.com/umple/umple/issues/1490

Gogolla, M., Büttner, F., & Richters, M. (2007). USE: A UML-based specification environment for validating UML and OCL. *Science of Computer Programming*, 69(1-3), 27–34. doi:10.1016/j.scico.2007.01.013

Husseini Orabi, M., Husseini Orabi, A., & Lethbridge, T.C. (2020). Umple-TL: A Model-Oriented, Dependency-Free Text Emission Tool. *Communications in Computer and Information Science*, 1161, 127-155.

Jayaraman, P., Whittle, J., Elkhodary, A. M., & Gomaa, H. (2007). *Model Composition in Product Lines and Feature Interaction Detection Using Critical Pair Analysis. In Model Driven Engineering Languages and Systems. MODELS 2007* (Vol. 4735). Springer.

Lethbridge, T. C. (2019). UmpleOnline as a Testbed for Modeling Empirical Studies: A Position Paper. In *Fourth International Workshop on Human Factors in Modeling (HuFaMo)*, (pp. 412-413). IEEE 10.1109/MODELS-C.2019.00064

Lethbridge, T. C., & Algablan, A. (2018). Using Umple to Synergistically Process Features, Variants, UML Models and Classic Code. In *International Symposium on Leveraging Applications of Formal Methods*, (pp. 69-88). Springer. 10.1007/978-3-030-03418-4_5

Lethbridge, T. C., Mussbacher, G., Forward, A., & Badreddin, O. (2011). *Teaching UML using Umple: Applying Model-Oriented Programming in the Classroom. In Software Engineering Education and Training (CSEE&T)*. IEEE.

Lundell, B., Lings, B., Persson, A., & Mattsson, A. (2006). *UML Model Interchange in Heterogeneous Tool Environments: An Analysis of Adoptions of XMI 2. In Model Driven Engineering Languages and Systems (MODELS)* (Vol. 4199). Springer.

Medvidovic, N., Egyed, A., & Rosenblum, D. S. (1999).Round-trip Software Engineering Using UML: From Architecture to Design and Back. *Second International Workshop on Object-Oriented Reengineering(WOOR'99)*, 1-8.

Mellor, S. J., & Balcer, M. (2002). *Executable UML: A Foundation for Model-Driven Architectures*. Addison-Wesley Longman.

Meservy, T. O., & Fenstermacher, K. D. (2005). Transforming software development: An MDA road map. *Computer*, 38(9), 52–58. doi:10.1109/MC.2005.316

Petre, M. (2013). UML In Practice. In *35th International Conference on Software Engineering (ICSE)* (pp. 722-731). IEEE.

Rhazali, Y., El Hachimi, A., Chana, I., Lahmer, M., & Rhattoy, A. (2020). *Automate Model Transformation From CIM to PIM up to PSM in Model-Driven Architecture. In Modern Principles, Practices, and Algorithms for Cloud Security.* IGI Global.

Rhazali, Y., Hadi, Y., & Mouloudi, A. (2016). CIM to PIM Transformation in MDA: From Service-Oriented Business Models to Web-Based Design Models. *International Journal of Software Engineering and Its Applications, 10*(4), 125–142. doi:10.14257/ijseia.2016.10.4.13

Rockstrom, A., & Saracco, R. (1982). SDL-CCITT specification and description language. *IEEE Transactions on Communications, 30*(6), 1310–1318. doi:10.1109/TCOM.1982.1095599

Umple. (2020a). *Umple User Manual.* Retrieved from http://manual.umple.org

Umple. (2020b). *Class Diagram of the Umple Compiler Generated by Umple.* Retrieved from http://metamodel.umple.org

Umple. (2020c). *Umple Compiler API of Generated Java Files.* Retrieved from http://javadoc.umple.org

UmpleOnline. (2020). Retrieved From http://try.umple.org

## KEY TERMS AND DEFINITIONS

**Association:** A UML and Umple modeling abstraction that connects classes and describes the links between instances that can be created at runtime. Associations in Umple result in generation of methods to manage links and maintain referential integrity.

**Aspect:** The representation of some part of software that describes how certain source code is to be blended into other source code, via a pattern-matching process.

**Attribute:** A data item listed in a class description; each instance of the class will have this data. In Umple, attributes are subject to constraints and result in the generation of accessor methods.

**Mixin:** A lightweight block of code that can be blended into a textual program or model to add features. In Umple, multiple mixins declaring the same class can be combined to build a class. The multiple mixins can be in separate files or a single file. Mixins are a syntactic feature, as no analysis is done prior to the combination; this in contrast with Traits.

**Mixset:** A set of mixins sharing the same name that can be made active by an Umple use statement in order to add a feature to a model in Umple.

**Trait:** A class-like modeling entity that groups various class features, such as associations, attributes, state machines and methods, to facilitate separation of concerns, feature-driven development, product lines and multiple inheritance. In contrast to a mixin, it has strong semantics so various errors can be detected.

**UML:** A widely used language using many types of diagrams to model software, including state machines and class diagrams.

**Umple:** A textual language for modeling software that incorporates many UML constructs as well as textual constructs such as mixins, mixsets, traits, and aspects.

# Chapter 2

# An Automatic Generation of Domain Ontologies Based on an MDA Approach to Support Big Data Analytics

**Naziha Laaz**

(iD) https://orcid.org/0000-0003-4709-6647

*MISC Laboratory, Faculty of Sciences, Ibn Tofail University, Kenitra, Morocco*

**Karzan Wakil**

*Research Center, Sulaimani Polytechnic University, Sulaimani, Iraq*

**Sara Gotti**

(iD) https://orcid.org/0000-0002-2513-2646

*MISC Laboratory, Faculty of Sciences, Ibn Tofail University, Kenitra, Morocco*

**Zineb Gotti**

(iD) https://orcid.org/0000-0003-3342-3248

*MISC Laboratory, Faculty of Sciences, Ibn Tofail University, Kenitra, Morocco*

**Samir Mbarki**

*MISC Laboratory, Faculty of Science, Ibn Tofail University, Kenitra, Morocco*

## ABSTRACT

*This chapter proposes a new methodology for the automatic generation of domain ontologies to support big data analytics. This method ensures the recommendations of the MDA approach by transforming UML class diagrams to domain ontologies in PSM level through ODM, which is an OMG standard for ontology modeling. In this work, the authors have focused on the model-driven architecture approach as the best solution for representing and generating ontology artifacts in an intuitive way using the UML*

DOI: 10.4018/978-1-7998-3661-2.ch002

*graphical syntax. The creation of domain ontologies will form the basis for application developers to target business professional context; however, the future of big data will depend on the use of technologies to model ontologies. With that said, this work supports the combination of ontologies and big data approaches as the most efficient way to store, extract, and analyze data. It is shown using the theoretical approach and concrete results obtained after applying the proposed process to an e-learning domain ontology.*

## INTRODUCTION

Although in its early days, ontology was only attractive as a base for artificial intelligence (Psyché et al., 2003), today's researches and new technologies tell us a completely different story, the power of these concept can be used almost everywhere. It surely isn't the limit, ontology's future looks bright and huge. Among the areas of application of domain ontologies is Big data. The big data is an abstract concept (Chen et al., 2014), it represents a significant amount of data so that its treatment becomes difficult and requires much technical knowledge. The ontology concept is on the cusp of its most exciting period to date, entering a new era where big data is starting to use semantic concepts to handle many requirements. Ontologies represents one of the Big data engines, because of the need to adapt the collection, processing and visualization of data according to the nature of each data.

The use of semantic technologies especially ontologies when representing complex datasets make it easier to understand the meaning and purpose of data. Moreover, the creation of domain ontologies is of paramount importance for future of big data. It will enhance the interpretation of information by identifying the corresponding business professional contexts. That's why, effective ontology modeling efforts have been conducted with respect to big data (Kouji Kozaki; Konys 2016; Nadal et al. 2018; Saber, Al-Zoghby, and Elmougy 2018). They are confident that the combination of big data and ontologies give new solutions for many problems, for example, ontology can provide semantics to add raw data, generalized concepts in ontology allow connections between data in various concept levels across domains. Furthermore, we can use ontology as given (and authorized) knowledge to analysis big data (Konys, 2016).

Despite such explosive increase of data, researchers are just beginning to address the fact that the treatment of these tasks require modeling tools that will allow them to automate the development of ontologies. So, it is strongly recommended to focus on technologies and materials to model ontologies. The integration time will be shorter, the implementation of projects will be easy, which will allow us to develop and diversify the use of user needs. On the other hand, we notice the great effort of the OMG group which has conducted several researches on the implication of ontologies in the model-driven engineering to exploit it later in application domains of different areas.

In the present work, we propose a solution for automating the ontology generation using MDA technologies. The approach is based on the two OMG standards; UML and ODM as a basis for ontology modeling. Domain ontologies are presented in an abstract way employing the graphical syntax of UML. The idea is to begin with UML representation of classes and then applying the concept of model to model transformation Language, to generate a target owl model and use it to get the source code of owl file. Domain ontology is designed as a PSM Model through ODM which is OMG standard for modeling ontology. However, we founded on UML to model the PIM level, because UML is advisable by MDA in PIM. As an illustration, we present along this paper the model-driven development process applied for e-learning UML class diagram to generate ontology documents respecting an RDF/XML format.

The structure of the paper is as follows: In the next section, we present the context of our research work. In Section III, we review previous efforts in ontology development regarding the generation of domain ontologies from UML class diagrams. Section IV describes our approach and gives an overview of model driven development process describing its different phases. In section V we show the results of our proposal by applying the model driven development process to an e-learning domain ontology. The paper ends with some conclusions.

## CONTEXT

The background of this work is presented under different subsections. Each of these subsections discuss the foundations of our proposal. In particular, Section II.A gives an overview of big data and its recognized, inherent characteristics. Also, we cite several advantages of the use of ontologies in a big data area. In section II-B, we define domain ontologies. For the last part in this section, we present and describe model-driven engineering and its standards used in this work UML and ODM, respectively.

### Big Data

Likewise, for other technology tendencies like Semantic web and Artificial Intelligence, Big data has become a buzzword around the world. Several definitions have been proposed for big data. In general, It means a very large data sets that no information management toolor classic database manager can really handle. This massive volume is divided into three categories specifically: Structured data, Semi structured and Unstructured data(Taneja & Gaur, 2018). The exploitation and management of "big data"

*Figure 1. The five Vs of Big Data*

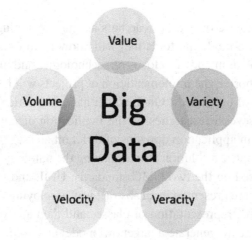

represents a technical and economic issue. Web giants, first and foremost Yahoo but also Facebook and Google, were the first to deploy this type of technology(Liu et al., 2018).

The figure above mentions the 5V's essential characteristics of Big data. They refer to five key elements to consider and optimize as part of a process to optimize the big data management (Storey & Song, 2017). The table 1 gives an overview of each of these characteristics:

*Table 1. 5V's Big data definition*

| Big Data Characteristic | Description |
|---|---|
| Volume | the volumes of data to be collected and analyzed are considerable and constantly increasing. |
| Variety | a wide variety of information from various sources, unstructured, organized, open, etc. The data can take very heterogeneous forms (texts, web analytics, images, etc.) |
| Velocity | a certain level of Velocity to reach, in other words frequency of creation, collection and sharing of these data. |
| Value | Be able to focus on data with real value. It is not easy to make sense of Big data analytics tools. |
| Veracity | It's a reliability of data. It raises issues of the meaning in the data itself such as word variation. |

we can identify five key technology families for the big data industry: text-mining, graph-mining, machine learning, data-visualization and knowledge description(ontologies). Efforts are made for one purpose, which is to simplify the analysis of big data sets by giving them meaning. Big data refers to a large scale that is used to represent a huge collection of datasets. The retrieval of data from these structures benefits from semantic knowledge. For this purpose, it is desirable to provide an ontology for data. The use of ontology is essential to integrate thinking and intelligent recovery of big data. Moreover, generalized concepts in an ontology can connect data in various concept levels across domains, they allow to add metadata ontology for annotating data, and they bring benefits for search and retrieval information(Konys, 2016). In addition, there are other advantages that ontologies offer to solve the difficulties faced in big data analytics.

## The Ontology Concept

Ontological engineering is born from the needs to represent knowledge in various fields especially artificial intelligence, Web technologies, database integration, big datasets(De Giacomo et al., 2018). This utility is motivated by the fact that ontologies allow systems to touch the semantic part of information and manipulate it by establishing representations and models, as well as, they are an effective way to manage and share knowledge in a particular area. Roche et al.(Roche, 2005)propose a definition of an ontology as a conceptualization of a domain to which one or more vocabularies of terms are associated. The concepts are structured in a system and participate in the meaning of the terms.

There are several kinds of ontologies for a wide variety of uses. Ontologies are therefore classified according to the formality of the languages used or the scope of the objects described by the ontology(Falquet et al., 2011).Among its types, mention Linguistic / Terminological Ontologies, Formal Ontologies, Domain Ontologies, Information Ontologies, etc.

Our aim is to assist in the design and generation of domain ontologies manipulated in the big data area. A domain ontology describes the vocabulary relating to a general domain such as medicine, education. It is defined for a given purpose and provides a shared understanding of a certain domain by a group of people. It's a structured set of concepts and relationships between them intended to represent the objects of a domain explicitly in a form that can be understood by both human and machines(Berners-Lee et al., 2001). In fact, it is formalized using five kinds of elements: classes, properties, datatypes, individuals and axioms. To clarify, classes have the same meaning of classes of objects modeled that exist in the modeling area, and individuals represent instances of classes. Properties represent attributes defined for characterizing classes. There are two kinds of properties; a property that link two classes or properties between a class and range of values. Datatypes are sets of literals such as strings or integers. All these declarations are grouped by axioms, in order to form complex descriptions from the basic entities. Besides, semantic technologies proposed by the W3C(*Extensible Markup Language (XML)*, 2017; *OWL - Semantic Web Standards*, s. d.; *RDF - Semantic Web Standards*, s. d.) are used to standardize the terms and concepts of each domain ontology, which facilitates communication and knowledge sharing. Domain ontologies have already shown their application in many domains, such as education, government, commerce, health, etc. This work focuses on the e-learning domain.

## Model Driven Engineering

According to(Brambilla et al., 2017), Model-Driven Engineering (MDE) isan engineering paradigm based on the principle of "all is model". The objective of MDE is to use models as a central concept in different levels of abstraction in the software development process, however, metamodels constitute the definition of a modeling language, since they provide a way of describing the whole class of models that can be represented by that language(Brambilla et al., 2017). Usually, in MDE, the implementation is (semi) automatically generated from the models. Its aim is to automate software development and increase it, thereby raising the level of abstraction of physical systems.

MDE is often confused with the Model Driven Architecture (MDA). MDA is a vision on MDE defined by the Object Management Group(OMG), and thus relies on the use of OMG standards. The MDA provides architecture for the design of software systems and focuses on the technical variability in software(Guide, 2015). Furthermore, this approach permits to understand complex systems and the real world through the definition of models in three different types (Blanc & Salvatori, 2011). The figure 2 shows the three MDA layers:

*Figure 2. Overview of the MDA Approach*
*(Blanc and Salvatori 2011)*

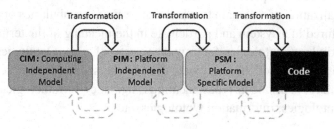

- **Computational Independent Model (CIM):** in which no computer considerations appear. It represents the system requirements, and describes the application and its environment and hides technical details of the system.
- **Platform Independent Model (PIM):** dedicated for analysis and design of the system. Models in this level describe structure and behavior of the application, but it does not include any technological details (operating system, programming language, hardware, network performance, etc.).
- **Platform Specific Model (PSM):** combine PIM specifications with system implementation in target platform to stipulate how the system uses a particular type of platforms which leads to include platforms specific details. Models in this level are closest to final code of application.
- **Code:** Represents the final result of the MDA process, the source code is obtained from the PSM using a generation engine. The final code generated can always be enriched or modified manually.
- **Model transformation**: is an important step in the MDA process, it is through transformations that models become productive elements of MDA. Performing the transformations ensures a traceability link between the different models of the MDA process. For this purpose, Model transformations are divided into two types: Model to Model (M2M) and Model to Text (M2T) transformations.
- **Reverse engineering:** means building models from existing applications (Raibulet et al., 2017). In this context, MDA also identifies inverse transformations: Code to PSM, PSM to PIM and PIM to CIM. In 2003, the OMG group lunched the ADM initiative in order to build and promote standards to modernize legacy systems.

The MDA approach advocates the use of OMG standards, among them UML(*About the Unified Modeling Language Specification Version 2.0*, 2017), MOF(GROUP, 2003) and XMI(X. OMG, 2000) (X. OMG, 2000), but does not exclude the use of other tools or languages. In the present work, we have exploited the two standards: ODM (Ontology Definition Metamodel), and UML (Unified Modeling Language) as central elements for design, transformation of models and generation of final code.

## Unified Modeling Language

The OMG publishes a variety of standard specifications, the best known is UML (Unified Modeling Language)(*About the Unified Modeling Language Specification Version 2.5.1*, s. d.). UML is the standard notation in the object-oriented modeling world advocating its use by the MDA(Miller et al., 2003). Its Metamodel integrates all the concepts necessary for the development of UML diagrams (use case, classes, sequences diagram ...), in addition, it provides a mechanism for extending UML modeling entities; notably classes, associations, properties etc., for building domain specific metamodel elements. The UML2.0 Infrastructure metamodel is split into around thirty packages to facilitate reuse. Its architecture is based on MOF(Meta Object Facility). MOF is a Meta Model Library considered as the foundation standard of the MDA four-layer architecture. MOF defines how UML models are exchanged between tools using XMI (XML Metadata Interchange). XMI is a serialization format for UML Models. The UML infrastructure is used at M2 and M3 levels as depicted in figure below.

On the other hand, class modeling concepts are the most widely used UML concepts (Shaikh & Wiil, 2018). According to the UML specification, a class model allows to express the conceptual model of information systems, even non-computer scientists use it for its simple graphical syntax that helps to understand the models easily. Moreover, several tools are available to model class diagrams like UML

*Figure 3. MDA four-layer MOF-based metadata architecture (Musumbu 2013)*

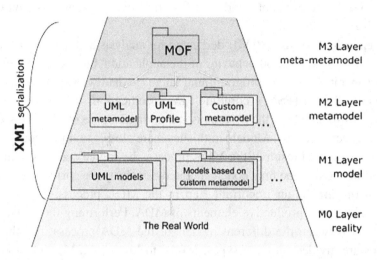

Designer(*UML Designer Documentation*, s. d.), etc. UML class model is a key ingredient of MDE. Several model-based approaches use only class diagrams have been proposed recently, we can cite (Elsayed & El-Sharawy, 2018; Esbai et al., 2017; Guskov et al., 2017; Hafeez et al., 2018; Rhazali et al., 2018; Sadowska, 2018).

## Ontology Definition Metamodel

The ODM specification has emerged in 2007. It defines a set of ontology metamodels; conforming to the MOF, and associated transformation methods (profiles and mappings)(ODM, 2007). ODM reflects an abstract syntax of different knowledge representation languages such as RDF, OWL or Topic Maps, etc. ODM defines five metamodels; RDFS, OWL, Topic Maps, Common Logic and Description Logic, two UML Profiles (RDFS/OWL Profile, Topic Maps Profile) and a set of QVT mappings from RDFS/OWL to Common Logic, Topic Maps to OWL and UML to OWL. This work uses two of technical artifacts defined by the present specification, which are the OWL and RDFS metamodels as depicted in figure 4.

*Figure 4. Dependencies between ODM metamodels*

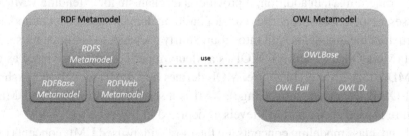

The ODM is applicable to conceptual modeling, formal taxonomy development, knowledge representation and ontology definition, and allows the design of ontologies using business models through mappings to MOF and UML, and this will facilitate their automatic generation (ODM, 2007).

The ODM plays a central role for bridging Semantic Web technologies and MDA based standards. The scope is to define semantics of several knowledge defined according to different formalisms, and thus, facilitate the exchange of knowledge models. By using these metamodels, it's possible to transform models expressed with UML syntax into ontologies(Musumbu, 2013).

with ODM, it would also be possible to profit more quickly from MDA's capabilities to develop ontology. There are two methods mentioned in ODM for the passage of a UML model to an RDF Schema model, either by using UML profiles or by transformation rules using language processing such as QVT, ATL, etc. We adopt the second method in order to generate our domain ontology linked to the graphical interfaces.

## RELATED WORK

This work proposes to use an enhanced MDA approach to facilitate the modeling of ontologies and to generate them automatically. Our proposal aims to encourage software analysts, developers, or designers that expect to easily use ontologies for improving Big data analytics and management, either for data integration and the implementation of big data management or data quality measurement, etc. On the other hand, several works based on MDA for ontology modeling exist in the literature. The most relevant are: (A\s smann et al., 2006; Bahaj & Bakkas, 2013; Belghiat & Bourahla, 2012; Brockmans et al., 2006; Gašević et al., 2007; Hillairet, 2007; Musumbu, 2013; Saripalle et al., 2013; Zedlitz et al., 2012)

A transformation from UML class diagrams to owl ontologies was presented by Belghiat et al. (Belghiat & Bourahla, 2012). Authors implement an application of the transformation based on graph transformation and by using the tool AToM3(De Lara & Vangheluwe, 2002). This approach has the advantage of generating owl file. But authors don't use transformation language like QVT or ATL. Nevertheless, they don't use ODM to generate ontologies and it's a great inconvenience because this meta model is considered one of standards defined by the object management group (OMG) for modeling ontologies.

Aÿmann et al. (A\s smann et al., 2006) describe the role of ontology in model-driven engineering. Authors present a scheme combining descriptive ontologies and prescriptive models in the meta-pyramid, the multi-level modelling approach of MDE. In this scheme, MDE starts from ontologies, refines, and augments them towards system models, respecting their relationships to prescriptive models on all metalevels.

Musumbu et al. (Musumbu, 2013) Propose an approach that use the benefice and advanced researches in Semantics Web, to combine it to Model Driven Architecture in the goal of making automatic business rules generation. This approach is based on merging MDA technologies and Semantics Web, but it does not allow an ontology generation from UML class diagrams while passing through the ODM metamodel. The authors of (Brockmans et al., 2006) presented an UML profile for OWL DL and OWL Full respecting ODM Metamodel. However, they did not achieve a real transformation based on the ODM standard while respecting the MDA architecture.

The last approach cited has some similarities with the work proposed by(Gašević et al., 2007). The proposed approach is based on the MDA architecture, using the UML profile of the ontologies as well as ODM. The model to model transformation was based on two phases, the first one consisted on an M2M transformation from Uml model to ODM model after that it executes another M2M transformation from ODM model to Xml Model and finally comes the phase of using an XML extractor they generate the owl file. This work done by these researchers has supported OMG's efforts in ontology development, and it is the only one that has covered the maximum of uml to odm transformation rules. Nevertheless, this approach has some lacks; use of two M2M transformations, no transformation language recommended by omg such as QVT. ODM implementation presented in (Hillairet, 2007) used the ATL language to develop the same approach presented by (Gašević et al., 2007).

In (Saripalle et al., 2013), an OWL translation of UML diagrams has been defined. Bahaj et al. (Bahaj & Bakkas, 2013) presented a method to convert a UML class diagram to an ontology using OWL / XML language but they don't use an MDA approach and its standards. On the other hand, Zedlitz et al. (Zedlitz et al., 2012) elaborate a QVT transformation between UML class diagrams and OWL 2 ontologies. The authors explicitly define the mapping rules between UML and OWL 2. however, this conversion has some limitations; doesn't support ABOX part of ontology and it would have been better if they used the ODM, furthermore, the authors talk about a QVT transformation while they have not used the MDA approach.

In this section, we highlighted interesting researches about ontology modeling in MDA. In brief, we can admit that all these approaches did not propose an MDA-based ontology generation process that exhibits the ODM standard, and the only one which generate owl file from ontology UML profile has gaps. This work represent an enhanced approach proposed for the generation of ontologies from UML class diagrams and ODM models using the MDA approach and QVT transformation to simplify their use in big data analytics.

## OUR PROPOSAL

This present work offers a new approach of the ontology development using OMG standards. It is based On an optimized and improved solution for automatically producing a standard format of domain

*Figure 5. The model driven development process*

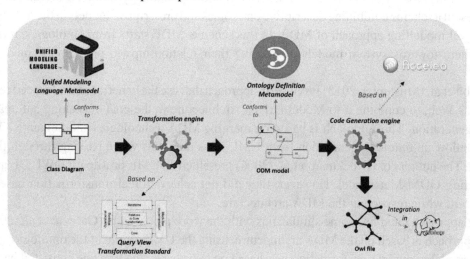

ontologies based on OMG standards. Therefore, with a simplified representation of ontology, different community in different domains, particularly Big data area, could use it.

So as to produce domain ontologies, a model driven development process is proposed in order to permit ontology modeling for big data analytics. The process of the desired approach relies on MDA standards, we cite UML and ODM standards. We choose for the process implementation Eclipse modeling tools. It supports MDA standards through a modeling framework (EMF) facility for the implementation of the standards.

As shown in figure 5, the process of producing domain ontologies contains three stages. In the first stage we start with the definition of the UML PIM metamodel and the ODM PSM metamodel, then we construct an abstract model according to UML metamodel to establish the following stage. In the second stage, we launch a M2M transformation so as to produce a model result describing eLearning domain. And eventually, we go to the last stage for establishing a M2T transformation that generates an ontology document, from the PSM model resulting from the second stage, which is conforms to RDF/XML serialization format.

## Construction Rules of PIM Level

UML was used in the PIM level to model the class diagram. The necessary steps and rules for constructing Class diagram are presented as follows:

- Identify and model **classes**; concepts having the same characteristics are gathered into classes.
- Define **attributes** and their admissible **values**; Characteristics distinguish one class from another.
- Identify and design **associations**; interconnections between the obtained classes
  - ○ Add meaningful names to associations.
  - ○ As a rule it is best to always indicate **multiplicities**; how many objects of each class are involved in a relationship. Multiplicities include minimums and maximums
  - ○ Names of associations or association classes are unique in an UML class diagram.
  - ○ An association may have a related **association class** that describes attributes of the association.
  - ○ Indicate **role** names when multiple associations between two classes exist
  - ○ Make associations bi-directional only when collaboration occurs in both directions.
- Identify **generalizations:** taxonomic relationships between a more general classifier named "superclass" and a more specific classifier named "subclass".
- Identify and make difference between **Aggregations and Compositions**. Aggregation is a specialization of association, highlighting an entire-part relationship that exists between a class named aggregate and a group of classes named constituent parts. The constituent parts can exist independently. However, composition is a much potent form of aggregation where the whole and parts have coincident lifetimes.
- An aggregation and composition have no associated class.
- Model a **dependency** when a relationship is in transition
- Never model implied relationships
- Never model every single dependency
- Design instances.

## Construction Rules of PSM Level

we choose for the PIM level of the process the UML metamodel to model class diagram which is very easy to construct. What is needed is to define ODM metamodel through a number of construction rules. we found many differences between what we call custom Ontology metamodels and ODM metamodel thing that renders the dynamic instance creation of the second one ambiguous. Elements in the other metamodels are arranged in different levels with their components, which is different from the representation of elements in the dynamic instance of ODM metamodel that keeps one level for all its components (OWLGraph, OWLOn-tology, OWLClass ...etc) with references for representing dependencies between them (see figure 6).

*Figure 6. References between metaclasses in ODM*

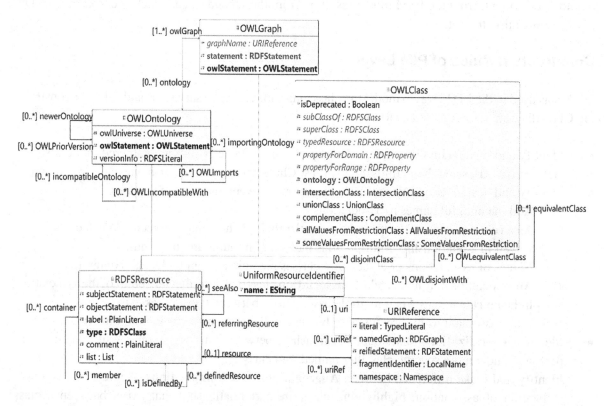

According to what we discussed before in section 2, we limit our process to the use of the two metamodels of ODM which are: OWL, that includes all concepts of RDFS and RDF, and RDFS for designing domain ontology. For constructing ODM components, it is necessary to affect a URI to each one for identification. We reference these URIs in the components via URIReference which has a "LocalName" and the referenced URI.

It remains to describe the rest of the construction rules as follows:

- "OWLGraph" is the root element.

- "OWLOntology" elements are referenced by "OWLClass" components.
- The elements which define the Properties for Domain and Range are "RDFSClass", "OWLObjectProperty" and "OWLDatatypeProperty".
- "ClassExpression" Specifies the different restrictions and extensions of classes, such as, *EquivalentClass, IntersectionClass, DisjointClass and ComplementClass.*
- "OWLClass" elements refer to Properties for Domain and Range and contain a Plain Literal that defines its name. OWL Classes is represented by RDFS Classes and OWL Properties are properties of RDF.
- RDFS defines two properties, rdfs:domain and rdfs:range that connect an rdf:Property with an rdfs:Class, allowing to distinguish various types of relations between various types of resources.
- Individual is represented by a subclass of "RDFSResource", "RDFSResource" is a superclass of "OWLClass". Single class is an instance of "OWLClass", so we can admit that classes are also resources
- "subClass" and "subproperty" in OWL are inherited from RDFS.

## M2M Transformation Rules

A mapping between two contents may be proceeded in three different methods: through a natural language, an algorithm in action language, or a model in a mapping language(Miller et al., 2003). The first method does not allow an automatic generation, it just gives an idea on the rules of mappings, for the second one, it does not give a clear vision on the output of the transformation. While the third method, specifies the transformation input and output models and allows a complete and precise transformation between them. We have opted for the third method via a model to model transformation language called QVT operational defined by OMG(Q. OMG, 2011). So, the Figure 7 displays the chosen method for applying a model to model transformation in our process.

*Figure 7. Adopted Method for M2M transformation*

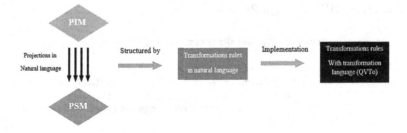

For mapping UML to ODM we consider all the UML metamodel (class diagram) components to be represented in the ODM standard. The table 2 shows our main transformation rules.

The M2M transformation admits the class model as the source model for the mapping. OWLGraph is the target to be built with an affected URI, we apply the same mapping for transforming package to OWLOntology. Actually, the concept of namespace is present in the two standards UML and OWL as "Package" in UML and "Ontology" in OWL. UML Class is transformed into OWLClass. The "ownedAttribute" relationship defines the attributes of each class. It is an "OrdredSet" of "Property" that can be mapped to either "OWLDatatypeProperty" or "OWLObjectProperty". If a property is a part of an association's "memberEnds" then the mapping will result "OWLObjectProperty", otherwise if the type of the property is "PrimitveType" then the property will be mapped to "OWLDatatypeProperty". "Domain" is the set of "OWLClass" that contains this "OWLDatatypeProperty". while "range" represents the type of "OWLDatatyoeProperty" which is defined by "RDFSClass"(see figure 8).

*Table 2. Mappings between UM and ODM concepts*

| UML | ODM |
|---|---|
| Model | OWLGraph |
| Package | OWLOntology |
| Class | OWLClass |
| AssociationClass | OWLClass |
| PrimitiveType | RDFSDataType |
| Enumeration | EnumeratedClass |
| Property | OWLDatatypeProperty |
|  | OWLObjectProperty |
|  | CardinalityRestriction |
|  | MaxCardinalityRestriction |
|  | MinCardinalityRestriction |
|  | SymmetricProperty |
|  | InverseFunctionalProperty |
| InstanceSpecification | Individual |
| Slot | OWLStatement |

*Figure 8. UML property to OWLDataTypeProperty*

```
mapping Property::Property2OWLDataProperties() : OWLDatatypeProperty {

    uriRef:=object URIReference{
            var ontologyName := self.owner.owner.oclAsType(Model).name;
            uri:=object UniformResourceIdentifier{
                name := addNamespace(ontologyName,self.name);
            }
        };

    domain += self.owner.oclAsType(Class).resolve(OWLClass);

    range += object RDFSClass{
            uriRef:= object URIReference{
            uri := object UniformResourceIdentifier{
                name:= getType(self.type.name);
            }
        }
    };
}
```

A Binary Association specifies a relationship between typed instances. It has exactly two ends represented by properties, each is connected to the end type. This association is mapped to OWLObjectProperty in a target model. The multiplicity of an UML class is mapped to (minimum and maximum) cardinality of the OWL object property.

*Figure 9. Dictionary of UML Types in QVTo Transformation*

```
helper getType(type:String) : String {
    var types: Dict(String,String):=Dict{
        'String'= 'http://www.w3.org/2001/XMLSchema#string',
        'Integer' = 'http://www.w3.org/2001/XMLSchema#nonNegativeInteger',
        'Boolean'= 'http://www.w3.org/2001/XMLSchema#boolean',
        'UnlimitedNatural'= 'http://www.w3.org/2001/XMLSchema#integer',
        'Byte'= 'http://www.w3.org/2001/XMLSchema#byte',
        'Currency'= 'http://www.w3.org/2001/XMLSchema#decimal',
        'Date'= 'http://www.w3.org/2001/XMLSchema#date',
        'Double'= 'http://www.w3.org/2001/XMLSchema#double',
        'Long'= 'http://www.w3.org/2001/XMLSchema#long',
        'Single'= 'http://www.w3.org/2001/XMLSchema#short',
        'Variant'= 'http://www.w3.org/2001/XMLSchema#string'};

    return types->get(type);
}
```

The dictionary shown in figure 9 defines different types of UML. Each type corresponds to an URI in ODM Model.

## Transformation Engine

The ontology file is derived directly from a PSM model using Acceleo template(Musset et al., 2006) without the need to use an XML extractor tool. We opted the use of RDF/XML type for the owl file generated, we define generation rules that bordered the construction of Ontology file. Our plugin allows to generate ontologies not only in RDF/XML format, but in other standard formats such as, JSON, OWL format, etc.

## RESULTS AND EVALUATION

This section shows an evaluation of our proposal's application to the case study presented in figure 10in order to validate its applicability and utility. The main goal of this evaluation consists of analyzing the Model-driven development process that can be functional in real application projects. The designed case study represents an e-learning domain. E-Learning systems help users from all around the world to take courses online using electronic devices such as computers, mobile phone, tablets, etc. It offers multiple advantages for the education process to different parties. For learners, e-learning allows them to directly interact with lessons for an engaging learning experience and they can learn at their own pace. For teachers, e-learning offers coherent course material that can be accessed anywhere and anytime, etc.

*Figure 10. e-learning Class Diagram*

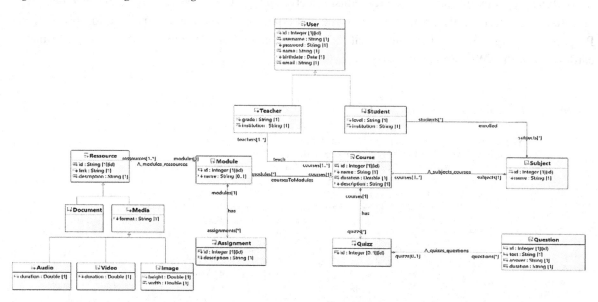

Big data has a relevant impact on eLearning by bringing more benefits, as a matter of fact it allows by a data-driven analytics to enhance the eLearning process, for example institutions and teachers can identify the most popular strategies that provide a better experience for individuals which will help

*Figure 11. Class Diagram Excerpt*

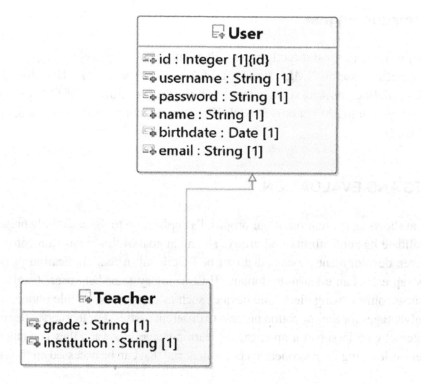

improve the efficiency of eLearning by advertising and suggesting to the users the most relevant and popular courses according to their preferences, etc. With that said, big data analytics can provide much of help for institutions in such a way that with less effort and less cost, can provide much better and effective user experience.

Once the e-learning system has been sufficiently modeled using the Class diagram, the model is used as an input for the transformation engine developed for the approach. Indeed, we will first generate a PSM model for the e-learning domain that respects the ODM metamodel. Then, it will become the input for the code generation part document that was developed using Acceleo.

The resulting file is an owl file representing an e-learning domain ontology. the result is very long either in the ODM model or the ontology generated. Using SPARQL queries we obtained the following result: Forty-six Subjects, 6 Predicates and thirty-seven Objects distributed as: fifteen classes, 5 object [properties]. So it is difficult to display all the results. that's why we chose to [show res]ults depicted in figure 11.

[The] owl classes(User, Teacher) are defined by "owl:class" tag and identi-[fied by the "about"] attribute. The "institution" data type property is represented by

*[PS]M model obtained from the QVTo transformation*

✦ Uniform Resource Identifier http://www.w3.org/2001/XMLSchema#string

"owl:DatatypeProperty" tag and identified by an Uri in the "rdf:about" attribute, this data type property belongs to the Teacher class presented in the "rdfs:domain" tag by a reference of its Uri in the "rdf:resource" attribute, the data type of this data type property is defined in the "rdfs:range" tag and referencing the type by an Uri in the "rdf:resource" attribute ;This data type property is valid for all the other ones.

The figure 13 presents a part of the output file in RDF/XML format, it describes the result of the M2T transformation. The Teacher class is a subclass of the User class, this relation is presented in the first one by an contained "owl:subClassOf" tag referencing the User class in "rdf:resource" tag containing its URI.

Many XML Namespaces are used to present our ontology, from which we mension: xmlns:owl="http://www.w3.org/2002/07/owl#". This ontology can be used in the development of semantic web applications through the integration of annotations into web pages(N. Laaz & Mbarki, 2019; Naziha Laaz & Mbarki, 2016).

*Figure 13. An OWL file excerpt of e-learning domain*

```
<owl:Class rdf:about="http://www.semanticweb.org/naziha/ontologies/ELearning#User">        User class
</owl:Class>

<owl:Class rdf:about="http://www.semanticweb.org/naziha/ontologies/ELearning#Teacher">      Teacher class
    <rdfs:subClassOf>
        <owl:Restriction>
            <owl:onProperty rdf:resource="http://www.semanticweb.org/naziha/ontologies/ELearning#teach"/>
            <owl:allValuesFrom rdf:resource="http://www.semanticweb.org/naziha/ontologies/ELearning#Teacher"/>
        </owl:Restriction>
    </rdfs:subClassOf>
    <rdfs:subClassOf rdf:resource="http://www.semanticweb.org/naziha/ontologies/ELearning#User"/>
</owl:Class>

<owl:DatatypeProperty rdf:about="http://www.semanticweb.org/naziha/ontologies/ELearning#institution">    institution dataPropery
    <rdfs:domain rdf:resource="http://www.semanticweb.org/naziha/ontologies/ELearning#Teacher"/>           for Teacher class
    <rdfs:range rdf:resource="http://www.w3.org/2001/XMLSchema#string"/>
</owl:DatatypeProperty>
```

## CONCLUSION

After many papers mainly devoted to the generation of domain ontologies, we focused here on using an approach based on standards. As a matter of fact, in this paper, we present an improved solution for generating domain ontologies automatically from UML class diagrams using an MDA approach. The objective of this paper is to stress on the big importance of ontology development in Big Data analytics. To this end, a model has been developed as an UML class diagram, transformed to ODM model, then used to obtain owl file respecting a standard syntax. As a result, we obtained an ontology files which can be shared with ontological engineering tools.

The proposed solution is one of the best useful development techniques for all software engineers. It can increase everyday productivity in big data and this ontology can easily be stored and implemented in many big data technologies such as Hadoop distributed file system. The future contribution will deal with deriving ontologies in other serialization formats such as JSON, OWL, etc.

# REFERENCES

Assmann, U., Zschaler, S., & Wagner, G. (2006). Ontologies, meta-models, and the model-driven paradigm. In *Ontologies for software engineering and software technology* (pp. 249–273). Springer.

Bahaj, M., & Bakkas, J. (2013). Automatic conversion method of class diagrams to ontologies maintaining their semantic features. *Int. J. Soft Comput. Eng., 2*.

Belghiat, A., & Bourahla, M. (2012). Automatic generation of OWL ontologies from UML class diagrams based on meta-modelling and graph grammars. *World Academy of Science, Engineering and Technology, 6*(8), 380–385.

Berners-Lee, T., Hendler, J., & Lassila, O. (2001). The semantic web. *Scientific American, 284*(5), 28–37. doi:10.1038cientificamerican0501-34 PMID:11341160

Blanc, X., & Salvatori, O. (2011). *MDA en action : Ingénierie logicielle guidée par les modèles*. Editions Eyrolles.

Brambilla, M., Cabot, J., & Wimmer, M. (2017). Model-driven software engineering in practice. *Synthesis Lectures on Software Engineering, 3*(1), 1–207. doi:10.2200/S00751ED2V01Y201701SWE004

Brockmans, S., Colomb, R. M., Haase, P., Kendall, E. F., Wallace, E. K., Welty, C., & Xie, G. T. (2006). A model driven approach for building OWL DL and OWL full ontologies. *International Semantic Web Conference*, 187–200. 10.1007/11926078_14

Chen, M., Mao, S., & Liu, Y. (2014). Big data : A survey. *Mobile Networks and Applications, 19*(2), 171–209. doi:10.100711036-013-0489-0

De Giacomo, G., Lembo, D., Lenzerini, M., Poggi, A., & Rosati, R. (2018). Using ontologies for semantic data integration. In *A Comprehensive Guide Through the Italian Database Research Over the Last 25 Years* (pp. 187–202). Springer. doi:10.1007/978-3-319-61893-7_11

De Lara, J., & Vangheluwe, H. (2002). AToM 3 : A Tool for Multi-formalism and Meta-modelling. *International Conference on Fundamental Approaches to Software Engineering*, 174–188. 10.1007/3-540-45923-5_12

Elsayed, E. K., & El-Sharawy, E. E. (2018). Detecting Design Level Anti-patterns; Structure and Semantics in UML Class Diagrams. *Journal of Computers, 13*(6), 638–655. doi:10.17706/jcp.13.6.638-654

Esbai, R., Erramdani, M., Elotmani, F., & Atounti, M. (2017). Model-to-Model Transformation in Approach by Modeling to Generate a RIA Model with GWT. *International Conference on Information Technology and Communication Systems*, 82–94.

Extensible Markup Language (XML). (2017). https://www.w3.org/XML/

Falquet, G., Métral, C., Teller, J., & Tweed, C. (2011). *Ontologies in urban development projects*. Springer Science & Business Media. doi:10.1007/978-0-85729-724-2

Gašević, D., Djurić, D., & Devedžić, V. (2007). MDA-based automatic OWL ontology development. *International Journal of Software Tools for Technology Transfer*, *9*(2), 103–117. doi:10.100710009-006-0002-1

Group, O. M. (2003). *Meta Object Facility (MOF) 2.0 Core Specification*.

GuideM. R. (2015). *2.0, OMG*.

Guskov, G., Namestnikov, A., & Yarushkina, N. (2017). Approach to the Search for Similar Software Projects Based on the UML Ontology. *International Conference on Intelligent Information Technologies for Industry*, 3–10.

Hafeez, A., Mussavi, S. H. A., Rehman, A.-U., & Shaikh, A. (2018). Ontology-Based Finite Satisfiability of UML Class Model. *IEEE Access: Practical Innovations, Open Solutions*, *6*, 3040–3050. doi:10.1109/ACCESS.2017.2786781

Hillairet, G. (2007). *ATL Use Case-ODM Implementation (Bridging UML and OWL)*. http://www. eclipse. org/m2m/atl/usecases/ODMImplementation

Konys, A. (2016). Ontology-Based Approaches to Big Data Analytics. *International Multi-Conference on Advanced Computer Systems*, 355–365.

Kozaki. (n.d.). *Ontology Engineering for Big Data* [Technologie]. https://fr.slideshare.net/KoujiKozaki/ontology-engineering-for-big-data

Laaz, Naziha, & Mbarki. (2016). Integrating IFML models and owl ontologies to derive UIs web-Apps. *Information Technology for Organizations Development (IT4OD), 2016 International Conference on*, 1–6.

Laaz, N., & Mbarki, S. (2019). *OntoifML : Automatic generation of annotated web pages from IFML and ontologies using the MDA approach: A case study of an EMR management application*. Scopus.

Liu, J., Pacitti, E., & Valduriez, P. (2018). A Survey of Scheduling Frameworks in Big Data Systems. *International Journal of Cloud Computing*, 1–27.

Miller, J., Mukerji, J., & Belaunde, M. (2003). *MDA guide*. Object Management Group.

Musset, J., Juliot, É., Lacrampe, S., Piers, W., Brun, C., Goubet, L., Lussaud, Y., & Allilaire, F. (2006). *Acceleo user guide*. See also http://acceleo. org/doc/obeo/en/acceleo-2.6-user-guide. pdf

Musumbu, K. (2013). Towards a Model Driven Semantics Web using the Ontology. *The 2013 International Conference on Advanced ICT for Business and Management (ICAICTBM2013), 700*.

Nadal, S., Romero, O., Abelló, A., Vassiliadis, P., & Vansummeren, S. (2018). *An integration-oriented ontology to govern evolution in big data ecosystems*. arXiv preprint arXiv:1801.05161

ODM. (2007). *Ontology Definition Metamodel–OMG Adopted Specification*. Object Management Group. http://www. omg. org/spec/ODM/1.0/Beta2/PDF/

OMG. (2000). *Metadata Interchange (XMI) Specification*. http://www. omg. org/docs/formal/05-05-01. pdf

OMG. (2010). *Unified modeling language (OMG UML), superstructure, version 2.3*. Object Management Group.

OMG. (2011). *Meta Object Facility 2.0, Query/View/Transformation Specification.*

Psyché, V., Mendes, O., & Bourdeau, J. (2003). Apport de l'ingénierie ontologique aux environnements de formation à distance. *Sciences et Technologies de l'Information et de la Communication pour l'Éducation et la Formation, 10*(1), 89–126. doi:10.3406tice.2003.858

Raibulet, C., Fontana, F. A., & Zanoni, M. (2017). Model-Driven Reverse Engineering Approaches : A Systematic Literature Review. *IEEE Access: Practical Innovations, Open Solutions, 5*, 14516–14542. doi:10.1109/ACCESS.2017.2733518

RDF - Semantic Web Standards. (n.d.). Consulté 18 février 2018, à l'adresse https://www.w3.org/RDF/

Rhazali, Y., Hadi, Y., Chana, I., Lahmer, M., & Rhattoy, A. (2018). A model transformation in model driven architecture from business model to web model. *IAENG International Journal of Computer Science, 45*(1), 104–117.

Roche, C. (2005). Terminologie et ontologie. *Langages, 1*(1), 48–62. doi:10.3917/lang.157.0048

Saber, A., Al-Zoghby, A. M., & Elmougy, S. (2018). Big-Data Aggregating, Linking, *Integrating and Representing Using Semantic Web Technologies. International Conference on Advanced Machine Learning Technologies and Applications*, 331–342.

Sadowska, M. (2018). A Prototype Tool for Semantic Validation of UML Class Diagrams with the Use of Domain Ontologies Expressed in OWL 2. In *Towards a Synergistic Combination of Research and Practice in Software Engineering* (pp. 49–62). Springer. doi:10.1007/978-3-319-65208-5_4

Saripalle, R. K., Demurjian, S. A., De la Rosa Algarín, A., & Blechner, M. (2013). A software modeling approach to ontology design via extensions to ODM and OWL. *International Journal on Semantic Web and Information Systems, 9*(2), 62–97. doi:10.4018/jswis.2013040103

Shaikh, A., & Wiil, U. K. (2018). Overview of Slicing and Feedback Techniques for Efficient Verification of UML/OCL Class Diagrams. *IEEE Access: Practical Innovations, Open Solutions, 6*, 23864–23882. doi:10.1109/ACCESS.2018.2797695

Storey, V. C., & Song, I.-Y. (2017). Big data technologies and Management : What conceptual modeling can do. *Data & Knowledge Engineering, 108*, 50–67. doi:10.1016/j.datak.2017.01.001

Taneja, R., & Gaur, D. (2018). Robust Fuzzy Neuro system for Big Data Analytics. In *Big Data Analytics* (pp. 543–552). Springer. doi:10.1007/978-981-10-6620-7_52

UML Designer Documentation. (2018). http://www.umldesigner.org/

Zedlitz, J., Jörke, J., & Luttenberger, N. (2012). From UML to OWL 2. In Knowledge Technology (pp. 154–163). Springer.

# Chapter 3
# An Overview of Knowledge Representation With Frames

**Vladislavs Nazaruks**
*Riga Technical University, Latvia*

**Jānis Osis**
*Riga Technical University, Latvia*

## ABSTRACT

*Knowledge can be represented in different formats. At present, knowledge representation as ontologies is the mainstream, while much less is heard about frames. In order to understand the state-of-the art of knowledge frames application, the authors overviewed recent research work in IEEE Xplore Digital Library, SpringerLink, ScienceDirect, and ACM Digital Library from 2000 till 2020. The overview touched such aspects as knowledge acquisition techniques, constituent parts of frames, the actual state of technologies used, capabilities of frames integration with other formats, and limitations. The results showed that native limitations of knowledge frames lead to creation of hybrid knowledge bases. However, hybrid systems also have known issues in performance and inconsistency of knowledge due to a conflict between paradigms. Moreover, a large part of technologies mentioned is not supported nowadays. The results can be useful for researchers who investigate whether to use knowledge frames for managing knowledge.*

## INTRODUCTION

Insufficient analysis of a problem domain is one of main causes of inadequacy of the proposed solution to customer's needs. There are several causes of the insufficient analysis, i.e., instability of the problem domain itself, informal or semiformal specification and representation means, provision of the domain knowledge for all stakeholders.

Unification, standardization and solid theory are three main things, joint use of which can solve this problem (Osis & Asnina, 2014). The result of unification is Unified Modelling Language (UML) and Business Process Model and Notation (BPMN). Standardization is an ongoing process. The results of

DOI: 10.4018/978-1-7998-3661-2.ch003

this process are open interfaces for common usage and integration. Development of the solid theory (or theories) has been just started and is the most difficult task. It requires accurate understanding of domain phenomena.

This research is one of the small steps towards finding the solid theory for software development. The main target is creation of the automated domain knowledge acquisition, analysis and transformation to source code. The authors assume that automatedly acquired domain knowledge can be kept and verified in a knowledge base and then used either for design model generation or for code generation. Since the current programming paradigm is the object-oriented one, the authors assume that knowledge frames (as a more similar structure) can be suitable means for knowledge representation, analysis, keeping and transformation.

In the given research, the authors overview research works that deal with knowledge frames. The objective is to summarize information about knowledge acquisition, frame elements, implementation technologies, existing limitations in implementation and integration with other knowledge representation formats. This research is an updated and extended version of results presented in (Nazaruks & Osis, 2017a). Additionally, the authors provide results of analysis of validity of found technologies used for knowledge systems. It is necessary since technologies (tools, frameworks, shells, languages, etc.) used for knowledge representation become obsolete very fast. New technologies take some successfully implemented principles or constructs from those outdated means. It allows understanding main trends in the field that appeared due to different stakeholders' needs.

The Background Section explains the authors' vision and background information in more detail. The section "Use of Knowledge Frames for Domain Knowledge Specification" gives an overview of the related research work. The section "Discussion on Findings" summarizes the results. The last two sections state a further direction of the research and describe main findings.

## BACKGROUND

Software development lacks rigor separation of concerns in specifications. Model Driven Architecture (MDA) (Miller & Mukerji, 2001) proposed by the Object Management Group (OMG) introduces three concerns (or viewpoints) and related models, namely, a computation independent model (CIM), a platform independent model (PIM) and a platform specific model (PSM). MDA can be defined as "an approach to system development and interoperability that uses models to express and direct the course of understanding, requirements elicitation, design, construction, deployment, operation, maintenance, and modification" (OMG, 2010).

The first model that can be used for problem domain analysis is a CIM. This model allows specifying a domain knowledge expressed as business rules and processes, data vocabulary and requirements to the system and to the software (Miller & Mukerji, 2001). Therefore, usually the representation formats are unstructured (informal) or semi-structured (semi-formal) text and graphical representations, e.g., BPMN (Yassine Rhazali, Hadi, & Mouloudi, 2016), Data Flow Diagrams (Kardoš & Drozdová, 2010), UML diagrams (e.g. use case and activity diagrams), user stories, business rules (Essebaa & Chantit, 2016), etc. Advantages of formal and structured formats is that they can be used for automated processing and inferring. Therefore, the question on what a format to use in order to specify and automatedly process enough domain facts and rules is still open.

As mentioned, a CIM is the first model and a starting point for further model transformations. Therefore, it is vitally necessary to describe a domain knowledge in it in the consistent and formal (i.e., computer understandable) format. The authors use a Topological Functioning Model (TFM) proposed by Jānis Osis (Osis, 1969)as such a CIM(Osis & Donins, 2017). The TFM allows specifying systems' functionality, behavior and structure. The systems could be of different types, e.g., mechanical and biological (Osis & Beghi, 1997; Osis, Gelfandbain, Markovich, & Novozilova, 1991) as well as software (Osis & Donins, 2017). This model is mathematical. Thus, its representation formats can be a list, a matrix, a graph. However, in order to automate knowledge processing and inferring the authors search a proper knowledge representation format to create a domain knowledge base built on principles of the TFM(Figure 1). Additional requirements to that format are existence of an inferring mechanism to avoid untrue facts and suitability for further transformations to source code via PIMs or PSMs. The transformations between the MDA models with a starting point at the CIM are under research at present (Rhazali, Hadi, & Mouloudi, 2015; Osis & Donins, 2017; Rhazali, Hadi, Chana, Lahmer, & Rhattoy, 2018; Rhazali et al., 2016). Besides that, the knowledge base should store facts about two domains, namely, a problem domain and a solution domain. Moreover, the two domain facts must be in consistency (Nazaruks & Osis, 2017b). All these aspects made the authors look at knowledge frames.

*Figure 1. The place of the knowledge base in the computation independent model*
*(Nazaruks & Osis, 2017a)*

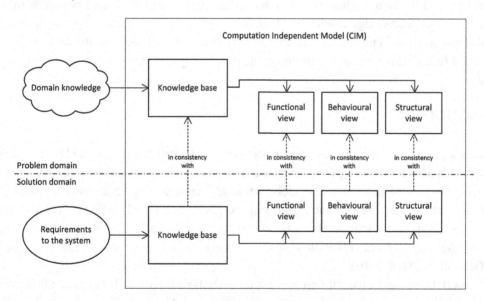

Besides knowledge frames, a knowledge can be represented as ontologies, concept networks, product rules etc. as well as in artificial (e.g., Esperanto, Conlang, Lingvata) or controlled natural languages. The artificial languages may help in translating semantics correctly from one language to another(Roux, 2013). However, this field is very specific and is out of scope of this paper. Each knowledge representation format has its own limitations usually in knowledge acquisition and representation (Kornienko, Kornienko, Fofanov, & Chubik, 2015) and search (Kornienko et al., 2015; Marinov, 2004).

According to Minsky's definition (Minsky, 1974), "a frame is a data structure for representing a stereotyped situation". A collection of frames linked together is called a frame system. Implementation of frame systems began from a Lisp-based language(Foster & Juell, 2006) At present, a number of languages can be used for the implementation. Frames and ontologies differ in their inferring mechanisms. Frames support the closed-world inferring paradigm (Detwiler, Mejino, & Brinkley, 2016), where all facts that are presented in the system are true. If some fact is not presented, that means that it is untrue. It allows avoiding errors in inferring mechanism related to the knowledge representation format. Ontologies support the open-world paradigm, where all facts that are not presented may also be true. This can lead to errors in inferring mechanism, but on the other hand may allow an engineer to discover new knowledge from the existing facts.

According to our vision (Figure 1), a declarative and procedural knowledge on a domain should be maintained in a format appropriate to model transformations within the object-oriented paradigm. Therefore, the following questions on frames and their application were set:

**Question 1:** How are facts entered into the frame systems: manually or automatedly?
**Question 2:** What domains of knowledge the frame systems are used for?
**Question 3:** What implementation technologies are used, and are they up to date?
**Question 4:** What are differences in frames structures?
**Question 5:** What limitations exist in frame systems and hybrid systems with frames?
**Question 6:** What knowledge representation formats frames are integrated with?

The authors have investigated the following publication databases: IEEEXplore Digital Library, SpringerLink, ScienceDirect, and ACM Digital Library. Search keywords used were "frame-based knowledge system", "frame-based knowledge base", "frame system", "knowledge frame", "knowledge base". The publication time is a period from 2000 to 2020.

In the ACM Digital Library, 14 publications on frames were found. Four of them were excluded since either were not related to the frames or contained only detailed information of frame elements. Ten publications were overviewed (Beltrán-Ferruz, González-Calero, & Gervás, 2004; Corcoglioniti, Rospocher, & Aprosio, 2016; Foster & Juell, 2006; Gennari, Mork, & Li, 2005; Grigorova & Nikolov, 2007; Kim, Lee, Jung, & Lee, 2008; Kramer & Kaindl, 2004; Marinov, 2004; Rector, 2013; Tan, Kaliyaperumal, & Benis, 2007).

In the ScienceDirect database, 8 publications were found and overviewed (Al-Saqqar, Bentahar, & Sultan, 2016; Bimba et al., 2016; Detwiler et al., 2016; Hernández & Serrano, 2001; Marinov, 2008; Shiue, Li, & Chen, 2008; Xue, Ghenniwa, & Shen, 2012; Zopounidis, Doumpos, & Matsatsinis, 1997).

In the SpringerLink database and the IEEE Xplore Digital Library, 2 publications were found and overviewed (Tettamanzi, 2006; Xue, Ghenniwa, & Shen, 2010).

The selected publications are overviewed in the chronological sequence. Since the publication year of the overviewed sources ends with 2016 (that is a quite long time for IT technologies), the validity (or actuality) of the mentioned technologies is overviewed.

## USE OF KNOWLEDGE FRAMES FOR DOMAIN KNOWLEDGE SPECIFICATION

Frames as a part of hybrid knowledge-based system are presented in (Hernández & Serrano, 2001), where they are integrated with product rules, constraints and other knowledge representation techniques. The knowledge base represents control knowledge and domain knowledge required for the emergency system. Design and implementation are done using Knowledge Structure Manager tool and the corresponding methodology.

The manual knowledge acquisition is described in (Beltrán-Ferruz et al., 2004), where the frame system represents Mikrokosmos system that is used in knowledge-based machine translations. The Mikrokosmos contains definitions of concepts that correspond to classes of things and events in the world. The world model is organized as objects, events and properties set in a complex hierarchy. The format of Mikrokosmos Ontology formally introduces its syntax and semantics using a BNF grammar. Ontology is saved in a text file using Spencer notation that is based on XML. Another possibility is to use notation called Beale that is based on Lisp. The reasoning is implemented using JENA and the DIG interface, as well there are two different inference engines: RACER and FaCT. For ontology implementation, they have developed an import plug-in for Protege 2.0. The frames used contain a concept name, slots, corresponding facets and filler(s). There are two kinds of slot fillers: (1) ATTRIBUTE or RELATION, that represent links between concepts in the hierarchy; (2) special ONTOLOGY-SLOTs dedicated to determining the structure of ontology. Possible descendants for the latter one are DEFINITION, DOMAIN, INSTANCES, INVERSE, IS-A, RANGE and SUBCLASSES. A filler generally contains either a name of a concept of the ontology or an instance. The authors mention that some special slots limit expressiveness. In the research, the authors provide mappings from Mikrokosmos Ontology frame system to descriptive logic language OWL that supports SHIQ logic. Because of the transformation, some knowledge is kept as annotations to description logic concepts due to the limitation of description logic expressiveness.

The authors in (Kramer & Kaindl, 2004) also discuss knowledge frame-based systems, which contain frames with slots with values and rules in form IF-THEN that are not attached to frames. The authors believe that evaluation of modularization metrics such as coupling and cohesion can help in assessment of technical quality of such systems that may suffer from inadequate representation of knowledge. This evaluation should help quickly understand potential problems with constructs in the knowledge base.

The implementation of frames using XML (eXtensible Markup Language) is discussed in (Marinov, 2004). Evolution of web-based knowledge modelling languages opens new opportunities for the application of Web-oriented frame-based knowledge representation. The new generation of such languages is DAMPL (DARPA Agent Markup Language), OIL (Ontology Inference Layer) and SHOE (Simple HTML Ontology Extension). They are system independent and web compatible thanks to XML and RDF support. The frame structure considered in the research is classical one, where a frame consists of slots, facets, and active slots with query procedures and daemons, which represent product rules. As the author mentions in (Marinov, 2008), tools for implementation of frame systems may be Protégé 2000, Conceptually Oriented Design/Description Environment (CODE4), and FramerD (a distributed object-oriented database).

The authors in (Gennari et al., 2005) investigate transformations between two fundamentally different knowledge representation formats, namely frame systems and relational databases. A frame-based system was developed in Protégé that subscribes to the Open Knowledge Base Connectivity. The authors declare that a frame-based system has greater expressiveness, and such transformation should lead to the loss of some information.

The author in (Tettamanzi, 2006) proposes a frame-based formalism for representing imprecise knowledge, combining it with fuzzy logic. The formalism is based on frames, but frames are simplified. According to this formalism, knowledge consists of three basic types of objects: (1) knowledge elements, which can be either atomic (atoms) or complex (frames); (2) fuzzy sets, or linguistic values; and (3) relations, which can be fuzzy rules or subsumption relations.

The list of the basic methods for knowledge representation (Grigorova & Nikolov, 2007) state that classification and inheritance in frame systems support knowledge engineering efficiently. The authors mention three disadvantages of frame-based knowledge base: (1) it should work with completely known object characteristics; (2) the knowledge domain has to be static; and (3) the fact that procedural knowledge is represented with programming code inside the frame does not allow reasoning about this knowledge (reasoning could be done with it). The authors declare that frames are a proper method for knowledge representation when the goal is realization of a natural language sentences analyzer.

In (Tan et al., 2007), the authors use ontologies as a structured and semantic representation of domain knowledge. The authors propose a method for building frame-based corpus for the domain of biomedicine based on domain knowledge provided by ontologies. They compared one frame to the corresponding frame in BioFrameNet and examined the gaps between the semantic classification of the target words in the domain-specific corpus and in FrameNet and PropBank/VerbNet.

The authors in (Kim et al., 2008) describe frame application for probabilistic dialog systems, namely, they have introduced a frame-based state representation. The frames have slots that can dynamically update their values, and frames can be grouped per indistinguishable user goal states. Knowledge acquisition methods and integration with other knowledge representation formats are not discussed.

Application of frames in banking expert systems, which requires fast and up-to-date decision-making, is discussed in (Shiue et al., 2008). The basic knowledge representation format for such systems are rules that in the long run lead to decrease of the understandability and accessibility of the knowledge base as well as to increase of the complexity of maintenance of knowledge rules. The knowledge acquisition is manual. The frames are chosen since they provide "an easy way for encapsulating declarative knowledge with procedural one". The frames contain slots with decision-making criteria, and corresponding procedures. Frame system maintenance foresees changing rules stored in objects. To create web-enabled interface for the expert system, the authors use Jess (Java Expert System Shell) and Object Web model, while an UML class diagram is used for representation of the model of the frame system. JavaBeans structures encapsulate the knowledge objects in the knowledge base. The limitation of such implementation is decrease of the performance of the system inference and execution, when the knowledge frame structure gets more complicated.

The authors in (Xue et al., 2010) propose a frame-based ontological view specification language (FOSL) that is based on the knowledge frame paradigm and uses XML as encoding. XML documents that hold knowledge frames allow development of web-enabled information systems. The authors suggest using the "ontological views" on the conceptualization of the domain, thus establishing a possibility of several such views, and integration of ontological languages. The language uses a concept of a frame that has four standard levels: frame, slot, facet, and data. The authors also indicate frame paradigm characteristics, i.e. a trade-off between the good expressiveness and the ease of inference. Continuing their research in (Xue et al., 2012), the authors analyze the capabilities of semantic integration on the basis of the frame-based ontological view, which can be created from the information model of an information system.

The interesting discussion about representation and inference possibilities of ontologies, frames and UML is given in (Rector, 2013). The author distinguishes knowledge representation systems into template-based (frames and UML) and axiom-based (ontology) by their inference mechanisms. It considers classical frame structures provided by Protégé-Frames.

The authors in (Sim & Brouse, 2014) uses Protégé-Frames tool for implementation of OntoPersona-URM model that consists of three interrelated ontologies. This system like a system in (Shiue et al., 2008) is foreseen to be web-enabled and able to check constraints and run queries on the ontology by using PAL plug-in toolset of Protégé-Frames.

The authors in (Al-Saqqar et al., 2016) use knowledge frames to represent agent knowledge and correspondent communicative commitments presented by modal logic in multi-agent systems. The knowledge frame-based system is integrated with model checking mechanism. However, it is not clear what method is used to acquire knowledge to the frame system.

The authors in (Bimba et al., 2016) provide very exhaustive survey on knowledge representation, implementation and acquisition techniques (for years 2000–2015), i.e. the linguistic knowledge bases, expert knowledge bases, ontology and cognitive knowledge bases. The authors stress that a use of production rules that contain expert knowledge is not suitable for every knowledge type. The authors found out that knowledge acquisition is manual through communication with domain experts with some automated methods such as LSPE and acquiring English sentences from the Open Mind Common Sense (OMCS) corpus. The authors have summarized that there are different applications for Natural Language Processing, Question Answering, Information extraction/retrieval, classification, knowledge discovery, engineering, health care, education, finance, environment, business, machine learning, robotics and forecasting. To implement linguistic knowledge bases, FrameNet, WordNet and ConceptNet supporting tools are used such as Sesame, SWI, NTLK, and ADW. Programming and mark-up languages used in such implementations may be XML, Python, Java, SQL, RDF, SPARQL, Perl, and JSON. In case of product rules in expert systems Prolog is also used. In most linguistic knowledge bases, frame elements, semantic networks and semantic graphs (of frames, lexical semantic associations between synsets and graphs) are used, while expert knowledge bases make a use of IF-THEN rules that join linguistic objects, values and operators. One of big limitations of linguistic knowledge bases are their dependence on volatile expert knowledge, and expensiveness and difficulty in building and expending the base. Besides that, frame nets cannot handle text coherence and link arguments across sentences. As the authors mention, FrameNets integration with other knowledge representation techniques is very difficult, and transformation to them requires additional effort in preserving richness of its annotations.

The authors in (Corcoglioniti et al., 2016) suggest a new approach called PIKES that is implemented as an open-source Java application. This approach is dedicated to analysis of any text in a natural language by means of several Natural Language Processing tools. The resulting net is implemented in RDF (Resource Description Framework) knowledge graph by means of extended RDFpro tool and support of SPARQL-like rule evaluation, where instances are linked to matching entities in DBpedia using OWL elements, and typed according to classes encoding VerbNet, FrameNet, PropBank and NomBank frame types.

The authors in (Detwiler et al., 2016) describe the transformation of the Foundational Model of Anatomy (FMA) represented in a frame system to the modern semantic web language OWL2. The main difficulty of the transformation lies in the difference between closed-world assumption made in frame systems and open-world assumption made in the ontology. The open-world assumptions may lead to mismatches in interpretations, since from its point of view even if some fact is not stated in the system, it does not mean that this fact is untrue (as it is in frame systems). Therefore, some untrue facts may be considered as possible. The frames in FMA are characterized by names, slots and facets (that are used as constraints to slot values). But there is no straight correspondence between slots and class properties in OWL, since slots may represent as frame structural properties as relations to other frames. Besides that, in frames the semantic of slots without values is not clearly defined. Although it is possible to have such slots in frames, in the ontology only those properties that must have values are to be listed.

## DISCUSSION ON FINDINGS

### Summary of Answers

Summarizing overview results here (Table 1, Table 2, Table 3), the authors can conclude that the most common way of entering knowledge into the frame system is manual, i.e. a knowledge engineer enters facts and assertions based on results of interviews with domain experts and other sources. Only in case of text analyzers automated entering is applied. However, the amount of human participation in this process is not clear.

*Table 1. Answers to Question 1 and Question 2*

| Characteristics | References |
|---|---|
| **Question 1. How are facts entered into the frame systems: manually or automatedly?** | |
| Manual | (Beltrán-Ferruz et al., 2004; Bimba et al., 2016; Detwiler et al., 2016; Shiue et al., 2008) |
| Automated | (Corcoglioniti et al., 2016; Grigorova & Nikolov, 2007; Xue et al., 2010, 2012) |
| Not discussed (assumed to be manual) | (Al-Saqqar et al., 2016; Gennari et al., 2005; Hernández & Serrano, 2001; Kim et al., 2008; Rector, 2013; Shiue et al., 2008; Sim & Brouse, 2014; Tan et al., 2007; Tettamanzi, 2006) |
| **Question 2. What domains of knowledge the frame systems are used for?** | |
| Emergency systems | (Hernández & Serrano, 2001) |
| Machine translation | (Beltrán-Ferruz et al., 2004; Bimba et al., 2016) |
| Biomedicine, health care | (Bimba et al., 2016; Detwiler et al., 2016; Tan et al., 2007) |
| Probabilistic dialog systems (forecasting) | (Bimba et al., 2016; Kim et al., 2008) |
| Banking expert systems | (Bimba et al., 2016; Shiue et al., 2008) |
| Not domain-specific (Natural language processing, question answering, information extraction/retrieval, classification, machine learning, robotics) | (Al-Saqqar et al., 2016; Bimba et al., 2016; Gennari et al., 2005; Grigorova & Nikolov, 2007; Kramer & Kaindl, 2004; Marinov, 2004, 2008; Rector, 2013; Sim & Brouse, 2014; Tettamanzi, 2006; Xue et al., 2010, 2012) |

(Nazaruks & Osis, 2017a)

The frame-based representation of declarative and procedural knowledge had a wide application. The last decade tendency is health care and biomedicine (mostly for ontologies of terms), forecasting and text/natural language processing (Question 2 in Table 1).

The most used implementation tool is Protégé-Frames (Table 2). Implementation languages differ from the specific knowledge representation languages like FOSL to general ones like Java. The overview

*Table 2. Answers to Question 3 "What implementation technologies are used, and are they up to date?"*

| Characteristics | References |
|---|---|
| Tools | Knowledge Structure Manager (Hernández & Serrano, 2001); Protégé 2.(Beltrán-Ferruz et al., 2004; Gennari et al., 2005; Marinov, 2008; Rector, 2013; Sim & Brouse, 2014); CODE4 (Marinov, 2004); Jess (Shiue et al., 2008); RDFpro (Corcoglioniti et al., 2016) |
| Reasoning | JENA and DIG interfaces that use RACER and FaCT inference engines (Hernández & Serrano, 2001) |
| Implementation Languages | Spencer notation based on XML (Beltrán-Ferruz et al., 2004); Beale based Lisp (Beltrán-Ferruz et al., 2004); XML, DAML, OIL, SHOE (Marinov 2004); UML for graphical representation (Shiue et al., 2008); Java (Bimba et al., 2016; Corcoglioniti et al., 2016; Shiue et al., 2008); FOSL (Xue et al., 2010); Python (Bimba et al., 2016); SQL (Bimba et al., 2016); SPARQL (Bimba et al., 2016; Corcoglioniti et al., 2016); Perl (Bimba et al., 2016); JSON (Bimba et al., 2016); Prolog (Bimba et al., 2016) |
| Databases | FramerD (Marinov, 2004) |
| Ontologies | BioFrameNet, FrameNet, PropBank/VerbNet (Corcoglioniti et al., 2016; Rector, 2013; Tan et al., 2007); DBpedia, NomBank (Corcoglioniti et al., 2016) |
| Web compatibility | XML (Bimba et al., 2016; Marinov, 2004, 2008; Sim & Brouse, 2014; Xue et al., 2010); RDF (Bimba et al., 2016; Corcoglioniti et al., 2016; Marinov, 2004, 2008); Web Object model (Shiue et al., 2008; Xue et al., 2010) |

(Nazaruks & Osis, 2017a)

*Table 3. Answers to Question 4 "What are differences in frames structures?"*

| Elements Used | References |
|---|---|
| Frame name | (Beltrán-Ferruz et al., 2004; Bimba et al., 2016; Detwiler et al., 2016; Kim et al., 2008; Kramer & Kaindl, 2004; Marinov, 2004; Shiue et al., 2008; Tettamanzi, 2006; Xue et al., 2010) |
| Slots | (Beltrán-Ferruz et al., 2004; Bimba et al., 2016; Detwiler et al., 2016; Kim et al., 2008; Kramer & Kaindl, 2004; Marinov, 2004; Shiue et al., 2008; Tettamanzi, 2006; Xue et al., 2010) |
| Facets | (Beltrán-Ferruz et al., 2004; Bimba et al., 2016; Detwiler et al., 2016; Marinov, 2004; Xue et al., 2010) |
| Fillers | (Beltrán-Ferruz et al., 2004; Bimba et al., 2016; Kim et al., 2008; Kramer & Kaindl, 2004; Tettamanzi, 2006; Xue et al., 2010) |
| Scripts, daemons, stored rules | (Bimba et al., 2016; Marinov, 2004; Shiue et al., 2008; Tettamanzi, 2006) |
| Separated rules | (Bimba et al., 2016; Kramer & Kaindl, 2004) |

(Nazaruks & Osis, 2017a)

showed that many frame-based knowledge systems are often integrated with other ontology nets. Besides that, there is a tendency to make frame systems more web-oriented (Table 2).

Limitations mentioned by the authors are inadequate representation of knowledge (Kramer & Kaindl, 2004), greater expressiveness that can lead pure ontologies to the loss of information in case of transformation into them (Bimba et al., 2016; Detwiler et al., 2016; Gennari et al., 2005), necessity to work with the completely known characteristics and static knowledge domain (Grigorova & Nikolov, 2007), representation of the procedural knowledge as programming code inside frames (Grigorova & Nikolov, 2007), and the fact that complex structures can decrease the performance of the system inference and execution (Shiue et al., 2008; Xue et al., 2010).

Integration with other knowledge representation systems such as product rules and business constraints (Hernández & Serrano, 2001), OWL (Corcoglioniti et al., 2016; Detwiler et al., 2016; Hernández & Serrano, 2001), fuzzy logic (Tettamanzi, 2006), and modal logic (Al-Saqqar et al., 2016) is possible. There are several successful attempts to adapt frames to new technologies, especially web technologies. This allows integrating frame-based knowledge systems with already existing ontologies and other knowledge representation techniques. This means that frame systems can be applied also for our purpose considering enumerated limitations and possibilities.

## Validity of Technologies

The technologies mentioned in the overviewed sources (Table 2) relate to the tools used for frame systems design and implementation, reasoning mechanisms, implementation languages and databases. Since the overviewed sources are published from 2001 till 2016 (that is a quite long period of time for IT technologies), the authors need to check their validity (or actuality) for the last six years, i.e. for the period from 2014 till 2019.

## Tools

The first mentioned tool is Knowledge Structure Manager (KSM). This tool was developed by members of the I&K Group and the Department of Artificial Intelligence of the Universidad Politécnica de Madrid (I&K Group, 2006). The last conference paper was published in 2006. Therefore, the authors can consider that this tool is outdated at the present.

The next frequently mentioned tool is Protégé 2 which appeared in the early 1990s. The Protégé project itself at Stanford University began in the 1980s (Musen & Protégé Team, 2015). The current version of the desktop version of the tool is Protégé 5 and it supports advanced features of OWL ontologies. A Web-based system (WebProtégé) allows almost the same functionality for many ontology-engineering tasks. Support of knowledge frames as a language for ontologies has not been migrated to the newer (Protégé 3, Protégé 4, Protégé 5) versions. The newer versions focus on the support of OWL and RDF(S). However, the authors claim that all versions are still available under an open-source license. The last update of the Protégé 2 is done in 2004.

CODE4 (Conceptually Oriented Description Environment) is a system for knowledge management that supports knowledge acquisition, analysis and retrieval (Skuce & Lethbridge, 2001). CODE4 has been implemented in Smalltalk and provided different views (hierarchical, graphical and property matrix) to the same knowledge source (Gómez-Pérez, Fernández-López, & Corcho, 2006). As the author, Doug Skuce, wrote (Skuce, 2000) starting from 2000 its ideas were implemented in the prototype called IKARUS (Intelligent Knowledge Acquisition, Retrieval, and Understanding System). However, it is also is not available in 2019.

The next one, Jess, is "a rule engine and scripting language" implemented in Java (Friedman-Hill, 2008). Jess is used for rule-based expert systems. It was inspired by CLIPS expert system shell. Jess uses the Rete mechanism to process rules. However, it seems inactive since 2016.

RDFpro is the last-mentioned tool. RDF (Resource Description Framework) is a model for knowledge representation, especially for metadata. RDF statements form a directed graph that could be queried to get existing or new knowledge. In order to understand and describe semantic knowledge vocabularies, taxonomies and ontologies are used. RDFPro (RDF Processor) is a public domain, Java command line tool and library for RDF models processing (Corcoglioniti, Aprosio, & Rospocher, 2015). RDFPro tool (DKM, 2016) executes RDF processor and allows implementing sequential and parallel composition in processing pipelines. Besides that, it supports reading/writing RDF models, smushing, rule executing and statistics gathering. The last update of this tool is done in 2016 and it is compatible with Java 8.

Therefore, the authors can call as a perspective tool Protégé 2 if it is still compatible with the current technologies and RDFPro. However, both of them are more applied for creation of ontologies and less for knowledge frames.

## Frameworks and Reasoners

Reasoning tools, mentioned in the sources, are JENA and DIG interfaces that use RACER and FaCT inference engines.

JENA is produced by Apache Software Foundation (The Apache Software Foundation, 2019). It provides an API for data extraction and writing into RDF models as well as for work with Web Ontology Language (OWL). The last update was done in 2019. JENA supports using the built-in OWL and RDFS reasoners as well as customer's reasoners. JENA API allows controlling prefixes, navigating and querying RDF models as well as manipulating with models as a whole (merging, finding differences and similarities). RDF models allow creation of frame-like systems. However, they have several inconsistencies with the original concept of a frame.

The DIG interface is a provider of uniform access to Description Logic Reasoners such as FaCT++ and RacerPro. It is used by JENA for reasoning over OWL ontologies. Reasoners to be used in a framework provide a support for the DIG interface (Turi, 2004). The DIG 2.0 interface standard is not available in 2019.

RACER and FaCT reasoners are examples of reasoners that can be used with JENA API. The list of reasoners includes more than 30 reasoners available in 2018 (The University of Manchester, 2018).

Thus, it is clear that selection of a reasoning API is highly dependent from the model used for knowledge representation, i.e., is it a pure RDF model or an OWL model. Moreover, selection of a reasoner also depends on a certain use case.

## Implementation Languages

Implementation languages can be grouped by a purpose: for the knowledge storage and interchange, representation in a graphical form, querying and implementation in a programming language.

Notations for frame storage include Spencer's notation based on XML (Extensible Markup Language), Beale notation based on Lisp, XML and JSON (JavaScript Object Notation) based formats. These notations use schemas as a structure for serialization of knowledge. The first two notations are specific ones and has been used in several scientific research projects. The last two notations are standardized notations widely used in industrial projects for information storage and interchanges in a formalized way.

Another group is web-oriented frame-based knowledge representation languages DAMPL, OIL and SHOE. DAMPL is a notation based on XML. It was developed during the research project DAML (DARPA Agent Markup Language) performed by the research center SRI International. This language was needed to unify time ontologies developed by several contractors and provide mappings from this unified representation to individual ontologies (DAML.org, 2006). OIL (Ontology Inference Layer) is a language used for ontology interchange. The OIL has three meta layers for ontology definition. In 2001 W3C organization has issued Annotated DAML+OIL Ontology Markup standard (Connolly et al., 2001). DAML+OIL had special effect on OWL language development (Horrocks, Patel-Schneider,

& van Harmelen, 2003). SHOE is a small extension to HTML language that allows annotating web-documents with machine-readable knowledge (Parallel Understanding Systems Group, 2001). SHOE was used for DAML+OIL language creation.

Another representative of this group is FOSL. The concept of ontology has been extended to an "ontological view" concept. This concept is formally specified in a Frame-based Ontological view Specification Language (FOSL) used for FRAME knowledge modelling approach with four-level architecture of a concept, properties and relationships, their details, and instances of concepts. FOSL is implemented using XML-based representation (Xue et al., 2012). The last mentioning of FOSL evolution was made in 2012.

Because of evolution of OWL as a standard recommended by W3C, the mentioned representation languages currently are not actively used.

Another language for graphical representation is UML (Unified Modelling Language). UML is used for graphical representation of RDF, DAML+OIL and OWL2 (De Paepe, Thijs, Verborgh, Mannens, & Buyle, 2017). The main difficulty of mapping UML to ontological constructs, especially RDF, is the notion of monotonicity (Baclawski et al., 2002). This means that inserting of a new fact cannot cause some known fact to become false. UML and object-oriented languages are not monotonic and cannot be used for validation of such cases. However, a graphical means provided by the UML are quite useful and are used at the present.

A group of querying languages includes SQL and SPARQL languages. SPARQL has been developed to query RDF models using specified "patterns". In comparison with SQL it has more advanced definition of a join conditions in queries. However, if RDF collections are stored in relational databases, then SQL language is a more natural choice. There are researches that attempt to map SPARQL to SQL for such cases (Kumar, Kumar, & Abhishek, 2011). This means that both languages are in use for ontologies querying and the selection depends on the data storage type.

A group of implementation languages includes Java, Python, Perl and Prolog (as well as not mentioned in the sources Lisp). The first three languages are used for ontology editors as APIs that can be used to build applications. Prolog and Lisp are traditional languages for rule engine implementations. There are no strict rules on selection of the programming language.

Thus, selection of languages for engines, APIs and storage formats as well as graphical representation must take into account their compatibility.

## Databases

Object-oriented, object-relational, relational and document databases can be used for knowledge storage.

Many publications show that relational databases are widely used for storing ontologies. However, there is a lack of ways for storing OWL 2 ontologies in object-oriented databases and just several researches are dedicated to this question (Zhang, Ma, & Li, 2015). FramerD mentioned previously – a portable distributed object-oriented database that is dedicated for maintaining and sharing knowledge bases – is not supported since 2005 (Beingmeta, 2005).

Relational databases support the close-world paradigm (similar to knowledge frames system) and are less suitable for the open world ontologies (Martinez-Cruz, Blanco, & Vila, 2012). In opposite, in case of frame systems, databases can be more suitable for RDF models, if XML-document based databases do not fit requirements.

## FUTURE RESEARCH DIRECTIONS

The further research is related to the design and implementation of the frame-based or hybrid knowledge base for knowledge necessary for software development. The base should keep a computation independent knowledge and support its transferring to functioning, behavioral and structural design models. The base should be flexible and compatible with web technologies.

## CONCLUSION

The results of literature analysis and availability of technologies illustrate that frames are implemented using RDF models or ontology specification languages that can be mapped to them. Structures of frames differ. However, the main elements such as frame names, slots, facets are widely used comparing to the "procedural" elements such as fillers, daemons and rules.

Analysis of technologies used for implementation showed that not all mentioned technologies are supported in the present. The reason is evolution of the OWL language and its supporting means. RDFPro and Protégé 2 are still available, but the question of their appropriateness is open. JENA framework and its supported reasoners are up-to-date and can be used for implementation of knowledge bases. Up-to-date languages for knowledge specification in documents are XML-based, OWL and UML. However, in case of knowledge frames all of them require correct mappings due to differences in implemented paradigms. Selection of a querying language and implementation language is rather dependent on certain project requirements. The mostly used storages are relational and XML-document databases.

## REFERENCES

Al-Saqqar, F., Bentahar, J., & Sultan, K. (2016). On the soundness, completeness and applicability of the logic of knowledge and communicative commitments in multi-agent systems. *Expert Systems with Applications, 43*, 223–236. doi:10.1016/j.eswa.2015.08.019

Baclawski, K., Kokar, M. K., Kogut, P. A., Hart, L., Smith, J., Letkowski, J., & Emery, P. (2002). Extending the Unified Modeling Language for ontology development. *Software & Systems Modeling, 1*(2), 142–156. doi:10.100710270-002-0008-4

Beingmeta. (2005). *FramerD*. Retrieved December4, 2019, from http://www.framerd.org

Beltrán-Ferruz, P. J., González-Calero, P. A., & Gervás, P. (2004). Converting Mikrokosmos frames into description logics. In *Proceedings of the Workshop on NLP and XML (NLPXML-2004): RDF/RDFS and OWL in Language Technology* (pp. 35–42). Association for Computational Linguistics.

Bimba, A. T., Idris, N., Al-Hunaiyyan, A., Mahmud, R. B., Abdelaziz, A., Khan, S., & Chang, V. (2016). Towards knowledge modeling and manipulation technologies: A survey. *International Journal of Information Management, 36*(6), 857–871. doi:10.1016/j.ijinfomgt.2016.05.022

Connolly, D., van Harmelen, F., Horrocks, I., McGuinness, D. L., Stein, L. A., & Lucent Technologies Inc. (2001). *Annotated DAML+OIL Ontology Markup*. Retrieved January26, 2020, from https://www.w3.org/TR/daml+oil-walkthru/

Corcoglioniti, F., Aprosio, A. P., & Rospocher, M. (2015). Demonstrating the Power of Streaming and Sorting for Non-distributed RDF Processing: RDFpro. *International Semantic Web Conference.*

Corcoglioniti, F., Rospocher, M., & Aprosio, A. P. (2016). A 2-phase frame-based knowledge extraction framework. In *Proceedings of the 31st Annual ACM Symposium on Applied Computing - SAC '16* (pp. 354–361). New York: ACM Press. 10.1145/2851613.2851845

DAML.org. (2006). *The DARPA Agent Markup Language Homepage*. Retrieved January26, 2020, from http://www.daml.org/

De Paepe, D., Thijs, G., Verborgh, R., Mannens, E., & Buyle, R. (2017). Automated UML-Based Ontology Generation in OSLO2. In E. Blomqvist, K. Hose, H. Paulheim, A. Ławrynowicz, F. Ciravegna, & O. Hartig (Eds.), *Proceedings of the 14th ESWC: Posters and Demos (Lecture Notes in Computer Science)* (pp. 93–97). Springer.

Detwiler, L. T., Mejino, J. L. V., & Brinkley, J. F. (2016). From frames to OWL2: Converting the Foundational Model of Anatomy. *Artificial Intelligence in Medicine*, *69*, 12–21. doi:10.1016/j.artmed.2016.04.003 PMID:27235801

DKM. (2016). *rdfpro - Home*. Retrieved January26, 2020, from https://dkm.fbk.eu/technologies/rdfpro

Essebaa, I., & Chantit, S. (2016). Toward an automatic approach to get PIM level from CIM level using QVT rules. In *11th International Conference on Intelligent Systems: Theories and Applications (SITA)2016*(pp. 1–6). IEEE. 10.1109/SITA.2016.7772271

Foster, J., & Juell, P. (2006). A visualization of the frame representation language. In *Companion to the 21st ACM SIGPLAN conference on Object-oriented programming systems, languages, and applications - OOPSLA '06* (p. 708). New York: ACM Press. 10.1145/1176617.1176685

Friedman-Hill, E. J. (2008). *Jess, The Rule Engine for the Java Platform*. Retrieved January26, 2020, from https://jessrules.com/jess/docs/71/index.html

Gennari, J. H., Mork, P., & Li, H. (2005). Knowledge transformations between frame systems and RDB systems. In *Proceedings of the 3rd international conference on Knowledge capture - K-CAP '05* (p. 197). New York: ACM Press. 10.1145/1088622.1088666

Gómez-Pérez, A., Fernández-López, M., & Corcho, O. (2006). *Ontological engineering: with examples from the areas of knowledge management, e-commerce and the Semantic Web* (1st ed.). Springer.

Grigorova, D., & Nikolov, N. (2007). Knowledge representation in systems with natural language interface. In *Proceedings of the 2007 international conference on Computer systems and technologies - CompSysTech '07* (p. 1). New York: ACM Press. 10.1145/1330598.1330670

Hernández, J. Z., & Serrano, J. M. (2001). Knowledge-based models for emergency management systems. *Expert Systems with Applications*, *20*(2), 173–186. doi:10.1016/S0957-4174(00)00057-9

Horrocks, I., Patel-Schneider, P. F., & van Harmelen, F. (2003). From SHIQ and RDF to OWL: The making of a Web Ontology Language. *Journal of Web Semantics, 1*(1), 7–26. doi:10.1016/j.websem.2003.07.001

I&K Group. (2006). *Knowledge Structure Manager.* Retrieved January 26, 2020, http://www.dia.fi.upm.es/grupos/I&K/KSM-home.htm

Kardoš, M., & Drozdová, M. (2010). Analytical method of CIM to PIM transformation in model driven architecture (MDA). *Journal of Information and Organizational Sciences, 34*(1), 89–99.

Kim, K., Lee, C., Jung, S., & Lee, G. G. (2008). A frame-based probabilistic framework for spoken dialog management using dialog examples. In *Proceedings of the 9th SIGdial Workshop on Discourse and Dialogue* (pp. 120–127). Columbus, OH: Association for Computational Linguistics. 10.3115/1622064.1622088

Kornienko, A. A., Kornienko, A. V., Fofanov, O. B., & Chubik, M. P. (2015). Knowledge in Artificial Intelligence Systems: Searching the Strategies for Application. *Procedia: Social and Behavioral Sciences, 166*, 589–594. doi:10.1016/j.sbspro.2014.12.578

Kramer, S., & Kaindl, H. (2004). Coupling and cohesion metrics for knowledge-based systems using frames and rules. *ACM Transactions on Software Engineering and Methodology, 13*(3), 332–358. doi:10.1145/1027092.1027094

Kumar, V. N., Kumar, A. P., & Abhishek, K. (2011). A Comprehensive Comparative study of SPARQL and SQL. *(IJCSIT). International Journal of Computer Science and Information Technologies, 2*(4), 1706–1710.

Marinov, M. (2004). Using XML to represent knowledge by frames. In *Proceedings of the 5th international conference on Computer systems and technologies - CompSysTech '04* (pp. 1-6). New York: ACM Press. 10.1145/1050330.1050350

Marinov, M. (2008). Using frames for knowledge representation in a CORBA-based distributed environment. *Knowledge-Based Systems, 21*(5), 391–397. doi:10.1016/j.knosys.2008.02.003

Martinez-Cruz, C., Blanco, I. J., & Vila, M. A. (2012). Ontologies versus relational databases: Are they so different? A comparison. *Artificial Intelligence Review, 38*(4), 271–290. doi:10.100710462-011-9251-9

Miller, J., & Mukerji, J. (2001). *Model Driven Architecture (MDA).* Architecture Board ORMSC. Retrieved January 26, 2020, from https://www.omg.org/mda/

Minsky, M. (1974). A Framework for Representing Knowledge. *MIT-AI Laboratory Memo 306.* Retrieved January 20, 2020 from https://courses.media.mit.edu/2004spring/mas966/readings.htm

Musen, M. A. (2015). The Protégé Project: A Look Back and a Look Forward. *AI Matters, 1*(4), 4–12. doi:10.1145/2757001.2757003 PMID:27239556

Nazaruks, V., & Osis, J. (2017a). A Survey on Domain Knowledge Representation with Frames. In *Proceedings of the 12th International Conference on Evaluation of Novel Approaches to Software Engineering (ENASE 2017)* (pp. 346–354). Porto, Portugal: SCITEPRESS - Science and Technology Publications. 10.5220/0006388303460354

Nazaruks, V., & Osis, J. (2017b). Joint Usage of Frames and the Topological Functioning Model for Domain Knowledge Presentation and Analysis. In *Proceedings of the 12th International Conference on Evaluation of Novel Approaches to Software Engineering (ENASE 2017)* (pp. 379–390). Porto: SciTe-Press. 10.5220/0006388903790390

OMG. (2010). The MDA Foundation Model. *SparxSystems*, 1–9. Retrieved January 20, 2020, from http://www.omg.org/cgi-bin/doc?ormsc/10-09-06.pdf

Osis, J. (1969). Topological Model of System Functioning (in Russian). *Automatics and Computer Science, J. of Academia of Sciences*, (6), 44–50.

Osis, J., & Asnina, E. (2014). Is modeling a treatment for the weakness of software engineering? In *Handbook of Research on Innovations in Systems and Software Engineering* (pp. 411–427). IGI Global.

Osis, J., & Beghi, L. (1997). Topological Modelling of Biological Systems. In D. A. Linkens & E. R. Carson (Eds.), *Proceedings of the third IFAC Symposium on Modelling and Control in Biomedical Systems (Including Biological Systems)* (pp. 337–342). Pergamon-Elsevier Science Publishing.

Osis, J., & Donins, U. (2017). *Topological UML Modeling: An Improved Approach for Domain Modeling and Software Development*. Elsevier. doi:10.1016/B978-0-12-805476-5.00005-8

Osis, J., Gelfandbain, J., Markovich, Z., & Novozilova, N. (1991). *Diagnostics on Graph Models (on the Examples of Aviation and Automobile Technology)*. Transport. (in Russian)

Parallel Understanding Systems Group. (2001). *SHOE: Simple HTML Ontology Extensions*. Retrieved January 20, 2020, from http://www.cs.umd.edu/projects/plus/SHOE/

Rector, A. (2013). Axioms and templates: distinctions and transformations amongst ontologies, frames, and information models. In *Proceedings of the seventh international conference on Knowledge capture - K-CAP '13* (p. 73). New York: ACM Press.

Rhazali, Y., Hadi, Y., Chana, I., Lahmer, M., & Rhattoy, A. (2018). A Model Transformation in Model Driven Architecture from Business Model to Web Model. *IAENG International Journal of Computer Science*, *45*(1), 14.

Rhazali, Y., Hadi, Y., & Mouloudi, A. (2015). A Methodology of Model Transformation in MDA: from CIM to PIM. *International Review on Computers and Software*, *10*(12), 1186-1201.

Rhazali, Y., Hadi, Y., & Mouloudi, A. (2016). CIM to PIM Transformation in MDA: From Service-Oriented Business Models to Web-Based Design Models. *International Journal of Software Engineering and Its Applications*, *10*(4), 125–142. doi:10.14257/ijseia.2016.10.4.13

Roux, C. (2013). *Can "Made Up" Languages Help Computers Translate Real Ones?* Retrieved January 20, 2020, from https://europe.naverlabs.com/Blog/Can-made-up-languages-help-computers-translate-real-ones/

Shiue, W., Li, S.-T., & Chen, K.-J. (2008). A frame knowledge system for managing financial decision knowledge. *Expert Systems with Applications*, *35*(3), 1068–1079. doi:10.1016/j.eswa.2007.08.035

Sim, W. W., & Brouse, P. (2014). Towards an Ontology-based Persona-driven Requirements and Knowledge Engineering. *Procedia Computer Science*, *36*, 314–321. doi:10.1016/j.procs.2014.09.099

Skuce, D. (2000). Integrating Web-Based Documents, Shared Knowledge Bases, and Information Retrieval for User Help. *Computational Intelligence*, *16*(1), 95–113. doi:10.1111/0824-7935.00107

Skuce, D., & Lethbridge, T. (2001). *CODE4 - Conceptually Oriented Description Environment*. Retrieved January 20, 2020, from http://www.csi.uottawa.ca/kaml/CODE4.html

Tan, H., Kaliyaperumal, R., & Benis, N. (2007). Building frame-based corpus on the basis of ontological domain knowledge. In *Proceedings of BioNLP 2011 Workshop* (pp. 74–82). Portland, OR: Association for Computational Linguistics.

Tettamanzi, A. G. B. (2006). A Fuzzy Frame-Based Knowledge Representation Formalism. In V. Di Gesú, F. Masulli, & A. Petrosino (Eds.), Lecture Notes in Computer Science: Vol. 2955. *Fuzzy Logic and Applications. WILF 2003* (pp. 55–62). Springer Berlin Heidelberg.

The Apache Software Foundation. (2019). *Apache Jena*. Retrieved January 20, 2020, from https://jena.apache.org/

The University of Manchester. (2018). *List of Reasoners | OWL research at the University of Manchester*. Retrieved January 20, 2020, from http://owl.cs.manchester.ac.uk/tools/list-of-reasoners/

Turi, D. (2004). *DIG 1.1 Reasoners API*. Retrieved January 20, 2020, from http://dig.sourceforge.net/javadoc-reasoners/1.1/

Xue, Y., Ghenniwa, H. H., & Shen, W. (2010). A Frame-based Ontological view Specification Language. In *The 14th International Conference on Computer Supported Cooperative Work in Design* (pp. 228–233). IEEE. 10.1109/CSCWD.2010.5471972

Xue, Y., Ghenniwa, H. H., & Shen, W. (2012). Frame-based ontological view for semantic integration. *Journal of Network and Computer Applications*, *35*(1), 121–131. doi:10.1016/j.jnca.2011.02.010

Zhang, F., Ma, Z. M., & Li, W. (2015). Storing OWL ontologies in object-oriented databases. *Knowledge-Based Systems*, *76*, 240–255. doi:10.1016/j.knosys.2014.12.020

Zopounidis, C., Doumpos, M., & Matsatsinis, N. F. (1997). On the use of knowledge-based decision support systems in financial management: A survey. *Decision Support Systems*, *20*(3), 259–277. doi:10.1016/S0167-9236(97)00002-X

## KEY TERMS AND DEFINITIONS

**Computation Independent Model:** One of three models in Model Driven Architecture that can be applied to specify business rules, business processes, data vocabulary and requirements to the system or software.

**Knowledge:** A fact that describes a phenomenon in a domain.

**Knowledge Frame:** A format for knowledge representation in computer science. It joins both declarative and procedural knowledge. Knowledge Frames support closed-world paradigm.

**Model Transformation:** A transformation process when a model is simplified, refined or otherwise changed according to mapping rules.

**Ontology:** A format for declarative knowledge representation in computer science. It supports open-world paradigm.

**Problem Domain:** An environment (or a field of expertise) that need to be investigated in order to improve or enhance its characteristics.

**Solution Domain:** A set of elements that can be applied in order to improve or enhance characteristics of a problem domain.

**Topological Functioning Model:** A formal mathematical model for specification of systems functional characteristics and causal relations among them based on the system theory and algebraic topology.

# Chapter 4
# MDE and MDA in a Multi–Paradigm Modeling Perspective

**Ambra Molesini**
(iD) https://orcid.org/0000-0003-0329-8618
*Università di Bologna, Italy*

**Enrico Denti**
(iD) https://orcid.org/0000-0003-1687-8793
*Università di Bologna, Italy*

**Andrea Omicini**
(iD) https://orcid.org/0000-0002-6655-3869
*Università di Bologna, Italy*

## ABSTRACT

*Since most complex software systems are intrinsically multi-paradigm, their engineering is a challenging issue. Multi-paradigm modeling (MPM) aims at facing the challenge by providing concepts and tools promoting the integration of models, abstractions, technologies, and methods originating from diverse computational paradigms. In this chapter, the authors survey the main MPM approaches in the literature, evaluate their strengths and weaknesses, and compare them according to three main criteria—namely, (1) the software development process, (2) the adoption of meta-model techniques, (3) the availability of adequate supporting tools. Furthermore, the authors explore the adoption of other promising approaches for the engineering of multi-paradigm systems, such as multi-agent systems (MAS) and systems of systems (SoS), and discuss the role of situational process engineering (SPE) in the composition of multi-paradigm software processes.*

DOI: 10.4018/978-1-7998-3661-2.ch004

# INTRODUCTION

Complex software systems are nowadays acknowledged to be inherently *multi-paradigm* – thatis, built out from with diverse components, differing in terms of the basic abstractions they are based on, the technologies they exploit, the way in which they behave, the autonomy degree, the intelligence, to name just a few. So, their engineering is a challenge, calling for a multiplicity of concepts and tools, as well as the suitable integration of models, abstractions, technologies, and methods originating from diverse computational paradigms. In turn, these also mandate for the adequate integration of heterogeneous software development processes, and the related methodologies (and tools). Since each of the aspects bringing diversity in systems is typically best modelled and developed according to its own specific paradigm (Kuhn, 2012)(Zambonelli & Parunak, 2003), non-trivial software systems end up with being intrinsically multi-paradigm in their very nature.

Along this line, Multi-Paradigm Modeling (MPM) approaches (Vangheluwe, 2002)aim at developing usable, effective, and coherent methods and techniques for the engineering of multi-paradigm systems – both physical systems, software systems, and their combinations.

Model Driven Engineering (MDE) moves precisely from the idea of *"using different models at different levels of abstraction for developing systems"* (Fondement & Silaghi, 2004): in fact, most MPM approaches build precisely on MDE notions, techniques and supporting tools.

To this end, MDE technologies introduce and combine two key ingredients:

- Domain Specific Modeling Languages (DSML) for *"formalizing the application structure, behavior, and requirements within given domains"* (Schmidt, 2006).DSML are often defined by meta-models, with transformations aimed at automatically generating (more specific) models from previous (more abstract) models.
- Model transformations to *"represent the automatic manipulation of a model with a specific intention"* (Syriani, 2011). The rules and mappings to do so are expressed at the meta-model layer, i.e. the layer where the transformation rules conceptually belong.

Because so many MPM approaches have been proposed over the years, finding one's way in such a field is anything but trivial: the differences among the available approaches range over several aspects and dimensions – from the more conceptual (i.e., developing processes, adopted abstractions, using of meta-modeling techniques) to the most practical ones (i.e., availability of effective tools, their learning curve, to name just some). Accordingly, choosing the adequate approach for a given application does not merely amount at listing the features, pros, and cons of the possible choices: what is needed is a key for understanding and choosing advisedly, possibly highlighting a uniform (pre-selected) set of *key aspects*, that enable a comparative analysis on a homogeneous basis. In order to work as an effective "choice helper" tool, the result of such a classification should be available not only in textual (verbose) form, but also in a more effective, concise form of eye-catching tables, for immediate reference at the reader's convenience.

This chapter is therefore organized as follows. First, we summarize the essential background as effectively as possible(Section **Background**), and overview the most relevant MPM approaches in the MDE&MDA perspective (Section **Multi-Paradigm Modeling: Overview**). Then (Section **Comparison and Discussion**) we discuss, compare and classify MPM approaches according to *the three main criteria*:

1. the software development process
2. the adoption of meta-model techniques
3. the availability/unavailability of adequate supporting tools

We also provide highlights on possible alternative views/approaches for engineering multi-paradigm systems beyond MPM (Section **Engineering Multi-Paradigm Systems beyond MPM**) and finally draw some conclusions.

## BACKGROUND

This section summarizes the basic concepts and aspects about development processes, methodologies, meta-models, modeling and meta-modeling languages.

The *development process* is likely the single issue in software engineering where the simultaneous exploitation of multiple paradigms impacts the most: so, it is also our main comparison criterion. Subsection **Developing Process** provides some background on the different notions of development process in the literature, and their relationship with the methodology notion.

The next key ingredient for the definition of new processes (and therefore another main classification criterion) is *Meta-models*, discussed in Subsection **Meta-models**. Because these are mostly defined via Unified Modeling Language (UML Home Page, 1997),Subsection **Meta-modeling Languages: UML & MOF** recaps its infrastructure and relationship with Meta Object Facility(MOF Home Page, 2002), the OMG-standard meta-meta-model used for defining the UML meta-model. Finally, Subsection **Model-Driven Engineering** presents the model-driven engineering approach.

### Development Processes

Defining a development process in a satisfactory way is not trivial, for it involves diverse elements and viewpoints. Different definitions can be found in the literature, focusing on specific aspects or adopting a specific viewpoint. Some major aspects that are typically found in all definitions are *(i) the structural aspect,* focusing on the key elements a development process is made of; *(ii) the organizational aspect*, referred in a broader sense to all the "surrounding" elements—people and people's roles, deliverables, milestones, timing, and schedules, up to (possibly) monetary and marketing issues; and *(iii) the technological aspect*, referring to all the support tools, guidelines, software infrastructures that the development process relies on.

The structural aspect is at the core of the definitions proposed in (Sommerville, 2007), according to which *"A software process is a set of activities that leads to the production of a software product (...). Four general activities can be identified, that are common to all software processes: specification, design and implementation, validation, and evolution."* In (Fuggetta, 2000), the author focuses on organizational and technological aspects: *"A software (development) process can be seen as the coherent set of policies, organizational structures, technologies, procedures, and deliverables needed to conceive, develop, deploy, and maintain a software product."*

Since no software process can be termed as ideal and successfully applied to any application scenarios (Brooks, 1987), different sorts of systems call for different software processes: their activities need to be *"organized in different ways and described at different levels of detail for different types of software"*(Sommerville, 2007). This consideration is at the base both of the identification of *process models* families, and of the definition of the so-called *Situational Method Engineering*(SME) (Brink-kemper, Saeki, & Harmsen, 1999) (Cossentino, Gaglio, Garro, & Seidita, 2007).

*Situational Method Engineering*(SME) (Brinkkemper, Saeki, & Harmsen, 1999) means to provide the basis for *"the composition of new, ad-hoc development processes for each specific need"*. The term "situation" here concerns the specific problem to be faced, the process requirements, the development context, the legacy environment, and other aspects. SME suggests the adoption of adequate building tools based on the reuse of *method fragments* (Cossentino, Gaglio, Garro, & Seidita, 2007)–that is, portions of (both existing and created ex novo) development process, taken from a specific repository.

Despite their strict relationship, software engineering methodologies and development processes are not the same: as sketched in (Cernuzzi, Cossentino, & Zambonelli, 2005),*"Methodologies focus more explicitly on how an activity or task should be performed in specific stages of the process,[while] processes may also cover more general management aspects concerning who, when, how much, etc."*. Although both aspects are obviously an engineer's concern, development processes focus on *phases*, *relationships among phases*, timing, roles, etc., while methodologies cope more specifically with the *specific techniques* adopted and *work products*. In this sense, development processes and methodologies can be seen as complementary—the development process being provided with suitable methodological guidelines that specify the tools to be used, the techniques to be adopted, the definition of the work products to be produced, best practices, etc.

## Meta-models

*Multi-Paradigm Modeling* (MPM) means to provide software designers with *"the most appropriate modeling abstractions for the particular problem domain, (automatically) transforming the resulting models into solution abstractions of the selected implementation platform"* (Vangheluwe, 2002). In this context, *meta-models* aim to formalize the modeling abstractions, their admissible relationships, and the mapping between abstractions belonging to different conceptual levels. Meta-models capture the rules that connect (i) the modeling abstractions, possibly from different conceptual layers, to each other, and (ii) the activities and roles that compose a development process or methodology.

Several definitions exist in the literature, e.g. (Bernon, Cossentino, Gleizes, Turci, & Zambonelli, 2004)(Gonzalez-Perez, McBride, & Henderson-Sellers, 2005): as the term suggests, they all share the idea that a meta-model is *"a model of a model"* (MDA Home Page, 2001).As highlighted in (Henderson-Sellers & Gonzalez-Perez, 2005),formalizing a methodology with ameta-modelis useful for several reasons – consistency check, planning extensions, etc. So, in order to be fruitful, meta-models should deal with all the multi-facet aspects of a methodology –process model, life cycle, activities, techniques, guidelines, up to the organization in the development team. In short, meta-models are *an essential tool from a 360-degree perspective* to study the completeness and expressiveness of a methodology, compare different methodologies (Henderson-Sellers & Gonzalez-Perez, 2005) and integrate methodologies (Cossentino, Gaglio, Garro, & Seidita, 2007).

## Meta-modeling Languages: UML & MOF

UMLis*"a general-purpose modeling language for describing artefacts in some domain of interest"*(Atkinson & Kuhne, 2001), purposely designed to be useable at multiple levels in a multi-layer architecture—in particular to describe its own meta-model, providing for compactness, conceptual economy, easier support for CASE (Computer-Aided Software Engineering) tools.

According to (Atkinson & Kuhne, 2001), four levels– normally referred to as *M0, M1,M2,* and*M3,* bottom-up – are adequate and enough for tool interoperability. The top layer, M3, provides the constructs for creating meta-models—that is, the meta-meta-models: a suitable example is MOF (Meta-Object Facility) (MOF Home Page, 2002). M2 is an instance of M3, which defines the modeling language to be used in M1: this is where the UML meta-model (an instance of MOF) is actually defined. M1 is an instance of M2 which defines the languages for describing the application domains: every user model is an instance of the UML meta-model. Finally, M0 expresses the actual run-time entities—instances of model elements defined in M1.

A crucial aspect in such architecture is the one-to-one relationships among UML and MOF: *"every model element of UML is an instance of exactly one model element in MOF"*(MOF Home Page, 2002). So, MOF defines how UML models can be exchanged between tools: this is due to the reuse of the core modeling concepts (belonging to the Core Package) between UML, MOF and other OMG meta-models. Such "meta-models' concepts sharing" is at the base of *Model Driven Architecture* (MDA).

Finally, *profiles* are UML's way to customize UML itself. The profile mechanism provides for adapting an existing meta-model (typically the UML meta-model) to a particular domain, thus enabling the definition of Domain-Specific Modeling Languages (DSML).

## Model-Driven Engineering

Model-Driven Engineering (MDE)promotes the development of software systems by focusing on the creation of basic models and then transforming such models, across multiple levels of abstraction down to code generation (Rhazali, El Hachimi, Chana, Lahmer, & Rhattoy, 2019).

Each MDE process defines (i) the models to be developed, (ii) in which order they should be developed, (iii) how a higher-level model is to be transformed into a lower-level one. The system under development is then first described by a model at the highest abstraction level (*Computation Independent Model*– CIM), and then iteratively transformed into a platform-specific model via subsequent refinements through different abstraction levels(Rhazali, Yassine, Hadi, & Mouloudi, 2016).Accordingly, the CIM level means to represent only the business process reality, while the next level –*Platform Independent Model*(PIM) – describes models in a way that is effective for analysts and designers. The lowest abstraction level is the *Platform Specific Model*– PSM –made basically of code models (Rhazali, El Hachimi, Chana, Lahmer, & Rhattoy, 2019).

Model Driven Architecture (MDA) (MDA Home Page) is OMG's vision of MDE, which relies on UML and MOF to define the structure, semantics, and notation of models.

The major goal of MDA is to develop sustainable models (both CIM and PIM models) to enable the automatic generation of all the application code, achieving a significant productivity gain (Rhazali, Yassine, Hadi, & Mouloudi, 2016). Despite being rooted on model transformations, MDA per se does not propose any methodological transformation process (Rhazali, Yassine, Hadi, & Mouloudi, 2016). Research efforts typically focus on the transformation from PIM to PSM, which are closely linked: instead, transforming the CIM level to the PIM level is rarely discussed in the literature, possibly because of their dissimilarity. A notable work about this crucial aspect is (Rhazali, Yassine, Hadi, & Mouloudi, 2016), where authors propose a methodology to master transformation from service-oriented CIM level to web-based PIM level. More recently(Rhazali, El Hachimi, Chana, Lahmer, & Rhattoy, 2019), a methodology has been proposed for the semi-automatic model transformation from CIM to PIM up to PSM.

## MULTI-PARADIGM MODELING: OVERVIEW

To get a sense of Multi-Paradigm Modeling (MPM), let us overview the most relevant works, focusing on the development process, meta-model definitions, and the availability of adequate documentation and supporting tools. The same criteria are reused in Section **Comparison and Discussion** for comparative analysis and in-depth discussion.

### The Basics

MPM as a stand-alone discipline dates back more than a decade. In the first workshop(Giese & Levendovszky, 2006), many committed with the definition proposed by Vangheluwe et al. since 2002 (Vangheluwe, 2002),which defined MPM as *"the integration of model abstraction, multi-formalism modeling and meta-modeling"*.

Moving from such definition, (Mosterman & Vangheluwe, 2002), (Mosterman & Vangheluwe, 2004) and (Denil, Vangheluwe, De Meulenaere, & Demeyer, 2012) introduce MPM approaches that explore and combine three aspects:

- *model abstraction*, concerned with *"the relationship between different models at different levels of abstraction"*;
- *multi-formalism modeling*, concerned with *"the coupling of and transformation between models, described in different formalisms"*;
- *meta-modeling*, concerned with *"the description (models of models) of classes of models—that is, the specification of formalisms"*.

MPM investigates their blending, by (i) combining, transforming, and relating formalisms one to each other; (ii) generating domain/problem-specific formalisms, methods, and tools; (iii) cross-checking the coherence among different views.

The main reason beyond this idea is that problem-specific formalisms and tools are desirable, yet their development is difficult and time-consuming; moreover, adopting a multi-formalism approach calls for *"interconnecting a plethora of different tools, each designed for a particular formalism"*(Lara & Vangheluwe, 2002). This is precisely where meta-modeling comes to help: while the introduction of a meta-layer enables DSML definition, the meta-layer information enables the generation of specialized tools for supporting newly-defined DSML. Together, they can cut the development cost of a customized tool, making the difference for actual DSML adoption. Moreover, since the generated tools represent the models through a common data structure, transformations between DSML become transformations between these structures.

Indeed, recent work by (Ciccozzi, Vangheluwe, & Weyns, 2019) investigate *blended modeling,* that is, *"the activity of interacting seamlessly with a single model (i.e., abstract syntax) through multiple notations (i.e., concrete syntaxes), allowing a certain degree of temporary inconsistencies."* In short, blended modeling aims to provide blended editing and multiple visualizing notations to interact with a set of concepts, usable for the different aspects of design, development and stakeholder communication in an MDE process.

## Multi-Paradigm Modeling With AToM3

To prove the effectiveness of the above ideas, Vangheluwe et al. developed the AToM[3] tool: its input is an Entity-Relationship meta-specification extended with suitable constraints, whereas its output is a new, model-specific tool customized for processing the models described in a given DSML. The meta-model drives the automatic generation both of the DSML and of its relative supporting tool(s).AToM[3] uses Abstract Syntax Graphs (Oliveira & Loh, 2013) to express models and graph grammar models(Ehrig, Engels, Kreowski, & Rozenberg, 1999) to express transformations, which take the form of graph re-writing. The meta-model of the DSML is in its turn represented as a *meta-metamodel*, like in the UML architecture: accordingly, new concepts are actually introduced at the meta-meta-level.

Although no specific description is provided about the process to be followed when developing an MPM application, it is apparently left as understood that engineers should first specify the meta-models of the different formalisms to be used: AToM[3] takes then care of generating the proper tools for each formalism. Once the tools are available, engineers can model the different pieces of the system adopting the most suitable formalism for each piece. The models (possibly represented in different formalisms) are then connected via *generic links* – AToM[3] way of enabling the connection between the different parts. As a final step, AToM[3] can automatically generate the source code according to user-defined transformations.

## A DSM-based MPM Approach for Simulation

Domain-Specific Modeling (DSM) is one of the basic MDE techniques. (Li, Lei, Wang, Wang, & Zhu, 2013)presents a DSM-based, MPM approach which exploits MDE for integrating Models & Simulations (M&S) paradigms (Balci, 2012): the goal is to build a simulation framework combining multiple M&S languages to describe the different domain behaviors.

This approach exploits several modeling methods—namely, (i) MDE models for the work products, with transformations and code generation for the development process; (ii) DSM to provide domain-specific solutions; and (iii) M&S formalisms to express the domain behaviors.

The simulation model development is structured in four top-down steps, which correspond to the four M&S layers:

1.    the *DSML layer*, addressing the conceptual modeling;
2.    the *M&S formalism layer*, devoted to model architecting and integration;
3.    the *model framework & specification layer*, concerned with the model design and formal analysis, based on the M&S formalism;
4.    the *executable model layer*, addressing the model implementation, based on SMP2/C++ transformations.

Authors(Li, Lei, Wang, Wang, & Zhu, 2013) move from the idea of decomposing a (complex) system into "a series of problem domains, defining domain-specific conceptual models for each domain". At the highest (DSML) layer, each sub-system is modeled via a DSML, whose meta-model (i.e., grammar) is designed by the joint effort of domain experts, language engineers and M&S experts. The next (M&S

formalism) layer exploits model specification and simulator algorithms to model the behavior and provide the denotational semantics for each DSML. Since a single formalism supports DSM for multiple domains, formal analysis methods can be applied to perform an overall analysis. The third layer (model framework & specification) is the architecture of the simulation system, aimed at providing "a structural foundation for the integration of simulation models of sub-systems across different domains".

Aiming at being technology-independent, DSM is described in terms of high-level concepts, abstracting from the general structure of the specific system. The model framework obtained embodies the architecture from the simulation viewpoint: it is a first-class artifact providing the foundations – intended as the structural elements and their mutual relationships – foreach domain. The model framework is then further combined with the behavior modeling, depicting the behavior patterns of each domain. The resulting model framework is finally mapped onto Simulation Model Portability 2(SMP2), a standard MDA model specification, to provide a platform-independent model.

The bottom (executable model) layer couples the structural aspects described in SMP2 with the behavioral code generated from the domain-specific models: such parts are finally integrated in the SMP2 framework for the generation of executable components (technically, this step is based on an SMP2/C++ mapping, performed via a custom C++ code generator in Eclipse).

## MPM in Model Transformation

(Syriani, 2011) proposes an MPM technique for the engineering of a *model transformation language*– the language expressing model transformations – in order to automate the model transformation itself. The approach, rooted in (Mosterman & Vangheluwe, 2004), adopts the MPM principles, in particular, *multi-abstraction* – which is *not* the same as model abstraction. Quoting the author, *"Model abstraction is a view of a system exhibiting some of its properties and hiding others, [while] multi-abstraction is the ability to express models at different abstraction levels"*.

The model transformation language is defined at the syntax level, while the semantics is modeled through meta-models and model transformations—the necessary enabling technologies. The aim is twofold: on the one side, to raise the abstraction level; on the other, to improve the mapping between model transformation languages and their corresponding domains, minimizing accidental complexity. The effectiveness of the resulting framework is illustrated by Syriani in the design and implementation of a model transformation language. However, emphasis is on expressiveness, rather than on the development process—in fact, no tools are actually provided.

## MPM in FTG+PM

In (Mustafiz, Denil, Lucio, & Vangheluwe, 2012)an MPM framework is proposed, called *Formalism Transformation Graph + Process Model* (FTG+PM), which is also based on MDE and adopting the MPM definition in (Mosterman & Vangheluwe, 2002). As its name suggests, the first component is a graph, whose nodes are languages and edges are transformations, while the second component models the software lifecycle and its transformations activities via UML 2.0 activity diagrams. Different modeling languages can be used at different abstraction levels: authors adopt UML modeling languages, domain-specific modeling languages, natural languages, and general-purpose languages, mainly meta-modeled via UML class diagrams.

Like any MDE process, FTG+PM includes several activities – from requirements to code synthesis – modeledat different abstraction levels, which depend on the different MDE phases: higher-level models (requirements models, domain-specific models) are transformed step-by-step into source code. Each abstraction layer is associated to the detailed tasks to be performed: quoting the authors, they are "first declared as transformation definitions in FTG, then instantiated as PM activities". Transformations represent the development glue: input models are turned onto one output model, all conforming to the meta-model.

The FTG+PM approach is supported by AToMPM(*A Tool for Multi-Paradigm Modeling*), which covers both the definition of meta-models and transformations, and the execution of the transformation chain.

## An Orientation Framework for Multi-Paradigm Modeling

Moving from the idea that each methodology is built upon some characteristic assumptions –its *paradigm*–, (Lorenz & Jost, 2006) observe that an effective modeling approach calls for best match of three key aspects:

- *purpose*, defined as "the motivation of the intended modeling effort"
- *object*, defined as "the real-world context under investigation"
- *methodology*, defined as "a comprehensive, integrated series of techniques or methods creating a general systems theory of how a class of thought intensive work ought to be performed".

Since it is often the case that no single set of modeling paradigm and methodology fits satisfactorily a given context and purpose, the intriguing idea is to try to combine different methodologies, in an MPM perspective, taking the "best-fit" methods from different methodologies. The assumption is that such an approach should match the reality more closely: at the same time, effectively combining different paradigms is an issue. A possible way to do so is to select the "best-fit" paradigm for each sub-problem and then build the multi-paradigm model in terms of interacting modules: however, choosing the best-fit paradigm/method for each part of the system is critical. While authors present some hints to face this point, little is actually said about the development process, the supporting tools, and the meta-model techniques.

## MPM in Software Architectures

In (Balasubramanian, Levendovszky, Dubey, & Karsai, 2014) authors discuss the multi-paradigm issues encountered during the development of a domain-specific architecture description language for distributed embedded systems.

Their software infrastructure, DREMS (Distributed Real-time Embedded Managed Systems) is aimed at *"designing, implementing, configuring, deploying, and managing distributed read-time embedded systems"*. The two major subsystems respectively deal with (a) modeling, analyzing, synthesizing, implementing, debugging, testing, and maintaining the software application, and (b) deploying and managing the application on a network.

Three main challenges are faced: (i) how to integrate the textual code inside the graphical modeling language; (ii) how to transform the high-level scheduling properties into the target platform schedule; and (iii) how to integrate different design-time analyses.

The first challenge derives from the use of a graphical UI on the user side and of a textual language in the underlying platform, which adopts the Component-Based Software Engineering (CBSE) approach: there, applications are made of reusable software components whose interfaces are specified via the Interface Definition Language (IDL)—an OMG standard for this purpose; code generators process IDL to generate stubs, which are then merged with the user logic to build the final component. In DREMS, the integration of the textual IDL language is performed by creating an add-on to the modeling language that parses the textual language for setting attributes onto the graphical elements.

The second challenge comes from the use of the DREMS temporal partition scheduler, which transforms the high-level scheduling constraints and artefacts (the process-partition assignment graph, and other details) into a detailed schedule usable by the underlying operating system. A schedule calculator then binds the individual temporal partitions to the DREMS schedule.

The third challenge originates from the need to integrate three automated analyses—namely, the security of communications, the network quality of service (QoS), and the software component schedulability. While security is granted via a multi-level security policy, the analysis of QoS requirements is based on the support for QoS profiles in the modeling language, which is capable to describe the evolution of the network parameters and the QoS requirements. Schedulability analysis involves the verification of system properties, and is performed by generating a suitable Colored Petri Net(Jensen & Kristensen, 2009).

The proposed solution goes beyond their specific case, and can be applied to similar situations, especially if aimed at providing an analogous level of tool automation. Because of the focus on domain-specific languages, however, other aspects –the development process, the supporting tools, the meta-model techniques – are left aside.

## Multi-Paradigm Design With Feature Modeling

(Vranic, 2005) introduces *Multi-Paradigm Design with Feature Modeling* (MPDfm), aimed at enabling explicit reasoning about "paradigms viewed as solution domain concepts", and at evaluating their "appropriateness for application domain concepts". A solution domain represents the language for describing a solution—typically, a programming language.

Application and solution domain are both modeled via *feature modeling* (Vranic, 2005), a modeling technique for multi-paradigm design. Application domain and feature models are subject to transformational analysis to define a suitable mapping between these domains. The mapping is expressed in the form of yet-another feature model, with the information about the application domain concepts and features (Vranic, 2005); overall, these determine the basic code structure. So, the development process is structured in four main steps: (i) application domain feature modeling; (ii) solution domain feature modeling; (iii) transformational analysis; and (iv) code skeleton design. The first two can proceed in parallel: then, the detailed design and implementation can follow the MPDfm approach.

Authors report that the method is verified, with good results, adopting feature modeling as the application domain and the AspectJ language as the solution domain; yet, no specific supporting tools seem to be available.

## Model-driven System Engineering for Virtual Product Design

(Dalibor, Jansen, Rumpe, Wachtmeister, & Wortmann, 2019) present a small Model-Driven System Engineering (MDSE) methodology to integrate the SysML paradigm with the CAD paradigm, that is, a method for integrating abstract system descriptions in the OMG Systems Modeling Language – SysML (SysML Open Source Project Home Page, 2003) with Computer-Aided Design (CAD) models. SysML is an UML subset extended with a graphical modeling language for systems engineering, while the Computer-Aided x (CAx) paradigm embraces various Computer-Aided methods such as CAD, Computer-Aided Engineering (CAE) and Computer-Aided Manufacturing (CAM).

The context is virtual product development, i.e. "a practice to support all phases of the product development process using a digital environment". CAD modeling methods are applied in all the development-relevant phases of the product life-cycle, to simulate, verify, validate, and manufacture the product, while minimizing the creation of physical prototypes. Their combination for virtual product development leads to the so-called "CAx process chain".

Authors introduce the idea of connecting such a chain with the SysML models (created with the Object-Oriented Systems Engineering Method-OOSEM). Process systems engineers would then be able to describe the system in SysML (via an ad-hoc profile), and integrate the model into the CAx process chain. The process starts with a SysML modeling activity, where the systems engineer creates an abstract system model specifying the elements of the physical parts of the system. The next step is to forward the parameters that are relevant for CAD modeling. Using the resulting CAD model in combination with additional information from the SysML diagram, engineers can perform additional CAE analyses and CAM modeling.

A suitable SysML Profile enables engineers to mark blocks of a SysML Block Definition Diagram as «CAD Element», and value properties that should serve as parametric design parameters as «CAD Parameter». Moreover, model information exchange in theSysML-CAD process chain is automated, via a special-purpose plug-in for the MagicDraw modeling environment (MagicDraw Home Page, 2019) that interchanges model information in a format suitable for Autodesk Inventor: so, the dimensions of concrete physical parts can be designed automatically.

Despite being very special-purpose, the approach seems quite appealing: however, it is strictly tied to the example proposed in the paper,so its application to other product seems not so trivial, especially due to the work necessary for adapting the automatic the exchange of model information.

## A Multi-paradigm Modeling Framework for Modeling and Simulating Problem Situations

(Lynch, Padilla, Diallo, Sokolowski, & Banks, 2014) propose a Multi-Paradigm Modeling Framework (MPMF) for modeling and simulating problem situations. The framework adopts three different levels of granularity (*macro*, *meso*, and *micro*) to analyze what is known and assumed about the problem situation. Such levels are then independently mapped to different modeling paradigms, which are combined to build up the comprehensive model and the corresponding simulation.

MPMF is based on Modeling and Simulation-System Development Framework (MS-SDF) (Diallo, Andreas Tolk, Gore, & Padilla, 2005), which defines a high-level approach on how to derive a model from a problem situation, and a simulation from the model. MS-SDF provides an effective approach to capture the information about the problem situation and represent it in a manner which is suitable for simulation, as well as to identify contradictions and inconsistencies.

In MS-DSF, three high-level constructs are introduced –*reference modeling, conceptual modeling*, and *simulation building*–that MPMF expands to support simulation *implementation*. The good level of *traceability* – another key MS-SDF feature – is also maintained in MPMF, thanks to the recursive layout of the framework in the modeling process.

In a multi-paradigm environment, the number of modeling paradigms to be handled represents a critical aspect to keep complexity manageable: accordingly, the number of modeling paradigms used to implement the simulation should be kept to the minimum.

In our knowledge, no tool or documentation are currently available for this framework.

## Multi-Paradigm Modeling Approach to Live Modeling

A different, more recent perspective to MPM, based on the above-discussed FTG+PM (Mustafiz, Denil, Lucio, & Vangheluwe, 2012), can be found in (Van Tendeloo, Van Mierlo, & Vangheluwe, 2019),aimed at adding *liveness* to modeling languages in a way that is reusable across multiple formalisms: the reason is that the support for live modeling has been identified as a key feature to advance the usability of model-driven techniques.

The basic idea is to transpose the essence of live programming to the modeling domain, in a generic way. Live programming concepts and techniques should be transposed to domain-specific executable modeling languages, clearly distinguishing between generic and language-specific concepts. However, domain-specific modeling means to handle (many) different domain-specific formalisms, each possibly with a handful of users, making it difficult to justify the investment for implementing live modeling techniques in an ad hoc way. So, to effectively support live modeling in the context of domain-specific formalisms, authors "deconstruct and reconstruct" the traditional live programming process. All the activities related to liveness are distilled into a single operation ("sanitization"): so, to make a formalism live, only sanitization needs to be updated, while the other aspects of live modeling can be reused.

Author considered three types of executable modeling formalisms: Finite State Automata(FSAs), Discrete Time Causal Block Diagrams (DTCBDs), and Continuous Time Causal Block Diagrams (CTCBDs). They are all supported, together with their live implementation, in the Modelverse tool(Van Tendeloo, Van Mierlo, & Vangheluwe, 2018), which supports all the necessary phases– language engineering, model transformations, process enactment –as well as the use of multiple interfaces. There, users first start the live modeling process which pertains to the desired formalisms, possibly providing an initial model. It is worth highlighting that only the design models are stored: simulation, instead, is always started anew. The enactment closely resembles the usual modeling interface, except for the presence of an extra simulation window –merely, an external program that visualizes the simulation results. In order to emphasize the uncoupling between model and formalisms, authors discuss three examples based on the exact same (parameterized)FTG+PM model, showing that only the sanitization operation is to be redefined for each formalism individually: the visual interfaces are untouched, as everything is based on process enactment. So, because of the independence between model and domain-specific formalisms, and thanks to the availability of an effective tool based on FTG+PM, this approach seems potentially applicable to a wide variety of modeling formalisms.

At the same time, Modelverse is a new tool, mainly based on the writing of Python code to create models via meta-model instantiation,(Van Tendeloo, Van Mierlo, & Vangheluwe, 2018),currently featuring no visual diagram support—a drawback which could limit actual usability, especially in more complex scenarios.

## COMPARISON AND DISCUSSION

This section aims to discuss comparatively the approaches introduced in Section 3 according to three main criteria:

1. the development process
2. the possible adoption of meta-models
3. the availability of suitable supporting tools

The very reason beyond the first criterion is well synthesized in (Sommerville, 2007): *"Different types of systems need different development processes (...) [so] the use of an inappropriate software process may reduce the quality or the usefulness of the software product to be developed and/or increased"*. This is particularly relevant for multi-paradigm systems, where the development process needs to adapt to diverse paradigms and application domains, in order to model the different parts of the system with a variety of abstractions.

The second criterion derives from meta-models being the conceptual and practical tool to bridge between (abstractions from) different paradigms: in fact, MPM approaches exploit meta-modeling techniques to define Domain-Specific Modeling Languages (DSMLs), which are then used for modeling specific sub-systems; in turn, these are further processed via (possibly automatic) transformations to map a DSML onto another.

The third criterion comes from the finding that the actual applicability of the multi-paradigm approach depends on the availability of effective supporting tools—both because of the inherent complexity and multi-facet nature of the development process, and specifically for the definition of the DSML and the related processing. At the same time, the actual usability of such tools is often critical also for experienced users, which makes it a crucial factor to be accounted for.

## Development Process Comparison

The analysis of the development process needs to start from the analysis of the process *model*.

Appropriate comparison criteria for this aspect can be derived from Sommerville's definition:

1. the kind (and structure) of process model
2. whether the process is adequately documented (other than, indirectly, reasonably easy to learn and apply).

As far as the first issue is concerned, one clear result is that, whenever a process model can be identified, it is a *transformational* process. This is not surprising, since a number of such approaches share the same root (Vangheluwe, 2002).

The second, often underestimated, issue is particularly critical in the MPM context since the development of adequate documentation does not follow the physiological evolution of the process itself, which is inherently complex because of the inter-twining of different paradigms. Unfortunately, documentation and tutorials are often outdated and do not reflect the new process requirements or design techniques. As a further consequence, the lack of suitable documentation negatively impacts on the learning process.

Table 1 summarizes the results of the comparison among the above-discussed approaches. Since the works by Vangheluwe, on which many approaches are based, refer to MDE principles and focus onto the automatic transformations among modeling domains/languages, the adoption of supporting tools like AToM³, AToMPM and Modelverse is an important factor. In many cases the presence of CASE tools *influences* the development process itself—indeed, the adoption of a given tool nearly imposes the process to be followed in the system development (Denil, Vangheluwe, De Meulenaere, & Demeyer, 2012), (Mosterman & Vangheluwe, 2002)(Mosterman & Vangheluwe, 2004)(Lara & Vangheluwe, 2002) (Mustafiz, Denil, Lucio, & Vangheluwe, 2012)(Van Tendeloo, Van Mierlo, & Vangheluwe, 2019). Alternatively, works inspired to the Features-Oriented software development, like (Vranic, 2005), adopt a transformational process model but blended with Features-Oriented ingredients.

The inadequate availability of up-to-date and complete documentation makes it often difficult not only to compare different development processes, but also to choose the most suited for the specific designer's situation. Of course, this problem is not peculiar only to the MPM community, but affects other communities, like e.g. the Agent-Oriented Software Engineering (AOSE) community, which also needs a standard way of documenting the development processes. This is why the IEEE-FIPA standardization organism supported in the last years the development of a standard Documentation Template (Cossentino, Seidita, Hilaire, & Molesini, 2014), based on a variant of SPEM 2.0 (Software & Systems Process Engineering Metamodel Specification. Version 2.0, 2008), which seems general enough to be potentially adopted also in domains other than AOSE—like, for instance, MPM.

As shown in Table 1, the only proposal adopting a formal approach – namely, SPEM – to deal with the documentation issue is (Denil, Vangheluwe, De Meulenaere, & Demeyer, 2012):however, it adopts the (older) SPEM 1.0, and only for modeling a single fragment of the development process. Other works opt for informal process documentation or examples to document their approaches: (Li, Lei, Wang, Wang, & Zhu, 2013) and (Mustafiz, Denil, Lucio, & Vangheluwe, 2012) are perhaps the ones providing the most complete documentation—with a positive impact on the learning process. Other approaches rely mostly on the supporting tools and related documentation for illustrating the development process, possibly suffering from the obsolescence problem of such documentation. In most cases, tools do not seem to be particularly suited for an easy learning, especially by non-expert designers.

## Meta-model Comparison

As meta-models are one of the most powerful conceptual tools to bridge between different paradigms, one obvious comparison criterion is whether they are adopted in a given MPM approach: if so, two further aspects concern which language(s) is used for their utterance and for which purpose(s) they are used. While most MPM approaches are actually rooted in (Mosterman & Vangheluwe, 2002), where meta-models are at the core, other approaches, like (Lorenz & Jost, 2006) and (Vranic, 2005), are based on different techniques—e.g., *features*.

Meta-models can then be seen as a sort of grammar specifying the syntax of a set of models, while model transformations specify the corresponding semantics: their combined use provides for the automatic generation of the modeling environment. So, meta-models both bridge between paradigms and set the practical foundation for automating the building of Domain Specific Modeling environments.

Table 2 reports the result of the comparison of the above approaches based on the metamodeling lens. When meta-modeling techniques are used, the most common representation language appears to be UML, possibly combined with Entity-Relationship (E-R): this is not surprising, since UML is the most

*Table 1. Comparison of the development processes.*

| Proposal<br>Authors and Bibliography Reference | Process Model<br>Type and Influence | Documentation | |
|---|---|---|---|
| | | **Formality** | **Examples** |
| (Denil, Vangheluwe, De Meulenaere, & Demeyer, 2012) | Type: transformational<br>Influence: AToM3 | *Formal (via SPEM 1.0)* | *Not provided* |
| (Mosterman & Vangheluwe, 2002) | Type: transformational<br>Influence: CASE tool | *Not provided* | *Not provided* |
| (Mosterman & Vangheluwe, 2004) | Type: transformational<br>Influence: CASE tool | *Not provided* | ✓ |
| (Vangheluwe, 2002) | Type: transformational<br>Influence: – | *Informal* | *Not provided* |
| (Lara & Vangheluwe, 2002) | Type: transformational<br>Influence: AtoM3 | *Not provided* | ✓ |
| (Li, Lei, Wang, Wang, & Zhu, 2013) | Type: transformational<br>Influence: N/A | *Not provided* | ✓ |
| (Syriani, 2011) | Type: not specified<br>Influence: – | *Not provided* | ✓ |
| (Mustafiz, Denil, Lucio, & Vangheluwe, 2012) | Type: transformational<br>Influence: AToMPM | *Informal* | ✓ |
| (Lorenz & Jost, 2006) | Type: not specified<br>Influence: – | *Not provided* | ✓ |
| (Balasubramanian, Levendovszky, Dubey, & Karsai, 2014) | Type: not specified<br>Influence: – | *Informal* | *Not provided* |
| (Vranic, 2005) | Type: transformational<br>Influence: features design | *Informal* | ✓ |
| (Dalibor, Jansen, Rumpe, Wachtmeister, & Wortmann, 2019) | Type: transformational<br>Influence: MDE | *Not provided* | ✓ |
| (Lynch, Padilla, Diallo, Sokolowski, & Banks, 2014) | Type: not specified<br>Influence: MS-SDF | *Not provided* | ✓ |
| (Van Tendeloo, Van Mierlo, & Vangheluwe, 2019) | Type: iterative<br>Influence: FTG+PM and Modelverse | *Informal* | ✓ |

used meta-modeling language. In other cases, however, either no assumption is made on the adopted language, or different languages are adopted.

In UML-based proposals, meta-models are typically used first at meta-level for creating the specific DSML, and then at a lower level for modeling specific sub-systems: automatic model transformations, based on the relationships defined at the meta-level, finally map a DSML onto another, transforming an input model onto a new model in a different (lower level) language.

## Tool Comparison

Tools must support not only the development process in general, but the specific abstractions and techniques that are peculiar to MPM: so, their design and implementation require a considerable development effort. The complexity and learning curve of the tools also needs to be evaluated, as it is often an obstacle also for experienced users.

In the approaches derived from (Vangheluwe, 2002), based on meta-models, tools are asked to support the definition of the desired DSML and the related transformation processing; other approaches have their own, different requirements. While most of the above-presented approaches are not supported by a specific tool, three of them do have one—namely, AtoM[3] (Lara & Vangheluwe, 2002), AToMPM(Syriani & Vangheluwe, 2012), and Modelverse(Van Tendeloo, Van Mierlo, & Vangheluwe, 2019). Their evaluation criteria should therefore include the tool power *vs.* complexity, the user-friendliness of the installation procedure, the learning curve, and the state of the documentation: results are summarized in Table 3.

All tools require their own (i.e., typically not the last) version of Python—namely, Python 2.3 for AtoM[3] and Python 2.7 for AToMPM and Modelverse, none of which is compatible with Python 3.x. Moreover, AToMPM adopts a client-server architecture, which requires that the server is properly configured to include a specific Python graphic package; the client instead just run inside Google Chrome, exploiting its JavaScript support. Modelverse, indeed, requires the SCCD compiler and runtime to be executed. They also require a proportionally long time to be learned and fruitfully exploited.

AtoM[3] may likely result too complicated for users with little experience in meta-model creation: in addition, users have to write by themselves the Python code for expressing pieces of models. On the other hand, it is well-documented— although the documentation and examples refer to an older version, with different GUI and functionalities, which makes it uneasy to follow the provided examples. AToMPM, instead, comes with a nice video and introductory tutorial slides: still, the lack of a complete

*Table 2. Comparing meta-models.*

| Proposal | Meta-models Adoption | Meta-modeling Language | Used for | |
|---|---|---|---|---|
| | | | DSML | Transformation |
| (Denil, Vangheluwe, De Meulenaere, & Demeyer, 2012) | ✓ | E-R + UML | ✓ | ✓ |
| (Mosterman & Vangheluwe, 2002) | ✓ | different languages | ✓ | ✓ |
| (Mosterman & Vangheluwe, 2004) | ✓ | UML | ✓ | ✓ |
| (Vangheluwe, 2002) | ✗ | (not applicable) | ✗ | |
| (Lara & Vangheluwe, 2002) | ✓ | E-R + UML | ✓ | ✓ |
| (Li, Lei, Wang, Wang, & Zhu, 2013) | ✓ | no assumption | ✓ | ✓ |
| (Syriani, 2011) | ✓ | UML | ✓ | ✓ |
| (Mustafiz, Denil, Lucio, & Vangheluwe, 2012) | ✓ | UML | ✓ | ✓ |
| (Lorenz & Jost, 2006) | ✗ | (not applicable) | ✗ | |
| (Balasubramanian, Levendovszky, Dubey, & Karsai, 2014) | ✓ | UML | ✓ | ✗ |
| (Vranic, 2005) | ✗ | (not applicable) | ✗ | |
| (Dalibor, Jansen, Rumpe, Wachtmeister, & Wortmann, 2019) | ✓ | UML | ✓ | ✗ |
| (Lynch, Padilla, Diallo, Sokolowski, & Banks, 2014) | ✗ | (not applicable) | ✗ | |
| (Van Tendeloo, Van Mierlo, & Vangheluwe, 2019) | ✗ | (not applicable) | ✗ | |

guide might force users to navigate menus and try out some modeling libraries to actually unleash its potential. Modelverse, however, requires users to write Python code in order to create their models.

*Table 3. Comparison of the supporting tools.*

| Tool | Installation Requirements | Learning Time | Documentation |
|------|---------------------------|---------------|---------------|
| AtoM3 | Python 2.3 | Considerable | documentation + examples (referred to an old version) |
| AToMPM | Python 2.7 + graphic package + JavaScript package | considerable | video + tutorial slides |
| Modelverse | SCCD compiler and runtime + Python 2.7 | considerable | documentation + technical report |

Another key point concerns *scalability*. Most of the above MPM approaches adopt the transformational process model and the MDE techniques, which means that the system under development is – roughly speaking – decomposed in multiple, independently-modeled sub-systems, and the code is finally generated via model transformations. However, most of the accompanying examples refer to rather simple situations, like the car windows system in (Mosterman & Vangheluwe, 2004), whose decomposition is equally simple and the involved paradigms are just two or three. So, more complex case studies, with multiple involved paradigms, would be required for an effective assessment of the applicability of MPM approaches to intricate scenarios such as pervasive computing (Satyanarayanan, 2001), pervasive intelligent systems (Mariani & Omicini, 2013), self-organizing systems (Di Marzo Serugendo, Gleizes, & Karageorgos, 2006).

# ENGINEERING MULTI-PARADIGM SYSTEMS BEYOND MPM

## The Multi-Agent Systems Paradigm

Due to its different perspective, the Multi-Agent System paradigm is mostly ignored in MPM field, despite its widespread adoption as a "*general-purpose paradigm for software development*" (Zambonelli & Parunak, 2003)– possibly because the MPM community traditionally focuses on application domains rooted in the M&S field(Balci, 2012). A notable exception is (Lorenz & Jost, 2006), where agent-based modeling is considered in the simulation context. However, the agent paradigm is widely acknowledged to be well-suited to model complex systems, thanks to features such as agent autonomy, sociality, and more generally to foundational notions of goals, actors, environment, etc. (Molesini, 2008) which make it possible to design complex, interactive systems at the "adequate" abstraction level—usually, higher than other paradigms. Moreover, application scenarios such as complex socio-technical systems (Bryl, Giorgini, & Mylopoulos, 2009) and pervasive intelligent systems (Mariani & Omicini, 2013) could likely benefit from a multi-paradigm approach that includes some key aspects of the MAS paradigm—for instance, to coordinate and govern the interaction among the many autonomous entities.

Yet, most MPM approaches could hardly be applied to the agent paradigm "as they are", since this would require that agent entities are transformed into suitable coordination "active entities" and vice-versa— would call for the agent paradigm to be integrated with other relevant paradigms, such as coordination (Papadopoulos, Stavrou, & Papapetrou, 2006)and event-based (Omicini, 2015) paradigms. In its turn, this would amount at (i) integrating the agent meta-model with the coordination meta-model, and (ii) creating a new development process by assembling fragments of agent-oriented methodologies with fragments of coordination methodologies. Analogously, integrating the agent paradigm with the event-based paradigm, as suggested in (Omicini, 2015), would require the suitable modeling of interactions between autonomous entities and the environment where they are immersed.

## Situational Process Engineering

Situational Process Engineering (SPE) techniques (Cossentino, Gaglio, Garro, & Seidita, 2007)(Cossentino, Seidita, Hilaire, & Molesini, 2014)– thatis, the evolution of the SME initially developed in the object-oriented field (Brinkkemper, Saeki, & Harmsen, 1999)–provide the conceptual and practical foundations for defining ad-hoc development processes, by suitably *re-combining* pieces (reusable *fragments*) of existing processes, so as to create a methodology that is specific for a given purpose.

Adopting SPE in a multi-paradigm context opens several challenges. First, the SPE approach cannot be used *as is*: integrating process fragments rooted on the same paradigm (and therefore sharing similar abstraction) is one thing, but doing the same with process fragments coming from methodologies based on completely different paradigms is all another story.

The availability of such fragments is another issue: while process fragments from AOSE methodologies are available for integration, fragments from other paradigms would need to be created from scratch. This is all but trivial, since fragment extraction requires a deep knowledge of the specific methodology; alternatively, the methodology should be very well documented in a standard way (Cossentino, Seidita, Hilaire, & Molesini, 2014)—another critical issue *per se*.

Suitably documenting such process fragments is one third, critical aspect. While the Documentation Template under development in the AOSE community could be of help for methodologies, the development of a standardized fragment documentation template is still a work in progress.

## The Intriguing Case of Systems of Systems

From an opposite perspective, paradigms could be used as *isolated worlds*, if each sub-system is modeled with a separate paradigm and sub-systems have little inter-dependencies on each other. The development of each sub-system could then follow its own development process, tailored to the specific paradigm.

An appealing approach could be to define a sort of "process orchestrator" to (i) manage the different sub-processes and their mutual inter-relationships in terms of time scheduling and interleaved activities, and (ii) analyze and design the interactions among sub-systems.

An example is represented by the so-called *System of Systems* (SoS)(Nielsen, Fitzgerald, Woodcock, & Peleska, 2015)—basically, a set of ad-hoc systems that put their resources and skills together, so that the resulting system provides more features and services than the simple sum of its parts. SoS move from the idea that "*the growing interdependency of systems contributes to an ever-emerging complexity*" (Ross, Ulieru, & Gorod, 2014): the use of multi-paradigm approach in that field is under investigation. A key challenge in this context is "*to identify the boundaries of the overall SoS and of its independent constituent systems*"(Nielsen, Fitzgerald, Woodcock, & Peleska, 2015), where "boundaries" refers both to technical (interfaces definition, integration, testing) and organizational aspects (governance, stakeholders).

Moreover, an open research aspect is how to possibly exploit the presence of a "process orchestrator" to structure the design at two levels—a (lower) level for each sub-system, and the orchestrator in charge of the global development process, obtained by integrating and scheduling the development process of each sub-system, at a higher level.

## Multi-Agent Systems for Systems of Systems

(Nielsen, Fitzgerald, Woodcock, & Peleska, 2015) argue that *"the space of SoS might be described in terms of eight dimensions"*—autonomy, independence, distribution, evolution, dynamic reconfiguration, emergence of behavior, interdependence, interoperability. Since these aspects fall well inside the MAS features, it is conceivable that the MAS paradigm can be exploited to address at least some of the SoS challenges: again, this is an open research issue.

## CONCLUSION

Summing up, MPM approaches typically adopt a transformational process model, with UML being the most common representation language for meta-modeling techniques. However, documentation is often unsatisfactory and inadequate to the learning curve, especially in case of non-expert designers. Tools are powerful, but also suffer from the inadequacy of documentation, tutorials, and effective examples.

Current MPM approaches seem not to consider the MAS paradigm, which could be of help to cope with complex scenarios such as pervasive intelligent systems, ubiquitous systems, and self-organizing systems. The perspective of a blend of MAS within MPM approaches is appealing, both for the intrinsic agent features and because of the chance, provided by SPE, to build ad-hoc development processes by combining process fragments rooted into different paradigms: this is an open research area. The emergence of the SoS paradigm (Nielsen, Fitzgerald, Woodcock, & Peleska, 2015), where multi-paradigm approaches are also investigated (Ross, Ulieru, & Gorod, 2014),opens another promising conceptual and technical framework for agent-oriented abstractions, technologies, and methodologies.

Interestingly enough, the term "paradigm" is left in the background in most of the above works in the "multi-paradigm" modeling field: typically, it is merely mentioned to highlight the simultaneous presence/application of different approaches, set of rules, methods, etc. "—yet, without pointing out what a "paradigm" is supposed to be, nor highlighting the possible paradigm shifts that, according to (Kuhn, 2012), inherently define the paradigm concept per se. This is not peculiar to the MPM field: looking wider, the same seems to hold for multi-paradigm programming (MPM), despite programming languages date back to the sixties.

Overall, with the growing complexity of software systems in all fields, it can be expected that the practice of combining ideas, methods, approaches, processes, methodologies –*paradigms*, in the broadest sense – from diverse fields, possibly far from each other, becomes increasingly common for conceptual, economical and practical reasons. At the same time, being "multi-paradigm" is much more than just "adopting" two paradigms in some way: suitable models, guidelines, and new ad-hoc research are needed to make this scenario actually fruitful.

## REFERENCES

Atkinson, C., & Kuhne, T. (2001). The essence of multilevel metamodling. In UML 2001 - The Unified Modeling Language. Modeling Languages, Concepts and Tools (Vol. 2185, pp. 19-33). Berlin: Springer.

Balasubramanian, D., Levendovszky, T., Dubey, A., & Karsai, G. (2014). Taming Multi-Paradigm Integration in a Software Architecture Description Language. In D. Balasubramanian, C. Jacquet, P. Van Gorp, S. Kokaly, & T. Meszaros (Ed.), *8th Workshop on Multi-Paradigm Modeling (MPM@MODELS 2014)* (vol. 1237, pp. 67-76). RWTH Aachen University: Sun SITE Central Europe. Retrieved from http://ceur-ws.org/Vol-1237/paper7.pdf

Balci, O. (2012, July). A Life Cycle for Modeling and Simulation. *Simulation*, *88*(7), 870–883. doi:10.1177/0037549712438469

Bernon, C., Cossentino, M., Gleizes, M.-P., Turci, P., & Zambonelli, F. (2004). Article In J. Odell, P. Giorgini, & J. P. Muller (Eds.), Agent Oriented Software Engineering V (Vol. 3382, pp. 62-77). Berlin: Springer. doi:10.1007/978-3-540-30578-1_5

Boehm, B. W. (1988, May). A Spiral Model of Software Development and Enhancement. *IEEE Computer*, *21*(5), 61–72. doi:10.1109/2.59

Brinkkemper, S., Saeki, M., & Harmsen, F. (1999). Meta-Modelling Based Assembly Techniques for Situational Method Engineering. *Information Systems*, *24*(3), 209–228. doi:10.1016/S0306-4379(99)00016-2

Brooks, F. P. (1987, April). No Silver Bullet Essence and Accidents of Software Engineering. *IEEE Computer*, *20*(4), 10–19. doi:10.1109/MC.1987.1663532

Bryl, V., Giorgini, P., & Mylopoulos, J. (2009, February). Designing Socio-Technical Systems: From Stakeholder Goals to Social Networks. *Requirements Engineering*, *14*(1), 47–70. doi:10.100700766-008-0073-5

Cernuzzi, L., Cossentino, M., & Zambonelli, F. (2005, March). rocess Models for Agent-Based Development. *Engineering Applications of Artificial Intelligence*, *18*(2), 205–222. doi:10.1016/j.engappai.2004.11.015

Ciccozzi, F. a., Vangheluwe, H., & Weyns, D. (2019). Blended Modelling – What, why and how. *First International Workshop on Multi-Paradigm Modelling for Cyber-Physical Systems*. Retrieved from https://msdl.uantwerpen.be/conferences/MPM4CPS/2019/wp-content/uploads/2019/09/mpm4cps2019_Blended.pdf

Cossentino, M., Gaglio, S., Garro, A., & Seidita, V. (2007). Method fragments for agent design methodologies: From standardisation to research. *International Journal of Agent Oriented Software Engineering*, *1*(1), 91–121. doi:10.1504/IJAOSE.2007.013266

Cossentino, M., Seidita, V., Hilaire, V., & Molesini, A. (2014). *FIPA Design Process Documentation and Fragmentation Working Group*. Retrieved from FIPA Design Process Documentation and Fragmentation Working Group: http://www.pa.icar.cnr.it/cossentino/fipa-dpdf-wg/

Dalibor, M., Jansen, N., Rumpe, B., Wachtmeister, L., & Wortmann, A. (2019). Model-Driven Systems Engineering for Virtual Product Design. *MPM4CPS 2019: First International Workshop on Multi-Paradigm Modelling for Cyber-Physical Systems*. Retrieved from https://msdl.uantwerpen.be/conferences/MPM4CPS/2019/wp-content/uploads/2019/09/Paper_MDSE4VirtualProductDesign.pdf

Denil, J., Vangheluwe, H., De Meulenaere, P., & Demeyer, S. (2012). *Calibration of Deployment Simulation Models: A Multi-Paradigm Modelling Approach. In 2012 Symposium on Theory of Modeling and Simulation — DEVS Integrative M&S Symposium (TMS/DEVS '12).* Society for Computer Simulation International. Retrieved from https://dl.acm.org/citation.cfm?id=2346629

Di Marzo Serugendo, G., Gleizes, M.-P., & Karageorgos, A. (2006, January). Self-Organization in Multi-Agent Systems. *The Knowledge Engineering Review, 20*(2), 165–189. doi:10.1017/S0269888905000494

Diallo, S., Andreas Tolk, A., Gore, R., & Padilla, J. (2005). Modeling and simulation framework for systems engineering. In D. Gianni, A. D'Ambrogio, & A. Tolk (Eds.), Modeling and Simulation-Based Systems Engineering Handbook (pp. 377-401). Boca Raton, FL: CRC Press. doi:10.1201/b17902

Ehrig, H., Engels, G., Kreowski, H.-J., & Rozenberg, G. (1999). *Handbook of Graph Grammars and Computing by Graph Transformation.* World Scientific. doi:10.1142/4180

Fondement, F., & Silaghi, R. (2004). Defining Model Driven Engineering Processes. In M. Gogolla, P. Sammut, & J. Whittle (Eds.), *3rd UML Workshop in Software Model Engineering (WiSME 2004)* (pp. 1-11). Lisbon, Portugal: Universidade Nova de Lisboa. Retrieved from http://ctp.di.fct.unl.pt/UML2004/workshop.html#ws5

Fuggetta, A. (2000). Software Process: A Roadmap. In *ICSE '00: Proceedings of the Conference on The Future of Software Engineering* (pp. 25-34). Limerick, Ireland: ACM Press. 10.1145/336512.336521

Giese, H., & Levendovszky, T. (Eds.). (2006). Proceedings of the Workshop on Multi-Paradigm Modeling: Concepts and Tools 2006. In *Proceedings of the Workshop on Multi-Paradigm Modeling: Concepts and Tools.2006/1.* BME-DAAI Technical Report Series. Retrieved from http://avalon.aut.bme.hu/\~mesztam/conferences/mpm06/mpm06\_proc.pdf

Gonzalez-Perez, C., McBride, T., & Henderson-Sellers, B. (2005). A Metamodel for Assessable Software Development Methodologies. *Software Quality Journal, 13*(2), 195–214. doi:10.100711219-005-6217-7

Group, O. (2008). *SPEM 2.0.* Tratto da Software & Systems Process Engineering Metamodel Specification. Version 2.0: https://www.omg.org/spec/SPEM/2.0/

Hardebolle, C., & Boulanger, F. (2009, November). Exploring Multi-Paradigm Modeling Techniques. *Simulation, 85*(11-12), 688–708. doi:10.1177/0037549709105240

Henderson-Sellers, B. (2002). Process Metamodelling and Process Construction: Examples Using the OPEN Process Framework OPF. *Annals of Software Engineering, 14*(1), 341–362. doi:10.1023/A:1020570027891

Henderson-Sellers, B., & Gonzalez-Perez, C. (2005, January). A Comparison of Four Process Metamodels and the Creation of a New Generic Standard. *Information and Software Technology, 47*(1), 49–65. doi:10.1016/j.infsof.2004.06.001

Jensen, K., & Kristensen, L. M. (2009). *Coloured Petri Nets. Modelling and Validation of Concurrent Systems*. Springer. doi:10.1007/b95112

Kuhn, T. S. (2012). The Structure of Scientific Revolutions (50th Anniversary ed.). Chicago: University of Chicago Press.

Lara, J. d., & Vangheluwe, H. (2002). Computer Aided Multi-paradigm Modelling to Process Petri-Nets and Statecharts. In A. Corradini, H. Ehrig, H. -J. Kreowski, & G. Rozenberg (Eds.), Graph Transformation (Vol. 2505, pp. 239-253). Berlin: Springer. doi:10.1007/3-540-45832-8

Larman, C., & Basili, V. R. (2003, June). Iterative and Incremental Development: A Brief History. *IEEE Computer, 36*(6), 47–56. doi:10.1109/MC.2003.1204375

Li, X., Lei, Y., Wang, W., Wang, W., & Zhu, Y. (2013). *A DSM-based Multi-Paradigm Simulation Modeling Approach for Complex Systems. In 2013 Winter Simulation Conference: Simulation: Making Decisions in a Complex World (WSC '13)*. IEEE Press. Retrieved from https://dl.acm.org/citation.cfm?id=2675983.2676133

Lorenz, T., & Jost, A. (2006). Towards an Orientation Framework in Multi-Paradigm Modeling: Aligning Purpose, Object and Methodology in System Dynamics, AGent-Based Modeling and DIscrete-EVent-Simulation. In A. Grosler, E. A. Rouwette, R. S. Langer, J. I. Rowe, & J. M. Yanni (Eds.), *24th International Conference of the System Dynamics Society* (pp. 2134-2151). Albany, NY: System Dynamics Society. Retrieved from https://www.systemdynamics.org/conferences/2006/proceed/papers/LOREN178.pdf

Lynch, C., Padilla, J., Diallo, S., Sokolowski, J., & Banks, C. (2014). A multi-paradigm modeling framework for modeling and simulating problem situations. In *Proceedings of the Winter Simulation Conference 2014* (p. 1688-1699). Savanah, GA: IEEE. 10.1109/WSC.2014.7020019

Mariani, S., & Omicini, A. (2013). Molecules of Knowledge: Self-Organisation in Knowledge-Intensive Environments. In *G. Fortino, C. Badica, M. Malgeri, & R. Unland (Eds.), Intelligent Distributed Computing VI.446* (pp. 17–22). Springer. doi:10.1007/978-3-642-32524-3_4

Molesini, A. (2008). *Meta-Models, Environment and Layers: Agent-Oriented Engineering of Complex Systems* (Ph.D Thesis). Alma Mater Studiorum - Università di Bologna, Dipartimento di Elettronica, Informatica e Sistemistica, Bologna.

Mosterman, P. J., & Vangheluwe, H. (2002, October). Guest Editorial: Special Issue on Computer Automated Multi-Paradigm Modeling. *ACM Transactions on Modeling and Computer Simulation, 12*(4), 249–255. doi:10.1145/643120.643121

Mosterman, P. J., & Vangheluwe, H. (2004). Computer Automated Multi-Paradigm Modeling: An Introduction. *Simulation, 80*(9), 433–450. doi:10.1177/0037549704050532

Mustafiz, S., Denil, J., Lucio, L., & Vangheluwe, H. (2012). The FTG+PM Framework for Multi-paradigm Modelling: An Automotive Case Study. In *6th International Workshop on Multi-Paradigm Modeling (MPM '12)* (pp. 13-18). New York, NY: ACM. 10.1145/2508443.2508446

Nielsen, C. B., Fitzgerald, J., Woodcock, J., & Peleska, J. (2015). Systems of Systems Engineering: Basic Concepts, Model-Based Techniques, and Research Directions. *ACM Computing Surveys, 48*(2), 1–41. doi:10.1145/2794381

NoMagic. (2019). *MagicDraw Home Page*. Retrieved 11 20, 2019, from NoMagic: https://www.nomagic.com/products/magicdraw

Oliveira, B. C., & Loh, A. (2013). Abstract Syntax Graphs for Domain Specific Languages. In *ACM SIGPLAN 2013 Workshop on Partial Evaluation and Program Manipulation (PEPM '13)* (pp. 87-96). New York, NY: ACM. doi:10.1145/2426890.2426909

OMG. (1997). *UML Home Page*. Retrieved from UML: http://www.uml.org

OMG. (2001). *MDA Home Page*. Retrieved from MDA: https://www.omg.org/mda/

OMG. (2002). *MOF Home Page*. Retrieved from MOF: https://www.omg.org/mof/

OMG. (2008). *Software & Systems Process Engineering Metamodel Specification. Version 2.0*. Retrieved from SPEM: https://www.omg.org/spec/SPEM/2.0/

Omicini, A. (2015). Event-Based vs. Multi-Agent Systems: Towards a Unified Conceptual Framework. In G. Fortino, W. Shen, J.-P. Barthès, J. Luo, W. Li, S. Ochoa, . . . M. Ramos (Eds.), *2015 19th IEEE International Conference on Computer Supported Cooperative Work in Design (CSCWD2015)* (pp. 1-6). Los Alamitos, CA: IEEE Computer Society. doi:10.1109/CSCWD.2015.7230924

Organization, S. (2003). *SysML Open Source Project Home Page*. Retrieved from SysML Open Source Project: https://sysml.org/

Papadopoulos, G. A., Stavrou, A., & Papapetrou, O. (2006, March). An Implementation Framework for {S}oftware {A}rchitectures Based on the Coordination Paradigm. *Science of Computer Programming, 60*(1), 27–67. doi:10.1016/j.scico.2005.06.002

Rhazali, Y., El Hachimi, A., Chana, I., Lahmer, M., & Rhattoy, A. (2019). Automate Model Transformation From CIM to PIM up to PSM in Model-Driven Architecture. In *Modern Principles, Practices, and Algorithms for Cloud Security*. doi:10.4018/978-1-7998-1082-7.ch013

Rhazali, Y., Hadi, Y., & Mouloudi, A. (2016). CIM to PIM Transformation in MDA: From Service-Oriented Business Models to Web-Based Design Models. *International Journal of Software Engineering and Its Applications, 10*(4), 125–142. doi:10.14257/ijseia.2016.10.4.13

Ross, W., Ulieru, M., & Gorod, A. (2014). A Multi-Paradigm Modelling & Simulation Approach for System of Systems Engineering: A Case Study. In *9th International Conference on System of Systems Engineering (SoSE 2014)* (pp. 183-188). Piscataway, NJ: IEEE. 10.1109/SYSOSE.2014.6892485

Satyanarayanan, M. (2001). Pervasive Computing: Vision and Challenges. *IEEE Personal Communications, 8*(4), 10–17. doi:10.1109/98.943998

Schmidt, D. C. (2006). Guest Editor's Introduction: Model-Driven Engineering. *IEEE Computer, 39*(2), 25–31.

Sommerville, I. (2007). *Software Engineering* (8th ed.). Edinburgh, UK: Addison-Wesley.

Syriani, E. (2011). A Multi-Paradigm Foundation for Model Transformation Language Engineering. McGill University.

Syriani, E., & Vangheluwe, H. (2012). *AToMPM Home Page*. Retrieved from AToMPM: http://www-ens.iro.umontreal.ca/$%5Csim$syriani/atompm/atompm.htm

Van Tendeloo, Y., Van Mierlo, S., & Vangheluwe, H. (2018). *Modelverse Home Page*. Retrieved from Modelverse: https://msdl.uantwerpen.be/git/yentl/modelverse

Van Tendeloo, Y., Van Mierlo, S., & Vangheluwe, H. (2019, October). A Multi-Paradigm Modelling approach to live modelling. *Software & Systems Modeling, 18*(5), 2821–2842. doi:10.100710270-018-0700-7

Vangheluwe, H. (2002). An Introduction to Multiparadigm Modelling and Simulation. In AI, Simulation & Planning in High Autonomy Systems (AIS 2002) (pp. 9-20). Lisbon, Portugal: Society for Modeling & Simulation International (SCS).

Vangheluwe, H. (2002). An Introduction to Multiparadigm Modelling and Simulation. In AI, Simulation & Planning in High Autonomy Systems (AIS 2002) (pp. 9-20). Lisbon, Portugal: Society for Modeling & Simulation International (SCS).

Vranic, V. (2005, June). Multi-Paradigm Design with Feature Modeling. *Computer Science and Information Systems, 2*(1), 79–102. doi:10.2298/CSIS0501079V

Zambonelli, F., & Parunak, H. V. (2003). Towards a Paradigm Change in Computer Science and Software Engineering: A Synthesis. *The Knowledge Engineering Review, 18*(4), 329–342. doi:10.1017/S0269888904000104

Chapter 5

# Cultivating Practitioners for Software Engineering Experiments in industry:
## Best Practices Learned From the Experience

**Guillermo López**

https://orcid.org/0000-0001-5850-1164
*Instituto Tecnológico de Aragon, Spain*

**Laura García-Borgoñón**

*Instituto Tecnológico de Aragon, Spain*

**Sira Vega**

*Universidad Politecnica de Madrid, Spain*

**Maria J. Escalona**

*University of Seville, Spain*

**Natalia Juristo**

*Universidad Politecnica de Madrid, Spain*

## ABSTRACT

*Controlled experiments are commonly used to evaluate software methods, processes, and tools. Literature presents that the validation of software engineering research results in industrial settings is a powerful way to obtain feedback about its value. However, to implicate industry and practitioners in experiments is not an easy task, and, even when a company is committed, frequently the number of practitioners involved is not enough to execute and validate the experiment. This chapter presents a guide of best practices that can be used in order to get a high number of participants that can validate research results from*

DOI: 10.4018/978-1-7998-3661-2.ch005

*the industry. These practices are oriented to create an attractive environment for companies to conclude that the participation in a research experiment can be interesting for them. In order to illustrate them, the chapter also introduces the authors' experiences when running an experiment about early testing at the University of Seville, where they followed these guidelines to successfully enhance the participation of 76 practitioners from 32 different software companies.*

# INTRODUCTION

Empirical studies are nowadays very common in software engineering (SE) and there is not any doubt that they can help to advance knowledge in the field (Juristo & Moreno, 2001). Empirical studies are needed to develop or improve processes, methods and tools for software development and maintenance (Runeson & Höst, 2009). Controlled experiments are a type of empirical study, which allow the identification of cause-effect relationships (Sjøberg et al. 2005). However, most controlled experiments in SE are running in the laboratory, and the experimental paradigm proposes that laboratory findings should be generalized experiments closer to the real world, such as: field experiments in industry.

In SE, field experiments are equivalent to run experimentation in industry (Vegas et al 2015). A major ambition of experimental SE is to provide software managers, who are in charge of decision-making in the software development industry, with evidence of how new technology can be introduced (Jedlistschka et al 2014). However, the experimental subjects used in the lab are typically students, with little or no professional experience (Dieste et al 2013). This situation has been hardly analysed in literature and it is an important gap for the field (Salman et al 2015). The few experiments run with practitioners are isolated experiences (that is, an experiment is conducted only once in a specific company) (Vegas et al 2015). Additionally, the experimental settings and materials tend to be artificial or only partially related to real projects (Escalona et al 2007). The systematic use of experiments as a way to cope with the decision analysis and resolution practices is far away from what would be desirable.

Industry-Academia Collaboration (IAC) in SE has been an important topic since the early years of SE (Garousi et al 2016), and it is an important challenge in software field experiments. In Vega et al. (2015), the authors report preliminary results regarding the difficulties encountered when they run experiments in industry. One of their main findings is that it is hard to get experimental subjects, even when a company agrees to run an experiment. The person committed to running the experiment hardly ever has enough power to enroll people, and the company internal organization is a critical factor in subject recruitment, therefore the research community has problems involving a large number of them in experiments. One option to this problem could be to try including a high number of companies in a same experiment, increasing the number of subjects. In any case, the research community has to find suitable initiatives that offer them enough subjects to run its SE field experiments.

The goal of this paper is to present a guide of best practices that involve a higher number of companies when running experiments in industry. To illustrate these guidelines, we present a real experiment carried out at the University of Seville, with a total of 97 practitioners registered (76 of them finally participating in the experiment) from 32 different software companies, to evaluate our research results in early testing. This experiments is oriented to value the suitably of a model-driven approach for early testing in the industry.

The remainder of this paper is organized as follows: Section 2 introduces the motivation for the research presented in this paper. Section 3 shows that the team should be established to achieve the goal of this proposal. Then, Section 4 presents the strategy we propose (as a set of best practices) to enroll a large number of participants in experiments with practitioners. Later, Section 5 describes our early testing experiment and illustrates how the proposed strategy is followed to get effective participation of companies and practitioners in the early testing experiment. Finally, the paper ends up with Section 6 by stating our conclusions. It is important to note that the aim of this paper is not presenting the results of our experiment, but to propose a strategy that can help research teams include a high number of companies in software engineering experiments to increase the number of subjects.

Describe the general perspective of the chapter. End by specifically stating the objectives of the chapter.

## BACKGROUND

Currently, the software industry decides which software development practices (methods, tools, technologies, etc.) to use in a project based on perceptions, bias and market-speak (Gibbs 1994). But engineering disciplines base their decisions on real objective data. However, no evidence exists today to demonstrate that using a particular software development method or tool will really improve productivity, development time or quality (Pfleeger 1999).

Engineering disciplines have used the scientific method to release them from the craft status (Shaw 1990).Evidence about software development can be gathered applying the experimental paradigm to software engineering (SE) (Wohlin et al 2012). The experimental paradigm helps to Davis (1992): (1) identify and understand the variables that play a role in the phenomenon under study and the connections between variables; (2) learn cause-effect relationships, and (3) establish laws and theories that explain behavior.

However, traditional SE experiment simplifies reality with one or more of the following (Juristo& Gómez 2010): students (rather than professionals); toy software (rather than real systems); exercises (rather than real projects); academic or an industrial tutorial (rather than developers' knowledge and experience); phases or techniques (rather than whole projects), etc. Experiments in academic laboratories with all these simplifications get results that are not very generalizable in the real world.

Researchers in SE tried to analyze why it is so difficult and complicated to carry out experiments in industry. To date, Höfer and Tichy(2006) found that 60% of SE experiments use students, whereas 22% were conducted with professionals and only 14% used both subject types. Sjoberg et al. (2005) found that students participated in 87% of the 103 papers on controlled experiments published from 1993 to 2002, whereas only 9% used professionals.

Therefore in Juristo (2016), some relevant aspects, like the cost of resources for an experiment in industry is hardly justified by the results and there seems to be a big gap between the cost-benefit relationship in companies. As a consequence, the author concludes that the reporting from the industry has to be different and be "industry oriented".

In a more general way, Vegas et al (2015) describes 15 difficulties to carry out experiments in industry and focus the problem on four main conclusions: (1) Environment of the industry offers more constraints than the research environment, at least, in their experiences. (2) Professionals were troubled, undermotivated, and performed worse than students. (3) Data had specific characteristics: there was missing data due to dropouts and it was highly variable. This might have had an influence on the reliability of the results.(4) Reporting used in scientific journals was not appropriate for practitioners who require more detailed, measurable and useful results, therefore reporting a higher value for them.

In any case, finding good practices, recommendations or good experiences that help to enhance in industrial experiments is still an open challenge in software engineering.

## PREPARING THE INFRASTRUCTURE

In the rest of this paper, best practices are presented and validated on a real and successful experiment. However, before presenting them, we will provide the guidance for the required conditions to execute a successful experiment. In most cases, an infrastructure is composed of the four elements below:

1. Experiment research group (ERG).
2. Sponsorship support group (SSG).
3. Management steering group (MSG).
4. Experiment participants group (EPG)

ERG is made up by research group members that will guide the experiment through its lifecycle. In most cases, it will be recommended that ERG includes someone who leads the group activities who is spokesperson for MSG and SSG. The mission of SSG is to facilitate and to help achieve the organizations commitment, which is represented at MSG to run the experiment.MSG comprises of all organization managers that participate in the experiment. Each MSG member is responsible for linking the experiment to her/his organization's vision, and allocating participants to run the experiment. EPG consists of subjects participating in the experiment, coming from different organizations participating in the project. These roles are referenced in the application of best practices.

## BEST PRACTICES TO INVOLVE PRACTITIONERS IN SOFTWARE ENGINEERING EXPERIMENTS

Our main objective is to try to attain a high number of practitioners when an industrial experiment in SE is running. To obtain a good number of subjects to value is difficult in the industry and we are going to propose a set of best practices to solve this problem. Our global strategy is to try to involve several companies at the same time, and try to get as many subjects as possible from each of them.

In order to reach this target, we are going to organize the best practices according to the lifecycle experimental phases proposed in Juristo & Moreno (2001): goal definition, design of the experiment, execution of the experiment, and analysis of the results. In the following sections, practices are described sequentially.

Each practice will be uniquely identified in order to allow them to be referenced throughout. The practice identifier begins with prefix P, followed by a number, which precedes the practice title.

Before starting to describe in detail each proposed practice, we would like to point out two important aspects that must be considered throughout the experimental life cycle, and which we will present as generic practices. Therefore, we will also establish an identifier for both generic practices, so that they will be able to be referenced in this paper as well as in future works.

**PG1. Conduct the experiment with an enterprise approach.** We must not forget that the required subjects of the experiment are professionals in the software industry area, so it is necessary to be aware of their constraints regarding time, perceiving values and benefits when we design the experiment.

**PG2. Appreciate participants' effort.** Valuation should be perceived by participants. Each participant is a key element in our experiment and this is something we need to transmit in order to obtain the best results. Praxis such as delivering customized material, explaining pursued goals or communicating the obtained results properly when running the experiment, are examples of tasks we can perform to make participants perceive the important role they play in the experiment.

## Goal Definition

We propose the following practices regarding the Goal Definition phase.

**P1. Obtain involvement and support from clients and partners**. In contrast to academic experiments, one of the main difficulties of industry experiments is how to initiate contact with companies to obtain their participation. In general, this practice aims to take advantage of the trust that the companies' contacts (both customers and partners) have demonstrated in us, before contacting unknown professional participants.

**P2. Maximize the spectrum of participants.** As much as possible, and always within the experiment limits, this practice establishes that it is interesting reducing constraints and maximizing categories and profiles of professional subjects that could be included as potential participants.

**P3. Communicate the experiment to the largest potential participants**. Once we have designed the experiment, and with the aim of increasing the number of registrations, this practice recommends the use of all available technologies (e.g, e-mails, social networks, whatsapp and forum, among others) in order to advertise the experiment, and let a large number of potential participants know more about it.

**P4. Provide a continued commitment of participants.** After attaining the first contact and having shown their potential interest in taking part in the experiment, this practice proposes effective action to ensure a successful contact with participants that may be direct and personal contact (e.g., by phone), this way they may formalize the previous verbal commitment and register interested people directly on the participants' list.

**P5. Obtain sponsorship of the experiment from institutions.** The different institutional entities as well as business associations or clusters are normally relevant points-of-contact for companies. Consequently, they can be a powerful influence of motivation to participants. Their endorsement for these kind of actions and their commitment in a subsequent valuation may be considered as a critical aspect for running a successful experiment. Thus, this practice suggests looking for this endorsement.

**P6. Interview with managers from participating organizations.** Large companies, which are potential suppliers of a number of participants in the experiment, might consider the necessity of another type of sponsorship: senior management sponsorship. This practice proposes to have a direct relationship with the senior management teams, preferably face-to-face meetings, where the main objective should be to awaken the companies' interest and obtain their support by participating in the experiment.

For this purpose, several key aspects should be taken into account:

- Transmit effectively the experiment's objectives.
- Expose the benefits that the organization could obtain if participating in the project, e.g, external objective evaluations compared to its competitors, presence in the experiment's advertising or collaboration with other sponsor institutions, among others.
- Present the plan for the experiment according to the organization's schedule availability.
- Have a specific staff list with potential members of the experiment.

## Design

We propose the following practices regarding the Design phase.

**P7. Plan and perform pilots.** As it is exposed in PG1, the experiment must have a professional approach. Therefore, it is necessary to ensure the proper running of the experiment, so that we can maximize the objectives' achievement effectively and efficiently. This practice raises the use of pilots as an evaluation exercise and previous testing to detect possible existing inefficiencies and failures during the design phase. So, a prior adjustment would be possible before executing the experiment.

There are two specific aspects, at least, that this practice proposes to pilot:

- Regarding the experiment content: assessment of explanatory material about the structure and contents, or adjust the agenda, among other aspects.
- Regarding the infrastructure to carry out experiments: properly prepare computer equipment (hardware and software) or adjust the number of places or room layouts, for example.

**P8. Contact participants in an appealing way**. It is necessary to show and offer the activity as something attractive for participants when designing the structure of the call. It will identify all the benefits that as a result of running the experiment the participants will have, such as: knowledge and awareness of innovative technologies, evaluation of tools previously to its market availability, networking or training course certification, for instance.

**P9. Define an accurate agenda.** Having a concrete and precise agenda is essential for the proper development of the experiment regarding the accomplishment of the planned timetable and objectives. In this practice, we propose that the development of the following aspects are taken into account and included in the experiment agenda definition:

- Incorporate specific and understandable activities for participants.
- Specify the activities schedule accurately, adjusting it to the experiments needs.
- Minimize time duration of participants involvement.
- Look for the participants' comfort, for example, reducing unwanted learning with known scenarios, restricting activities complexity or mitigating the fatigue effect that could effect to the experiment results, among other issues.
- Include aspects related to networking, such as time for a coffee break, the possibility of lunch or dynamics for participants' presentation.

**P10. Establish a strict schedule for running the experiment**. Business professionals' availability and time are always limited. This practice suggests that one way to overcome timing problems is to propose complementary and alternative disjoint calls, in order to facilitate the choice that best suits each participant.

**P11. Use online resources to manage the experiment**. Data management in the experiment is a key factor for further analysis and discussion of results. Therefore, in this practice we suggest the use of online tools that allow you to:

- Simplify the access (availability of time, site or systems, for instance) and use of participants.
- Collect previous information about participants (personal, academic or professional data).
- Carry out continuous monitoring of the progress of participants' registration, in order to take appropriate corrective action.
- Collect preferences and constraints regarding participants' needs while the experiment is running.
- Gather expectations of participants when they accept to participate in the experiment.

**P12. Monitor registration against plan**. In many cases, there is an associated risk related to the real participation of professionals in the experiment, due to the experiment is not part of their daily activity, but an external and extra commitment. It occurs despite senior managers' agreement to allow their staff to take part in the experiment. Therefore, this practice arises the need to monitor and control the list of participants' registration, in order to know the evolution and take necessary corrective actions before conducting the experiment.

**P13. Establish the experiment plan.** Although all activities related to wooing professionals for their participation in the experiment are not technical tasks, they should be considered as important actions in each of experiment phases. In consequence, they should be included in the project plan of the experiment. This practice proposes to establish and maintain an experiment plan where all aspects, technical and social, are included like in a project plan.

**P14. Design the experiment for heterogeneity**. Due to the proposal of enlarging the participants' spectrum, there is a high possibility of having a high heterogeneity among subjects. Therefore, this practice presents the need to take into account this heterogeneity when the experiment is being designed, both in terms of content and support throughout the execution.

**P15. Establish the experimental infrastructure.** In Juristo & Moreno (2001), authors point several difficulties related to the infrastructure in experiments with professional subjects. They are the following ones:

- The high number of dropouts due to interference caused by being developed in the usual workplace.
- The lack of appropriate resources (rooms, computers, tools, systems or licenses, among others) for conducting the experiment.
- The difficulty for people from other companies to participate in the project because they are possible competitors.

Therefore, this practice proposes the selection of independent facilities for all participants. Also necessary resources should be available and accessible for all subjects in the experiment. To locate the experiment at the university facilities could also encourage company-university relationship, which is an objective that experiment in industry promotes.

## Execution

This Section exposes the practices related to the Execution phase as follows.

**P16. Send previous reminder.** This practice aims to mitigate the risk regarding the lack of the experiment prioritization against participants' daily work. This practice would reinforce previous practices performed during definition and design phases. At this point, it is recommended to send a reminder few days before the execution date, with a dual objective: on the one hand, to avoid forgetting the committed session, and on the other hand, to ensure, as soon as possible, the previously confirmed attendance.

**P17. Promote networking.** This practice raises the use of designed places and moments for networking, promoting meetings and collecting information about participants' expectations and needs with view to future collaborations beyond the current experiment.

**P18. Comply with the agenda.** Along the experiment, it is essential to comply with planned tasks at the assigned time to do them. Therefore, this practice proposes the inclusion of a timekeeper role within the ERG, with the main objective of following as much as possible the planned timetable.

**P19. Satisfy participants' expectations.** In order to achieve sufficient participation in the experiment, some benefits should be offered to participants. These benefits have already been showed at registration tools. This practice suggests that it is mandatory to cope with expectations as well as carry out actions that allow us to know the level of satisfaction of such expectations. An example would be a customer satisfaction survey. As known, conducting the survey is a task that should be also included in the agenda.

Accomplishment of this practice reinforces the fact that it is necessary to meet generated expectations during recruitment phases to avoid feeling of bad experience.

## Analysis

We propose the following practices regarding the Analysis phase.

**P20. Satisfy commitments.** This practice shows that it is necessary to meet the planned outcomes when the experiment has been run with things such as: attendance certificate, availability of results and related information, among others. Time in research is often longer than time in business. Therefore, response time performing this practice should be as short as possible.

**P21. Evaluate results of experiment participation.** After running the experiment, all information related to participation, initial expectations and results of customer satisfaction survey is available. This practice proposes that, although this data is not a specific part of the experiment analysis, it is necessary to evaluate them in order to extract information and learned lessons that will allow us to look for improvement aspects in future experiments.

**P22. Maintain interest of participants.** Once professionals have made a big effort in getting involved in the experiment, their interest in this field should not be wasted. For that purpose, organizers should take advantage of different actions such as: communicating or delivering the results in order to maintain a communication channel where different doubts could be raised, different links to download results, news and all material related to the experiment could be provided.

**P23. Manage steering committee interest.** Unlike the above practice, which was focused on subjects, this practice refers to companies' interest, represented by their steering committees. In this case, it is recommended to hold face-to-face meetings to give feedback about specific organization's results and status in the area as well as about future collaborations proposals.

## SUCCESSFUL CASE STUDY: EARLY TESTING EXPERIMENT

This section presents the experiment run by IWT2, as a successful experience dealing with the application of the best practices described in the section above. Thus, we will describe the experiment setting according to Juristo & Moreno (2001). Then, we will highlight how our proposal of best practices was implemented in the early testing experiment, and finally, we will summarize the obtained results in the application of best practices.

### Description of the Experiment

The goal of the experiment was to analyze the adequacy of the paradigm guided by models (or MDE-Model Driven Engineering) (Top¸cu et al. 2016) as basis technique for developing functional tests in an early phase (early testing). The participants were staff of companies (small, medium and large) and software organizations (private and public) with representation in Spain. They mainly came from Andalusia, but we also gathered people from other cities, such as Madrid or Barcelona. Participants were not required a particular profile, apart from being a software engineer that do some kind of software testing in their daily work. Thus, junior and senior testers, test managers or developers who do testing in a timely manner were able to participate.

This heterogeneous group required the collection of demographic data of each participant in order to guarantee a proper randomization, and thus a right profile of participant. For this purpose, an electronic registration form was used[1]. The content of this form is summarized in Table 1.Initially, 97 participants registered to participate in the experiment, although some of them were not able to attend it. Finally, 76 practitioners from 32 different software companies participated. There were two research questions in the experiment:

- RQ1: Is developer effort affected by MDE when generating functional test cases?
- RQ2: Is the quality of the functional test cases generated affected by MDE?

*Table 1. Participants' data gathered in the registration form*

| | |
|---|---|
| **Personal Data** | • Name<br>• Surname<br>• NIF<br>• BirthDate<br>• Phone<br>• Email<br>• Gender |
| **AcademicData** | • Degree<br>• Year of finishing the last degree<br>• Any special course related with testing (such as TestQA) |
| **Professional Data** | • Company<br>• Position: Manager, Analyst, Designer, Programmer, Scholar employer, Other<br>• Years of experience in testing or any other fields (like programming or commercial activities, among others): Experience in testing, Test Manager, Junior Tester, Senior Tester<br>• Percentage of time dedicated to testing per week: Less than 25%, Between 25% and 50%, Between 50% and 75%, More than 75%<br>• Typical testing carried out in: Unit Testing, Integration Testing, Functional Testing, System Integration, Acceptance Testing |

We have an associated hypothesis (H) for each of these questions as shown below:

- H01: The effort to build a test case using MDE is the same as using manual development.
- H02: The control and quality of test cases generated using MDE is the same as using manual development.

The experiment has one factor: functional definition method. The control is manual method while the treatment is MDE method with the support of NDT-Suite (García-García et al 2012) solution. NDT-Suite is a set of tools to support NDT (Navigational Development Techniques) (Escalona & Aragon 2009). It is not the aim of this paper to present NDT in detail but it is worth highlighting that it is a model-driven methodology that offers suitable support for the application of MDE in software development. NDT covers the whole software lifecycle, from requirements to maintenance, and even supports other management activities like quality assurance, project management and software security assurance. NDT has been successfully applied to a high number of real projects. However, companies never valued methodologically its suitability. As NDT covers a high number of tools and software phases, we had to decide which were the most interesting for our first experiment with companies. One of the most important characteristics of NDT is its support for early testing activities. Testing is currently a critical phase for software companies because they usually have poor resources (Gutierrez et al 2012). Thus, we selected this phase, concretely functional phase. The experiment aims to study if, in fact, experts consider these solutions as suitable for enterprise environment.

The response variables measured in the experiment are:

- RQ1 requires to measure developer effort. The selected metric was **resolution time**.

- RQ2 is a little more complicated. Initially, as our experimental objects came from real projects (as it is explained later), we had the code of the system in the first version (and also in the final one). Thus, if experts detected a good number of errors or mistakes, we could consider they defined a good set of functional tests. However, it was not possible. Tests defined manually by our experts did not identify any errors (later we will analyze the reason), so we reconsidered this way of evalu-

*Table 2. Timetable for the experiment*

| Time | Content |
|---|---|
| 15:30-16:00 | Welcome and presentation |
| 16:00-16:30 | Presentation of examples and material |
| 16:30-17:00 | Defining functional testing manually |
| 17:00-17:30 | Coffee Break |
| 17:30-19:00 | Training course: knowing MDE. Presenting NDT and NDT-Suite |
| 19:00-19:30 | Defining functional testing automatically |
| 19:30-19:45 | Final interview |
| 19:45-20:00 | Closing and _Final conclusions |

ation, and the used metric was the evaluation of two experts about **the tests' quality**. It means that two experts worked on the functional test definition, assessed the participants' tests and gave a mark between 0 (very bad) and 4 (very good).

The experiment followed a factor-two level (control and treatment) within subjects design. The experimental operation is presented in Table 2[2]. The experiment had two differentiated parts. In the first one, participants were asked to exercise the control. This implied that functional tests should be generated manually. We did not offer any support or extra learning because we aimed to assess the knowledge of our expert. In the second part, after a training session, we asked participants to generate functional tests using MDE with NDT. After that, each participant filled out a form.

According to the experiment definition presented in Table 2, each participant had to perform two tasks, one manually, and another one automatically using MDE, concretely, NDT and NDT-Suite as shown in Table 3.

*Table 3. Experiment design*

|  | **Manual** | **Automatic** |
|---|---|---|
| Group 1 | D1F | D2F |
| Group 2 | D2F | D1F |
| Group 3 | D1D | D2D |
| Group 4 | D2D | D1D |

Our design was exposed to a number of validity threats, such as fatigue and learning. We believed that we had managed to address those effects in our experiment by applying the following strategies:

- Fatigue effect: The fact that each subject had to analyze two problems meant that two sessions were required to run the experiment. If those sessions were performed in close succession, subjects may experience fatigue, resulting in a drop in their effectiveness as the experimental session progressed. To avoid that pernicious effect, the experimental sessions took only 4.5 hours with a break for coffee to relax. Therefore, fatigue would not affect the second session, which was developed in similar conditions to the first one.
- Learning effect: The source of the learning effect is performance of the same experimental task by the same experimental subject on repeated occasions. In this experiment, each subject analyzed two completely different domains, and therefore the information was unlikely to be reusable from the domain-aware problem (AP1) to domain-ignorant problem (IP1). On the other hand, elicitation was performed using the open interview, and subject skills were a priori unlikely to improve substantially after a mere 30-minute course (actual elicitation sessions were even shorter) and over the 2 days between sessions.

## Implementing Best Practices in the Experiment

This section explains how the best practices illustrated in Section 4 has been used in our early testing experiment to get a large number of participants. It has been organized around three moments: before running the experiment, while running the experiment and after running the experiment.

### Before Running the Experiment

The first idea was to obtain the support of the Regional Government of Andalusia (2020), as a way to comply with P5 and P1. We contacted with the person in charge of decision-making related to IT (Information Technologies) digital policy who is General Director of Digital Policy in the Regional Ministry of Treasure and Public Administration in Andalusia (P5). He is a very relevant person and a significant contact, as well as a key customer for companies in Andalusia (P1). The manager of our team hold personal meeting with him. She met him several years ago and she presented him the experiment asking for his endorsement. She explained in detail (30 minutes approximately) the importance of that kind of experience among University-Public Administration-Companies, mainly in a current strategy line for IT testing.

The support we were looking for was critical for our experiment. In invitation to participate in the experiment, we could detail that we were also supported by the Regional Government of Andalusia, which recognized our experiment as a very innovative initiative for the community. After that, as a second action we prepared an invitation, as we cited in practice P3, and a website with the definition of our experiment. In this invitation, we detailed some critical aspects[3]:

1. The support of the Regional Government of Andalusia and the Senior Manager's endorsement.
2. A set of advantages for our participants, as described below.
3. A very concrete agenda, as we presented in Table 2.

Thus, we satisfied practices P8, P9 and P13. These aspects were an attractive claim for companies for several things:

1. The support of the Regional Government of Andalusia was critical because they have key clients for companies in our environment and they also set the pace and make global decisions about IT that are crucial for IT companies located in Andalusia. Thus, the fact of participating in an initiative with the University of Seville in Software Testing endorsed by the General Director gives companies a relevant position in the community.
2. The advantages in the presentation were critical, since we offered two points. This action directly corresponds to P8.
   a. First, advantages for participants: we offer a personal certificate of participation, a free course in early testing and a free evaluation of their work in the experiment, where our experts value their knowledge by means of a personal assessment.
   b. Second, we consider some advantages for companies, thus, if a company participates with at least five participants, it will be awarded with an especial certificate of participation, which results very attractive for them, mainly for public contracts regarding testing in Andalusia.

3.  The definition of a very concrete agenda was also a relevant aspect, which confirms that we have coped with practice P9. People in companies are very busy. For them, to spend time in an experiment is often very difficult. With a concrete agenda, we help them close and reserve the period of time dedicated to the experiment. Besides, we planned three different sessions, so as to enable them to select the most appropriate one concerning their availability. So, with this action, we have also complied with P10.

However, our experience working with companies confirms that an official invitation is not enough. Today, we receive a high number of emails and we consider a lot of them as spam. For this reason, if we only send the invitation, it will probably be received in the spam folder. Thus, together with the official invitation, we sent personal emails to people in companies, as it was established in P4. Sending the invitation, we learned that it was very important:

1.  Use personal emails, with a personalized text for each receiver. Our mails were not sent to companies as general emails. They were sent to particular people (our own contacts or our contacts' contacts or event contacts provided by the Regional Government of Andalusia). Each email was different and each one enclosed an invitation. In the email, we asked participants to resend the invitation to other people who may work with them.
2.  Make phone calls or use other ways of communication, such as whatsApp or any other social net, since we considered that busy people usually ignore unrelevant emails. Obviously, this kind of calls involve a high cost. In light of this, it was mainly the director of the team who carried out this task. For companies, calls made by the boss, acquire a more relevant character and they are frequently given more importance.

*Table 4. The number of contacts did by the IWT2 leader*

| | |
|---|---|
| Number of sent mails | 337 |
| Number of phone calls directly related to the experiment | 131 |
| Number of sent whatsapp messages directly related to the experiment | 350 |

Table 4[4] displays the number of mails, whatsapp messages and calls sent to invite people to participate in the experiment.

However, despite this dedication, we thought that it was not enough. For our experiment, it was essential to count on different profiles, for example Small and medium enterprises (SMEs), big companies and public companies. Besides, we looked for different levels of experts, both junior and senior, as we exposed in P2. Thus, in cases of key participants or companies, we even asked for a face-to-face meeting, as it was established in P6. Thus, for instance, we held a personal meeting with the manager team of two important multinational companies whose testing factory headquarters are located in Seville, to ask for their participation in the project. Experiments were planned (and later executed) between November 4th and 5th. In total, three different sessions were executed; one on Wednesday afternoon and the other two on Thursday morning and afternoon. We did not plan the schedule of the meetings independently but in liaison with companies and mainly with bosses along the face-to-face meetings that we held with them (P6).

*Table 5. Number of face-to-face meetings held by the group leader during the call*

| SMEs Visits | Public Companies Visits | Big Companies Visits | Total |
|---|---|---|---|
| 4 | 4 | 5 | 13 |

Table 5 presents the number of meetings that the leader of the team held with companies. They are classified in SMEs, big companies or public companies. We consider that it was key to have these meetings in companies' headquarters. It obviously entailed a cost of moving for the team since some of them were even located out of Seville. However, we can assure that all visited companies participated in the experiment. Some of them, even aimed to replicate the experiment in their own companies.

At last, to finish with the preparation of our experiment, we defined an online registration form, which was described in Table 1, as we established inP11. The strategy of designing an online registration form was also a clever idea, since it allowed us to satisfy several practices:

1.  We could follow up the number of participants, so that, if a company or person was not inscribed, we could insist by either making some more calls or by sending more emails (P12).
2.  In the form, we included some demographical and personal data (like experience or level of test knowledge, among other) which was essential for a good definition of our experiment (P14).
3.  Each participant could select the best section for him/her, which was critical to assure that we could assume the number of participants in each section (P10).

Due to the right execution of the experiment was a critical aspect for our future relationships with the participating companies, we had the intention to make sure that any technical problem would be solved before running the experiment. For that purpose, we carried out a pilot in Zaragoza as we established in P7. We counted on the support of the Aragón Institute of Technology (2020), which in turn, invited 17 companies. During this experience, we were able to assure that our schedule was good planned, that some aspects of the early testing course had to be changed to be clearer for participants, as well as some other improvements.

In order to satisfy practice P15, we executed the experiment in a room at School of Computer Science at the University of Seville, giving relevance to the preparation of the class. Thus, in addition to Zaragoza's pilot, three days before the experiment we carried out a new pilot in the same room where the experiment would take place, with five students in the last course of the degree, just to check if software was right, computers were available, and web connection was working correctly, among other aspects. This pilot was essential because we had time to repair some computers with software problems (just technical problems with Enterprise Architect installation or internet connection).

## Running the Experiment

Some days before the agreed date of the experiment, we sent personal emails to each participant as a reminder of the starting time and the agenda, as we established in P16. Those emails were aimed not only to remember the appointment, but also to guarantee that people was going to attend or not the meeting. As we introduced in Section 5.1, we worked with two different systems and with two kinds of use cases for each of them: four examples in total. With on-line supporting, we divided cases among our participants in order to assure a good distribution of each of them. The email enabled us to guarantee that we had a good number of examples and a right distribution. However, we also considered other elements which highly influenced the corporative and public image of our group and our experiment. They were mainly four listed as follows:

1.  As we established in PG2, each participant was important to run the experiment successfully. We wished that participants felt valued, so each of them received a folder with personalized documentation for the experiment. In fact, we were sponsored by Fidetia, which provided folders, pens and notebooks, by offering a very serious and interesting view of our experiment.
2.  The coffee break was seen as a relevant moment that allowed improving networks and relations among participants. We planned to offer some coffee, although we then considered that as the experiment involved a short period of time, to move our participants from one place to another was not a good idea. Therefore, we used a classroom with a special area for the coffee break, and so, we satisfied practice P17.
3.  As we introduced in P18, our participants valued time as a very positive aspect, thus to accomplish the agenda was a critical aspect: to be on time was essential to collaborate with companies, because time means money and they usually have very busy and complex agendas.
4.  Another important aspect to take into account was fulfilling participants' expectations, as established in P19.

## After Running the Experiment

There were still some pending activities after the execution of our experiment and, therefore, we followed the practices related to the analysis phase in order to demonstrate our participants the positive effect of taking part in university experiments. The compiled information lets us know about some aspects that we have never considered before about the use of early testing and the view that experts have of our tools. However, analyzing these conclusions is not the aim of this paper.

In practice P21, we posed the needed of doing something similar to a customer satisfaction survey. In Table 6, we present a very relevant graphic obtained from OPINA (2020) with the result of a very

*Table 6. Satisfaction results*

| Blue: It is not interesting | 0% |
| --- | --- |
| Green: I consider I did not learn anything | 2% |
| Red: Yes, but I wanted to get more learning | 45% |
| Pink: Yes, I like it and I learn | 47% |

particular question that we asked to each participant. This Figure responds to a question in the last questionnaire of the experiment: do you consider this kind of experience between university and companies as a relevant issue?

As it can be concluded from this survey, a high number of our participants deemed the experiment very interesting and they thought that this kind of collaboration would be very suitable for improving their jobs. They also added that it was such an interesting working day that could offer very relevant solutions to improve their own businesses. For that reason, we state that the research community should improve this kind of collaboration because a large number of participants (98%) thought this kind of experience as something relevant for them.

Once the experiment was carried out, we also continued applying practices to keep the interest of our partners companies and participants up. Firstly, according to practice P22, after the execution of the experiment, we sent a personal email with the global figures the project entailed (number of participants, number of companies, and some others), just to demonstrate the interest of the results. Additionally, we sent a letter to Junta de Andalusia and we published especial news about the successful experiment in our university social networks. Besides, each participant could freely download the examples, tools and manuals used during the experiment and have direct connection with the research team in case he or she decided to know more about early testing.

Two weeks after the experiment, participants received their certificate of participation via email and we offered them the possibility to also get the original copy. This action complied with practice P20. During the next three months (December, January and February) the team worked in the analysis of the outcomes. When finished, we wrote a new email to our participants, giving them the possibility to know their results. Along the experiment, we guaranteed the confidentiality of the results, that means that we could not provide information about each participant and result, but we offered them to show their personal results and their position in comparison to other participants. It means that we could met participants who demanded it and, depending on their profile, we could compare their results with other participants with the same profiles and as well as we could give them, under our consideration, some key recommendations.

We started a direct contact with new companies and after that experience, we have also strengthened the communication with companies we had worked before, by means of demonstrating that the experiment was also relevant for them, in order to accomplish practice P23. For this reason, the results have led to a new phase. We closed face-to-face meetings with managers in companies by offering both a detailed evaluation about the current situation of their experts, and a theoretical evaluation of their situation free of charge. Obviously, we had to be very careful with those meetings not to be seen as conceited. Companies know very well their businesses, thus, we only offered a constructive opinion according to our experiment's results.

## Results

97 professionals were registered for the experiment. Some of them were people who had previously worked with us in projects (they could be considered our clients in technology transfer projects). There were also new people that collaborated for the first time with the University.

As previously mentioned, the experiment was carried out on November 4th and 5th. It was planned as a half-day (4.5 hours, see Table 2) activity, in which participants would work at the School of Computer Science at the University of Seville. At the beginning of the session, we asked them to fill in a registration form that included personal data as well as academic and professional information similar to that showed in Table 1. The objective was to guarantee that nobody would make an error in his/her inscription.

As it has been commented, information, both inscriptions and interviews at the end of the experiment were recorded by means of online forms, designed with a tool named OPINA. This is a free tool that we frequently use because it is very versatile and lets us explore and export results in Excel.

The first part of the experiment, the manual definition of tests was manually written in paper. We have this information classified and it comprises the starting and finishing time for each participant (it is essential for answering the first RQ).

Moreover the second part of the experiment was the generation of tests in an automated way. For this purpose, participants used NDT-Suite as previously mentioned. NDT-Suite can be briefly described as a specific Unified Modeling Language (UML) (OMG 2020) profile which enables us to apply NDT in real environments. NDT-Suite also implements all necessary transformations among models. All this framework is integrated into Enterprise Architect (2020) tool. Using this environment, each participant was able to (1) generate tests associated with his/her use cases and (2) generate different office documents with the structure of each test and result. This process was performed in an automatic and systematic way, but we keep results of each participant's performance in order to control this part of the experiment. We also recorded the time spent by each participant (i.e., starting and finishing marks).

Thanks to comply with the best practices we established to get a high number of participants in software industry experiments, ours was a success. Nevertheless, our experiment not only provided good results; during the execution we had also some problems and negative aspects to solve and that is why we would like to highlight them. The first one was related to the number of PCs. We reserved a classroom in the School of Computer Languages and Systems and we had to face up a very simple problem. In the form designed to book classes, the School recommended a maximal number of people to stay in the class at the same time. Thus, we considered that this number involved the total number of computers in the classroom as well. In consequence, the class was designed with one computer for two people and we had to divide participants in two different groups. It was important in the session of Wednesday morning since it brought together the largest number of participant. It was really a misfortune that could be avoided as we performed a test on Monday and we did not realize it. Moreover, we had to change the execution at that moment, and we even used our personal laptops to decrease the effect it would provoke on the time table of the experiment. As a result, we suffered a delay of 30 minutes approximately.

Although we had 97 people registered, only 76 subjects participated in the experiment. The remaining subjects were re-assigned to groups in order to maintain the design balanced and, in turn, to mitigate this problem.

Another drawback was a conceptual decision made in the definition of the experiment. We considered that it could be interesting to execute the experiment with people of different level of knowledge: juniors, seniors, managers, and soon. The results obtained with this decision were really good butt hey entailed a considerable problem in the execution of the experiment, because along the Early Testing course we had a very heterogeneous audience. We reduced the effect of this problem involving many team members (more than 15 people participated in each session), who assisted and helped some of the youngest people[5].

## CONCLUSION AND FUTURE WORKS

Industry-academia collaboration has been an important topic since the early years of software engineering. There is a critical need to both industry and academia to collaborate. In the specific case of software experiments, it is an important challenge to get the participation of subjects coming from the industry as well as to involve companies.

By following a software experiment process, this paper has presented a set of guidelines (best practices) for involving a high number of companies and experimental subjects from industry when running experiments with practitioners. A total of 23 best practices have been formulated and organized according to the life cycle experimental phases: goal definition, design of the experiment, execution of the experiment and analysis of the results. An ideal support infrastructure to run the experiment has been successfully presented as well.

In order to validate our proposal, these guidelines have been used in a real experiment, executed at the University of Seville in collaboration with the Technical University of Madrid and Aragón Institute of Technology, in which we have engaged a total of 97 practitioners registered (76 of them finally participating in the experiment), from 32 different software companies to evaluate our research results in early testing.

We detected some limitations because in this experiment we involved several companies at the same time, our approach has to be tested in other environments (for instance, with only a validation in a concrete company).

As a future work, we would like to improve and redefine these best practices for experiments to be able to incorporate other type of empirical strategies, such as surveys and case studies, and make them become a practical guideline to follow in industry-academia collaborations. Moreover, we would like to publish and get information about the experiment with the obvious aim of improving our tools. Besides, after the success of this first experience, we are looking forward repeating it with other areas of NDT like quality, project management or requirements management.

It is also worth pointing out that many companies (e.g. companies from Zaragoza) that took part in the experiment, have asked to repeat it with their staff at their headquarters. Finally, this paper will conclude with a global consideration: this study has confirmed that communication and collaboration between academia and companies is possible. Nevertheless, communication has to be in two directions.

If we aim to involve companies in our experiments, we will have to consider their situation and availability make it as easy as possible, without being detrimental to our scientific method.

## ACKNOWLEDGMENT

This research has been supported by the Pololas project (TIN2016-76956-C3-2-R) of the Spanish Ministry of Economy and Competitiveness and Research grant PGC2018-097265-B-I00 of Spanish Ministry of Science, Innovation and Universities.

# REFERENCES

Davies, P. (1992). *The mind of God: the scientific basis for a rational world*. Simon & Schuster.

Dieste, Juristo, & Danilo. (2013). Software industry experiments: a systematic literature review. *Proceedings of the 1ˢᵗ International Workshop on Conducting Empirical Studies in Industry*, 2–8.

Escalona, M. J., Gutierrez, J. J., Villadiego, D., & Le'on, A. (2007). *Practical Experiences in Web Engineering*. Springer, US.

Escalona & Aragon. (2008). A model-driven approach for web requirements. *IEEE Trans. Software Eng.*, *34*(3), 377–390.

Garc'ıa-Garc'ıa. Alba, Garc'ıa-Borgon~'on, & Escalona. (2012). Ndt-suite: A model-based suite for the application of NDT. *Web Engineering-12th International Conference, ICWE2012 Proceedings*, 469–472.

Garousi, V., Petersen, K., & Ozkan, B. (2016). Challenges and best practices in industry-academia collaborations in software engineering: A systematic literature review. *Information and Software Technology*, *79*, 106–127. doi:10.1016/j.infsof.2016.07.006

Gibbs, W. W. (1994). Software's chronic crisis. *Scientific American*, *271*(3), 72–81. doi:10.1038cientif icamerican0994-86 PMID:8091191

Group, O. M. (n.d.). *Unified Model Language V2.5*. http://www.omg.org/ spec/UML/2.5/

Guti'errez, J. J., Escalona, M. J., & Mejías, M. (2015). A model-driven approach for functional test case generation. *Journal of Systems and Software*, *109*, 214–228. doi:10.1016/j.jss.2015.08.001

H¨ofer & Tichy. (2006). Status of empirical research in software engineering. *Empirical Software Engineering Issues. Critical Assessment and Future Directions, International Workshop*.

IN2. (n.d.). *Opina*. http://opinahq.com

Jedlitschka, A., Juristo, N., & Rombach, D. (2014). andH.D.Rombach.Reportingexperiments to satisfy professionals' information needs. *Empirical Software Engineering*, *19*(6), 1921–1955. doi:10.100710664-013-9268-6

Juristo & Moreno. (2001). Basics of software engineering experimentation. Kluwer.

Juristo & Gomez. (2010). *Replication of software engineering experiments. In Empirical Software Engineering and Verification-International Summer Schools, LASER 2008-2010*. Revised Tutorial Lectures.

Juristo, N. (2016). Experiences conducting experiments in industry: the ESEIL fidipro project. Proceedings of the 4th International Workshop on Conducting Empirical Studies in Industry, 1–3.

Pfleeger, S. L. (1999). Albert Einstein and empirical software engineering. *IEEE Computer*, *32*(10), 32–37. doi:10.1109/2.796106

Runeson & Host. (2009). Guidelines for conducting and reporting case study research in software engineering. *Empirical Software Engineering*, *14*(2), 131–164.

Salman, I., & Tosun, A. (2015). Are students representativesof professionals in software engineering experiments? *37th IEEE/ACM International Conference on Software Engineering, ICSE 2015*, 666–676.

Shaw, M. (1990). Prospects for an engineering discipline of software. *IEEE Software*, *7*(6), 15–24. doi:10.1109/52.60586

Sjøberg, D. I. K., Hannay, J. E., Hansen, O., Kampenes, V. B., Karahasanovic, A., & Liborg, N. (2005). A survey of controlled experiments in software engineering. *IEEE Trans. Software Eng.*, *31*(9), 733–753.

SparxSystems. (n.d.). *Enterprise Architect*. http://www.sparxsystems.com

Top¸cu, O., Durak, U., & Oguztu¨zu¨n, H. (2016). Distributed Simulation - A Model Driven Engineering Approach. In Simulation Foundations, Methods and Applications. Springer.

Vegas, Dieste, & Juristo. (2015). Difficulties in running experiments in the software industry: Experiences from the trenches. *3rd IEEE/ACM International Workshop on Conducting Empirical Studies in Industry*, 3–9.

Wohlin, C., Runeson, P., Ho¨st, M., & Ohlsson, M. C. (2012). Experimentation in Software Engineering. Springer.

## ENDNOTES

[1]  Questionnaire is available in Spanish in http://iwt2.org/opina/c/290. It was developed using Opina.

[2]  This table represents an afternoon section. In the web of the experimenthttp://iwt2.org/experimentacion-en-testing-temprano/ more information is available.

[3]  It is available in the website of the experiment http://iwt2.org/experimentacion-en-testing-temprano.

[4]  This table only presents speci_c calls and mails for the experiment. The experiment was also referred in other meetings or environments, but they are not present here.

[5]  It is very important to stick out that this help did not consist in carrying out the experiment, but only in solving concepts related to metamodels, transformations or even functional test definition. Our team did not influence the expert's execution of the experiment.

# Chapter 6
# Integration of Agile Methodologies and Model-Driven Development:
## Case Study-Based Comparison

**Imane Essebaa**

*Computer Science Laboratory of Mohammedia, Hassan 2 University of Casablanca, Morocco*

**Salima Chantit**

*Hassan 2 University of Casablanca, Morocco*

**Mohammed Ramdani**

*Computer Science Laboratory of Mohammedia, Hassan 2 University of Casablanca, Morocco*

## ABSTRACT

*Agile methods (AM) and model-driven engineering (MDE) are two principal domains of software development. AM proposes best practices in information programming, while MDE focuses on technical part of software development. Both of these domains are in the way of improvement and evolution in order to facilitate the development of IT projects. However, these areas evolve separately despite the great number of researches that focus on improving development project' techniques. Thus, in this chapter the authors present an overview of their approach "Scrum with MoDAr-WA", that aims to improve Scrum Agile methodology by combining two variants of MDE: model-driven architecture and mode-based testing with the V development lifecycle used to deal with sprint development in Scrum methodology. Then they present a comparison study between the standard Scrum process and Scrum with MoDAr-WA approach in order to highlight the authors' contribution to improve agile methodologies.*

DOI: 10.4018/978-1-7998-3661-2.ch006

# INTRODUCTION

Software Development evolves in a fast manner and becomes more and more important in different application areas. Thus, dealing with this issue becomes an important area of researches where two main areas were proposed: Agile Methodologies and MDE.

Agile methodologies focus on best practices of programming and their integration in the development process. It is an approach that defines a disciplined management of software development projects: Agility recommends iterative and incremental method to develop software systems. The other domain is the Model Driven Engineering (MDE) which is an Object Management Group (OMG) proposition to deal with this issue. MDE is a paradigm based on the use of models throughout the life cycle of an application as it enhances every step of software development from design until code and testing, by defining different variants describe the general perspective of the chapter. End by specifically stating the objectives of the chapter. such as Model-Based Testing that aims to generate automatically test cases from Modelsa nd Model Driven Architecture (MDA) where models are the core of this architecture. In fact, MDA defines three levels of abstraction beginning with the Computation Independent Model (CIM), which is transformed into Platform Independent Model (PIM) that is in its turn transformed into Platform Specific Model (PSM) from which the source code is generated. The two first transformations are of Model-to-Model type while the last one is Model-to-Text transformation.

The researchers note that both, MDE and Agile Methodologies (AM) aim to easily manage frequent requirements changes; AM focus on a methodological aspect that defines the process to develop and test the system while MDE is more concerned by an architectural aspect that aims to automate model's transformations in order to ensure traceability and completeness between different levels.

Several works have been made on these two domains that allow them to evolve but unfortunately separately. Indeed, few works have focused on how to combine MDE and Agility, which constitutes the main idea of this paper where the authors aim to overview their proposed approach that combines Scrum with MoDAr-WA (Model Driven Architecture for Web Application; an approach that aims to automatically generate source code for web applications). Then, in order to make a comparison study, they applied Standard Scrum process and Scrum with MoDAr-WA approach on a "Rental Car Agency" system, and according to some criteria the comparison was made.

This paper is organized as follows; the second section summarizes the concepts elaborated in this paper. In the third section, some previous works made in this context were presented and discussed. The following section (Section 4) overviews the proposed approach that will compared to a strands scrum development process. Finally, the paper is finished by a conclusion and some of the authors' future works.

# BACKGROUND

## Agile Methodologies

The "Agile Manifesto" published in in February 2001 (Beck et al., 2015) based on analysis of previous experiences that allow to propose good practices to developers. The agile principle introduced by the agile manifesto is related to time invested in analysis and design (Dyba & Dingsoyr, 2009). Agility, a paradigm for a new vision of an organization, asserts itself as an alignment and coherence tool between internal forces and external challenges that give dynamism to an enterprise (Vickoff, 2001). Agile methodology is a loom to project management, classically used in software development. It helps teams respond to the changeability of building software through incremental, iterative work cadences, known as sprints. Agile methods are methodologies essentially dedicated to the management of IT projects. They are based on adaptive and iterative development cycles depending on the evolving needs of the client. There are several agile methods for the management of the IT project in its various phases of development, in this work the researchers focus on Scrum methodology

## Model Driven Development

### Model Driven Architecture

The MDA (Model Driven Architecture) is an initiative of the OMG (Object Management Group) released in 2000 (Soley, 2000). The basic idea of the MDA approach is theseparation of the functional system specifications and its implementation on a particular platform. The MDA approach lies in the context of the Model Driven Engineering which involve the use of model and metamodels in the different phases of development lifecycle.

MDA defines three viewpoints:

- CIM (Computation Independent Model): This level is used by Business Manager and Business Analysts that model the system requirements and describe the business activities to meet the business objectives;
- PIM (Platform Independent Model): This level describes the Business Logic of the system regardless of technical platform;
- PSM (Platform Specific Model): that adds to PIM the technological aspects of the target platform. It is called also the model of code.

The transition from one level to another is realized by applying transformations to source elements, to generate target elements. There are two types of model transformations; Model to Model transformation(M2M) that are used to move from CIM to PIM, and from PIM toPSM. The second type is Model to Text(M2T) which is used for the generation of source code from PSM (PSM to Code).

### Model Based Testing

Testing a system is an activity performed to identify software problems and failures in order to improve the quality of a program. The Model-Based Testing (MBT) is a variant of test techniques that are based on explicit behaviour models, describing the expected behaviours of the System Under Test (SUT), or the behaviour of its environment, built from functional requirements. The MBT is an evolutionary approach that aims to generate automatically from models, test cases to apply on the (Utting & Legeard, 2007).

## Paper Question

Provide broad definitions and discussions of the topic and incorporate views of others (literature review) into the discussion to support, refute, or demonstrate your position on the topic.

## RELATED WORKS

Being aware of the importance of Model Driven Engineering with its both variant MDA and MBT, agile methodologies and development lifecycles, many works were made on these domains in order to improve development process taking into account managing system changes. However, it is noted that these domains evolve separately and their combination was discussed in few works that are presented in the following of this section.

Kulkarni et al. (2011) discuss and argue in their paper why agile methodology can't be used with Model Driven Engineering, then they propose a modification to make on agile methodologies in order to combine them with MDE. Indeed, this paper describes a new Software Development process that combines Scrum and MDE. In this approach authors proposed the use of Meta Sprints that run in parallel to Sprints in order to validate models, they suggest two to three months as timescales for meta sprints where clients must provide feedback on models and prototyping, which is opposite to agility principles. As a matter of fact, that agility recommends that the feedback of clients must be in period less than what was proposed in this approach.

Alfraihi (2016) analyses the challenge of combining Agility and Model Driven Development, the paper describes an approach that aims to increase the adaptability of these domains by proposing a framework that facilitate Agility and MDD, this approach proposes recommendations, guidelines, and procedure to can use Agile MDD in practice. However, even if this approach proposes some practices to implement the Agile MDD but it does not take account of the architecture of the MDD, Model Driven Architecture, and how to benefit from the different abstraction levels to produce sustainable software systems.

In the paper, Wegener (2002) presents a study made on the context of the combination of agility and Model Driven Development, then to propose issues that show how this combination impacts organizations, process and architecture, this paper presents a comparison of different approaches proposed to use Agility and Model Driven Development.

Mahe et al. (2010) present their first reflections about the fusion of the MDA and Agility in order to have a combination with improved properties than the additions of the two approaches, they propose a canvas based on processes and agile practices in both modelling and meta-modelling level.

## PROPOSED APPROACH

In this section, the authors highlight their approach of the combination of MDD variants (MDA, MBT) and a Scrum Agile Methodology (previously detailed in medi2018).

The researchers' approach aims to improve the product development phases of the scrum methodology by using in each sprint the V-life cycle combined with the two important variants of MDE; Model Driven Architecture used to automate the left branch steps of V-life cycle until codegeneration, and model-based Testing that automate test generation in the right branch.

This approach is divided into three main parts; at first, they aim to describe the process of each sprint of scrum methodology using the V-life cycle. The second part aims to cover the V-life cycle left branch phases with the different MDA levels in order to automate the code generation from PSM level which is automatically generated from the PIM level which is in its turn the result of automatic transformations of the CIM level. The third part is to generate the different tests in V-life cycle from models that are describe in the different MDA levels.

The main goal behind the approach of integrating of MDA and MBT in V-life cycle process used in each sprint of scrum methodology is to deal with system' change requirements.

This approach is illustrated by the presented Figure 1.

*Figure 1. Overview of Scrum methodology with MoDAr-WA approach*

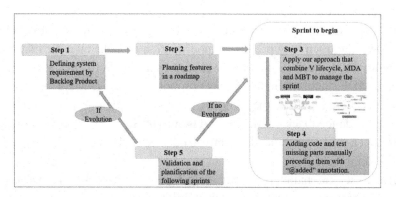

The authors' proposal is divided into 5 main steps:

- **Step 1:** Defining system requirement in the Backlog Product.
- **Step 2:** Planning the features in a RoadMap.
- **Step 3:** For the sprint to begin, it is proposed to use V-life cycle combined with MDA in left hand and MBT in right one as described in section 1.2.2 and 1.2.3.
- **Step 4:** Adding code missing parts manually in the generated code and also in tests preceding them with "@added" annotation.
- **Step 5:** Validation and Planning of following sprints. In this step two cases are identified:
  - If there is no system evolution: Restart from step 3 for the next sprint
  - If there is an evolution: Restart from step 1 and keep the old code except the parts preceded by "@added" annotation of features that still exist in the system (added code of deleted features is deleted automatically after the new execution)

Details of each step in the approach is presented in the paper (medi2018), and its application on a Rental Car Agency.

In the next section, the researchers focus on an agile standard software development process, in order to highlight their contribution on agile methodologies.

## CASE STUDY: RESULTS, COMPARISON AND DISCUSSION

In order to well illustrate the ideas detailed in the approach section, the authors present in this one their application on the Rental Car Agency system. The application has three users' profiles that have different privileges:

- Customer: A person who can view the cars available in the agency, rates and pro-motions and may subscribe. A client must register and authenticate in the system to search for available cars and book a car by indicating the reservation date and time;
- Manager: A Manager must also authenticate to view all cars, add, edit or remove cars. He can also view the bookings made by customers waiting for validation to decide to accept or refuse them;
- Administrator: Once authenticated into the system, the administrator has the privilege of modifying and deleting a customer account, as well as the management of managers' account (add, change, or delete).

As the aim of this paper is to make a comparison between results of two software development paradigms; Standard Software Development process used in Scrum Agile Method, and the "Scrum with MoDAr-WA" approach, which is a Model Driven Software Development process combined with Agility.

Results of the use of the standard software development process in scrum method, are detailed bellow, as a continuity of the results presented in the paper (Essebaa, 2018c), where the authors described an application of Scrum with MoDAr-WAon Rental Car Agency.

For that end, they start by defining the backlog product of the project, to plan the Roadmap, which describes different sprints of first project' requirements, before any evolution. In this example, and same as the Scrum with MoDAr-WA process, the users plan three sprints to develop the system, where each one takes 2 weeks.

The Figure 2 describes the Roadmap of the Rental Car Agency system.

*Figure 2. Scrum Roadmap of Rental Car Agency System*

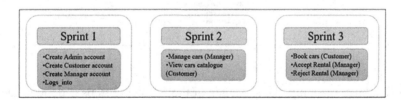

The next steps of this process will follow the standard software development paradigm; analysis, design, development and tests. These steps should be carried by different stakeholders. Indeed, the designer should analyse the system' requirements to propose a design solution. Then this design is used by the developer as a graphic description of code to develop. Finally, the final application code is tested by a tester. These steps are performed using conception, development and testing tools, which are allied by information manually and used separately.

Even though, these steps are organized using communication and project management tool, but this organization is manually made, hence the process take a long time to be done. Moreover, the involvement of several stakeholders in the development of the system, may induce a lack of traceability between all the steps, in addition to a misunderstanding of the system, or several points of views, which may result from the different system' analysis.

In this section some evolutions to the system (addition, deletion and modification of features) are made, in order to visualize the process of models' transformation and test generation in V lifecycle combined in scrum, the evolution will be as follow:

- Modifications: "View car catalogue" feature will be available for all users not only customers, this modification engender a new actor "User" that it will be a generalization of "Customer" actor, this modification requires changing the actor of "register" method too.
- Addition: In the new system, "Customer" will be able to validate its rental by "payment", The addition of a feature may engender some modifications to old ones, for example the verification of car availability will be made automatically by a system.
- Deletion: The addition of "payment" feature requires to delete "manage rental" feature of "Manager" that allowed him to accept or reject the rental, in the new system the customer can validate its rental from the system, before proceeding to payment option the system must be able to check if the chosen car is available for date specified by the customer.

After analysing the system requirements' evolution, another features are dispatched on the next sprints as presented in Figure 3.

*Figure 3. Scrum Roadmap of Rental Car Agency system after requirements' changes*

After the new Roadmap planning, the sequence of the following steps is done in the same way presented earlier: analysis, design, development and tests.

Same to the previous sprint, the new developments and changes are performed manually, thus it slows down making of the final application. Furthermore, there is a risk of producing a lack of traceability then system documentation.

In order to perfect the comparison, which is the purpose of this paper, the authors defined several objective criteria to demonstrate the contribution of the approach to agile methodology:

Traceability: compare if the used methods ensure the traceability between source elements and target source code;

- Ease of Development: compare application code development time needed;
- Ease of making changes: in addition to time needed to add changes, they check which method is easy to add changes (add, modify or delete a requirement);
- Automatic system documentation: compare which method allows to have an automatic documentation of the system, in all development steps (from requirement to source code);

- Test Automation: check the possibility to automatically generate test cases, for each step of development.

*Table 1. Overview o the comparison study' results*

| Method\Criteria | Traceability | Ease of Development | Ease of making requirements' Changes | Automatic System Documentation | Test Automation |
|---|---|---|---|---|---|
| Scrum with MoDAr-WA | Y | Y | Y | Y | P |
| Agile Standard Development Process | N | N | P | N | N |

The Table 1 describes the result of this comparison (Legend: Y: Yes, N: No, P: Partially).

As shown in the table, the authors' proposed approach Scrum with MoDAr-WAensures in a complete way the most of comparison criteria: traceability, ease of development and making changes and automatic system documentation. Indeed, as the Scrum with MoDAr-WAapproach is based on models that design all MDA levels (CIM, PIM and PSM), it allows having automatic system documentation, and due to the automatic transformation rules implemented between different MDA levels until code generation, the Scrum with MoDAr-WAapproach ensures traceability from the system requirements until system' source code. Moreover, the automatic transformations guarantee a fast development and making changes.

However, at this level the test automation is partially covered by MoDAr-WA approach, due to the non-implementation of transformation rules proposed to generate test cases

Concerning the agile standard development process presented in this paper, this method allows partially making changes, however the other criteria are not covered. Indeed, the development, tests and system documentation are made manually by different stakeholders, which influence the traceability between system development steps.

In fine, according to the previous analysis, it is possible to conclude that combining MDD practices with scrum agile methodology improves quality of development, and helps respecting agility values.

## CONCLUSION

The primary objectives of this book chapter are to present a contribution of Authors' approach "Scrum with MoDAr-WA", that aims to improve Scrum Agile methodology by combining two variants of MDE; Model Driven Architecture and Mode-Based testing with the V development lifecycle used to deal with sprint development in Scrum methodology. Then they present a comparison study between the standard Scrum process and Scrum with MoDAr-WA approach, in order to highlight their contribution to improve agile methodologies.

The Scrum with MoDAr-WA approach combines two important variants of Model Driven Engineering; MDA and MBT, with V lifecycle in order to ensure the quick and performing development process. In this approach the researchers automate left branch of V-life cycle by automating two types of transformation; M2M transformations applied between PIM and PSM levels, and M2T transformations to generate code from PSM level. Their approach consists on modelling PIM level by BCD andSSD that are automatically generated from CIM level, then using automated transformation rules DSD for MVC web application, is generated, the second part is an approach to automatically generate code from PSM. Concerning the right branch, they propose an approach that automate test generation form models.

Finally, the authors focused in this chapter on a comparison study between "Scrum with MoDAr-WA" approach and standard scrum process. Thus, the authors executed the both approached on "Rental Car Agency" system, and according to several criteria, the comparison was performed.

In their future works, the authors plan to:

- Apply their approach on other case studies to improve it;
- Extend their approach to cover all agile methodologies, and even propose a new methodology combining best practices of software development and model transformation.

# REFERENCES

Acceleo. (2006). https://www.eclipse.org/acceleo/

Alfraihi, H. (2016). Towards improving agility in model-driven development. *Joint Proceedings of the Doctoral Symposium and Projects Showcase Held as Part of STAF 2016 co-located with Software Technologies: Applications and Foundations (STAF 2016)*, 2-10.

Dyba, T., & Dingsoyr, T. (2009). *What do we know about agile software development?* doi:10.1109/MS.2009.145

Essebaa, I., & Chantit, S. (2018). 2018c Scrum and V Lifecycle Combined with Model-Based Testing and Model Driven Architecture to Deal with Evolutionary System Issues. In E. Abdelwahed, L. Bellatreche, M. Golfarelli, D. Méry, & C. Ordonez (Eds.), *Model and Data Engineering*. MEDI. doi:10.1007/978-3-030-00856-7_5

Essebaa, I., & Chantit, S. (2018a). A combination of v development life cycle and model-based testing to deal with software system evolution issues. *Proceedings of the 6th International Conference on Model-Driven Engineering and Software Development*, 528-535. 10.5220/0006657805280535

Essebaa, I., & Chantit, S. (2018b). Tool support to automate transformations from SBVR to UML use case diagram. *Proceedings of the 13th International Conference on Evaluation of Novel Approaches to Software Engineering*, 525-532. 10.5220/0006817705250532

Kulkarni, V., Barat, S., & Ramteerthkar, U. (2011). Early experience with agile methodology in a modeldriven approach. *Model Driven Engineering Languages and Systems, 14th International Conference,MODELS 2011 Proceedings*, 578-590.

Mahe, V., Combemale, B., & Cadavid, J. (2010). *Crossing model driven engineering and agility – preliminary thoughts on benefits and challenges*. Academic Press.

MOF. (2009). *Omg, meta object facility (mof)2.0query/view/transformation specification*. https://www.omg.org/spec/QVT/1.0/PDF

Papyrus. (2010). https://eclipse.org/papyrus/

Soley, R. (2000). *Model driven architecture (mda)*. http://www.omg.org/cgibin/doc?omg/00-11-05

Utting, M., & Legeard, B. (2007). *Practical Model-Based Testing: A Tools Approach*. Morgan Kaufmann-nPublishers Inc.

Vickoff, J. P. (2001). *Agile why not?* www.entreprise-agile.com

Wegener, H. (2002). Agility in model-driven software development? implications for organization, process, and architecture. *OOPSLA 2002 Workshop on Generative Techniques in the Context of Model Driven Architecture*.

# Chapter 7
# The Contribution of MDA in Software–Defined Network:
## A Survey

**Adra Hammoud**

https://orcid.org/0000-0003-1817-5899
*Ibn Tofail University, Morocco*

**Mohamed Lahmer**
*Moulay Ismail University, Morocco*

**Samir Mbarki**
*Ibn Tofail University, Morocco*

**Fatima Sifou**
*Mohamed V University, Morocco*

## ABSTRACT

*Software-defined networking is changing the way we design and manage networks. This prominent paradigm based on the separation of control and management plane is highly heterogeneous with different devices from various technologies and leads to an incredible growing of materials. As SDN expands in size of devices and complexity, it faces greater administrative and management challenges. The paradigm of MDA was introduced using NETCONF/YANG as a way to model in order to deal with these management challenges and soften the development of SDN applications. The researchers joined the MDA and its related concepts as model-driven engineering to SDN to implement a platform called model-driven networking increasing the level of abstraction on development. This chapter presents a comprehensive survey of the research relating to MDN paradigm. It starts by introducing the basic concepts of SDN. Next, it presents the concepts related to MDA, and the YANG which is a modeling language. Last, it highlights the studies introducing the MDN paradigm and its benefits in SDN applications.*

DOI: 10.4018/978-1-7998-3661-2.ch007

# INTRODUCTION

According to latest research from strategy analytics(« Number of connected devices reached 22 billion, where is the revenue? », 2018), which reflects an enormous augmentation in terms of using networks, as a result, the management of networks may become more challenging and complex. Software defined networking (SDN) is changing the way we design and manage networks. It enables the network programmability, via an external controller. The application development in this context is still complex due to the difficulties of integration and compatibility, as the new programmed network had to be incorporated in the existing environment. To cope with these challenges, researchers introduced an approach based on the model driven architecture (MDA) paradigm to raise the level of abstraction in development and ease the integration of SDN networks in the existing networks. This chapter book surveys latest developments in this active research area of SDN. The researchers first present basic concepts of SDN with the aforementioned two characteristic features, potential benefits, main components and faced challenges of SDN. Secondlythey dwell on SDN implementation (Openflow) and a related work about a comparison of the existent SDN controllers, which leads to their presentation of Mininet as the most powerful testing platform. Subsequently the model driven architecture (MDA) is introduced as a paradigm allowing the ease of development in SDN environment. Finally, they highlight some related work using MDA in SDN networks, and conclude this chapter book with some suggested open research challenges.

# BACKGROUND

The key idea of SDN is to decouple the control plane from the data plane and allow flexible and efficient management and operation of the network via software programs. Nevertheless, the application development in this context is still complex for such recent technology. Moreover, there is a strong need for methodologies and tools exploring the abstraction levels potentials supported by SDN. In the move to this architecture, model-driven templating plays a pivotal role in helping develop and deliver new services more quickly(Abel Tong, 2016). In this context, many researches have been proposed using the Model-Driven Architecture and its concepts to ease the application development within the new paradigm. A novel Software-Defined Networking (SDN) Controller architecture that is founded on Model-Driven Software Engineering (MDSE) concepts was presented (Jan Medved et al., 2014). It supports both the "classic" OpenFlow-based approach to SDN and emerging model-driven network management/programmability technologies, such as NETCONF/YANG. (Felipe A. Lopes et al.,2015)introduced a new approach based on the Model-Driven Engineering (MDE) paradigm, called Model Driven Networking (MDN). MDN relies on a Domain-Specific Modelling Language (DSML) to create SDN applications. This proposal increases the level of abstraction on development, therefore reduces the complexity to implement SDN applications. These applications should be built in a more customized fashion, and seamless integrated with existing SDN infrastructure and control. (JoãoEurípedes Pereira Júnioretal., 2019) proposed a Model-Driven Development (MDD) approach to SDN application development and integration so as to ensure high-quality network services. The suggested method is based on the use of ontology-driven conceptual modeling to understand the behavior of existing and to improve the network architecture's elements in order to optimally interface and integrate into models. These models are transformed into source code that respects the requirements of existing components and enforce the requirements of SDN applications been developed leading to higher continuity and lower time to market and maintenance cost of SDN services. These models also promote communication and learning improvements in developer community accelerating the development process and minimizing risks. (Clemm. A, et al., 2017) Defined an abstract (generic) YANG data model for network/service topologies and inventories. The data model serves as a base model which is augmented with technology-specific details in other, more specific topology and inventory data models. In case of facing a new network controller, developers are forced to re-implement their solution. Although Openflow is the interface between the controller and the network infrastructure, the interoperability between different controllers and network devices is crowded and the closed ecosystems are increasing.

## 1. BASIC CONCEPTS

### a) SDN Definition

SDN is a fascinating technology which is evolving over the time, which enables computer networks programming. As defined in(« Software-Defined Networking (SDN) Definition », 2019b), Software-Defined Networking (SDN) is an emerging architecture characterized by its dynamism, manageability, cost-effectiveness, and adaptability, making it ideal for the high-bandwidth, dynamic nature of today's applications. This architecture decouples the control and data plane. The control plane contains all the functions enabling the network control to become directly programmable and the data plane is the underlying infrastructure to be abstracted for applications and network service. The introduction of SDN offers an opportunity to improve network performance globally and aims to have a holistic view of the network.

### b) SDN Main Characteristics

In traditional networks, the control plane decides how to handle the traffic, it is coupled with data plane which is responsible for forwarding traffic according to decisions made by the control plane. This coupling causes various network management tasks (debugging configuration problems, controlling routing behavior...). To overcome these challenges, SDN occurs. It has two significant characteristics. On one hand SDN separates the *control plane* from the *data plane*. On the other hand, an SDN strengthen the control plane (various dataplane elements will be controlled by a unique software program). The SDN control plane controls the network's data-plane elements (routers, switches, and other middle boxes) directly via a well-defined Application Programming Interface (API).

### c) Traditional Architecture vs. SDN Architecture

The architecture is the convergence point which made the distinction between the traditional network model and the SDN one. In the traditional model, the control and data plane are coupled as shown in the figure 1, consequently, every vendor configure his protocol, hardware and material, which may introduce errors and misconfigurations. In case of birth of a new technology, the vendor changes all the devices to be adapted with the new technology. This shift is very expensive in terms of price and time, and may cause a lot of bugs. Furthermore, traditional networks are rigid and complex to manage and control. As a result of the high cost and the potential to integrate new technologies in networks, a number of standardization efforts around SDN are ongoing.

*Figure 1. Traditional architecture of networks*

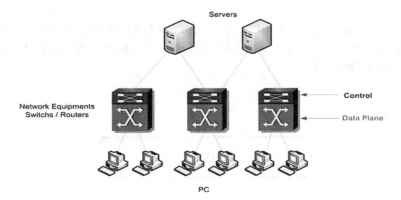

In the SDN model, the control and data plane are decoupled. Control logic is moved to an external machine called SDN controller. The network is programmable through software

applications running on top of the SDN controller that interacts with the underlying data plane devices. This is a fundamental characteristic of SDN, considered as its main value proposition. The architecture of the SDN model is detailed in the figure 2. SDN lets network managers configure, manage, secure, and optimize network resources very quickly via dynamic, automated SDN programs, which they can write themselves because the programs do not depend on proprietary software (Xia, Wen, Foh, Niyato, &Xie, 2015, p. 1–3).

*Figure 2. SDN architecture*

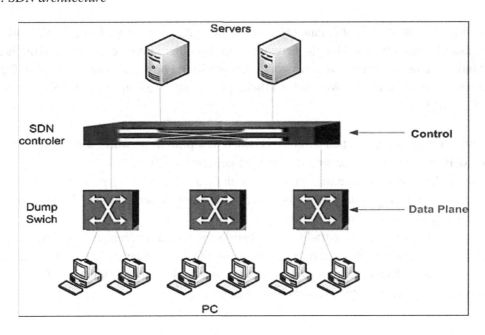

## d) SDN's Main Components

In addition to three functionality layers (data plane, control layer and application layer), there are two gateway layers, the southbound interface and the northbound interface respectively, connecting them one by one as shown in figure 3.

*Figure 3. SDN components*

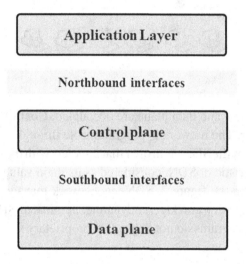

## e) Benefits of SDN

The decoupling of control and data plane offers many benefits to Software Defined Network.It is the key to the desired flexibility, breaking the network control problem into pieces, and making it easier to create and introduce new abstractions in networking, simplifying network management and facilitating network evolution and innovation. We dwell on these aforementioned benefits of SDN (Xia, Wen, Foh, Niyato, &Xie, 2015, p. 1–3):

1.  Improving Configuration: when a device is added to a present network, some configurations are required, hence, errors may occur and affect the network function.
2.  Improving Performance: Current approaches often focus on enhancing performance of a subset of networks or the quality of user experience for some network services. The introduction of SDN offers an opportunity to improve network performance globally.
3.  Encouraging Innovation: in the traditional networks, new ideas coping with challenges are almost blocked. The innovation into existing networks is complicated, because of the increase of configurations in the slight change. However, SDN facilitate innovation and introduction of new paradigms by providing a programmable platform to implement.

*Table 1. SDN layers and their functionalities*

| Layer | Functionality |
|---|---|
| Data plane | Contains the network's elements responsible of dispatching the traffic and support the OpenFlow protocol shared with the controller |
| Control plane | It is the brain of the system, it provides a global visibility of the network and the infrastructure devices. It communicates and controls upper and lower layers with APIs through Interfaces. |
| Management plane | Automates applications via the network by means of open programmable interfaces. |
| Northbound API | Transfers the information to switches and routers of network and ensure the communication between network applications and the controller. |
| Southbound API | Defines the protocol associated with a series of programming interfaces for the communication between the data and the control planes, it communicates with the applications and deploy services. |

## f) SDN Limits or Challenges

The knowledge on SDN attacks is very limited and deployments are still looking for solutions to secure SDN infrastructure. Some security challenges can appear in SDN networks such as network centralized control and programmability feature (Asturias, 2017, p. 1–3):

Network centralized control: SDN networks rely on the central SDN controller. This backing on the machine controller bring new security challenges. A single mistake could cause a lot of damage. By compromising the SDN controller, an attacker could control the whole network. In that respect, controller is the single point of failure and source of attack representing an aim for attackers(Azab& Fortes, 2017, p. 1–3).

Programmability (a double-edged sword): programmability is the main characteristic of SDN networks, it enables to increase automation and flexibility. However, when a new system is introduced, new vulnerabilities or faults are systematically introduced. SDN is exposed to more risks when it provides programmatic access to users. SDN may face some challenges in terms of integration and compatibility, as the new programmed network has to be incorporated in the existing environment.The application development in this context is still complex for such recent technology.

## g) SDN Models

According to (Durand, 2015), we can quote different model of SDN:

1. Individual programmability of every device. In this model an application interacts directly with every device via APIs. The application is centralized or can be located directly on the network device to realize specific tasks.
2. Programmability via a controller: in this model, an application gives an abstract and global command to a controller, which translate this query to a sequence of instruction to the network devices involved. The controller hides the network complexity. We can identify many cases according to the sort of exchanged instruction between the controller and devices.
3. Creation of a virtual network overhead the physical one: in this model, applications create their own network « overlay », we talk about the network function virtualization, when routers, switches and firewalls are virtualized elements in servers.

*Figure 4. SDN models*

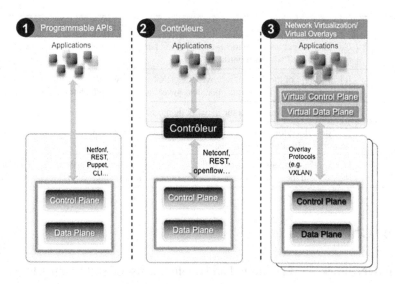

## 2. SDN IMPLEMENTATION

## a) Openflow Protocol

In 2007, Martin Casado created a company called Nicira, and was concurrently preparing his thesison OpenFlow protocol, and he used this protocol to create the first Open vSwitch. In April 2008, the first paper about OpenFlow protocol was published, and it was on march 2011, when the Open Networking Foundation was formed. Historically, the term SDN did not come into use until a year after OpenFlow made its appearance in 2008, which is a protocol serving as an intermediary between the machine controller and devices.

*Figure 5. SDN history*

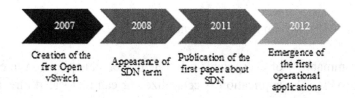

The separation of the control plane and the data plane can be achieved through an API located between the switches and the SDN controller. The controller practice direct control over the state in the data plane elements via this well-defined application programming interface (API). Various protocols ensuring the communication between SDN controller and the switches occur such as Opflex(« OpFlex:Opflex Architecture », s. d., p. 1–3)OVSDB (A Linux Foundation Collaborative Project, 2016, p. 1–3) and OpenFlow. The most significant example of such an API is OpenFlow(McKeown et al., 2008, p. 1–3)

which is a protocol used to regulate the communication flow between the controller and the switch, it also could be used in switching devices and controllers interfacing. This protocol defines the particular messages and message formats exchanged between controller (control plane), and device (data plane) and specifies how the device should react in various situations, and how it should respond to commands from the controller. This famous protocol provides convenient flow table manipulation services for a controller to insert, delete, modify, and lookup the flow table entries through a secure TCP channel remotely (Alshnta, Abdollah, & Al-Haiqi, 2018, p. 1–3). (Samociuk, 2015, p. 1–3), describes three possibilities of creating the secure channel for communication between switches and controllers using OpenFlow, and examine how to secure the OpenFlow architecture with an authentication mechanism that reduces the possibility of spoofing a device. An OpenFlow switch has one or more tables of packet-handling rules (flow tables). Each rule matches a subset of traffic and performs certain actions (dropping, forwarding, or flooding) on the traffic. An OpenFlow switch can behave like a router, switch, firewall ..., depending on the rules installed by a controller application (Feamster, Rexford, &Zegura, 2014, p. 1–3). The design of controller platforms followed the creation of the OpenFlow API, and enabled the creation of many new control applications.

*Figure 6. OpenFlow Architecture*

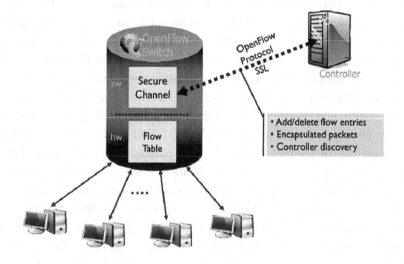

## b) SDN Controller

An SDN controller is the kernel of SDN network, it serves to link the applications to devices and support various protocols to configure the network devices. The SDN controller behaves like an Operating System (OS), as it is the key point of control in SDN network. By taking the control plane off of the network hardware and running it instead as software, the centralized controller facilitates automated network management and makes it easier to integrate and administer business applications (« What is SDN controller (software-defined networking controller)? - Definition from WhatIs.com », s. d., p. 1–3). Information about the network (the belonging of the devices to the network, their capabilities and collecting network statistics) are transmitted to switches/routers and application through the SDN controller.

This crucial part of Software Defined Network is referred as Network Operating System (NOS). There are a number of controllers which are implemented in different languages, which provides a flexibility to choose a controller depending on the application. Some of the well-known controllers are DISCO, Beacon, NOX, POX, OpenDaylight, Floodlight andRyu, everyone had its performance and features. (Zhu, Karim, Sharif, Du, &Guizani, sous presse) and (El Khalfi, El Qadi, &Bennis, 2017)conducted a comparative study between the existing SDN controllers, and inferred that the tools used vary significantly in features and capabilities, hence, it was infeasible to compare results of one tool with another.

## c) Mininet as SDN Testing Platform

SDN is not yet a widespread technology, hence, very few network simulators support the OpenFlow protocol. Furthermore, implementing network with large number of devices is very complex and expensive. To overcome these issues, researchers suggested virtual mode strategy as in Mininet(« Mininet Overview », 2018, p. 1–3), which is the most significant simulator for prototyping and emulating these kind of technologies. Mininet is a network emulator, or a network emulation orchestration system (Team, s. d., p. 1–3). It runs a set of hosts, switches, routers and links on a single Linux Kernel. According to (Keti & Askar, 2015)Mininet is able to provide to network programmers to create software defined network prototype in a simple way, including the capability to interact, adapt, share, and provides a smooth path to running it on hardware . This network emulator has a set of commands used to configure a network with a number of Openflow enabled switches and hosts attached to them. The external OpenFlow controllers could be used in conjunction with Mininet to totally emulate a real world situation where a network comprising of OpenFlow enabled switches is controlled by an OpenFlow controller. Mininet is characterized by various features, as flexibility, applicability, interactivity, scalability, besides being realistic and share-able. Several studies (Keti&Askar, 2015), (Juba, Huang, & Kawagoe, 2013), (Lantz, Heller, &McKeown, 2010b) and (Kaur, Singh, & Singh Ghumman, 2014)have been conducted to compare Mininet to other testing platforms as Emulab, VINI, GENI, FIRE, POX controller. These works highlighted many capabilities of Mininet emulator in SDN paradigm, as the number of default topologies (minimal, single, reserved, linear and tree) and the ability of connection with remote controllers. They concluded that Mininet offers ease of use, performance accuracy and scalability and choose it as one of the most powerful tools in emulating the SDN and virtual networks. In Mininet, when loads are high and CPU resources are multiplexed in time, the performance accuracy may reduce or disappear, hence, the availability of a host to send a packet is not guaranteed. It cannot operate different OS kernels at once, all hosts share the same filesystem. These are the major limitations of Mininet platform.

## 3. THE CONTRIBUTION OF MDA IN SDN

## a) Introduction to MDA

Over the last years, The integration of new technologies in the existing systems had been hard and complex. The Object Management Group (OMG) has worked hard and for a long time, to allow developers opportunity to integrate their new applications with old and even with future ones. An architecture which provides integration and interoperability is crucial. MDA is an architecture proposed by the OMG to standardize services and technologies and provide an independent platform model. As introduced

*Figure 7. A multiple level topology with N and two hosts per switch in Mininet*

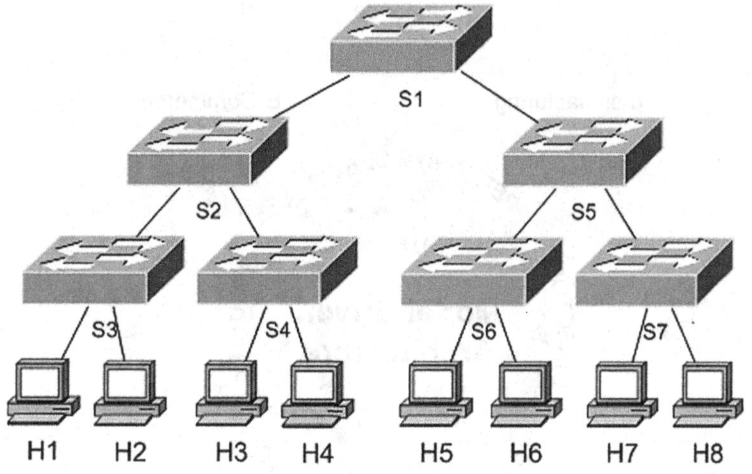

in (Nakamura, Tatsubori, Imamura, & Ono, 2005), MDA is as an approach to application design and implementation. Even at the early stages of development, abstract system models are built, and they are further improved to the next concrete level. As shown in the figure below, the MDA is supported by the Unified Modeling Language (UML), the Meta-Object Facility (MOF), XML Metadata Interchange (XMI), and the Common Warehouse Meta-model (CWM). MDA provides a raise in terms of level of abstraction using specific modeling languages and by separating business knowledge from implementation technology. It also applies automatic transformations and manage metadata centrally. MDA is used in various fields as finance, E-commerce, healthcare, telecom,...etc, and can be advantageous to gain adaptability, support for system evolution, integration, increases productivity, improves quality and maintainability, reduces cost and development time etc.

## b) Model-Driven Engineering (MDE)

Model driven Engineering (MDE) or Model Driven Software engineering (MDSE) is a promising approach used to reduce the complexity in software development. It focuses on creating and exploiting conceptual domain models. This software development methodology highlights the abstract representation of a specific application domain. It is used in SDN development to value its benefits, this paradigm combines as described by(C. Schmidt, 2007, p. 1–3):

- *Domain-specific modeling languages* whose type systems formalize the application structure, behavior, and needs within particular domains. A DSML compose a MDE technology and consists of meta-models to define the domain concepts and relationships.
- *Transformation engines and generators* that analyze certain aspects of models and then synthesize various types of artifacts, such as source code, simulation inputs, XML deployment descriptions, or alternative model representations.

MDE generate a framework which is based on relationships between various models, normalized mappings, patterns enabling model generation and code generation from models. This framework can

*Figure 8. Architecture of MDA*

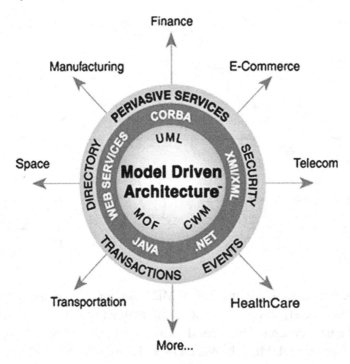

support a data modeling language regardless of the model'sdomain type. YANG has emerged as the most prominent data modeling language for the networking domain.

## c) YANG as a Data Modeling Language

YANG is a data modeling language that uses trees to model configuration and state data manipulated by the Network Configuration Protocol (NETCONF), NETCONF remote procedure calls, and NETCONF notifications. YANG « Yet Another Next Generation » is developed at the IETF « Internet Engineering

*Figure 9. Three levels architecture of MDE*

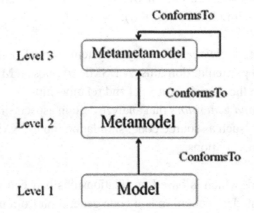

Task Force ». To overcome the blocking techniques used in the configuration management of devices and services, researchers used YANG and NETCONF as a solution to these challenges. Relying on (Medved,Varga, Tkacik, & Gray, 2014) implementation of YANG architecture in the OpenDaylight Project Hydrogen release, they proved that YANG is in addition an Interface Description Language (IDL) to describe SDN network and network device APIs. (Hazboun, 2015)Implemented a protocol called I2RS which is based on NETCONF, while its data models are based on YANG modeling language.This protocol focuses on routing operations in networks by offering operators standardized programmatic interfaces to the routing information stored in their devices. YANG and NETCONF are the prominent choices to manage network, ensure the interoperability of devices in SDN paradigm. The figure below describes the concept of NETCONF/YANG in case of devices having different types.

*Figure 10. Concept of NETCONFIG/YANG*

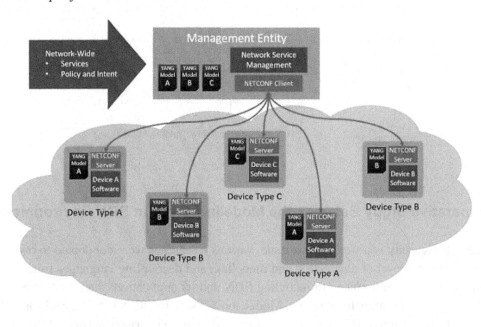

## d) Model Driven Networking

Model-Driven Networking (MDN) is a modeling framework to create and describe applications and environments in Software-Defined Networking (SDN). It is used to raise the abstraction level for developing SDN applications, and it is focused on identifying the benefits of a model-based approach for the SDN field (alencar, s. d., p. 1–3). MDN paradigm have been applied in several studies, (Lopes, Santos, Fidalgo, &Fernandes, 2015) presented the MDN approach based on a Domain-Specific Modelling Language (DSML) to create SDN applications. This study proved that MDN raises the level of abstraction on development, therefore, reduces the complexity to implement SDN applications and avoid conflicting policies. (Lopes, Lima, Santos, Fidalgo, & Fernandes, 2016) Showed how the MDN framework can be a practical solution to create applications from controllers and to allow verification of SDN applications. This proposed framework is composed of CASE tool and Domain-Specific Modeling Language

(DSML).The figure below as presented in (A. Lopes, Bauer, Stenio, &Fernandes, 2016), explains the MDN architecture and its main components. This architecture is based on DSML that help to overcome several issues in developing SDN applications, such as validation and dependency between languages and controllers.

*Figure 11. MDN Architecture*

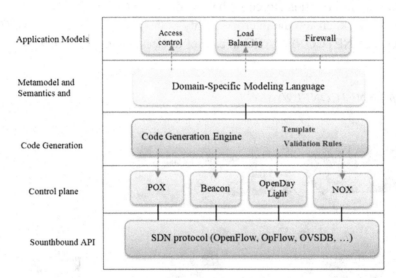

## e) A Comparative Study Between the Modeling Tools in SDN Environments

SDN switch heterogeneity is a well-known issue, various researches were conducted to overcome this issue by increasing the level of abstraction and modeling, and decoupling languages from the controllers. Various works were introduced to modeling SDN and its applications such as Minied it, Virtual Network Descriptor, Common Information Model for SDN (CIM-SDN), MDN and OpenDaylight. According to (Lopes, Santos, Fidalgo, &Fernandes, 2015), a comparison between Minied it, VND, CIM-SDN and MDN was introduced, based on various features. The comparison leads to nominate the Model Driven Networking as the efficient solution, so as it is the only one supporting Domain Specific Modelling Language (DSML) which raises the level of abstraction on development. The MDN paradigm is also applied to soften the issue of complexity to implement SDN applications and explicitly support infrastructure heterogeneity. However, the birth of Open Daylight has impacted, as it leverages Model Driven Software Engineering (MDSE) defined by the OMG. The Open Daylight architecture is based on Model-Driven Service Adaptation Layer (MD-SAL) which can overlay any specific modeling language. The MD-SAL allows easy creation of Model to Model translations and evolutions of the existing system. This authorization of abstraction and modeling position The OpenDaylight platform as a potential Next Generation management system (Medved, Varga, Tkacik, & Gray, 2014, p. 1–3). This platform contains approximately 110 YANG models already present in the project.

## CONCLUSION

With the increase of connected devices, the traditional networks are no more easy to manage. Many reasons forced the birth of Software Defined Network as a shift in the development and evolution of networks. One of the reasons is that the SDN allows the separation of control and data plane which are vertically integrated in the traditional network. Another critical reason, devices are strictly dependent to versions and products. The main idea in SDN is the programmability of forwarding devices via southbound interfaces. However, current issues in developing SDN applications could occur such as: validation of applications and dependency between programming languages and controllers. To address these issues, MDN was proposed as a solution given that is based on DSML. This chapter book highlight the prominent function of modeling software development and its advantages in SDN environment through the various studies presented in this context. The most significant benefit is the raise of level of abstraction which reduces the complexity and ease the development.

There are several ways to enhance and extend our work. First, we highlight the significant function of Model Driven Service Abstraction Layer (MD-SAL) in the architecture which provides OpenDaylight the ability to support any protocol talking to the network elements as well as any network application. MD-SAL provides a framework for Authentication, Authorization and Accounting (AAA), and enables automatic identification and hardening of network devices and controllers. Then, we explain the role of MDA in reducing the issues of access control in SDN environments, relying on OpenDaylight as a flexible and powerful controller.

## REFERENCES

A Linux Foundation Collaborative Project. (2016). *Ovsdb : description.* Consulté à l'adresse http://docs. openvswitch.org/en/latest/ref/ovsdb.7/

Agborubere, B., & Sanchez-Velazquez, E. (2017).OpenFlow Communications and TLS Security in Software-Defined Networks. *2017 IEEE International Conference on Internet of Things (iThings) and IEEE Green Computing and Communications (GreenCom) and IEEE Cyber, Physical and Social Computing (CPSCom) and IEEE Smart Data (SmartData).* 10.1109/iThings-GreenCom-CPSCom-SmartData.2017.88

Alencar, F. (n.d.). *Felipealencar/mdn.* Consulté le 10 décembre 2019, à l'adresse https://github.com/ felipealencar/mdn

Alshnta, A. M., Abdollah, M. F., & Al-Haiqi, A. (2018). SDN in the home: A survey of home network solutions using Software Defined Networking. *Cogent Engineering, 5*(1). Advance online publication. doi:10.1080/23311916.2018.1469949

Asturias, D. (2017, mars 21). *9 Types of Software Defined Network attacks and how to protect from them.* Consulté à l'adresse https://www.routerfreak.com/9-types-software-defined-network-attacks-protect/

Azab, M., & Fortes, J. A. B. (2017). Towards proactive SDN-controller attack and failure resilience. *2017 International Conference on Computing, Networking and Communications (ICNC).*10.1109/ ICCNC.2017.7876169

Bjorklund, M. (2010). *YANG - A Data Modeling Language for the Network Configuration Protocol (NETCONF)*. IETF., doi:10.17487/rfc6020

CTAN. (n.d.). Consulté le 11 décembre 2019, à l'adresse http://www.ctan.org/tex-archive/macros/latex/contrib./supported/IEEEtran/

Durand, J. (2015). *SDN pour les nuls*. Consulté à l'adresse https://hepia.infolibre.ch/Virtualisation-Reseaux-2018-2019/Le_SDN_pour_Les_Nuls_Jerome_Durand_JRES_2015.pdf

El Khalfi, C., El Qadi, A., & Bennis, H. (2017). A Comparative Study of Software Defined Networks Controllers. *Proceedings of the 2nd International Conference on Computing and Wireless Communication Systems - ICCWCS'17*.10.1145/3167486.3167509

Feamster, N., Rexford, J., & Zegura, E. (2014). The road to SDN: An Intellectual History of Programmable Networks. *Computer Communication Review*, *44*(2), 87–98. doi:10.1145/2602204.2602219

Floodlight OpenFlow Controller. (n.d.). Consulté le 10 décembre 2019, à l'adresse http://www.project-floodlight.org/floodlight/

Gude, N., Koponen, T., Pettit, J., Pfaff, B., Casado, M., McKeown, N., & Shenker, S. (2008). NOX: Towards an Operating System for Networks. *Computer Communication Review*, *38*(3), 105–110. doi:10.1145/1384609.1384625

Hazboun, E. (2015). The Interface to the Routing System. *Innovative Internet Technologies and Mobile Communications*, *WS2015*, 25–31. doi:10.2313/NET-2016-07-1

Home. (n.d.). Consulté le 10 décembre 2019, à l'adresse https://www.opendaylight.org/

Juba, Y., Huang, H.-H., & Kawagoe, K. (2013). Dynamic Isolation of Network Devices Using OpenFlow for Keeping LAN Secure from Intra-LAN Attack. *Procedia Computer Science*, *22*, 810–819. doi:10.1016/j.procs.2013.09.163

Kaur, K., Singh, J., & Singh Ghumman, N. (2014).Mininet as Software Defined Networking Testing Platform. *International Conference on Communication, Computing & Systems (ICCCS–2014)*.

Keti, F., & Askar, S. (2015). Emulation of Software Defined Networks Using Mininet in Different Simulation Environments. *2015 6th International Conference on Intelligent Systems, Modelling and Simulation*.10.1109/isms.2015.46

Lantz, B., Heller, B., & McKeown, N. (2010a). A network in a laptop. *Proceedings of the Ninth ACM SIGCOMM Workshop on Hot Topics in Networks - Hotnets '10*.10.1145/1868447.1868466

Lantz, B., Heller, B., & McKeown, N. (2010b). A network in a laptop: Rapid Prototyping for Software-Defined Networks. *Proceedings of the Ninth ACM SIGCOMM Workshop on Hot Topics in Networks - Hotnets '10*.10.1145/1868447.1868466

Lopes, F., Bauer, R., Stenio, F., & Fernandes, L. (2016). Capability-Aware SDN Application Models: Dealing with Network Heterogeneity. *IEEE Computer*.

Lopes, F. A., Lima, L., Santos, M., Fidalgo, R., & Fernandes, S. (2016). High-level modeling and application validation for SDN. *NOMS 2016 - 2016 IEEE/IFIP Network Operations and Management Symposium*. 10.1109/noms.2016.7502813

Lopes, F. A., Santos, M., Fidalgo, R., & Fernandes, S. (2015). Model-driven networking: A novel approach for SDN applications development. *2015 IFIP/IEEE International Symposium on Integrated Network Management (IM)*. 10.1109/INM.2015.7140372

McKeown, N., Anderson, T., Balakrishnan, H., Parulkar, G., Peterson, L., Rexford, J., Shenker, S., & Turner, J. (2008). OpenFlow: Enabling Innovation in Campus Networks. *Computer Communication Review, 38*(2), 69–74. doi:10.1145/1355734.1355746

Medved, J., Varga, R., Tkacik, A., & Gray, K. (2014).OpenDaylight: Towards a Model-Driven SDN Controller architecture. *Proceeding of IEEE International Symposium on a World of Wireless, Mobile and Multimedia Networks 2014*. 10.1109/WoWMoM.2014.6918985

Mininet. (n.d.). *Mininet/mininet*. Consulté le 10 décembre 2019, à l'adresse https://github.com/mininet/mininet/wiki/Introduction-to-Mininet

MininetOverview. (2018). Consulté à l'adresse http://mininet.org/overview/

Nakamura, Y., Tatsubori, M., Imamura, T., & Ono, K. (2005). Model-driven security based on a Web services security architecture. *2005 IEEE International Conference on Services Computing (SCC'05) Vol-1*. 10.1109/SCC.2005.66

Number of connected devices reached 22 billion, where is the revenue? (2019, mai 23). [Post de blog]. Consulté à l'adresse https://www.helpnetsecurity.com/2019/05/23/connected-devices-growth/

Open Networking Foundation. (2015). *OpenFlow Switch Specification*. Consulté à l'adresse https://www.opennetworking.org/wp-content/uploads/2014/10/openflow-spec-v1.3.0.pdf

OpFlex. Opflex Architecture. (n.d.). Consulté à l'adresse https://wiki.opendaylight.org/view/OpFlex:Opflex_Architecture

Pereira Júnior, J. E., de Oliveira Silva, F., de Souza Pereira, J. H., & Rosa, P. F. (2019). Interfacer: A Model-Driven Development Method for SDN Applications. *Advanced Information Networking and Applications*, 643-654. doi:10.1007/978-3-030-15032-7_54

Pinheiro, B., Chaves, R., Cerqueira, E., & Abelem, A. (2013). *CIM-SDN: A Common Information Model extension for Software-Defined Networking. In 2013 IEEE Globecom Workshops*. GC Wkshps. doi:10.1109/glocomw.2013.6825093

Ryu S. D. N. Framework. (n.d.). Consulté le 10 décembre 2019, à l'adresse https://osrg.github.io/ryu/index.html

Samociuk, D. (2015). Secure Communication Between OpenFlow Switches and Controllers. *The Seventh International Conference on Advances in Future Internet*, 32-37.

Schmidt, D. (2007). Cover Feature Model-Driven Engineering. *IEEE Computer*, 25-31.

Software-Defined Networking (SDN) Definition. (2019a). Consulté à l'adresse https://www.opennetworking.org/sdn-definition/

Software-Defined Networking (SDN) Definition. (2019b, mars 18). Consulté le 29 janvier 2020, à l'adresse https://www.opennetworking.org/sdn-definition/

Team, M. (n.d.). *Mininet: An Instant Virtual Network on your Laptop (or other PC) - Mininet.* Consulté le 10 décembre 2019, à l'adresse http://mininet.org

Tong, A. (2016, décembre 13). *Why Model-Driven Templating Matters with SDN and NFV networks - Ciena.* Consulté le 29 janvier 2020, à l'adresse https://www.ciena.com/insights/articles/Why-Model-Driven-Templating-Matters-with-SDN-and-NFV-networks.html

Wang, S.-Y., Chou, C.-L., & Yang, C.-M. (2013). EstiNetopenflow network simulator and emulator. *IEEE Communications Magazine, 51*(9), 110–117. doi:10.1109/MCOM.2013.6588659

What is SDN controller (software-defined networking controller)? - Definition from WhatIs.com. (n.d.). Consulté le 10 décembre 2019, à l'adresse: https://searchnetworking.techtarget.com/definition/SDN-controller-software-defined-networking-controller

Xia, W., Wen, Y., Foh, C. H., Niyato, D., & Xie, H. (2015). A Survey on Software-Defined Networking. *IEEE Communications Surveys and Tutorials, 17*(1), 27–51. doi:10.1109/COMST.2014.2330903

Zhu, L., Karim, M., Sharif, K., Du, X., & Guizani, M. (sous presse). SDN Controllers: Benchmarking & PerformanceEvaluation. *IEEE JSAC.*

# Chapter 8
# Towards a Generation of Class Diagram From User Stories in Agile Methods

**Samia Nasiri**

https://orcid.org/0000-0002-4245-652X

*ENSAM, Moulay Ismail University of Meknes, Morocco*

**Yassine Rhazali**

https://orcid.org/0000-0003-1488-0216

*ISIC Research Team of ESTM, LMMI Laboratory of ENSAM, Moulay Ismail University of Meknes, Morocco*

**Mohammed Lahmer**

*ISIC Research Team of ESTM, LMMI Laboratory of ENSAM, Moulay Ismail University of Meknes, Morocco*

## ABSTRACT

*Model-driven architecture (MDA) is an alternative approach of software engineering that allows an automatic transformation from business process model to code model. In MDA there are two transformation kinds: transformation from computing independent model (CIM) to platform independent model (PIM) and transformation from PIM to platform specific model (PSM). In this chapter, the authors based on CIM to PIM transformation. This transformation is done by developing a platform that generates class diagram, presented in XMI file, from specifications that are presented in user stories, which are written in natural language (English). They used a natural language processing (NLP) tool named "Stanford Core NLP" for extracting of the object-oriented design elements. The approach was validated by focusing on two case studies: firstly, comparing the results with the results other researchers; and secondly, comparing the results with the results obtained manually. The benefits of the approach are aligned with agile methods goals.*

DOI: 10.4018/978-1-7998-3661-2.ch008

# INTRODUCTION

Requirements Engineering is a process of collecting and defining the services to be implemented in the future system[1]. In traditional project management, the specifications are not flexible. This obliges computer scientists to think from the beginning about project details. But in the agile approaches, the customer is regularly involved in the realization of the project. Indeed, he can add or modify requirements. Therefore, the product is delivered in several versions. In agile methods such as Scrum. The requirements are presented in many documents called User Stories. A user story often uses the following format type: As a <type of user>, I want <some goal > so that <some reason >[2].

Since the appearance of MDA, several research projects have been carried out to transform PIM to PSM and PSM to code, but very few researchers have examined the problems related to the transformation of CIM into PIM in an agile context. The MDA guide[3] states that the requirements of a system are gathered in a Computational Independent Model (CIM), which represents what the system is supposed to do. In our research, the User stories model represents the CIM level. This model describes the requirements of the system. PIM is another level of MDA which represents application design such as structural and dynamic view, independently of the technical platform. In this respect, our goal aims to automate transformation from CIM level user stories-based to the PIM level XMI-based. XMI file generated by our solution describes a UML class diagram.

In the Software Development Life Cycle, developers start with the requirements specification phase, and after, they need to carry out the design phase, which is an essential task. This phase is very critical because, if some functional needs are missing or contains ambiguity, then the software will be provided incomplete to the customers. Our proposed approach allows automating transformation from requirements specification to the design phase. Our objective aims to improve the extraction rules of the object-oriented design elements, and to generate a class diagram. Given that the user stories are written in natural language (English), so we need to use natural language processing techniques (NLP) to automate the transition from the user story to the design phase; these techniques can extract design elements that will be useful in the design phase, and manage the dependency between several user stories. The structure of this paper is as follows: This section introduces agile methods, MDA, and user stories. In section 2, we present the related work of our proposal, then, we compare the research work. However, we detail our proposal approach, and we present the main algorithm of the platform in Section 3. Then, we present a case study by discussing in section 4. In section 5, we discuss related work. At finally, conclusion and future work are presented in section 6.

# RELATED WORK

Several approaches have been developed in natural language processing (NLP) to generate the conceptual model from unrestricted text requirements. But few researchers have generated a class diagram or conceptual model based on user stories.

In (Mich, 1996), and (Mich & Garigliano, 2002), the researchers propose semi-automatic approaches by developing a tool called LOTIFA which allows extracting objects from user needs without distinguishing between classes, and attributes. However, in (Mich & Garigliano, 2002), the computer scientist intervenes to refine the results obtained.

In (Zhou & Zhou, 2004), the searchers suggest an approach to automate transformation from text requirements to the conceptual model, their goal was to predict the relationship between two concepts and to distinguish betwixt a class and an attribute; indeed, machine learning was used to automate the acquisition of linguistic patterns from training examples. In (Deeptimahanti & Babar, 2009) a tool called UMGAR was developed that generates three models: use cases, conceptual model, and collaboration diagram, indeed, syntactic rules were defined to extract artifacts by using Stanford parser NLP tool. In (Elbendak et al., 2011), the authors describe requirements model obtained by a semi-automatic transformation from requirements presented in textual use case diagram, though, this search based on ClassGen tool programmed in Java language, indeed, this tool identifies nouns, verbs, adjectives and adverbs in textual use case diagram to form class diagram. Many researchers in (Herchi & Abdessalem, 2013), (Thakur & Gupta, 2017), (Lucassen et al., 2017), and (Javed & Lin, 2018) are based on the (Elbendak et al., 2011) study, especially in the rules definition phase of design elements extraction from the use case model, however, a limitation of their method is oriented to simple sentence structures. In (Herchi & Abdessalem, 2013), a platform called DC-Builder was developed, that accepts as input a textual data represented by user needs expressing in natural language, then, the platform identifies the class names, their attributes, and their associations to classify them in a structured XML file. However, this initial file will be refined using the ontology domain, next, the tool input file is a general requirement document but not user stories, also, the class diagram generated didn't contain the multiplicity. In (Vidya Sagar & Abirami, 2014) there is no corpus of standard phrases that can be used in needs language, as reference terms represent an unrestricted requirement document. The researcher has developed 38 rules that may not be enough to cover all kinds of sentence structures. In (Thakur & Gupta, 2017), the authors suggest an approach that produces a class diagram from use case specifications, parts of speech tags (POS tags) and typed dependencies (TD), (POS tag) was used to reach their objective. Then, the author applied TD rules to extract design components such as classes, attributes, relationships, and operations, however, the developed tool analyses simple sentences. The rules used to extract attributes are not valid in most sentence structures, due to the failure of consecutive names processing. In (Lucassen et al., 2017), The authors developed a Visual Narrator tool in python, this tool generates a conceptual model output as a Prolog program or OWL ontology 2. However, they generated only the entities and relationships, but not the class diagram. Furthermore, they did not extract the attributes of each entity.

In (Elallaoui et al., 2018), the searchers used the TreeTagger analyzer (NLP tool) and developed a JAVA plugin to generate the use case diagram from user stories, the plugin does not handle sentences containing compound names. Besides; it does not support inclusion or exclusion relationships between use cases. The authors in (Javed & Lin, 2018) study, the conceptual model was generated from an unrestricted format such as general requirements, user stories, or use cases; indeed, new rules are defined for extracting attributes from requirements text. But attribute extraction rule is based on a set previously designed verb. The author uses a set of verbs that indicate attributes; this extract attribute approach is not effective. The researcher has not defined rules for generalization.

## PROPOSED APPROACH

In this section we are presenting our approach for extracting design elements, our implementation was done in python language using *Stanford Core NLP* tool[4]. Figure 1 shows the architecture of the proposed approach.

*Figure 1. The architecture of the proposed approach*

The CIM level represents a set of user stories, which are a basis for generating PIM. Through an automatic transformation, the XMI file is created to describe a class diagram at the PIM level. The overview and steps followed in our approach are presented in Figure 2.

*Figure 2. Steps of the proposed approach*

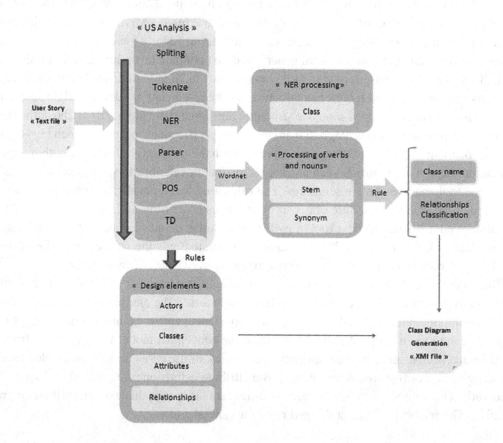

## User Stories Analysis

Like all-natural language processing tools, the processing of a text goes through several steps:

1.  **Splitting**: decomposition of the text into several sentences
2.  **Tokenizing:** Each sentence is split into words: in our case, each user story is split into words.
3.  **POS:** Part of Speech tagging or word-category disambiguation, is the process of marking up a word in a text as corresponding to a particular part of speech; the identification of words as nouns, verbs, adjectives, adverbs, etc[5]. Each word of the user story is tagged using *Stanford Core NLP*. Figure 3 shows an example of a user story with its part of speech.

*Figure 3. Example of a user story with its Part Of Speech*

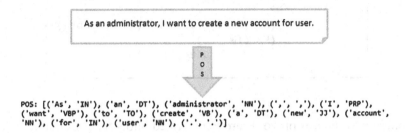

Table 1 represents the majority of part of speech tags and their significance[6].

*Table 1. POS and their significance*

| POS Tag | Significance |
|---|---|
| NNP<br>NNPS<br>NNS | noun plural<br>proper noun, singular<br>proper noun, plural |
| VB verb<br>VBD verb VBG verb VBN verb<br>VBP verb VBZ verb | base form<br>past tense<br>gerund/present participle<br>past participle<br>Sing. present, non-3d take<br>3rd person sing. present |
| WDT | determiner which |
| WP | pronoun who, what |
| PRP | possessive pronoun my, his, hers |
| RB | adverb |
| RBR | adverb, comparative |
| RBS | adverb, superlative |
| CC | coordinating conjunction |
| DT | determiner |
| IN | preposition/subordinating conjunction |
| JJ | adjective |
| JJR | adjective, comparative |
| JJS | adjective, superlative |

*Figure 4. Syntactic parser example*

```
(ROOT
  (S
    (PP (IN As)
      (NP (DT an) (NN administrator)))
    (, ,)
    (NP (PRP I))
    (VP (VBP want)
      (S
        (VP (TO to)
          (VP (VB create)
            (NP
              (NP (DT a) (JJ new) (NN account))
              (PP (IN for)
                (NP (NN user)))))))))
    (. .)))
```

4.  **Syntactic parser:** Sequences of words are transformed into structures that indicate how the sentence's units relate to each other. Figure 4 represents the syntactic parse of the user story previously shown.

5.  **Typed Dependencies:** *Stanford Core NLP* tool offers the typed dependencies that represent grammatical relationships between the words of a sentence to extract textual relations. It is denoted by a triple relation between two pairs of words[7].

The verb is considered as the root of the sentence. All other words are directly or indirectly related to the root via the dependency links.

*Figure 5. Typed Dependencies example*

```
('ROOT', 'ROOT-0', 'want')
('case', 'administrator', 'As')
('det', 'administrator', 'an')
('nmod', 'want', 'administrator')
('punct', 'want', ',')
('nsubj', 'want', 'I')
('mark', 'create', 'to')
('xcomp', 'want', 'create')
('det', 'account', 'a')
('amod', 'account', 'new')
('dobj', 'create', 'account')
('case', 'user', 'for')
('nmod', 'account', 'user')
('punct', 'want', '.')
```

The triple relationship that represents dependency is in the form (dep_name, governor, dependent). The Dep_name is a typed dependency that connects the governor and dependent.

The representation of dependency is available to extract textual information. Dependencies are delivered from user stories using python (figure 5). The typed dependencies are shown in Figure 5 and other dependencies are elaborated in Table 2, it corresponds to the user story presented previously.

*Table 2. User Stories and Typed Dependencies*

| Typed Dependencies | Example |
|---|---|
| **nsubj** | · I want to……<br>· *I* is a subject of a sentence<br>· (**nsubj**, want, **I**) |
| **dobj** | · (**dobj**, Enter, **Login**)<br>· A login is a direct object of the verb *Enter* |
| **conj** | Conjunction between login and password.<br>(**conj**, login, password) |
| **nmod** | As a visitor, I want …….<br>(**nmod**, want, visitor) |
| **compound** | (**compound**, address, email) |
| **amod** | · As a customer, I can change my address which is characterized by postal code, city, and number.<br>· (**amod,** postal, code)<br>· It is equivalent to compound name adjective-noun |
| **nmod:Poss** | · As a manager, I can add the film's title.<br>· **nmod: poss** is a dependency between film and title |

## Extraction Rules of Class Diagram Elements

To build a class diagram from several user stories, we need first to extract the components of the diagram such as (classes, Attributes, relationships, and operations).

Given that a user story represents one or more features performed by an actor, then, we must first extract actors. In this section, we are presenting the rules for extracting actors and other components of the class diagram. These rules are based on Part Of Speech (POS) to determine verbs, nouns, and adjectives. Moreover, typed dependencies (TD) were used to identify the subject, the object, the compound name (noun-noun) or (adjective-noun). POS and TD are provided by the NLP tool called *Stanford Core NLP*.

Figure 6 shows different states and transitions to extract the design elements.

### Actors Extraction

A user story often uses the following format type: As a <type of user>, I want <some goal > so that <some reason >; type of user represents the actor. The rules for extracting actors in a user story are presented in Table 3.

*Figure 6. The state diagram for extracting design elements*

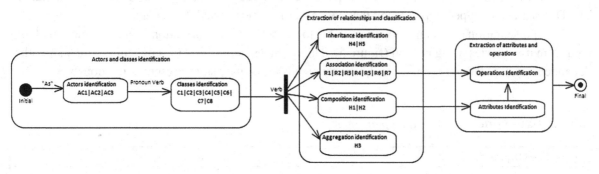

*Table 3. Rules of Actors extraction*

| Rules | Description |
|---|---|
| AC1 | The first name after *As* is an actor; if it is not a compound noun. |
| AC2 | If the first name after *As* is a proper name, followed by another name, then the second name is an actor. |
| AC3 | The compound noun after *As* is an actor. If the first noun in a compound noun is an adjective and the second noun is an actor, then there is an inheritance relationship between this latter and the compound noun which is an actor. |

Example 1: Consider the user story: *As a site administrator, I can create a new event that* contains a compound noun *site administrator* which is an actor according to the rule (AC3).

Example 2: Consider the user story: *As a manager, I want to create a new account.* Rule (AC1) indicates that *manager* is an actor.

Example 3: Consider the user story: *As John an instructor, I can create a description of my course.*

*Instructor* is as an actor according to the rule (AC1).

## Class Extraction

The majority of researchers are agreed about the class rule which states that *all nouns are classes*. This rule is wrong because if all names are classes, many useless classes will be detected. These are generally not relevant and can lead to confusion between the design elements in the conceptual model. So not all the nouns are classes, maybe attributes or actors.

While handling sentences in distinct structures, we have loosed these general rules following:

- Direct Objects in a user story are classes or attributes.
- Actor (subject) is a class if it has a relationship with another class.
- The noun in *nmod* dependency is a class or an attribute.
- In the compound noun, the first may be a class and the second attribute.

Subject: nmod(A,B)

- *The subject of the sentence is a potential entity;* (Elbendak et al., 2011), (Vidya Sagar & Abirami, 2014), (Thakur & Gupta, 2017), and (Javed & Lin, 2018).
- By analyzing different structures of user stories, we have found that the subject is not always a class; the subject can be a pronoun, in this case, we use Stanford coreference to replace the pronoun by its reference;e.g. if the pronoun is *I* or *We*, then, the subject is replaced by the name of the actor. We have changed the rule adopted by the authors: t*he actor is a class if there is a relationship with another class.*

## Verb

The verb in a sentence of the user story is a relationship or an operation of a class.

## Direct Object: obj(A,B)

- *The objects of the sentence are entities;* (Elbendak et al., 2011), (Vidya Sagar & Abirami, 2014), (Thakur & Gupta, 2017), and (Javed & Lin, 2018).
- The direct object is a class, there are two cases: simple class and class with a compound noun that one of a noun is a direct object. In this case, the two nouns constituting the compound noun are combined to form a compound class.

*Table 4. Rules of classes extraction*

| Rules | Description |
|---|---|
| **C1** | · The subject of a sentence is a class, provided that it is a noun and not a pronoun.<br>· *As an administrator, I can upload videos, so that visitors can watch those videos.*<br>A visitor is a subject so it's a class. |
| **C2** | · The direct object of the sentence is a class,<br>· *As a visitor, I want to be able to view the site.*<br>Site is a class because it's a direct object. |
| **C3** | The rule C2 is applied but the direct object is part of a compound noun:<br>If the direct object is part of a compound noun then an extraction process of the second noun is performed, therefore these nouns are combined to form a class.<br>· *As an administrator, I can manage a site page.*<br>Page is a direct object and it is part of the compound noun, then the Site page class is extracted.<br>· *As a visitor, I can change my email address.*<br>email address is a class. |
| **C4** | The name that precedes the possessive apostrophe is a class:<br>· *As a manager, I want to enter a product's price.*<br>*Product* is a class |
| **C5** | In this rule, (nmod, A, B) dependency is used if A and B are a noun.<br>If A is a class then B is a class. |
| **C6** | C5 is applied but a noun is not composed |
| **C7** | The name after (*of, for, to*) is a class:<br>· *As a visitor, I can input a publication date to any item.*<br>*item* is a class |
| **C8** | Conjunction between classes: If a noun is a class and it is in conjunction with another noun then the latter is a class:<br>· *As an administrator, I can consult the information about the product and orders.*<br>If *product* is a class then *orders* is a class. |

Table 4 describes the extraction rules of classes with examples.

## Relationships Extraction

Table 5 designates the extraction rules of classes with examples.

*Table 5. Rules of Relationships extraction*

| Rules | Description |
|---|---|
| R1 | The verb is an association between the direct object of the sentence and the actor: verb (dobj, Actor) |
| R2 | (nmod,A,B) dependency<br>The verb (A) is an association between B and the subject of the sentence:<br>A (B, subject) |
| R3 | (nmod,A,B) dependency<br>The verb (A) is an association between B and the actor: A (B, Actor) |
| R4 | Verb with preposition |
| R5 | Prepositions like *of, to, for,* and *about*, detect an association between the class which is before preposition and another that is after it. |
| R6 | In (nmod,A,B) dependency which A and B are nouns determine an association. |
| R7 | Possessive case: "s'", "my", "his"… determine an association; Correlation of pronouns with nouns to extract the associations using co-reference of Stanford core NLP. |
| H1 | The verb in *nmod* TD must belong to the list of composition relationships indicators that are: *contain, part of, consist, include, have, comprise…* |
| H2 | Compound noun: if both of nouns are classes then there is a composition relationship between them. |
| H3 | If the verb in nmod TD is among a list of verbs that indicate a relationship aggregation: (participate, ..) |
| H4 | If the subject and the direct object of the sentence are classes, and the verb that connects the two objects is *to be*, then the class (the object) is the parent class, this rule determines inheritance relationships |
| H5 | These indicators: *is a type of, is kind of*, determine inheritance relationship |

In these rules R5, R6, R7; if one of the classes linked by the association has no attributes and is not linked to another class, then it becomes an attribute of the other class.

## Attributes and Operations Extraction

The extraction of attributes is based principally in composition relationships. these rules are presented in table 5. Some classes are converted into attributes are that make up a class and they are not in composition relation with other classes. After attributes extraction, we can detect operations of classes by extracting each relationship in which attribute is present.

## Stemming and Lemmatization

Stemming is the process of reducing a word at its root that is based on the root of a word called a lemma. Root research is important in Natural Language Processing (NLP). These techniques are used to prepare text, words, and documents for further processing. To avoid extracting classes in the plural and the same singular, we used *Wordnet* to avoid redundancy in classes. Likewise, for verbs that represent relationships, *Wordnet* makes verbs form their basic form. This tool is used to found synonyms of verbs indicating composition relationships.

## Named Entity Recognizer (NER)

NER identifies sequences of words in a text that are the names of elements, such as a person, company names, duration, and time. In a class diagram, the notion of time is not integrated, that's why we used the *NER* process to refine the results obtained through the transformation rules. As a result, the extra classes have been removed. In the compound noun: adjective-noun, we used *NER* to ignore the following adjectives: weekly, daily ..., likewise in the noun such as past, and future. *NER* is also used to replace an Actor which is a proper noun by a *Person*, in particular, the actors who are classes.

## Example of Application Rules

In this section, we present a set of user stories and we indicate which rule is applied to detect actors and Oriented Object design (see rules applied in appendix). Our approach based on *Typed Dependencies*. The extraction of the attributes is done after determining the relationships between the classes. If the compound class has no attributes, then this one becomes an attribute.

## Extraction Algorithm

To extract the UML class diagram components, and also the actors, from a set of user stories, we followed the steps described in the algorithm presented below:

```
1: Procedure (Stories S, Actors A, Classes C, Rels R, Attributes ATT, Operations Op)
2:    for each s in S
3:       p=POS(s)
4:       t=word_tokenize(s)
5:       dep=dependency_parse(s)
6        A=extract_Actor(s)
7:       C=extract_class(s)
8:    for each  s in S
9:        R= Extract_all_relationships(s)
10: comp=   filtrate_composite_rel(R)
11: for each c in C
12:     if  c in comp then
13:     ATT=extract_attribute(comp)
14: for each r in R
15:      If  ATT in r
16:        Op=r
```

The algorithm takes as input a set of user stories S and empty sets of classes C, attributes ATT, relationships R, and operations Op. Then C, ATT, R, and Op are filled while applying extraction rules. The loop in line 2 consists to browse and parse each user story. At (line 3-4), the part of speech and tokenization are applied to classify each word in a user story. Afterward, the typed dependencies are detected. The first iteration extracts the actors and classes (lines 6-7). In the second iteration relationships are obtained (line 9). At line 10, composition relationships are extracted from the list of relationships (R), some classes are transformed into attributes based on the composition relationships (lines 11-13). The relationships containing the attribute are considered operations (lines 14-16).

## Generated Class Diagram

XMI (XML Metadata Interchange) is an Object Management Group (OMG) standard for exchanging metadata information via Extensible Markup Language (XML) [8]. Effectively, XMI is proposed to help programmers using Unified Modeling Language (UML) with different languages and software modeling tools to exchange their data models with each other[7]. The developed tool generates an XMI file which is an Ecore file created with *pyecore API*. Ecore file is the Eclipse Modeling Framework (EMF) meta-model, which illustrates the names of the classes, their attributes, and their types, as well as the methods and relationships with their classifications. Also, PlantUML[9] API is used to visualize the class diagram. These treatings were done in python.

## CASE STUDIES

In this section, we show two case studies to illustrate our method of transforming the CIM level based on user stories to the PIM level. To compare the performance of our tool and the (Lucassen et al., 2017) tool named Visual narrator, we used similar user stories in two cases study.

## Case Study Number 1

The input of our platform is a text file that regroups all user stories of the case study, as shown below.

The following user stories[10] represent event management: booking and purchase an event ticket ...

```
As a Visitor, I can create a new account.
As a Visitor, I can log in.
As a Visitor, I am able to log out.
As a Visitor, I want to choose an event, so that I can book a ticket for that
event.
As a Visitor, I want to filtrate on event type, so that I can only see event
of the type I want.
As a Visitor, I can rename my account.
As a Visitor, I can change my account password.
As a Visitor, I want to search for an event.
As a Visitor, I am able to purchase multiple tickets.
As a Visitor, I want to see the ticket price.
```

*Table 6. Classes and their attributes*

| Classes | Attributes |
|---|---|
| Account | Password |
| Visitor | personal_details |
| Ticket | Price |
| Ticket | Type |
| Event | Type |
| Payment methods | - |

*Table 7. Relationships results*

| Relationships |
|---|
| Create (account, Visitor) |
| Have (account, Visitor) |
| Rename (account, Visitor) |
| Choose (event, Visitor) |
| Search (event, Visitor) |
| See (event, Visitor) |
| Choose (payment_methods, Visitor) |
| Buy (ticket, Visitor) |
| Book (ticket, Visitor) |
| Purchase (ticket, Visitor) |
| Receive (ticket, Visitor) |
| Have (ticket, event) |

```
As a Visitor, I want to choose payment methods, so that I can buy a ticket.
As a Visitor, I want to choose a type of ticket.
As a Visitor, I want to provide my personal details to purchase a ticket.
As a Visitor, I want to receive a purchased ticket.
```

*Table 8. Generation of classes operations*

| Classes | Operations |
|---|---|
| Visitor | provide(personal_details) |
| Account | change(password) |
| Event | Filter(type) |
| Ticket | see (price) |
| Ticket | choose(type) |
| Event | choose(type) |

The final results of the design elements extraction for the given user story, after applying extraction rules, are presented in tables below.

Classes and their attributes are indicated in Table 6. The relationships results are shown in Table 7. Table 8 indicates operations results.

The classes detected in the Visual narrator tool are: *Visitor, Account, System, Event, Ticket, Event-Type, Type, AccountPassword, Password, TicketPrice, Price, Detail, and Method.*

*hasType (Event, EventType), hasPrice(Ticket, TicketPrice), hasPassword(Account, AccountPassword), canLogOut(Visitor, System), canLogIn(Visitor, System), canLogOut(Visitor,System),* these relationships are among the relationships detected in visual narrator and not detected by our approach. Table 9 shows the total items detected by (Lucassen et al., 2017) and our approach.

*Table 9. Total of design elements detected by (Lucassen et al., 2017) and our approach*

|  | Actors | Classes/Entity | Attributes | Relationships | Operations |
|---|---|---|---|---|---|
| **(Lucassen et al., 2017)** | 1 | 13 | 0 | 19 | 0 |
| **Our approch** | 1 | 5 | 5 | 12 | 6 |

Table 10 shows the total items manually detected and using our approach. In our approach, the actors (Visitor is an actor) and the classes are the first to detect, afterward the relationships and their classifica-

*Table 10. Total of design elements detected manually and automatically*

|  | Actors | classes | Attributes | Relationships | Operations |
|---|---|---|---|---|---|
| **Manually** | 1 | 5 | 5 | 12 | 6 |
| **Automatically** | 1 | 5 | 5 | 12 | 6 |

*Figure 7. Generated class diagram from user stories*

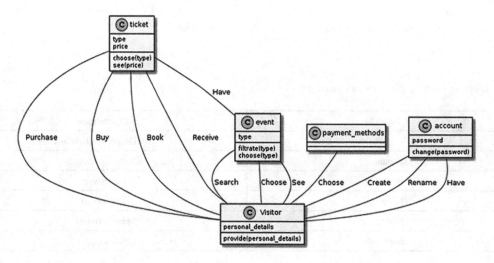

tions. Based on the composition relationships, the attributes are generated. Finally, the methods of the classes are extracted.

Figure 7 represents the generated class diagram of the case study.

Given this user story: *As John, I can change my account password*, Table 9 shows how the previous user story will be treated according to (Lucassen et al., 2017) and our approach.

*Table 11. Comparison between (Lucassen et al., 2017) approach and our approach*

| Our Approach | (Lucassen et al., 2017) Approach |
|---|---|
| If the actor is a proper name, then I use *NER* of *Stanford core NLP* tool and I add the returned name to the list of classes ®*Person is a class* The subject is a class, but if It refers to proper noun then we use NER | · A proper noun is an entity · The subject is an entity then *John is an entity* |
| The account is a class and password is an attribute | · The compound entity is created account_password · The relationship: IS_A(password,account_password) represents inheritance relationship |

Comparison between (Lucassen et al., 2017) approach and our approach is indicated in Table 11.

According to (Lucassen et al., 2017) approach, multiple compound classes, and inheritance relationships will be created, which will encroach the result with unnecessarily compound classes, and inheritance relationships which caused by the lack of attribute extraction rules.

## Case Study Number 2

The following user stories represent inline course management: videos, quizzes, and others[11]:

```
As an instructor, I can upload a video to be part of a course so that the vis-
itor can watch those videos.
As an administrator, I can delete any course or event, so I can remove things
that will no longer occur.
As a site editor, I can update any course or event so that I can fix things
the original author has not.
As an instructor, I can see the thumbnail image for each video. So that the
thumbnail image is one I like rather than randomly selected.
As an instructor, I can create a quiz to include in a video so that visitors
can take those quizzes to ensure they are learning.
As an instructor, I can properly sequence the elements of course.
As an instructor, I indicate whether a forum is part of a course.
As an instructor, I can see the schedule for a course so that the visitor can
consult the weekly elements.
As an instructor, I can add subtitles to any video so that it is more acces-
sible.
As a visitor, I can create an account so that I can track my progress.
As an instructor, I can create an event.
```

As a visitor, I can see an event that is characterized by a name, description, start date, end date, and address.
As an administrator, I can see that the participant is a type of visitor.
As an instructor, I can turn a course into an event, so I can correctly classify anything that was entered incorrectly.
As a visitor, I can manage my account so that it reflects my current information.
As a visitor, I can view a list of all the courses I have taken, so that I have access to that historical information and did not call someone instead.
As an administrator, I can set the listing fee per Other Course or Event.
As an instructor, I want to insert publication date of elements, so that items become available when I want and not sooner.
As an instructor, I can create a quiz so that the participant can assess their learning.
As a participant, I can take a quiz as part of a course.
As a participant, I see if I pass a quiz after I finish taking it.
As a participant, I can see which quiz I have passed, not passed, or not yet taken when viewing the course outline so that I know which quiz I need to take or possibly re-take.
As an instructor, I want quiz responses stored in the database so that I can see how people are doing at various questions, perhaps so I can fix one that is worded poorly.
As a participant, I want to receive feedback after each quiz question so that I can see if I got the question right or wrong.
As a participant, I can answer questions in a different order.
As a participant, I can get an answer via video rather than text so that I watch rather than read an answer.
As a participant, I can participate in several events.
As an instructor, I can store responses of quiz questions.

Tokenization, lemmatization, stemming, POS: are used for user story processing. After, the dependencies between words are applied for each user story.

The extraction of design elements is based on the definition of rules. To do this; the dependencies are harnessed and analyzed to extract design components.

Firstly, the actors and classes will be extracted (Table 12) and subsequently the relationships (Table 14). Attribute extraction is based on the composition relationships between classes (Table 13). Our approach is to first extract all the names either simple or compound and will be classes. Later, if a class composes another class and it is not in a composition relation with another class, so the class will be transformed into an attribute. The next step will be to add operations to the corresponding classes (Table 15).

If the actors appear in the relationships generated, then these actors will be added to the list of classes. In this case study, all actors are classes.

Classes that are not connected to other classes such as *Text, Oiginal_author*, and *Items* are deleted automatically from the class diagram but if we add a user story in the input file in which have an association about the class, in this case, this class will be visible and its relationship will be extracted

*Table 12. Generated Actors and classes*

| Actors | Classes |
|---|---|
| Instructor | Course |
| Administrator | Video |
| Visitor | Elements |
| Site editor | Learning |
| Participant | Listing fee |
| | Quiz |
| | People |
| | Items |
| | Feedback |
| | Event |
| | Questions |
| | Order |
| | Text |
| | Original_author |
| | Answer |
| | Anything |

*Table 13. Classes and their attributes*

| Classes | Attributes |
|---|---|
| Course | Schedule, Outline, Forum |
| video | Subtitles, Thumbnail_ image |
| Elements | Publication_date |
| Event | Name, Address, Description, Start_date, End_date |
| Visitor | Account Progress |
| Question | Response |
| Site editor | Things |

automatically. *The account* in this case study is an attribute because it has not characteristics, unlike the first case study, the account has a *password*.

Figure 8 represents part of the generated class diagram of the case study.

To compare the performance of our tool and (Lucassen et al., 2017) tool, we used similar user stories. Table 16 shows the total of design elements detected by our approach and (Lucassen et al., 2017) approach.

In Visual narrator, 7 actors are extracted, among these actors; *Editor* is detected instead of *site editor,* the Editor class is wrong because of the absence of rule to extract compound actors (noun-noun). Regarding relationships, 30 are detected, in which 28 are correct, the others are: *hasImage(Thumbnail, Thumbnail_Image),* and *hasquestion(quiz, quiz_question).* In Visual narrator, the inheritance rule applied

*Table 14. Relationships and their type*

| Relationships | Type |
|---|---|
| watch (answer, participant) | Association |
| delete (course, administrator) | Association |
| turn into (course, event) | Association |
| turn (course, instructor) | Association |
| have (course, site_editor) | Composition |
| update (course, site_editor) | Association |
| contains (elements, course) | Composition |
| sequence (elements, instructor) | Association |
| consult (elements, visitor) | Association |
| delete (event, administrator) | Association |
| create (event, instructor) | Association |
| turn (event, instructor) | Association |
| participate (event, participant) | Aggregation |
| update (event, site_editor) | Association |
| see (event, visitor) | Association |
| receive (feedback, participant) | Association |
| assess (learning, participant) | Association |
| set (listing_fee, administrator) | Association |
| see (people, instructor) | Association |
| create (quiz, instructor) | Association |
| pass (quiz, participant) | Association |
| take (quiz, participant) | Association |
| Answer (question, participant) | Association |
| include in (quiz, video) | Composition |
| take (quiz, visitor) | Association |
| contains (video, course) | Composition |
| upload (video, instructor) | Association |
| watch (video, visitor) | Association |
| Is a type of (visitor, participant) | Inheritance |
| Receive(question, participant) | Association |
| Get(question, participant) | Association |
| contains(question, quiz) | Composition |
| Classify(Anything, Instructor) | Association |

to the composite noun which is wrong; this contributes to incorrect relationships which will influence the generated conceptual model.

*Table 15. Generation of classes operations*

| Classes | Operations |
|---------|------------|
| Course | View(outline) |
| Course | See(schedule) |
| Elements | Insert (publication_date) |
| Question | Store(reponse) |
| Site_editor | Fix (things) |
| Site_editor | Remove (things) |
| Video | Add (subtitles) |
| Video | See (thumbnail_image) |
| Visitor | Create (account) |
| Visitor | Manage (account) |

In this case study, the classes such as *Image, Thumbnail, Thumbnail_Image,question, quiz_question;* are extracted which leads to redundant classes. The other incorrect classes are *Date* instead of *publication_date, Part, List, Information*, and *Fee* instead of *Listing_Fee*.

The researchers did not define rules for extracting attributes. Table 17 shows the accuracy of automated and manually approaches.

The incorrect relationship is *Classify (Anything, Instructor)*, it is extracted because the class *Anything* is detected as a class.

The results obtained with our approach proposed in the two case studies show that our technique is more improved compared to that of (Lucassen et al., 2017) with a very high level of precision 98% by comparing these results with that obtained manually.


## ANALYSIS AND DISCUSSION BASED ON ANALYTICAL SURVEY

In this section, we present an analysis and discussion based on an analytical survey. The summarizes works that allow transforming textual requirements into conceptual models are indicated in Table 18.

Most searchers did develop a platform to generate the UML diagrams (class diagram) or entity-relationship model from unrestricted general requirements. Furthermore, the processing to extract actors using nominal compounds in user stories has been missing in most research. Also, some attribute extraction rules lead to design errors. Among the proposed approaches, there are just three approaches that parse user stories. The first, (Lucassen et al., 2017), deals with the user stories, but the rules presented are not too detailed and output is a conceptual model without attributes. The second, (Elallaoui et al., 2018), parse user stories to generate use cases but not a class diagram. In the third approach, (Javed & Lin, 2018), the authors did not even mention the extraction rules conceptual model elements, they are focused on the transformation rules from general requirements, and even in the case study, they have not described it about user story. They represent the results immediately.

Our approach is the unique method that defined extraction rules for composition relationships from user stories.

*Figure 8. Generated class diagram from user stories*

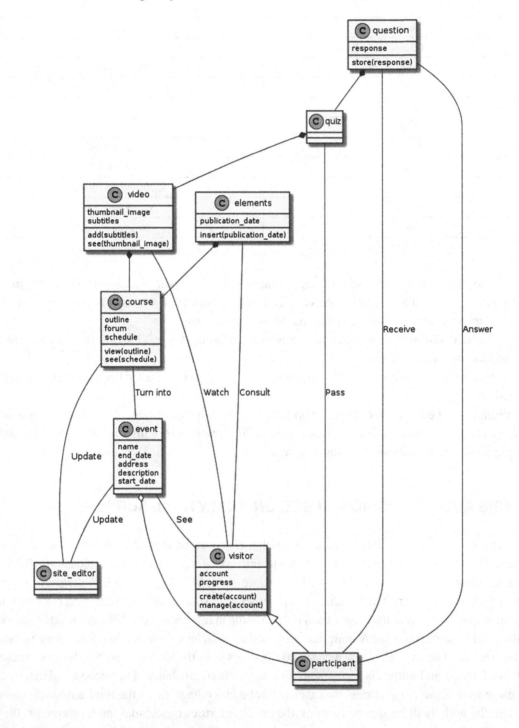

## CONCLUSION AND FUTURE WORK

In this paper, we have proposed an approach to automate the transition between user stories and the analysis phase, to extract the components of the class diagram. Our approach is based on the use of typed

*Table 16. Total of design elements detected by our approach and (Lucassen et al., 2017) approach*

|  | Actors | Classes/Entity | Attributes | Relationships | Operations |
|---|---|---|---|---|---|
| (Lucassen et al., 2017) | 7 | 9 incorrect classes from 28 classes | 0 | 30 | 0 |
| Our approch | 5 | 17 | 15 | 32 | 10 |

*Table 17. Total of design elements detected manually and automatically*

|  | Actors | Classes | Attributes | Relationships | Methods |
|---|---|---|---|---|---|
| Manually | 5 | 16 | 15 | 32 | 10 |
| Automatically | 5 | 17 | 15 | 33 | 10 |
| Recall | 100% | 99% | 100% | 97% | 100% |
| Total Recall: 98% |  |  |  |  |  |

dependencies offered by *Stanford core NLP* for improving and defining new extraction rules to extract required Oriented Object artifacts. The accuracy obtained on the generated design elements reaches 98%, for this reason, the results obtained using our approach are very satisfactory. The main advantages of the proposed technique are:

- Treating different types of sentence structure in User Stories.
- Efficient management of compound nouns for classes extraction.
- Refined classes have been obtained following a transformation of some classes into attributes using composition relationships, and some relationships to operations.

We believe that our proposed approach can serve to facilitate the design of analytical tasks in the team. Next, minimize time and costs. The benefits of our approach are aligned with agile methods goals.
In the future, our work can be enhanced by:

- Defining new rules to extract cardinalities of the class diagram.
- Applying artificial intelligence techniques to generate new rules, especially, to detect aggregation relationships.
- Using test criteria with user stories to build dynamic UML diagrams such as the Activity diagram.

# REFERENCES

Deeptimahanti, D. K., & Babar, M. A. (2009). An automated tool for generating UML models from natural language requirements. *ASE2009 - 24th IEEE/ACM International Conference on Automated Software Engineering*. 10.1109/ASE.2009.48

*Table 18. Analysis class diagram elements detected by the existing automated approaches*

| Related Works | Approaches and Tools | Input | Output | |
|---|---|---|---|---|
| | | | Model | Design Elements |
| (Elbendak et al., 2011) | · Development of a *ClassGen* tool<br>· The output is an initial class diagram requires manual intervention to refine it | Text requirement | Class diagram | Classes, attributes, relationships, aggregation, and Inheritance |
| **(Herchi & Abdessalem, 2013)** | · Developed Platform *DC-Builder*<br>· Output: XML file<br>· Use of the domain of ontology to refine the results obtained based on heuristic rules | Text requirement | Class diagram | Classes, attributes, relationships, aggregation, and composition |
| (Vidya Sagar & Abirami, 2014) | Using Stanford Parser and *Wordnet* to generate a class diagram | Text requirement | Class diagram | Classes, attributes, operations, relationships, aggregation, composition, and inheritance |
| (Thakur & Gupta, 2017) | · Part Of Speech tags (POS tags) and typed dependencies (TD), were used to extract design elements.<br>· Using the Stanford NLP parser, and Java language.<br>· Graphviz API is used to visualize the class diagram | Use case specifications written in MS Excel file | Class diagram | Classes, attributes, operations, relationships |
| **(Lucassen et al., 2017)** | · Development of a *Visual Narrator* tool in python and the Spacy API.<br>· The tool generates a conceptual model output as a Prolog or ontology program OWL 2. | User stories | Conceptual model | Entities and relationships |
| **(Elallaoui et al., 2018)** | · Using the *Treetagger* analyzer (NLP tool).<br>· Development of a JAVA plugin to generate the use case diagram | User stories | Use cases | Actors and use cases |
| **(Javed & Lin, 2018)** | Visual C # language and Stanford CoreNLP 3.8 APIs are used to build the conceptual model. | User Stories, text requirements, and use cases | Conceptual model | Classes, attributes, Relationships |
| Proposal approach | · Using the Stanford CoreNLP tool, Wordnet API, and Python language.<br>· PlantUml API is used to visualize class diagram in PNG image.<br>· *Pyecore* API is used to generate XMI file which is an *Ecore* file | User stories | Class diagram | Classes, attributes, operations, relationships, aggregation, composition, and Inheritance |

Elallaoui, M., Nafil, K., & Touahni, R. (2018). Automatic Transformation of User Stories into UML Use Case Diagrams using NLP Techniques. *Procedia Computer Science, 130*, 42–49. doi:10.1016/j.procs.2018.04.010

Elbendak, M., Vickers, P., & Rossiter, N. (2011). Parsed use case descriptions as a basis for object-oriented class model generation. *Journal of Systems and Software, 84*(7), 1209–1223. Advance online publication. doi:10.1016/j.jss.2011.02.025

Herchi, H., & Ben Abdessalem, W. (2013). *From user requirements to UML class diagram*. https://gate.ac.uk/

Javed, M., & Lin, Y. (2018). Iterative process for generating ER diagram from unrestricted requirements. *ENASE 2018 - Proceedings of the 13th International Conference on Evaluation of Novel Approaches to Software Engineering,* 192–204. 10.5220/0006778701920204

Lucassen, G., Robeer, M., Dalpiaz, F., van der Werf, J. M. E. M., & Brinkkemper, S. (2017). Extracting conceptual models from user stories with Visual Narrator. *Requirements Engineering, 22*(3), 339–358. Advance online publication. doi:10.100700766-017-0270-1

Mich, L. (1996). NL-OOPS: From natural language to object oriented requirements using the natural language processing system LOLITA. *Natural Language Engineering, 2*(2), 161–187. Advance online publication. doi:10.1017/S1351324996001337

Mich, L., & Garigliano, R. (2002). *NL-OOPS: A requirements analysis tool based on natural language processing*. Management Information Systems.

Thakur, J. S., & Gupta, A. (2017). *Automatic generation of analysis class diagrams from use case specifications*. https://arxiv.org/abs/1708.01796

Vidya Sagar, V. B. R., & Abirami, S. (2014). Conceptual modeling of natural language functional requirements. *Journal of Systems and Software, 88*, 25–41. Advance online publication. doi:10.1016/j.jss.2013.08.036

Zhou, N., & Zhou, X. (2004). Automatic Acquisition of Linguistic Patterns for Conceptual Modeling. *INFO 629. Artificial Intelligence*, 1–19. http://daviszhou.net/Research/INFO629Prj.pdf

## KEY TERMS AND DEFINITIONS

**Coreference Resolution:** Is a task of recognizing the token in a sentence that refers to the same underlying real-world entities.

**Lemma:** Lemma in NLP applications allows recognizing different tokens as instances of the same word; like the infinitive form of a verb, the singular plural of the most noun.

**NER:** Is text analysis that allows classifying the named entities under various predefined classes.

**POS Tagger:** Specifies parts of speech to each word such as noun, verb, adjective,

**Stanford Core NLP:** Is a natural language software that provides a set of human language technology tools, including the part-of-speech (POS) tagger, the named entity recognizer (NER), the parser, the coreference resolution system.

**Tokenization:** Tokenization is the process of splitting a sentence into a list of words.

**Typed Dependencies:** Designate grammatical relationships between the words in a sentence.

## ENDNOTES

1    https://www.geeksforgeeks.org/software-engineering-requirements-engineering-process/
2    https://www.mountaingoatsoftware.com/agile/user-stories
3    https://www.omg.org › 00-2_MDA_Guide_v1.0.1.pdf.
4    https://stanfordnlp.github.io/CoreNLP/
5    https://en.wikipedia.org › wiki › Part-of-speech_tagging
6    https://cs.nyu.edu/grishman/jet/guide/PennPOS.html
7    https://nlp.stanford.edu/software/dependencies_manual.pdf
8    https://whatis.techtarget.com/definition/XMI-XML-Metadata-Interchange
9    https://pypi.org/project/plantuml/
10   https://github.com/MarcelRobeer/StoryMiner/blob/master/example_stories.txt
11   https://www.mountaingoatsoftware.com/agile/user-stories

# APPENDIX

User Stories with applied rules are presented in Table 19.

*Table 19. User Stories with applied rules*

| User Story | Design Elements | | | | | | |
|---|---|---|---|---|---|---|---|
| | Actor | | Classes | | Attributes | Relationships and Operations | |
| | Name | Rule | Name | Rule | Name | Name | Rule |
| As an administrator, I want to create a new account | Administrator | AC1 | account | C2 | - | Create (account, administrator) | R1 |
| - As an administrator, I want to register a number of room in a system.<br>- As an administrator, I can change the description for any material<br>- As an administrator, I can store a list of materials that are contained in the room. | Administrator | AC1 | Room<br>Materials | C7<br>C7 | Number<br>Description | · Contains (number, room) is an association relationship. But because number is not linked to other classes, then, it becomes an attribute. In this case, R5 rule detects an attribute, and it will be removed from the list of classes.<br>· Because *number* is an attribute, then, register*(number)* is an operation in *room* class.<br>· *Description* is an attribute of *material*.<br>· *Change(description)* is an operation in *material* class<br>· Contained(room,materials) is a composition relationship but materials is not an attribute of *room* because it has an attribute(number). | R5<br>R5<br>H1 |
| As a manager, I want to know if the user has received the weekly SMS sent by the system | manager | AC1 | Sms<br>User<br>system | C5<br>C1<br>C2 | | · Sent by (system, sms)<br>· Received(sms, user) | R4<br>R2 |
| As Rayan the manager, I want to enter a film's title | manager | AC2 | film | C4 | title | · *title* is an attribute.<br>· Enter*(title)* is an operation of *film* class. | R7 |
| As an administrator, I can create an account for the customer. | Administrator | AC1 | Account<br>Customer | | | · Have (account, customer) is an association.<br>· Create (Administrator, Account) | R5<br>R3 |
| As a registered user, if my profile is created then I can change my address that is characterized by a city, postal code and number | Registered user<br>If *user* is already extracted as an actor, then, an inheritance relationship link actors: user and a registered user | AC3 | Address<br>Profile | | City<br>Postal code | · Have(manager, profile) is an association<br>· Change (manager, address)<br>· Characterized by(address,city)<br>· Characterized by(Address,postal code)<br>· Characterized by (Address, number)<br>The three latter composition relationships detect attributes of *address* class. | R7<br>R3<br>H1<br>H1<br>H1 |

# Chapter 9
# Extending the Knowledge Discovery Metamodel to Support Tasks and Presentation Behaviors of Design Knowledge

**Zineb Gotti**
https://orcid.org/0000-0003-3342-3248
*MISC Laboratory, Morocco*

**Samir Mbarki**
*MISC Laboratory, Morocco*

**Sara Gotti**
https://orcid.org/0000-0002-2513-2646
*MISC Laboratory, Morocco*

**Naziha Laaz**
https://orcid.org/0000-0003-4709-6647
*MISC Laboratory, Morocco*

## ABSTRACT

*Currently, the main objective of all programmers and designers is to render interactive systems usable and effective. So, users can complete their tasks and achieve their goals. To ensure that, programmers and designers require good understanding of system characteristics and functionality. This work focused on an approach to automate the process of extracting the system information. The approach is based on the ADM initiative as the best solution for system's evolution. The OMG ADM Task Force defines a set of standards to facilitate that, like Knowledge Discovery Metamodel, captures design knowledge needed for the construction of future user interfaces. Actually, KDM allows abstract structural and semantical aspect representation. However, no support exists for expressing behavior of system content, interaction, user control, and activities of the front-end applications. The authors hope to alleviate this lack by extending KDM model to fulfill the needs of complete abstract model construction.*

DOI: 10.4018/978-1-7998-3661-2.ch009

# INTRODUCTION

Interactive systems evolution is a software engineering field that requires a thorough analysis to build and preserve a model of the important system characteristics and functionality, that includes their user interfaces graphical structure and navigation, as well as the widgets they contain, and the properties of those widgets. It provides support for transforming an existing system user interfaces to modern ones with new requirements.

This paper presents an approach that analyses the automatic process of user interfaces characteristics and functionalities extracting. It is based on recording, processing and checking the legacy system structure and behavior. It is a model-based approach in which the knowledge extracted from system assets is captured and examined in models that conform to an abstract meta-model, namely the knowledge discovery meta-model (KDM) (OMG, 2016a).

However, this direct models reconstruction involves code parsing of different user interfaces code blocks. The process proposes a multi-step procedure and transformation, which analyses the structure and behavior of system artifacts. The approach is based on the ADM initiative (OMG, 2003).

The resulting models contain all retrieved information presented at a higher abstraction level respecting the KDM meta-model.

During the process, the authors use Object Management Group (OMG) standards and techniques to capture the design knowledge needed to build future user interfaces of modernized system.

Actually, the KDM is one of these standards. It is a meta-model for representing information about existing software system artifacts, their elements, and operational environment; it allows the structural and semantical aspect representation in a high level of abstraction. However, no support exists for expressing the behavior of content, interaction, user control and activities of the front-end applications.

The process extends the OMG's KDM. So, the KDM model extension result contains all the necessary information, it covers all the typical development needs on reverse engineering.

This paper is organized as follows. Section 2 describes the ADM approach and its KDM standard and covers also the related works. Section 3 defines the ADM based process and details its different phases. It describes also the extended KDM meta-model named XKDM used for modeling user interaction and control. Section 4 discuss the research gaps and explain the validation of our approach. Section 5 concludes the benefits of the extended meta-model.

# BACKGROUND

As cited before, ADM provides standards in the field of reverse engineering. These standards are based on models and meta-models for modernizing legacy software systems. The KDM metamodel is the main one.

To support modernization activities, OMG defined the KDM standard that presents a platform-independent representation of the software systems to be analyzed.

KDM is a meta-model used to represent system artifacts at a high level of abstraction. It is the basic element for the ADM approach.

The main purpose of the KDM specification is to gain comprehension of source code. It provides a knowledge intermediate representation of existing software systems (OMG, 2016a). It captures precise knowledge about the existing applications and makes the interoperability between the reverse engineering tools possible.

An ADM-based process using KDM starts by analyzing the different legacy software artifacts in order to build a higher-abstraction level model in a bottom-up mode through reverse engineering techniques (Pérez-Castillo et al., 2012).

Obviously, the KDM represents the core of the ADM initiative because it provides a summary of the application structure and a common interchange format intended to represent existing software assets, thus allowing tool interoperability.

KDM is organized in several packages each one corresponds to an architectural view of the system (for example, platform, user interface, or data) and represents software artifacts as entities and relations. These packages as detailed in Table 1, are classified into four abstraction layers to improve modularity and separation of concerns: infrastructure, program elements, runtime resource, and abstractions (OMG, 2016a).

*Table 1. KDM layers*

| Layer | Packages | Detail |
|---|---|---|
| Infrastructure | Core, kdm, and Source | It is the lowest abstraction level; it defines a small set of concepts used systematically throughout the entire KDM specification. |
| Program Elements | Code and Action | It represents the code elements and their associations. It consists of a set of meta-model elements common between different programming languages to provide a language-independent representation. The program elements layer represents the logical view of a legacy system. |
| Resource | Data, Event, UI and Platform. | it represents the higher-level knowledge of the existing software system. This layer focuses on those things that are not extracted from the syntax at the code level but rather from the runtime incremental analysis of the system. |
| Abstractions | Conceptual, Structure and Build | It defines a set of meta-model elements for representing domain-specific knowledge as well as to provide a business overview of legacy information systems. |

## RELATED WORKS

Software modernization is a new software engineering field that requires evolutionary maintenance to solve reengineering problems. The ADM approach guarantees this increase in evolutionary maintenance. So many researches, both on model-driven engineering and software modernization, have been conducted.

In (Gotti&Mbarki, 2016), the authors proposed an ADM based approach for developing separate models capturing tasks, presentation and dialog structures and behaviors. The extraction process is based on analyzing and understanding the legacy system behavior and structure.

In (Gotti et al., 2018), the authors have focused on the ADM approach for the interactive Nooj system's evolution. They used a set of standards to facilitate interoperability between modernization tools: The Knowledge Discovery Meta-model and Abstract Syntax Tree Meta-model. These standards capture all design knowledge needed for the construction of the future Nooj user interfaces respecting web technologies.

The KDM model is an OMG standard that provides a common representation of programs written in a number of programming languages. It is extensible to support all the information needed for a good high level of abstraction presentation.

Perez-Castillo et al. in (Pérez-Castillo et al., 2012)have extended KDM's Event model to represent event logs. They have used the Extension Family mechanism that allows to create Stereotypes comprising different Tag Definitions and integrate event logs in KDM.

In (Durak, 2015), the authors extended the knowledge discovery meta-model by adding a package named simulation model. it enables using architecture-driven simulation modernization. The extended meta-model is named the simulation knowledge discovery meta-model.

The authors in (Mirshams Shahshahani, 2011) defined KDM as a standard that supports a number of procedural and object-oriented programming languages. But it does not support the aspect-oriented programming languages. So, they extend KDM to support AspectJ, perhaps the most popular aspect-oriented language. However, while Mirshamset al. have based her extension on an aspect model created by themselves, Santos et al. in (Santos et al., 2019) have created a KDM extension for aspect-oriented programming based on Evermann's profile (Evermann, 2007) that encompasses all the aspect-oriented concepts presented in AspectJ and in other aspect-oriented languages.

## OVERVIEW OF APPROACH

In this article, authors opted for a modernization process that is based on the ADM initiative as the best solution for the legacy system's adaptive and perfective maintenance. This modernization process is guided by the horseshoe model as figured in Figure 1.

*Figure 1. ADM horseshoe model*
*(OMG, 2003)*

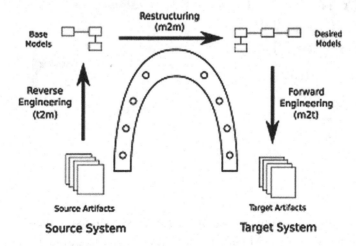

The horseshoe model allows an abstract representation of the legacy source system in order to improve its understandability and its migration to the target modernized system.

The migration process consists of three phases (Chikofsky& Cross, 1990): reverse engineering, restructuring, and forward engineering.

- **Reverse engineering:** It is the process of information extraction from the source code for building code models. authors propose for that, a method to retrieve important elements such as the components of the graphical user interface and their interrelationships. All the information generated was incorporated into concrete PSM models which are ASTM and GUIM in our case. After that, the extracted models will be presented in another form or at a higher level of abstraction defined in KDM models.
- **Restructuring:** It takes as input the abstract representation obtained from the previous step and converts it into an enhanced representation at the same level of abstraction. It is a model to model transformation while maintaining the user interfaces external behavior.
- **Forward engineering:** It takes the abstract representation result and generates the physical implementation of the target system as a lower level of abstraction.

All these phases are well explained in these previous works (Gotti et al., 2018),(Gotti&Mbarki, 2016).

This paper presents an approach that focuses only on the reverse engineering phase applied to interactive system in order to capture all information about user interfaces structure and behavior at a high level of abstraction. Figure 2 explains the approach.

*Figure 2. Overview of the process*

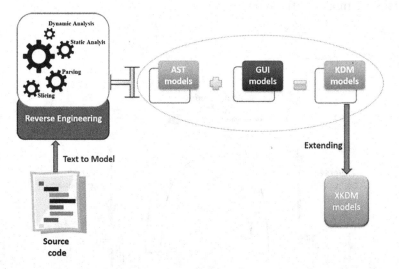

The first step is to analyze the source code of the legacy system using the JDT parser(Eclipse JDT, n.d.)to discover its corresponding PSM code models. It enables the extraction of GUI knowledge and business logic from the system and stores it in concrete models such as ASTM that expresses the syntax of the source code, and GUIM that represents the graphical components, their interrelationships, and their properties.

The parser implements a visitor pattern that allows visiting all the nodes of the compiled source code. The engine traverses all nodes defined in the abstract syntax tree and calls the appropriate method on each node (ClassVisitor, AnnotationVisitor, FieldVisitor, and MethodVisitor) using the visit () method (see Figure 3). It uses some techniques like parsing and slicing (Harman &Hierons, 2001)to identify the system business rules and GUI information and ignore irrelevant details.

*Figure 3. Source code parsing*

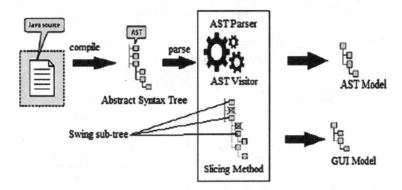

After that, authors transform these two models into the KDM model to present all information retrieved at a higher level of abstraction. Thus, they launch a Model to Model transformation implemented with QVTo language (OMG, 2016b). The inputs of this transformation are the ASTM and GUIM models and the output is the KDM model.

To validate the process of knowledge extraction, authors tested it on a Java library application with complex user interfaces. Figure 4 shows the result of the first step presented in ASTM and GUIM code models of the illustrated source interface.

ASTM and GUIM result models gather all GUI information: the GUI components, their interrelations, the structural aspect of the application and the events attached to each graphical component. The ASTM result model represents the class structure of the selected source interface, while the GUIM model encapsulates containers and widgets of the mainframe and their properties.

Figure 5 provides the result of the model to model transformation that represents the abstract level of the migration process presented in the KDM model. This model represents the logical structure of the view and the spatial relationships between the user interface components.

KDM is the key element of the ADM approach; it is used to model software system artifacts, basically the structural and semantical aspect in a high level of abstraction. It is used to statically represent the main components of the existing user interface. But the information related to user interactions and tasks is missing. It does not well express the interaction and user control of the front-end applications and does not determine how and when a user task is executed, and how these results may impact on other parts of the system.

Moreover, to be usable the approach generated system needs to be effective. In another way, the system has to support the tasks the user wants to do and the subcomponents of such tasks.

*Figure 4. Parsing code Result*

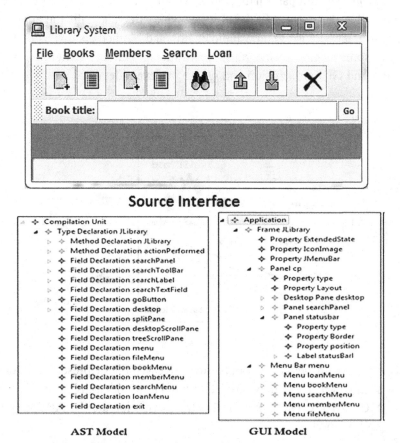

This analysis conduct to make a decision for extending the OMG's KDM to have a complete abstract representation of existing systems containing all necessary information needed during the migration process.

In this paper, the main goal is to propose a new representation of KDM with new included packages. This extended representation is termed XKDM. As shown in Figure 6, XKDM extends KDM with both the interaction and user control packages.

## Interaction Package

The Interaction package describes user interactions and front-end behavior used for passing context information between two elements of display. Figure 7 illustrates the two main added meta-classes of the interaction package, responsible for representing the content-dependent navigation with the transmission of parameters expressed by DataFlow meta-class and LinkParameter meta-class.

Actually, the runtime behavior is created from the execution of the graphical user interface (Gotti&Mbarki, 2016).In other words, the behavior is defined by events and the effect of an event is represented by a connection flow, which connects the event to the component affected by the event.

There are two types of connection flow:

*Figure 5. A model to model transformation KDM result*

*Figure 6. Extending KDM meta-model*

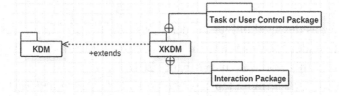

- **The UIFlow:** captures the behavior of the user interface as the sequential flow from one instance of Display to another (OMG, 2016a). This element is already presented in the existent KDM meta-model.
- **The DataFlow:** is a kind of connection used for passing context information between UI elements.

DataFlows are triggered any time a parameter is available to transfer to a target element. The dataflow is used to represent parameter passing without user interaction.

This element is not presented in the KDM meta-model, so authors decided to add it as a meta-class in the Interaction Package to enable communication between UI elements by means of parameter passing. They deduced that after a deep analysis of IFML specification (Brambilla, 2014), (Laaz et al., 2018).

*Figure 7. XKDM Interaction Package*

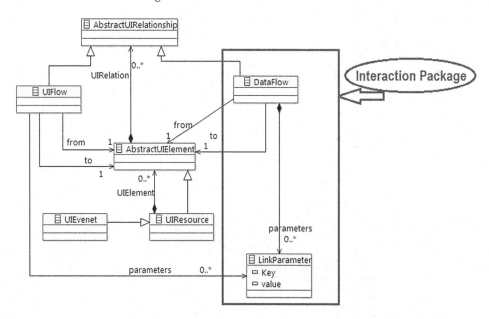

Moreover, when a UIFlow is followed, information may be propagated from the source to the target UI element through link Parameters. Also, when an event is triggered, connection flows are followed and parameter values flow from source to target UI elements.

To present this important element in the KDM, a LinkParameter meta-class has been added to the Interaction Package. LinkParameter is a typed name element. It may correspond to elements of the user interface (UIfields as example).

## The User Control Package

The user control package, as depicted in Fig. 11, describes how the user interfaces activities should be implemented, in order to understand its limits, problems, and characteristics. This package is deduced from performed analysis in this work (Gotti & Mbarki, 2016).

This package consists of one or more top-level tasks, linked by a named TaskRef relation with the UIResource meta-class of the KDM UI package.

These tasks are associated with operators in order to describe the relations between them: Interleaving, Order independence, Synchronization, Parallelism, Choice, Disabling, Suspend-Resume, Enabling, Iteration, and Optional operators.

These Tasks are grouped into many categories:

- **User task:** An internal cognitive activity.
- **System task:** Performed by the application itself.
- **Interaction task:** User actions that may result in immediate system feedback.
- **Abstract task:** A task that has subtasks belonging to different categories.

*Figure 8. Task or user control Package*

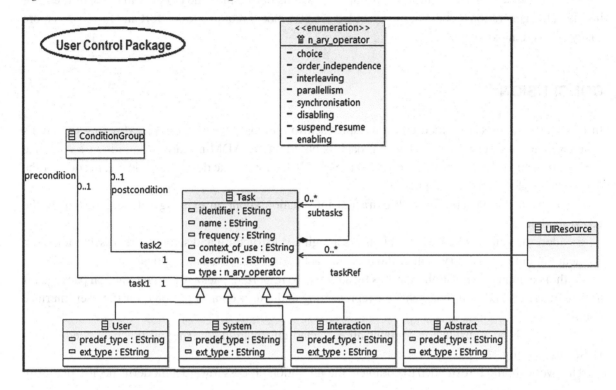

A precondition is an instance of the ConditionGroup class. It indicates what must be true before the task is carried out. While a post-condition indicates what will be true after the task execution.

## DISCUSSION

ADM provides a methodology based on models like KDM for software modernization, but it lacks in providing adequate means to recover all knowledge needed(Durak, 2015).

The contribution of this work proposes a metamodeling approach that defines meta constructs for the knowledge discovery necessary for the future user interfaces construction which are the user interactions and tasks.

This approach has extended the KDM metamodel to support all the information needed for the construction of the modernized system from one and complete abstract model. The new XKDM extended metamodel allows the structural and semantical aspect representation, and also the behavior of system content, interaction, user control and activities of the front-end application.

Although, as we discussed in related works, our previous work in (Gotti & Mbarki, 2016) has shown the ability of an ADM based approach to represent existing code (reverse engineering) in three complementary models capturing tasks, presentation and dialog structures and behaviors. It seems to be more appropriate to use the approach detailed in this work (see figure 2) with the new extended XKDM metamodel, since it includes all the necessary elements to complete the modernization process.

We can evaluate the performance of the approach considering the time to perform the activities. For instance, the generation process of the extended XKDM model requires less effort and its reuse is more easily adapted in existing tools

## CONCLUSION

In this work, authors have focused on an approach to automate the process of extracting the GUI's characteristics and functionality. The approach is based on the ADM initiative that allows a complete presentation about user control, dialog structures and behaviors of the design knowledge, needed for the construction of the future user interface.

For that, this work represents all extracted information about an existing software system in the KDM model.

Besides, the generated KDM model allows a high level structural and semantic representation of an application, but it does carry neither the user interaction nor the front-end applications activities.

Authors extend it to fulfill these needs by adding two important packages: an interaction package for user interactions and front-end behavior representing and a user control package for the user interface control.

The XKDM model extension contains all extracted information covering all practical needs on reverse engineering.

This work should be extended to complete the migration process toward a modern specific platform.

## REFERENCES

Brambilla, M. (2014). *The IFML book – OMG's Interaction Flow Modeling Language explained* (1 edition). Morgan Kaufmann. https://marco-brambilla.com/2015/02/10/the-ifml-book-omgs-interaction-flow-modeling-language-explained/

Chikofsky, E. J., & Cross, J. H. (1990, January). Reverse engineering and design recovery: A taxonomy. *IEEE Software*. https://ieeexplore.ieee.org/document/43044

Durak, U. (2015). *Extending the Knowledge Discovery Metamodel for architecture-driven simulation modernization*. Academic Press.

Eclipse, J. D. T. J. (n.d.). *Eclipse Java development tools (JDT) | The Eclipse Foundation*. Retrieved March 19, 2019, from https://www.eclipse.org/jdt/

Evermann, J. (2007). A meta-level specification and profile for AspectJ in UML. *Proceedings of the 10th International Workshop on Aspect-Oriented Modeling*, 21–27. 10.1145/1229375.1229379

Gotti, Z., & Mbarki, S. (2016). *Java Swing Modernization Approach—Complete Abstract Representation based on Static and Dynamic Analysis*. ICSOFT-EA. doi:10.5220/0005986002100219

Gotti, Z., Mbarki, S., Gotti, S., & Laaz, N. (2018). Nooj Graphical User Interfaces Modernization. In S. Mbarki, M. Mourchid, & M. Silberztein (Eds.), *Formalizing Natural Languages with NooJ and Its Natural Language Processing Applications* (pp. 227–239). Springer International Publishing. doi:10.1007/978-3-319-73420-0_19

Harman, M., & Hierons, R. (2001). An overview of program slicing. *Software Focus*, *2*(3), 85–92. doi:10.1002wf.41

Laaz, N., Wakil, K., Mbarki, S., & Jawawi, D. N. A. (2018). Comparative Analysis of Interaction Flow Modeling Language Tools. *Journal of Computational Science*, *14*(9), 1267–1278. doi:10.3844/jcssp.2018.1267.1278

Mirshams Shahshahani, P. (2011). *Extending the Knowledge Discovery Metamodel to Support Aspect-Oriented Programming* [Masters, Concordia University]. https://spectrum.library.concordia.ca/7329/

OMG. (2003). *ADM Platform Task Force | Object Management Group*. https://www.omg.org/adm/

OMG. (2016a). *About the Knowledge Discovery Metamodel Specification Version 1.4*. https://www.omg.org/spec/KDM/

OMG. (2016b). *About the MOF Query/View/Transformation Specification Version 1.3*. https://www.omg.org/spec/QVT/About-QVT

Pérez-Castillo, R., de Guzmán, I. G.-R., Piattini, M., & Places, Á. S. (2012). A case study on business process recovery using an e-government system. *Software, Practice & Experience*, *42*(2), 159–189. doi:10.1002pe.1057

Pérez-Castillo, R., de Guzmán, I. G.-R., Piattini, M., & Weber, B. (2012). Integrating event logs into KDM repositories. *Proceedings of the 27th Annual ACM Symposium on Applied Computing*, 1095–1102. 10.1145/2245276.2231949

Santos, B. M., Landi, A. de S., Santibáñez, D. S., Durelli, R. S., & de Camargo, V. V. (2019). Evaluating the extension mechanisms of the knowledge discovery metamodel for aspect-oriented modernizations. *Journal of Systems and Software*, *149*, 285–304. doi:10.1016/j.jss.2018.12.011

# Chapter 10
# Model Transformation Approach According Model–Driven Architecture From BPMN to UML Up to IFML

**El Mustapha MELOUK**

*MISC Laboratory, EST Kenitra, Ibn Tofail University, Morocco*

**Yassine Rhazali**

🆔 https://orcid.org/0000-0003-1488-0216

*ISIC Research Team of ESTM, LMMI Laboratory of ENSAM, Moulay Ismail University, Meknes*

**Youssef Hadi**

*MISC laboratory, Morocco & EST Kenitra, Morocco & Ibn Tofail University, Morocco*

## ABSTRACT

*The main key in MDA is the model's transformation. There are two transformation kinds into MDA: CIM to PIM and PIM to PSM. Most researchers focused on transformation from PIM to PSM because there are several points in common between these two levels. But transforming CIM to PIM is rarely discussed in research subjects because they are two different levels. This chapter presents a methodology to master model transformation from CIM to PIM up to PSM respecting MDA. The methodology is founded on creating a good CIM level, through well-chosen rules, to facilitate transformation to the PIM level. However, the authors establish a rich PIM level, respecting the three classic modeling views: functional, dynamic, and static. The method conforms to MDA by considering the business dimension in the CIM level, through BPMN which is the OMG standard for modeling business process. Nevertheless, they used UML models into the PIM level because UML is recommended by MDA in this level. Then, they use IFML the OMG standard for representing web interface model in PSM level.*

DOI: 10.4018/978-1-7998-3661-2.ch010

## INTRODUCTION

Transformation between different levels of MDA (OMG-MDA, 2015) begins by CIM to PIM transformation, which allows building computation models from computation independent models. This transformation, reformulates technically the contents of the CIM models inside models of the PIM level, this ensures that business processes requirements are not lost into the MDA procedure; this allows obtaining quality design models that validates the business requirements. However, models independent of platform have to be adapted to a specific platform, during transformation from PIM to PSM, through adding information of a specific platform into PIM models.

Some standards provide a semi-automatic transformation from PIM to PSM. But the transformation from CIM to PIM, at the moment, is not supported by any standard. Indeed, most searches define multiple methodologies for transforming PIM level models to PSM level models; because there are several points in common between these two levels. However, transforming CIM level to PIM level is rarely discussed in research subject because these levels are totally different. Our objective is that CIM models do not stay a simple documents established by business managers and used by software specialists, Indeed, the goal is to construct into CIM several productive models allow providing PIM models automatically.

In this paper, we propose a semi-automatic transformation from the CIM level to the PIM level. For that, we use well defined rules, so as to obtain concentrated CIM models that simplify the transformation to the PIM level. Then, we determine a set of well chosen rules for automating the transformation from the CIM level to the PIM level. Next we ensure PIM to PIM transformation by adapting PIM models with web oriented user interface. According to MDA, the CIM level is represented by business process models. However, we build business process models by the BPMN notation in the CIM level because the BPMN represents the specialized standard for modeling business process supported by OMG. UML (Unified Modeling Language) (Mileset al., 2006) is advocated by MDA in the PIM level. For this reason, we divide PIM models in accordance with the three UML classic modeling views including functional, static, and dynamic view. The use case diagram model is the first model of the PIM level which defines the functionality of the information system (functional view), the state diagram model presents the system states (dynamic view), the class diagram model represents the system classes and their relationships(static view) and all classes are structured into packages in package diagram model (static view). Next we use IFML, the OMG standard of user interface modeling, for adapting PIM models with web-oriented user interface. For automating CIM to PIM transformation and PIM to PIM transformation, our approach is based on transformation rules which are implemented by ATL (Atlas Transformation Language) (Jouault et al., 2006).

Our approach is the unique method based on construction rules for structuring CIM in order to facilitate the transformation toward the PIM. Our methodology describes clear transformation rules because each rule is presented by three ways: human language, ATL language and graphic presentation. Our goal in this approach is not just move from the CIM level to the PIM level, but our objective is to attain a rich PIM level that can be transformed thereafter into the PSM level.

The remainder of the paper is presented as follows: In section 2, we show the related works concerning transformation from the CIM level to the PIM level. The section 3 presents our proposal by describing the construction rules of the CIM models and the transformation rules that allow moving from CIM to PIM and from PIM to PIM. An illustration of our method in a case study is shown at section 4. Section 5 discusses the performance evaluation of our transformation approach. Finally, we conclude by specifying the ongoing future work in section 6.

## RELATED WORK

In this section, we survey the related work concerning the transformation from CIM level to PIM level in the MDA approach.

Kherraf et al. (Kherraf et al., 2008) presents an approach based on patterns and archetypes to transform the CIM level to the PIM level. The authors apply patterns to structure the CIM level, and use archetypes to shift to the PIM level. This method is based on two steps for modeling the CIM level. At the first step, authors use an activity diagram and a use case diagram of UML 2 to represent business processes and at the second step, they involve a detailed activity diagram for modeling system requirements. Then the requirement elements are transformed to the system components as a first step in the PIM level. Finally, a set of four archetypes (Lefebvre, 2005; Coad et al., 1999) contribute in the transformation from the system components to the class diagram.

A feature-oriented and component-based method to transform the CIM level to the PIM level is presented by Zhang et al. (Zhang et al., 2005).The authors use the feature model for structuring requirements in the CIM level. This model contains features and relationships between them. This approach uses software architecture for presenting the PIM level which contains a set of components and interactions between them. However, responsibilities are considered as connectors between features and components to simplify the transformation from CIM to PIM.

An analytical method is proposed by Kardoš et al. (Kardoš et al., 2010) for passing from the CIM level to the PIM level. The authors represent business process in CIM through the Data Flow Diagram (DFD) (Qing Li, 2009; Hoffer, 2004). However, the PIM level is based on four UML diagrams including activity diagram, use case diagram, sequence diagram, and domain model.

Rodríguez et al. (Rodríguez et al., 2007.a) defines a transformation method from secure business process to use case diagram. This approach presents business process in CIM level through secure business process model defined in BPMN. However, a set of transformation rules are defined in Query/View/ Transformation (QVT) (OMG-QVT, 2015), checklists, and refinement rules allow authors to obtain the use case diagram which represents requirement and analysis design in the PIM level. In (Rodríguez et al., 2007.b; Rodríguez et al., 2010) Rodríguez et al, based on the same previous approach but UML2 activity diagram is added in secure business model, and PIM level enlarged by class diagram.

A transformation approach from the CIM level to the PIM level for information system service-oriented development was proposed by De Castro et al. (Castro et al., 2011).The authors define business view in the CIM level by using BPMN for business process modeling, and use value model (Gordijn et al., 2003) for identifying services. Then ATL language is used for passing to the information system view in the PIM level which is defined by two extensions of UML use case diagram and two extensions of UML activity diagram.

A transformation approach from business requirements towards agent-based execution is presented by Hahn et al. (Hahn et al., 2010). The authors use BPMN to define the CIM level. However, SoaML (OMG-SoaML, 2012) model is used to model agents in the PIM level. This approach based on ATL language for transforming from the CIM level to the PIM level.

A transformation approach from model-driven goal-oriented requirement to data warehouses is presented by mazón et al. (Mazón et al., 2007). The authors define the CIM level with UML profile using the i* modelling framework (Yu, 1997). However, Query / View / Transformation (QVT) is used to shift towards the PIM level which is presented by data warehouse design.

An approach where activity diagrams generated automatically from use case is presented by Gutiérrez et al. (Gutiérrez et al., 2008). The authors propose a QVT-based approach to generate a transformation from functional requirements represented by use case in the CIM level toward activity diagram which define the PIM level.

While in (rhazali et al., 2015.c) we have proposed a disciplined approach for transforming CIM level towards PIM level. The approach is based on BPMN and UML 2 activity diagram to model business process. The PIM level includes use case diagram, state diagram and class diagram. This approach is founded on a set of transformation rules for passing from the CIM level to the PIM level.

In another work (rhazali et al., 2015.b), we have proposed a transformation method from CIM to PIM. The approach is based on BPMN and UML 2 activity diagram to model business process. The PIM level includes models of state, class and package diagram. This approach is founded on an improved methodology for moving from CIM to PIM.

We also established another method for transforming CIM to PIM (rhazali et al., 2015.d). The approach is based only on UML 2 activity diagram to model business process. The PIM level includes models of state diagram, class diagram and package diagram. This approach is founded on a set of transformation rules for shifting from the CIM level to the PIM level.

In (Rhazali et al., 2016a) the authors propose an approach for transforming business process models to analysis and design model. This approach allows establishing business process in CIM by basing on SoaML models. However, PIM models are presented by UML 2 use case diagram, state diagram, class diagram and web diagram presented by SoaML: software component.

In (Rhazali et al., 2016b) the authors represent an approach to move from CIM to PIM; they define the business process by using BPMN. However, the PIM level is established by UML. This approach founded MVC design pattern.

In (Rhazali et al., 2017a) the authors define a method to transform from CIM level to PIM level; they define the business process by using UML activity diagram. However, the PIM level by UML diagrams models. In PIM level this approach is founded also in SoaML and IFML.

In (Rhazali et al., 2018; Rhazali et al., 2019) the authors represent an approach to shift from CIM to PIM; they define the business process by using BPMN. However, the PIM level is established by the three UML view point. This approach founded also in web model to define PIM level.

In (Rhazali et al., 2015a) the authors establish a transformation method for moving from CIM to PIM. This method based on BPMN notation for presenting the business process models. Then, PIM models are established by the three classical modeling views. This method focuses on analytic survey that allows moving from CIM level to PIM level through a semi-automatic transformation.

## PROPOSED METHOD OF TRANSFORMATION FROM CIM TO PIM

Computation Independent Model (CIM) means that this model does not disclose any information related to the system. According to OMG (OMG-MDA, 2015), CIM level is presented by business process models which are supposed to be representative of the real world. According to OMG-BPMN, 2011), BPMN is a specialized standard for modeling business, and all the benefits of most standards of business process converge to BPMN.

In our approach, we modeled business process in the CIM level through BPMN. The most interesting of our methodology is the consideration, at the beginning, that we are in the process of creating business models that will be automatically transformed to information system models. We carefully used a set of selected rules to establish business models that will contain rich information to achieve the transformation easily. Our approach preserves the business knowledge throughout the transformation towards the PIM level. This enables producing an information system with quality.

We divided models of the PIM level according to the three classical modeling views (Roques, 2004; Shin et al. 2000; Demuth, 1999) including functional, static, and dynamic view. Some research indicates that UML is recommended by MDA in the PIM level (Blanc, 2005; Kleppe, 2003). However, the intersection of our UML 2 models and modeling views is presented as follows: The model of the use case presents functional view, the model of the state diagram interprets the dynamic view and the model of the class diagram shows the static view. Then, we structure all classes in packages through model of the package diagram that represents the static view of the information system. Finally we use IFML, the OMG standard of user interface modeling, for adapting PIM models with web-oriented user interface, to facilitate thereafter the transformation toward the PSM level.

The model transformation is based on a set of transformation rules. These rules may be described by human language that has less value. However, in the model transformation, algorithms and programming languages are more precise, but model transformation languages are considered to be the most efficient for describing model transformation. In our proposal, all PIM level models are obtained via an automatic transformation or a semi-automatic transformation from CIM level. Then IFML model is resulted through semi-automatic transformation from PIM models. The transformation is realized through well concentrated rules implemented in ATL.

In the following subsections, each transformation rule is described in human language, in ATL language, and represented with a schema. Before executing the transformation process, the designer can intervene, only for selecting not transformable elements (task, data object ...). However, each rule verifies if the element is transformable, for that, at the beginning of each rule, we called the helpers described with OCL language.

## Construction Rules of the CIM Level

The rules of construction the BPMN collaboration diagram model:

- Define a medium sub-processes (not complexes sub-processes). In fact, each sub-process must be comprised between 4 and 10 tasks.
- If a sub-process contains less than 4 tasks, or represents an additional operation to another sub-process, we can merge various sub-processes into one, provided that, the sub-process do not exceed 10 tasks.
- Avoid the representation of the tasks, and show only manual tasks.
- The model does not show all possible cases, but it just represents the general sequence of the business processes.
- Based only on sub-processes and their relations.
- Show the maximum of the actors which collaborate in the realization of enterprise business processes.

The rules of construction the BPMN business process diagram model:

- Detailing individually each sub-process as various tasks (the task constitutes the fundamental unit in the BPMN business process diagram).
- Avoid the manual tasks
- Represent gateways in this model.
- Show the most exceptional paths.
- Add a data object containing object state at the output of each task.

## Transformation Rules From CIM to PIM

Transformation from BPMN models to use case model:

The (Figure 1) show the transformation rules from BPMN models towards use case model.

The ATL rule (R1) allows transforming non-manual "task" to "use case". To ensure that the "task" is non-manual, we called a helper function "isManual". However, if a "task" has "gateway xor" in "out" the "use case" transformed with relationship "extend" in "in", and vice versa. If a "task" has "sequence flow" in "in" the "use case" transformed with relationship "include" in "out", and vice versa. If a "task" belongs to a "sub-process" the "use case" transformed belongs to "package". The ATL rule (R2) transforms "collaborator" to "actor", then, the ATL rule (R3) allows transforming "gateway xor" between two "tasks" to relationship "extend" between two "use cases". In the ATL rule (R4), a "sequence flow" between two "tasks" corresponds to relationship "include" between two "use cases". In this latter rule, before the transformation, we verified that "sequence flow" is not returning back, which corresponds to the ATL rule (R5). In the ATL rule (R6), a "sub-process" is transformed to a "package".

Transformation from BPMN model to state diagram model:

Figure 2 shows the transformation rules from BPMN models towards state model.

The ATL rule (R7) allows transforming "data object" to "state". However, the state is recovered by the helper "state". In the ATL rule (R8) we transform "exclusive fork" to "decision point". The ATL rule (R9) allows transforming "exclusive joint" to "junction point". In the ATL rule (R10) each "parallel fork" is transformed to "fork state". The ATL rule (R11) transforms "parallel join" to "join state". In the ATL rule (R12) a "parallel joint and fork" is transformed to a "join and fork state". The ATL rule (R13) transforms "exclusive joint and fork" to "junction point". In the ATL rule (R14) we transform "start event" to "initial state". The ATL rule (R15) allows transforming "end event" to "final state". In the ATL rule (R16) each "sequence flow" is transformed "transition". However, two helpers function "source" and "target" are called to affect respectively the source and destination for the transition.

Transformation from BPMN model to class diagram model:

Figure 3 shows the transformation rules from BPMN models to class model.

The ATL rule (R17) allows transforming "state" to "method". In the ATL rule (R18) each "data object" is transformed to a "class".

Transformation from BPMN models to package model:

Figure 4 shows the transformation rules from BPMN models towards package model.

The ATL rule (R19) allows transforming "group" to "package". In ATL rule (R20) each "sub-process" that does not belong to any group is transformed to "package". Then, the helper "subprocessBelongs-Group" verifies if a sub process belongs to a group.

In ATL rule (R21) each set of "classes" become from the same "group", will be placing in the "package" that matches the "group". In ATL rule (R22) "classes", resulting from the same "sub-process" which

*Figure 1. Transformation rules from BPMN models to use case diagram model.*

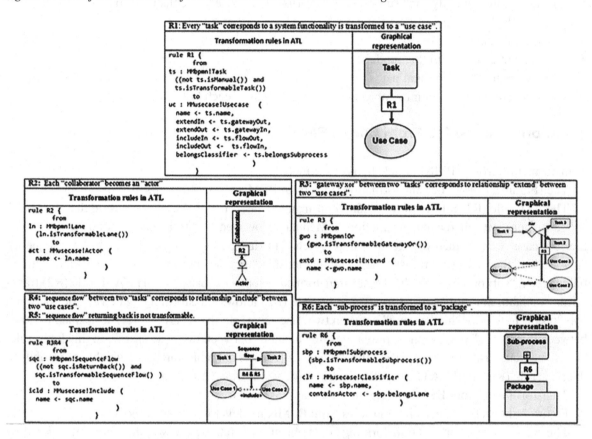

belongs to no "group", will be placing in the package that corresponds to the "sub-processes". However we use in rules (R21, R22) the helper "dataBelongsGroup" checks if a "data" belongs in a "group".

Transformation from PIM models to IFML model:

Fig. 5 shows the transformation rules from CIM models towards IFML model.

## CASE STUDY

In this section, we present a case study of booking services to illustrate our transformation approach from the CIM level to the PIM level.

Customer can browses the available room catalogues and can also shows information concerning each room, then decides to choose a room for reservation or not . At any time, the customer has the option to add, update or delete his bookings. Once booking options are selected, the customer starts booking while presenting payment information. The booking agent starts the process of booking and declares the reservation of rooms with the options specified by the customer. Then, the maid prepares manually the room with specified options. The butler checks the room quality and ensures the availability of each option. Finally the receptionist delivers the room at the customer. Finally the receptionist delivers the room at the customer.

*Figure 2. Transformation rules from BPMN model to state diagram model.*

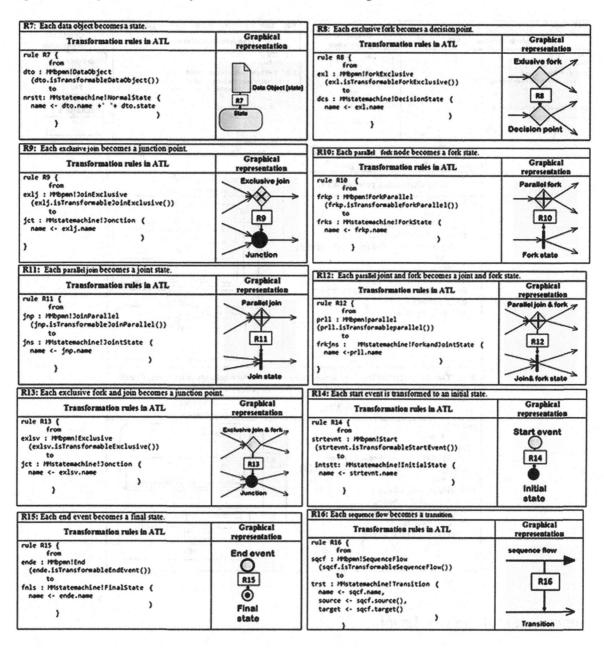

*Figure 3. Transformation rules from BPMN model to class diagram model.*

*Figure 4. Transformation rules from BPMN model to package diagram model.*

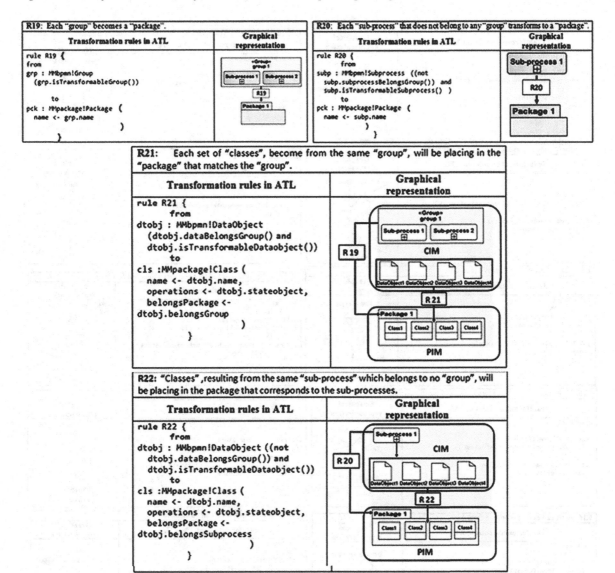

## Presentation of the CIM Level

The model of business process represented by BPMN collaboration diagram is illustrated in (Figure 6). In this model we just represented the sub-processes and their sequence, but we avoided identification of tasks and connections between them for presenting a general business process. However, we have presented the maximum of collaborators in order to represent a true business process, in which there is collaboration between several potential business partners.

The representation of several collaborators facilitates the task of transformation from CIM to PIM. Indeed, when passing to the use case diagram model, collaborators will be transformed to actors. Nevertheless, we presented medium sub-processes. Thus, the customer must presents the sub-processes

*Figure 5. Transformation rules from PIM models to IFML model.*

| | | |
|---|---|---|
| **R23:** Each "display" method, into class diagram, becomes "web page" container with "list" view component plus OnSelect event | rule R23 {<br>from<br>opr: MMclass!Operation<br>(opr.isTransformableOperation()and<br>opr.isDisplay())<br>to<br>cnt : MMIFML!Container (<br>name <- '«WebPage»'+opr.name )<br>vc : MMIFML!ViewComponent (name <- '«List»',<br>containerBelongs<- cnt.name )<br>ose : MMIFML! OnSelectEvent (<br>ViewComponentBelongs<-vc.name ) } | 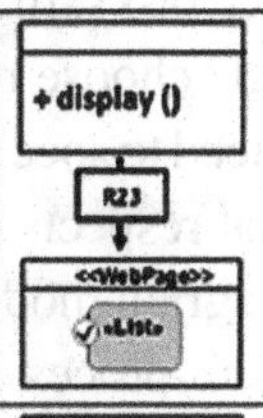 |
| **R24:** Each "delete" method, into class diagram, becomes "web page" container with "delete" action plus simple event | rule R24 {<br>from<br>opr : MMclass!Operation<br>(opr.isTransformableOperation()and<br>opr.isDelete())<br>to<br>cnt : MMIFML!Container (<br>name <- '«WebPage»'+opr.name)<br>ac : MMIFML!Action ( name <- 'Delete',<br>containerBelongs<- cnt.name )<br>se : MMIFML! SimpleEvent (<br>ViewComponentBelongs<-ac.name ) } | 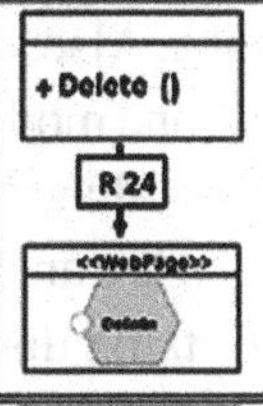 |
| **R25:** Each "add" or "modify" method, into class diagram, becomes "web page" container with "form" view component plus OnSubmit event | rule R25 {<br>from<br>opr : MMclass!Operation<br>(opr.isTransformableOperation()and<br>(opr.isAdd() or opr.isModify()))<br>to<br>cnt : MMIFML!Container (<br>name <- '«WebPage»'+opr.name )<br>vc : MMIFML!ViewComponent (<br>name <- 'Form'+ opr.name,<br>containerBelongs<- cnt.name )<br>ose : MMIFML! OnSubmitEvent(<br>ViewComponentBelongs<-ac.name ) } | 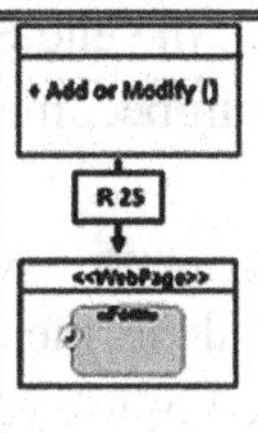 |
| **R26:** Each state into state diagram (or method into class diagram) becomes "web page" container | rule R26 {<br>from<br>opr : MMclass!Operation<br>(opr.isTransformableOperation()and not<br>(opr.isAdd()) and not (opr.isModify())and not<br>(opr.isDelete()))<br>to<br>cnt : MMIFML!Container (<br>name <- '«WebPage»'+opr.name )<br>} | 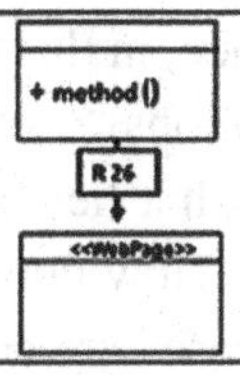 |
| **R27:** Each transition, into state diagram becomes navigation flow | rule R27 {<br>from<br>trs : MMstatemachine!Transition<br>(opr.isTransformableTransition())<br>to<br>cnt : MMIFML!NavigationFlow (<br>name <- trs.name,<br>input <- trs.input,<br>output <- trs.output )<br>} | 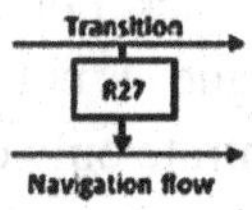 |
| **R28-R29:** Each fork state, into state diagram, becomes "menu" view component with several simple events corresponding transition in output fork state | rule R28 {<br>from<br>fs : MMstateMachine!FokState<br>(fs.isTransformableForkState())<br>to<br>vcp: MMIFML!ViewComponent (<br>name <- '«Menu»'+fs.name ) }<br>rule R29 {<br>from<br>ft : MMstateMachine!Transition<br>(ft.isTransformableForkState()and<br>ft.Outputisforkstate())<br>to<br>sev: MMIFML!SimpleEvent ( name <- ft.name,<br>ViewComponentBelongs <-<br>ft.NameForkStateOutput() ) } | 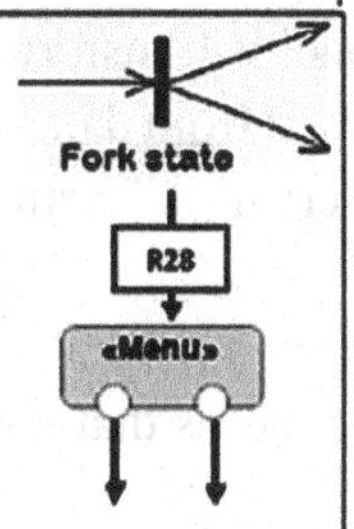 |
| **R28-R29:** Each fork state, into state diagram, becomes "menu" view component with several simple events corresponding transition in output fork state | rule R30 {<br>from<br>ds : MMstateMachine!DecisionState<br>(ds.isTransformableDecisionState())<br>to<br>vcp: MMIFML!ViewComponent (<br>name <- '«Menu»'+ds.name ) }<br>rule R31 {<br>from<br>tr : MMstateMachine!Transition<br>(tr.isTransformableDecisionState()and<br>tr.OutputisDecisionState())<br>to<br>sev: MMIFML!SimpleEvent (name <- tr.name,<br>ViewComponentBelongs <-<br>tr.NameDecisionStateOutput() )} | 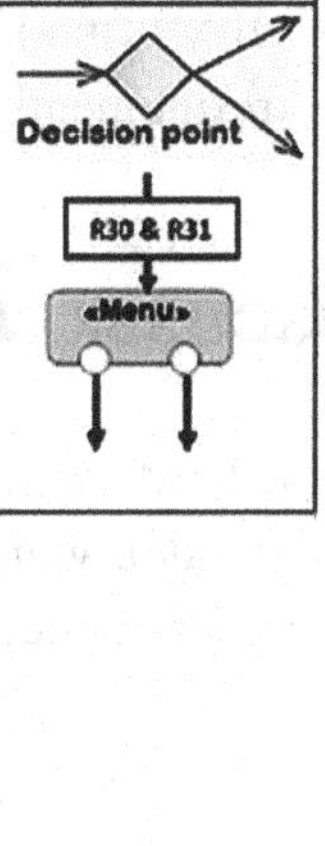 |

"choose room", "start reservation" and "present information", but the sub-process "start reservation" cannot contain more than three tasks. In this way, we have merged "choose room" and "start reservation" as a single sub-process called "choose rooms for reservation".

Finally, in this model we need to specify all manual tasks. We can make various refinements into initial model to achieve a model that respects our rules. The second model in the CIM level is represented as a BPMN business process diagram model. In this last model, we detail each sub-process individually as several tasks. However, the sub-process "choose room for reservation" is detailed (Figure 7). Then, we have identified all possible paths. Also we presented a data object with its state in the output of each task.

The (Figure 8) shows the second model in the PIM level, which is the state diagram model, transformed from model of business process diagram. First, data object is transformed to state and the sequence flow that lies between two tasks is transformed to a transition. E.g. the data object "Catalogue" with the state "displayed" becomes "Catalog displayed" in the state diagram model. However, the start event is transformed to an initial state; the end event becomes a final state; the exclusive fork is transformed to a decision point; exclusive join become junction point, finally an exclusive fork & join node becomes a junction point.

However, the sub-process "choose room for reservation" is transformed to a package. Then the collaborator "customer" who realizes the sub-processes becomes actor and next the tasks that detail the sub-processes are transformed to use cases. Gateway xor which lies between two tasks becomes relationship "extend". For instance, in this model there is a Gateway xor between two tasks "specify room" and "add accommodation options "; so the two correspondents use cases are connected via an "extend" relationship. Sequence flow that lies between two tasks becomes relationship "include". However, in this model there is sequence flow between the two tasks "display catalogue" and "specify room", so the two corresponding use cases are connected via an "include" relationship. So, we do not show the sequence flows which return back. For example, the relationship between the tasks "add accommodation options" and "display catalogue" is not specified in this model, so as not to complicate the model, and so that the use case will concentrate only on the identification of functionalities and not on the sequences.

The (Figure 9) presents the ultimate goal of the PIM level which is the establishment of a model of class diagram. This model is transformed from the model of BPMN business process diagram. In this model, class is transformed from data object. Then the states of an object become functions in the class. So, the data object "reservation" with state "started" transformed to class "reservation" that contains the method "start".

The (Figure 9) presents a model of package diagram. So the group "realize reservation" becomes package. Then, the sub-process that not belongs to any group, such as "deal accommodation" becomes a package.

The (Figure 10) show IFML model obtained from PIM models by respecting transformation rules. Then, we can realize few refinements.

## ANALYSIS AND DISCUSSION

The (Figure 11) shows the CIM meta-model, which is designed as BPMN meta-model and the (Figure 12) shows the PIM meta-model, which is presented by use case meta-model, state meta-model, class meta-model and package meta-model.

*Figure 6. BPMN collaboration diagram model*

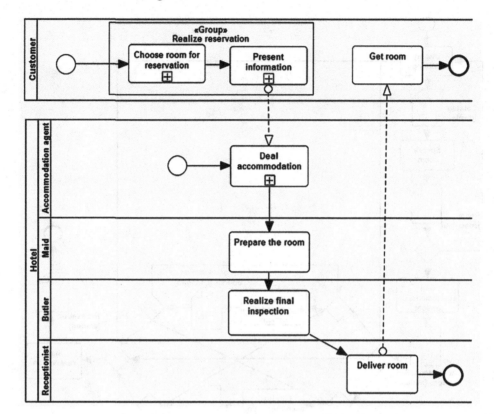

## Analysis

The CIM level:

There is a current which is based only on system requirement for modeling the CIM level like in (Gutiérrez et al., 2008; Fatolahi et al., 2008; Wu et al., 2007), but this level is independent of computation. Other hybrid stream is founded on business process and system requirement for modeling the CIM level as in (Kherraf et al., 2008). In these approaches, system requirement are early modeled in CIM level to facilitate transformation towards PIM level. In our approach, we modeled business process in CIM level through BPMN. Because, business process is independent of computation and BPMN is the OMG standard for business process modeling.

The PIM level:

There is no approach in the related work which covers the three modeling views except (Kardoš et al., 2010; rhazali et al., 2015.c). As well, several approaches do not model the classes in the PIM level as (Zhang et al., 2005; Rodríguez et al., 2007.a; Castro et al., 2011; Hahn et al., 2010; Mazón et al., 2007; Gutiérrez et al., 2008; Wu et al., 2007), although without classes the model of source code, PSM, isn't easily obtained by transformation. Our approach covers the three modeling views. However, in static view we based on class model, and package model for organizing classes.

Transformation:

*Figure 7. BPMN business process diagram model*

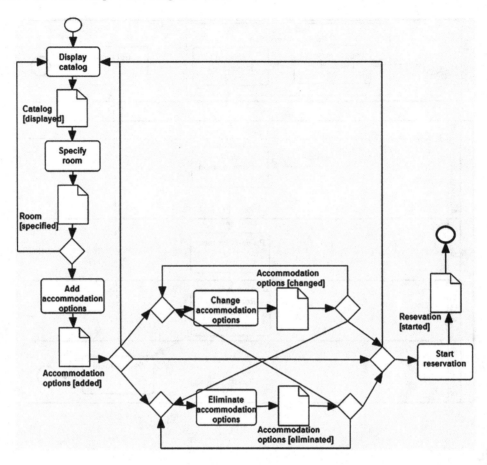

There is no approach which defined a source and target metamodels except (Castro et al., 2011; Gutiérrez et al., 2008). But without metamodels, an automatic transformation of models is impossible. However, most approaches define the transformation in a human language like in (Kherraf et al., 2008;

*Figure 8. PIM models: I use case diagram model, II state diagram model.*

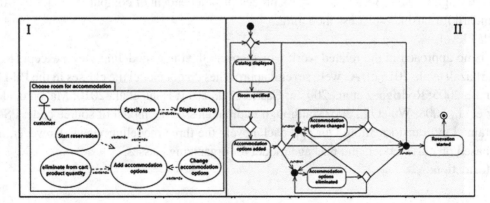

*Figure 9. PIM models: III class diagram model, IV package diagram model*

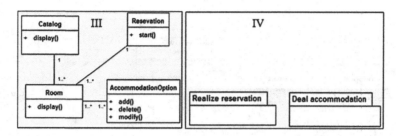

Gutiérrez et al., 2008; Bousetta et al., 2013; Fatolahi et al., 2008; Wu et al., 2007; Rhazali et al., 2014; rhazali et al., 2015.c). Since, there is one approach (Zhang et al., 2005) based on algorithm to describe transformation, but transformation must be implemented with a transformation language as in (Rodríguez et al., 2007.a; Rodríguez et al., 2007.b; Rodríguez et al., 2010; Castro et al., 2011; Hahn et al., 2010; Mazón et al., 2007; Gutiérrez et al., 2008). Our approach based on source metamodel, target metamodel, and transformation rules described into transformation language.

Assessment methodology:

In practice, there is no approach which is developed personal tool for supporting transformation. But there is one approach (Castro et al., 2011)based on Eclipse tool to implement transformation from CIM to PIM. Our approach is approved with practice case. The most transformation approaches are approved by theoretical case study like in (Kherraf et al., 2008; Zhang et al., 2005; Kardoš et al., 2010; Rodríguez et al., 2007.a; Rodríguez et al., 2007.b; Rodríguez et al., 2010; Mazón et al., 2007; Gutiérrez et al., 2008; Mokrys et al., 2012; Bousetta et al., 2013; Fatolahi et al., 2008, Rhazali et al., 2014, rhazali et al., 2015.c). Then, two approaches not approved (Hahn et al., 2010; Wu et al., 2007).

*Figure 10. IFML model*

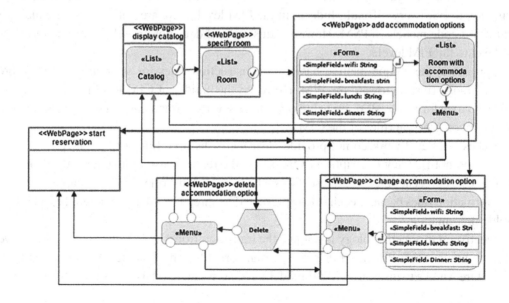

*Figure 11. CIM meta-model: BPMN meta-model*

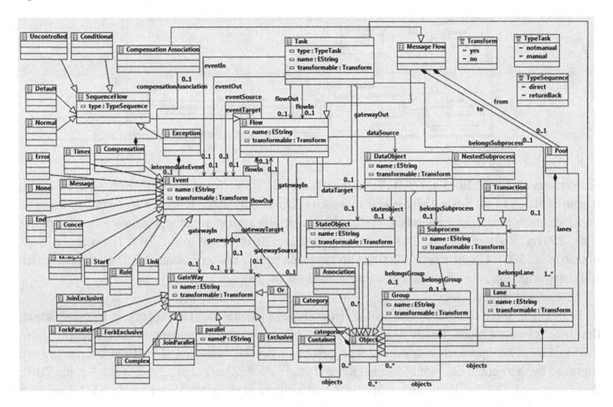

## Discussion

We find that the approach (Castro et al., 2011) validates most of our evaluation criteria. This approach allows building the CIM level on the basis on value model that is not a business modeling standard. Then the PIM level is presented just by the models of the use case and the activity diagram, which makes the transformation to PSM very difficult. Indeed, in the PIM level, there are not classes on which we base to move toward code models in PSM. However, this method does not provide clear rules to transform the CIM level to the PIM level.

Our approach is the unique method based on construction rules for structuring CIM in order to facilitate the transformation toward the PIM. However, the builder of CIM level must produce models intended to be transformed to PIM, by using optionally several refinements on the base models and by respecting our construction rules of the CIM.

Approaches of related work do not provide clear and structured transformation rules. In most approaches, we do not find any description of the rules; the reader must deduce the rules from the case study. In the rest approaches there are subsections which contain just rules hints. Our approach describes clear transformation rules because each rule is presented by three ways: human language, ATL language and graphic presentation.

Our objective in this methodology is not just the transition from the CIM level to the PIM level, but our goal is to attain a rich PIM level that can be transformed to the PSM level represented by IFML. Indeed in future we like to insert new MDE modeling ideas found in (Osis & Asnina, 2014; Nazaruks &

*Figure 12. PIM meta-model: (I) use case meta-model, (II) state meta-model, (III) class meta-model, (IV) package meta-model.*

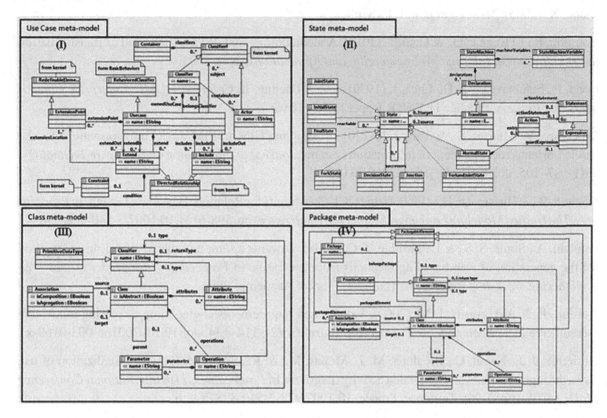

Osis, 2017a; Osis, 1969; Osis & Donins, 2017; Osis & Beghi, 1997; Osis, Gelfandbain, Markovich, & Novozilova, 1991; Osis & Donins, 2017; Nazaruks & Osis, 2017b) and by inserting ontologies principles (Laaz & Mbarki, 2019; Laaz & Mbarki, 2016).

## CONCLUSION AND FUTURE WORK

One of the major challenges in the software development process is the definition of an approach that allows moving from models that describe the working of the business to models which present the analysis and design of software.

Based on MDA, our approach provides an efficient solution to the problem of transformation of business models represented in CIM level to analysis and design models, modeled in PIM level (Rhazali et al., 2017b) up to platform model in PSM. The future work intended to improve the rules of construction of the CIM level and the rules of transformation to the PIM, then, to PSM, in order to implement these transformations to a tool. Indeed

# REFERENCES

Blanc, X. (2005). *MDA en action*. Ed. Eyrolles.

Bousetta, B., El Beggar, O., & Gadi, T. (2013). A methodology for CIM modeling and its transformation to PIM. *Journal of Information Engineering and Applications*, 2(3), 1–21.

Coad, P., Lefebvre, E., & De Luca, J. (1999). Java Modeling. In *Color With UML: Enterprise Components and Process*. Prentice Hall PTR Upper Saddle River.

De Castro, V., Marcos, E., & Vara, J. M. (2011). Applying CIM-to-PIM model transformations for the service-oriented development of information systems. *Journal of Information and Software Technology*, 53(1), 87–105. doi:10.1016/j.infsof.2010.09.002

Demuth, B., & Hussmann, H. (1999). Using OCL Constraints for Relational Database Design. In *Proceedings, The Unified Modeling Language, Second Int. Conference* (pp. 598-613). 10.1007/3-540-46852-8_42

Fatolahi, A., Somé, S. S., & Lethbridge, T. C. (2008). Towards a semi-automated model-driven method for the generation of web-based applications from use cases. In *Proceedings, 4th Model Driven Web Engineering Workshop* (pp 31-45). Toulouse, France: Academic Press.

Gordijn, J., & Akkermans, J. M. (2003). Value based requirements engineering: Exploring innovative e-commerce idea. *Requirements Engineering Journal*, 8(2), 114–134. doi:10.100700766-003-0169-x

Gutiérrez, J. J., Nebut, C., Escalona, M. J., Mejías, M., & Ramos, I. M. (2008). Visualization of use cases through automatically generated activity diagrams. In *Proceedings, 11th International Conference MoDELS'08*. (pp83-96). Toulouse, France. 10.1007/978-3-540-87875-9_6

Hahn, C., Dmytro, P., & Fischer, K. (2010). A model-driven approach to close the gap between business requirements and agent-based execution. In *Proceedings, 4th Workshop on Agent-based Technologies and applications for enterprise interoperability* (pp. 13–24). Toronto, Canada: Academic Press.

Hoffer, J. A., & George, J. J. A. (2004). Valacich, Modern System Analysis and Design. Prentice Hall.

Jouault, F., Allilaire, F., Bézivin, J., Kurtev, I., & Valduriez, P. (2006). ATL: a QVT-like transformation language. *Proceedings of the 21st ACM SIGPLAN symposium on Object-oriented programming systems, languages, and applications*. 10.1145/1176617.1176691

Kardoš, M., & Drozdová, M. (2010). Analytical method of CIM to PIM transformation in Model Driven Architecture (MDA). *Journal of Information and Organizational Sciences*, 34(1), 89–99.

Kherraf, S., Lefebvre, É., & Suryn, W. (2008). Transformation from CIM to PIM using patterns and Archetypes. In *Proceedings, 19th Australian Software Engineering Conference* (pp. 338–346). 10.1109/ASWEC.2008.4483222

Kleppe, A., Warmer, G. J., & Bast, W. (2003). *MDA Explained: The Model Driven Architecture: Practice and Promise*. Addison-Wesley.

Laaz, Naziha, & Mbarki. (2016). Integrating IFML models and owl ontologies to derive UIs web-Apps. *Information Technology for Organizations Development (IT4OD), 2016 International Conference on*, 1–6.

Laaz, N., & Mbarki, S. (2019). *OntoifML : Automatic generation of annotated web pages from IFML and ontologies using the MDA approach: A case study of an EMR management application.* Scopus.

Lefebvre, E. (2005). Building Platform-Independent Models with Business Archetypes and Patterns. *Proceedings of the Montreal Conference on eTechnologies, 127*.

Li, Q., & Chen, Y.-L. (2009). *Modeling and Analysis of Enterprise and Information Systems.* Springer Berlin Heidelberg. doi:10.1007/978-3-540-89556-5

Mazón, J., Pardillo, J., & Trujillo, J. (2007), A model-driven goal-oriented requirement engineering approach for data warehouses. In *Proceedings, Conference on Advances in Conceptual Modeling: Foundations and Applications, ER Workshops* (pp. 255–264). 10.1007/978-3-540-76292-8_31

Miles, R., & Hamilton, K. (2006). *Learning UML 2.0.* O'Reilly Media.

Mokrys, M. (2012). Possible transformation from Process Model to IS Design Model. In *Proceedings, 1th International Virtual Conference* (pp. 71–74). Academic Press.

Nazaruks, V., & Osis, J. (2017a). A Survey on Domain Knowledge Representation with Frames. In *Proceedings of the 12th International Conference on Evaluation of Novel Approaches to Software Engineering (ENASE 2017)* (pp. 346–354). Porto, Portugal: SCITEPRESS - Science and Technology Publications. 10.5220/0006388303460354

Nazaruks, V., & Osis, J. (2017b). Joint Usage of Frames and the Topological Functioning Model for Domain Knowledge Presentation and Analysis. In *Proceedings of the 12th International Conference on Evaluation of Novel Approaches to Software Engineering (ENASE 2017)* (pp. 379–390). Porto: SciTe-Press. 10.5220/0006388903790390

OMG-BPMN. (2011). *Business Process Model and Notation (BPMN)-Version 2.0.* OMG.

OMG-MDA. (2015). *Object Management Group Model Driven Architecture (MDA)MDA Guide rev. 2.0.* OMG.

OMG-QVT. (2015). *Meta Object Facility (MOF) 2.0 Query/View/Transformation Specification, V1.2.* OMG.

OMG-SoaML. (2012). *Service Oriented Architecture Modeling Language (SoaML) – Specification for the UML Profile and Metamodel for Services (UPMS).* OMG.

Osis, J. (1969). Topological Model of System Functioning (in Russian). *Automatics and Computer Science, J. of Academia of Sciences, (6),* 44–50.

Osis, J., & Asnina, E. (2014). Is modeling a treatment for the weakness of software engineering? In *Handbook of Research on Innovations in Systems and Software Engineering* (pp. 411–427). IGI Global.

Osis, J., & Beghi, L. (1997). Topological Modelling of Biological Systems. In D. A. Linkens & E. R. Carson (Eds.), *Proceedings of the third IFAC Symposium on Modelling and Control in Biomedical Systems (Including Biological Systems)* (pp. 337–342). Pergamon-Elsevier Science Publishing.

Osis, J., & Donins, U. (2017). *Topological UML Modeling: An Improved Approach for Domain Modeling and Software Development.* Elsevier. doi:10.1016/B978-0-12-805476-5.00005-8

Osis, J., Gelfandbain, J., Markovich, Z., & Novozilova, N. (1991). *Diagnostics on Graph Models (on the Examples of Aviation and Automobile Technology)*. Transport. (in Russian)

Rhazali, Y., El Hachimi, A., Chana, I., Lahmer, M., & Rhattoy, A. (2019). *Automate Model Transformation From CIM to PIM up to PSM in Model-Driven Architecture. Modern Principles, Practices, and Algorithms for Cloud Security*. Igi-Global., doi:10.4018/978-1-7998-1082-7.ch013

Rhazali, Y., Hadi, Y., Chana, I., Lahmer, M., & Rhattoy, A. (2018). A model transformation in model driven architecture from business model to web model. *IAENG International Journal of Computer Science, 45*(1), 104–117.

Rhazali, Y., Hadi, Y., & Mouloudi, A. (2014). Transformation Method CIM to PIM: From Business Processes Models Defined in BPMN to Use Case and Class Models Defined in UML, International Journal of Computer, Electrical, Automation. *Control and Information Engineering, 8*(8), 1453–1457.

Rhazali, Y., Hadi, Y., & Mouloudi, A. (2015a). A Methodology of Model Transformation in MDA: From CIM to PIM. *International Review on Computers and Software, 10*(11), 1186. Advance online publication. doi:10.15866/irecos.v10i12.8088

Rhazali, Y., Hadi, Y., & Mouloudi, A. (2015b). A Methodology for Transforming CIM to PIM through UML: From Business View to Information System View. *Proceedings, Third World Conference on Complex Systems*. 10.1109/ICoCS.2015.7483318

Rhazali, Y., Hadi, Y., & Mouloudi, A. (2015c). Disciplined Approach for Transformation CIM to PIM in MDA. In *Proceedings, 3rd International Conference on Model-Driven Engineering and Software Development* (pp. 312 – 320). DOI: 10.5220/0005245903120320

Rhazali, Y., Hadi, Y., & Mouloudi, A. (2015d). Transformation Approach CIM to PIM: From Business Processes Models to State Machine and Package Models. *Proceedings, the 1st International Conference on Open Source Software Computing*. 10.1109/OSSCOM.2015.7372686

Rhazali, Y., Hadi, Y., & Mouloudi, A. (2016a). CIM to PIM Transformation in MDA: From Service-Oriented Business Models to Web-Based Design Models. *International Journal of Software Engineering and Its Applications, 10*(4), 125–142. doi:10.14257/ijseia.2016.10.4.13

Rhazali, Y., Hadi, Y., & Mouloudi, A. (2016b). Model Transformation with ATL into MDA from CIM to PIM Structured through MVC. *Procedia Computer Science, 83*, 1096–1101. doi:10.1016/j.procs.2016.04.229

Rhazali, Y., Hadi, Y., & Mouloudi, A. (2016c). A Based-Rule Method to Transform CIM to PIM into MDA. *International Journal of Cloud Applications and Computing, 6*(2), 11–24. doi:10.4018/IJCAC.2016040102

Rhazali, Y., Hadi, Y., & Mouloudi, A. (2016d). A new methodology CIM to PIM transformation resulting from an analytical survey. In *Proceedings, 4th International Conference on Model-Driven Engineering and Software Development (MODELSWARD)* (pp. 266-273). 10.5220/0005690102660273

Rhazali, Y., Hadi, Y., & Mouloudi, A. (2017a). A model transformation in MDA from CIM to PIM represented by web models through SoaML and IFML. In *Colloquium in Information Science and Technology, CIST* (pp. 116-121). DOI: 10.1109/CIST.2016.7805027

Rhazali, Y., Hadi, Y., & Mouloudi, A. (2017b). *Transformation des modeles depuis CIM vers PIM dans MDA*. Noor Publishing.

Rodríguez, A., García-Rodríguez de Guzmán, I., Fernández Medina, E., & Piattini, M. (2007a). Towards CIM to PIM transformation: from Secure Business Processes defined in BPMN to Use-Cases, Business Process Management. *Proceedings of the 5th International Conference on Business Process Management*. 10.1007/978-3-540-75183-0_30

Rodríguez, A., García-Rodríguez de Guzmán, I., Fernández Medina, E., & Piattini, M. (2007b). CIM to PIM Transformation: A Reality. In IFIP International Federation for Information Processing, Volume 255, Research and Practical Issues of Enterprise Information Systems II. Boston: Springer.

Rodríguez, A., & García-Rodríguez de Guzmán, I. (2010). Semi-formal transformation of secure business processes into analysis class and use case models: An MDA approach. *Journal of Information and Software Technology, 52*(9), 945–971. doi:10.1016/j.infsof.2010.03.015

Roques, P. (2004). *UML in Practice: The Art of Modeling Software Systems Demonstrated through Worked Examples and Solutions*. Wiley.

Shin, M. E., & Ahn, G. J. (2000). UML-based representation of role-based access control. *Proceedings of the 9th IEEE International Workshops on Enabling Technologies: Infrastructure for Collaborative Enterprises*. 10.1109/ENABL.2000.883728

Wu, J. H., Shin, S. S., Chien, J. L., Chao, W. S., & Hsieh, M. C. (2007). An Extended MDA Method for User Interface Modeling and Transformation. *Proceedings of the 15th European Conference on Information Systems*, 1632.

Yu, E. (1997). Towards modeling and reasoning support for early-phase requirements engineering. *Proceedings of the 3rd IEEE International Symposium on Requirements Engineering*. 10.1109/ISRE.1997.566873

Zhang, W., Mei, H., Zhao, H., & Yang, J. (2005). Transformation from CIM to PIM: A Feature-Oriented Component-Based approach. In *Proceedings, MoDELS* (pp. 248-263). 10.1007/11557432_18

# Chapter 11
# Towards a Systematic Derivation of an Analysis Model From Business Process Models in the Context of Model–Driven Architecture

**Nourchène Elleuch Ben Ayed**
*Higher Colleges of Technology, UAE*

**Wiem Khlif**
*University of Sfax, Tunisia*

**Hanêne Ben-Abdellah**
*Higher Colleges of Technology, UAE*

## ABSTRACT

*The necessity of aligning an enterprise's information system (IS) model to its business process (BP) model is incontestable to the consistent analysis of the business performance. However, the main difficulty of establishing/maintaining BP-IS model alignment stems from the dissimilarities in the knowledge of the information system developers and the business process experts. To overcome these limits, the authors propose a model-driven architecture compliant methodology that helps software analysts to build an IS analysis model aligned to a given BP model. The proposed methodology allows mastering transformation from computation independent model to platform independent model. The CIM level expresses the BP, which is modelled through the standard BPMN and, at the PIM level represents the aligned IS model, which is generated as use case diagram, system sequence diagrams, and class diagram. CIM to PIM transformation accounts for the BP structural and semantic perspectives to generate an aligned IS model that respects the best-practice granularity level and the quality of UML diagrams.*

DOI: 10.4018/978-1-7998-3661-2.ch011

## INTRODUCTION

Each enterprise needs to have a clear vision of its Business Processes (BP) in order to increase both the quality of its products/services and its profits. A BP is described by a set of business models that encapsulate the core business logic in terms of strategies, tasks and policies. The activities of a business process manipulate and generate data that represent the daily transactions within the enterprise. To facilitate the management of this data and fulfill this need, an enterprise relies on an Information System (IS).

The IS development that supports the business activities and objectives of the enterprise has been an active niche of research in software engineering, in particular, under the scope of Process-Aware Information Systems (PAIS)(Dumas, Van Der Aalst, & Hofstede, 2005). The tight correlation between the IS and BP prompted researches (Qazi, Rehman, Saif Kazmi, N., & R., 2011)to consider deriving and extracting the PAIS requirements from business process models, rather than adopting classical requirements engineering techniques, such as brainstorming, interviews, surveys, focus group, etc... Indeed, a perfect alignment between the PAIS and BP models maximises the return on investment and is key to the success of an enterprise (Aversano, Grasso, & Tortorella, 2016).However, the BP and PAIS modelling are carried out separately and the transition between them is still manual.

Model Driven Architecture (MDA) (OMG, 2014)is recognized in the academic and industrial communities as a promising approach for moving the complexity of system development from programming to modeling. It overcomes several development challenges through the separation of concerns, emphasizing modeling, and using model transformations. According to OMG, an MDA-based development life cycle can start by the creation of a Computation Independent Model (CIM) from which a Platform Independent Model (PIM) can be derived. The CIM depicts the business model of th esystem without presenting its construction details, and the PIM describes the structure and behavior of the system independent of any platforms. Given a Platform Description Model (e.g., CORBA, RMI...), the PIM can be transformed into one or more Platform Specific Models (PSM) from which the code is generated. Since MDA does not prescribe specific guidelines for CIM construction, the latteris not considered in major MDA implementations.

Few works have considered the CIM construction and its derivation to PIM (Kriouile, Addamssiri, & Gadi, 2015). Most of the approaches have addressed the generation of IS functional user requirements, represented by UML use case diagrams, from the business specification. They differ in the use case diagram elements they derive: the use cases and their related actors (Rhazali, Hadi, & Mouloudi, 2016); use cases and their textual documentation (Siqueira & Silva, 2014); the relationships between use cases (Berrocal, García-Alonso, Vicente-Chicote, & Murillo, 2014). However, none of these approaches derives a use case diagram that is documented with system sequence diagrams—a common way to detail the abstract functional user requirements modeled by the use cases. In addition, they differ in the degree of automation of the proposed approach. Furthermore, few works have looked into the assessment (i.e., quality, precision, coverage) of the generated diagrams (Abrahão, Gravino, Insfrán, Scanniello, & Tortora, 2013)(Vachharajani, Vasant, & Jyoti, 2016).

This work aims to bridge the gap between organization's business processes and the information systems that support them by using model driven paradigms. It proposes a model-driven development methodology called DESTINY (moDel-driven procESs-aware requiremenTs engineering methodologY) that automatically generates a detailed UML analysis model from business process models to build a process-aware information system. Our approach accounts for the alignment between the BP and IS in order to provide a consistent way to generate an analysis model that fulfills the business needs and expectations. More specifically, we show in this paper how to generate a set of coherent UML diagrams, representing the PIM, from a BPMN model representing the CIM. The analysis model is composed of a documented UML use case diagram, a domain class, and system sequence diagrams, which can be later used by IT staff to build a PAIS. To do this, we first carry out pre-treatments on the BPMN model to allow for a quasi-automatic analysis model's generation. The pre-treatments consists on the use of the business context as a means to encapsulate semantic information pertinent to the business logic and organizational aspect, the definition of a set of linguistic syntactic patterns to annotate the BPMN model, and the use of Jacobson stereotypes to tag the performers of the BPMN model. Then, we tackled the differences in the semantics and granularity levels between UML and BPMNby defining a set of transformation rules that account for both the structural and informational perspectives of the BPMN model. The transformation from the CIM to the Use Case Diagram (UCD) is pattern-based; whereas the transformation from the CIM to the System Sequence Diagrams (SSD) and Class Diagram (CD) is a 1:n mapping. In fact, the 1:1 mapping between the BPMN meta-model and use case meta-model elements is not sufficient to preserve the semantics of neither the business domain nor the modeling languages. To overcome this deficiency, we identify and enumerate a set of patterns that respect the semantics of both the source and target languages as well as the semantics of the business domain. We defined BPMN model fragments representing user-system interactions based on the structural and semantic perspectives of BPMN models. It is important to mention that all the transformation rules produce UML diagrams that are compliant with OMG specification and can be used with standard UML tools.

We tested our methodology on a set of business process models from the literature. First, we examined the performance of the transformations experimentally through the calculation of recall and precision rates. These measures aim to compare the performance of our methodology to the human performance by analyzing the results given by our methodology to those supplied by the expert. For each element type of the class diagram (class, attribute, association, etc…), use case diagram (use case, actor, etc…), and system sequence diagram (object, message, parameters, etc…), the recall and precision rates are calculated. The high scores for both ratios mean that the generated analysis model covers the whole domain precisely in accordance with the experts' perspective. Second, we measured the quality of generated diagrams by using well-known quality metrics (Chidamber & Kemerer, 1994)(Lorenz & Kidd, 1994) (Abreu & Melo, 1996)(Briand, Devanbu, & Melo, 1997)(Harrison, Counsell, & Nithi, 1998)(Genero, Piattini, & Caleron, 2005)(Amstel, Lange, & Chaudron, 2007) and best-practice quality criteria(El-Attar & Miller, 2012). The results showed the conceptual soundness of the methodology. Overall, compared to existing works, our approach contributes to the BP-IS alignment and IS design domains by proposing semantic and structural transformation rules that aim to obtain the class diagram.

The remainder of this paper is structured as follows: Section 2 introduces the background of this research. Section 3analyses the main related work that deals with existing approaches for generating UML diagrams from BPMN Models. Section 4 presents a detailed description of DESTINY methodology. Section 5 illustrates our methodology through a case study and evaluates the quality of the generated diagrams by considering the recall and precision rates as well as quality measurement of the produced diagrams. Finally, in section 6, we summarize the presented work and outline its extensions.

## BACKGROUND

### Business Process Modelling

In Nowadays organization, the goals of any enterprise are accomplished through a set of coordinated activities called Business Processes (BP). The BPis considered as a first class business asset since it encapsulates the core business logic in terms of strategies, tasks, and policies. It constitutes the backbone of any organization. BPis defined as sets of related activities providing specific outputs for a customer or market. Many business process modelling techniques and languages exist in the literature such as UML(OMG, OMG Unified Modeling Language (OMG UML). formal/2015-03-01, 2015), Data Flow, and BPMN(Business Process Model and Notation)(OMG, BPMN. Business Process Model and Notation (BPMN). formal/2011-01-03, 2011).BPMN is widely used to model the BP in terms of nodes, gateways, lanes, and pools. The nodes represent the activities and/or tasks of the process. The gateways control the flow between the nodes by allowing parallel or alternative execution paths. The lanes organize the activities and gateways according to function or role. The pools categorize the lanes.

### Model Driven Architecture

Model Driven Architecture (MDA)(OMG, Model Driven Architecture (MDA)-MDA Guide rev. 2.0, 2014)is recognized in the academic and industrial communities as a promising approach for moving the complexity of system development from programming to modeling. It overcomes several development challenges through the separation of concerns, emphasizing modeling, and using model transformations. According to OMG, an MDA-based development life cyclecan start by the creation of a Computation Independent Model (CIM) from which a Platform Independent Model (PIM) can be derived. The CIM depicts the business model of thesystem without presenting its construction details, and the PIM describes the structure and behavior of the system independent of any platforms. Given a Platform Description Model (e.g., CORBA, RMI...), the PIM can be transformed into one or more Platform Specific Models (PSM) from which the code is generated. Since MDA does not prescribe specific guidelines for CIM construction, the latter is not considered in major MDA implementations.

All MDA models are orchestrated according to the four-layer meta-modeling architecture:

1. M0 (Reality Layer) contains a runtime representation of models. They can be either the business processes or the information system.
2. M1 (Model Layer) defines, with a concrete syntax, the conceptual and transformation models. It includes all MDA models (CIM, PIM, PSM, and Transformation Models).
3. M2 (Meta-Model Layer) contains the meta-models which serve as an abstract syntax to define the models of M1.
4. M3 (Meta-Meta-Model Layer) where all meta-models of the previous layer are conforming to MOF (OMG, OMG Document Number: formal/2015-06-05, 2015).

### Information System Model Quality

An IS model is an abstract and graphical representation of IS functionalities, structure, and/or behavior. It may be composed of many diagrams. The quality of IS model is a major determinant for the quality of the delivered IS. To assess, measure, and evaluate the quality of IS models, software metrics are used. Since UML constitutes the defacto language to analyze and design an IS, multiple authors have proposed many sets of software metrics in the literature (Chidamber & Kemerer, 1994), (Lorenz & Kidd, 1994), (Abreu & Melo, 1996), (Briand, Devanbu, & Melo, 1997), (Harrison, Counsell, & Nithi, 1998), (Genero, Piattini, & Caleron, 2005) to assess the quality of UML diagrams. For instance, (Chidamber & Kemerer, 1994) propose a suite of metrics to measure internal design quality characteristics of a class diagram, e.g., complexity, coupling, cohesion. (Amstel, Lange, & Chaudron, 2007)propose four approaches to analyze the quality of sequence diagrams that are formal model checking techniques to identify ambiguities, metrics to measure coverage properties, a series of checks to identify syntactic defects, and common interactive behavior patterns. (El-Attar & Miller, 2012) propose a set of anti-patterns to evaluate the validity of the use cases' construction and composition.

## RELATED WORK

In this section, we summarize existing works on aligning BPM to IS model.

In (Kardoš & Drozdová, 2010), the authors describe a method of transformation among CIM and PIM level of MDA. In the case of CIM level, business process models are represented by DFD and the textual description of processes while in case of PIM level, UML models, especially use cases are utilized. Using these models, a BP transformation into UML diagrams is discussed.

In (Rhazali, Hadi, & Mouloudi, 2016), the authors transform any activity in a BPMN model into a use case despite of the different levels of granularity of the modeling languages. In addition, they use ATL to specify CIM-to-PIM transformations that structure the produced class diagram according to the model view controller (MVC) architectural style pattern.

In (Siqueira & Silva, 2014), based on model-driven engineering concepts, this study proposes a semi-automatic transformation from an enterprise model to a use case model. The enterprise model is used as a source of information about the stakeholder requirements and domain knowledge, while the use case model is used as software requirements model. This study presents the source and target metamodels, and transformation rules.

Similar to our approach, (Berrocal, García-Alonso, Vicente-Chicote, & Murillo, 2014) present a pattern-based and model-driven approach for deriving IT system functional models from annotated business models. First, they explain how to annotate the BPMN business models with information useful for deriving the functionalities. Then, they introduce a set of patterns aimed to help identifying the functionalities and the relationships existing among them from the annotated BP model.

In (Suchenia, et al., 2017), the authors describe how to transform a BPMN model into a UML sequence diagram. As the UML model natively supports modeling time issues, the proposed solution can be used for validating such issues by business analysts, software engineers, etc.

(Cruz, Machado, & Santos, 2012) study mainly the usage and data persistence in BPMN 2.0. They propose a set of rules to generate a data model from the business process model. Then, the data model may be used as a starting artifact in the IS software development process.

The approach presented by (De la Vara, Fortuna, Sanchez Diaz, Lima Werner, & Borges, 2009) proposes guidelines to extract the domain class diagram from an extended version of BPMN 1.2. Furthermore, the authors focus on annotated data objects to allow data dependency representation and data instance differentiation as well as SQL queries generation. (Meyer, Pufahl, Fahland, & Weske, 2013)

(Przybyłek, 2014)combine techniques from both the fields of Business Process Engineering and Requirements Engineering and define a Business-oriented approach to requirements elicitation. This approach enables traceability between business processes and system requirements.

Table 1 summarizes the most relevant works related to CIM-to-PIM transformations, which we compared to answer the following research questions: What languages are used to define source and target models? Is the semantics of the modeling languages considered in the transformation? Is the transformation completeness considered? Is the transformation formalized? Overall, the above works related to BP-IS models in (Rhazali, Hadi, & Mouloudi, 2016)(Meyer, Pufahl, Fahland, & Weske, 2013)are purely structure-based; They ignore the remaining aspects of a BP, which do affect the performance of a BP. For example, the type of semantic relations between classes is not captured, like the composition, heritage, etc. Furthermore, sequence system diagram is crucial since it is a popular notation to specify scenarios of the processing of operations as its clear graphical layout gives an immediate intuitive understanding of the system behavior. Our proposed method combines both aspects in order to obtain a use case diagram, sequence system diagrams and class diagram that cover the structural and semantic aspect. To do so, we use the business context concept.

*Table 1. Synthesis of related works.*

| Related Works | (Rhazali, Hadi, & Mouloudi, 2016) | (Kriouile, Addamssiri, & Gadi, 2015) | (Berrocal, Garcıa-Alonso, Vicente-Chicote, & Murillo, 2014) | (Siqueira & Silva, 2014) | (Kardoš & Drozdová, 2010) | (Suchenia, et al., 2017) | (De la Vara, Fortuna, Sanchez Diaz, Lima Werner, & Borges, 2009) |
|---|---|---|---|---|---|---|---|
| CIM model | BPMN | BPMN UCD | BPMN | Enterprise Model | DFD | BPMN | BPMN |
| PIM Model | UCD, CD, PD& SD | CD & SD | UCD | UCD | UCD, AD, SSD& CD | AD | CD |
| Mapping | 1:1 | 1:1 | n:m | n:m | 1:1 | 1:1 | 1:1 |
| Transformation Completeness | No | No | Yes | No | No | No | No |
| Transformation Formalization | ATL | QVT | ATL | QVT | No | No | No |

## DESTINY Methodology

DESTINY (a moDel-driven procESs-aware requiremenTs engineering methodologY) is an MDA-compliant method that derives the IS functional requirements from a given BP model. Our approach accounts for the alignment between the BP and IS in order to provide a consistent way to generate an analysis model that fulfills the business needs and expectations.In its initial edition, DESTINY generates from a given BPM described in the BPMN standard a use case diagram without any behavioral description of its use cases. In this book chapter, we refine the initial generation rules of DESTINY to produce more precise use case diagram. In addition, we extend it with a set of transformation rules to generate the documentation of each use case with a system sequence diagram that describes its normal scenario. Furthermore, we propose a set of transformation rules to generate the corresponding sequence and class diagrams.

More specifically, we propose the concept of *business context* as a means to define the IS scope by delimiting the boundaries of the BP model. In addition, we refine the use case size and scope by proposing a new fragmentation method of the BP model. We define new rules to generate coherent system sequence and use case diagrams from the BP model. Finally, we complement DESTINY by a set of transformation rules to generate the class diagram.

Towards this end, we designed DESTINY according to the MDA four-layer meta-modeling architecture. The DESTINY method for CIM-to-PIM transformation operates at the meta-model level. The BPMN model constitutes the CIM and the use case, system sequence, and class diagrams represent the generated PIM.

*Figure 1. DESTINY conceptual process for BP-driven IS analysis model generation.*

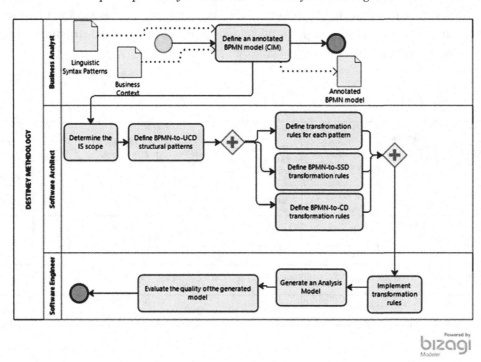

As illustrated in Figure 1, the DESTINY approach operates in four phases:

1.  The pre-processing phase during which the *Business Analyst* first prepares the input BPMN model to insure that it is well-structured and well-defined. This requirement guides the transformations and alleviates the complexity of the identification of use cases, messages in the sequence diagrams and methods in the class diagram. To handle this requirement, on the one hand, we rely on the BPMN syntactic meta-modeling rules; on the other hand, we have defined a set of linguistic syntactic patterns to annotate the BPMN model as well as a business context to enhance it with semantic information related to the business logic and organizational aspect. In addition, we use the Jacobson stereotypes to tag the performers of the BPMN model.

2. The transformation-definition phase during which the *Software Architect* defines the CIM-t to-PIM transformations. DESTINY adopts two types of transformations: pattern-based for the CIM to the Use Case Diagram (UCD) transformation, and 1-n mapping for the CIM to the System Sequence Diagrams (SSD) and class diagram transformation.

3. The transformation-implementation phase during which the *Software Engineer* formalizes /implements the transformation rules, which provides for the automated generation of the PIM model (a use case diagram, a set of system sequence diagrams and a class diagram).

4. The evaluation phase during which the quality analyst calculates the metric values to assess the quality of generated model as well as computes the recall and precision to evaluate the performance of the transformation rules.

## Linguistic Patterns and Business Context

We defined a set of Linguistic Syntax Patterns (LSP) and a business context to guide the business expert in the annotation of the business processes. The LSPs are used to define the description field of a BPMN element (LSP1) and label the BPMN tasks (LSP2), while the business context is used to complement the BPMN elements with semantic information related to their functional and organizational perspectives.

The following section summarizes the syntax of the linguistic patterns. We mean by *BusinessObject* any entity that describes the business logic. The *NominalGroup* is a set of pre/post-modifiers, which are centered around a *HeadWord* that constitutes the *BusinessObject*. The pre-modifiers (respectively post-modifiers) can be a noun, an adjective, or an ed/ing-participle (respectively, a noun, an adjective, or adverb). The *VerbalGroup* indicates the relationship type between *BusinessObjects*. The *Quantifier* gives an idea of the multiplicity. We note that the expression between brackets is optional.

**LSP1:** BusinessObject+VerbalGroup+[Quantifier] +BusinessObject
**LSP2:** ActionVerb I CommunicationVerb + BusinessObject I NominalGroup + [[to ReceiverName] I [from SenderName]]

Besides applying the linguistic patterns, the software analyst prepares the BPMN model by annotating it with its *businesscontext,* which encapsulates the functional and organizational perspectives. The functional perspective represents the process elements being performed which are *Activities* (simple tasks or complex sub-processes). The organizational perspective represents *where* and *by whom* process elements are performed, which is mainly reflected by the *Pool* and *Lane* concepts.

The business context of BPMN activities contains the following information:

1. *Actor ID is a* unique identifier of the actor responsible for performing the activity.
2. *Actor Description* indicates the relationships between the activity and the involved actors.
3. *Lane ID* is the unique identifier of the lane, which contains the activity.
4. *Upstream and downstream ID* is the unique identifier of the activity on which this activity directly depends.
5. *Extended attributes* describe the activity properties. Each attribute can be a pure value or a complex one representing a business entity. This distinction is extracted from their description.
6. *Activity Description* indicates the relationships between the business entities and/or the activity's extended complex attributes. The relationships' semantic follows the first linguistic pattern (LSP1).

7.   *Resources* are the data objects/stores that are required by an activity to fulfill its goal. Each resource has a name, extended attributes, and description, which have the same semantic than the activity's extended attributes and description.

In addition, we augment the lane/Pool with the following information to define its business context:

1.   *Lane/Pool ID* is the unique identifier of the lane/pool.
2.   *Lane Description* (respectively *Pool Description*) indicates the semantic relation between the lane (respectively pool) and the tasks/data object or stores (respectively the lanes or tasks/data object or stores) that belong to it.
3.   *Extended attributes* describe the lane/pool properties and have the same semantics of activities.
4.   *Actor_Description_Lane*indicates its type that can be either an entity or a performer. The performer is classified into two categories: the business worker who is internal to the organization, and the business actor who is external to the BP.

## Transformation Definition Strategy

Once the BPMN model is prepared, the *Software Architect* can start the definition of the CIM-to-PIM transformations: The transformation from the CIM to the Use Case Diagram (UCD) is pattern-based; whereas the transformation from the CIM to the System Sequence Diagrams (SSD) and Class Diagram (CD) is a 1:n mapping. In fact, the 1:1 mapping between the CIM and use case meta-model elements is not sufficient to preserve the semantics of neither the business domain nor the modeling languages. To overcome this deficiency, the software architect should identify and enumerate a set of patterns that respect the semantics of both the source and target languages as well as the semantics of the business domain. To do so, we defined BPMN model fragments representing user-system interactions based on the structural and semantic perspectives of BPMN models. Recall that a use case represents a set of actions that the system(s) should or can perform in collaboration with one or more business workers or business actors, and it should provide some observable result to them. A business worker represents an abstraction of a human that acts within the business to realize a service, while a business actor represents a role played by some person or system external to the modeled business and interacting with the business. As such, the activities performed by the business actors are out of the information system scope, and are ignored in the identification of BPMN-to-UCD patterns.

Structurally, we defined a *pattern* as a fragment $F$ in a BPMN process model $P$, that is a connected, directed sub-graph of $P$ starting at one activity and ending at another activity such that $F$ contains the maximum number of activities between either two gateways, a start node and a gateway, or a gateway and an end node. We exclude the gateways from $F$ because they do not represent a system activity.

In terms of the business domain semantics, a pattern may include special business event labels (*i.e.,* send, receive, acknowledge, etc.), activity's business objects (*i.e. request, document, invoice, etc*), and lane/pool labels (*i.e. department, agent, unit, etc*). These labels, along with their synonyms, guide the DESTINY transformations, as we will illustrate in the following sections.

Since each use case is obsolete without a textual or graphical description, we associated with each BPMN-to-UCD pattern a set of BPMN-to-SSD rules to model the use case behavior, which is 1:n mapping between the concepts of BPMN and sequence diagram. To end this purpose, we lightly extended the BPMN meta-model to handle the business context. We added attributes and two new classes that are*Description* and *ExtendedAttributes*. For each BPMN element, we associate a *Description* that adds a specific information to BPMN elements in terms of the relationships between them. The *Extended Attributes* class specifies the properties of each BPMN element. The business context is also used to generate the class diagram.

## Source and Target Meta-Models

To simplify the definition of the transformation rules, we extended the source meta-model, i.e. BPMN (OMG, BPMN. Business Process Model and Notation (BPMN). formal/2011-01-03, 2011), by adding six classes and some attributes in the original classes, as well as the target metamodel, i.e. UML use case meta-model (OMG, OMG Unified Modeling Language (OMG UML). formal/2015-03-01, 2015)by adding two classes and four attributes. These additions are lightweight extensions; they do not modify the semantics nor the syntax of the standard BPMN and UML; they merely are used to facilitate the navigation of a BPMN model. The meta-classes marked in gray constitute the elements that we added (See Figure. 2).

*Figure 2. Extract of the used BPMN and Use Case Metamodel*

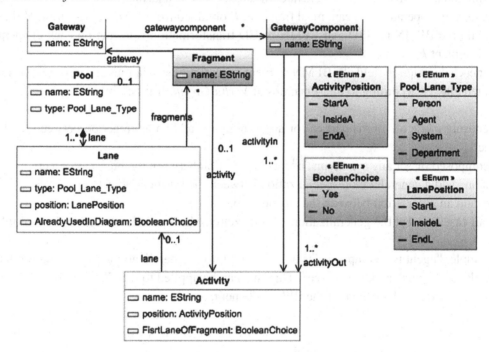

The six added classes to the BPMN metamodel, are: "fragment" to classify the activities located between the gateways; "GatewayComponent" to identify the entry and the exit activities; "Pool_Lane_Type" to identify the type of the pool/lane and in case the type is "department", a naming rule will be applied; "LanePosition" to identify the primary actor of the fragment; and"ActivityPosition" to identify the name of the first activity in the fragment; and "BooleanChoice" for the added attributes in the classes "Activity".

The base meta-classes are *UseCase, Actor, Extend* and *Include*. Each Use Case might include or extend other Use Cases. We added the meta-class *"InheritanceRelation"* to facilitate the addition of an inheritance relationship between actors representing Lanes and actors representing Pools. We added also the meta-class *"ActorUCRelation"* to identify whether the relationship between the actor and the use case is a one-way or two-way relation.

## Transformation Rules

The analysis model is typically composed of the Use Case Diagram (UCD), a set of System Sequence Diagrams (SSD), and the domain Class Diagram (CD). Each SSD details/documents a use case by describing the behavior through the actors involved in the interaction, the system, and the operations.

The first step of IS analysis model generation consists of the definition of the IS scope. We assume that the business analyst has respected the linguistic syntactic patterns, defined the business context and annotated each pool/lane, representing the performers, by business actor or business worker tags. All activities performed by a business actor are out of scope. They will be ignored in the generation of the use case diagram. However, some of them will be used to derive the system sequence and class diagrams.

The second step of IS FUR generation consists of the elaboration of a set of transformation rules from an annotated BPMN model to generate an aligned UML analysis model. The BPMN-to-UCD transformation rule operates on a canonical fragment *F* obtained from the decomposition of the BPMN model; While the BPMN-to-SSD and BPMN-to-CD transformation rules act on each element of the canonical fragment *F*.

**R1.** For each description field of a BPMN element, extract the associations and multiplicities between the generated classes according to the semantics of *VerbalGroup*. If it is:

1. "is entirely made of" or "is part of" or any synonyms, add an aggregation between the business objects;
2. "is composed of" or any synonyms, add a composition between the business objects;
3. "Is a/an",add a generalization/specialization between the business objects;
4. Else, add an association between the business objects;
5. For all cases, except the generalization/ specialization, the quantifiers indicate the multiplicity.

For example, "agent is an employee"is transformed into a generalization/specialization relation between the classes "agent" and "employee". This rule can be applied to the CD.

**R2.** For each extended attribute of the BPMN element, add:

1. either an attribute to the class corresponding to the BPMN element, if its extended attribute is a noun that merely represents a pure value;
2. or a new class with the name *extendedAttributeLabel*, and an association between the two generated classes by applying **R1**, if the extended attribute is a complex noun.

Figure 3 illustrates the class diagram corresponding to the annotated data object in terms of extended attributes and description. The description indicates a relationship between the *Purchase order* data object and one of its extended attributes: *orderLine(Each Purchase order is composed of order lines)*. The extended attributes of purchase order data object are *orderNumber*, *deliveryDate*, *orderDate*, and

*Figure 3. R2 illustration.*

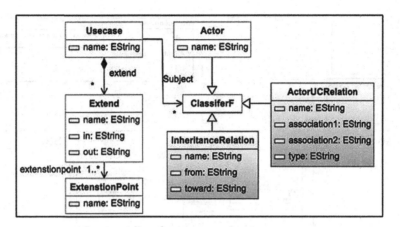

*OrderLine.* All of them are transformed into class attributes, except the *orderLine,* which is transformed into a class.

**R3.** For each Pool/lane:

1. *UC* and *SSD:*
   a. For each lane whose label is a synonym to "person", "agent", "System"transform it to the corresponding actor that has the lane name.
   b. For each pool/lane whose label is a metonymy of "department", "unit", "division" or "management", transform it to the actor where the name represents the concatenation of the pool/lane name and the word "Agent".
2. *CD:*
   a. Transform it to a package and class.
      i. The package name depends on the participant type which is a performer or an entity. If the participant is a perfomer, then the package name is a concatenation of the lane name and the word "space" or "area". Else, the package name is a concatenation of the lane name and the word "management".
      ii. The class name corresponds to the pool/lane name. The class has as many attributes to the extended attributes of the corresponding pool/lane (See **R2**). The class can have many associations depending on the pool/lane description (See **R1**).
   b. For each lane, the package corresponding to the pool includes the package corresponding to the lane's pool (See Figure 4).

**R4.** For each pool:
**R4.1.** If the pool includes only business workers, then (See Figure 4):

1. *UCD:* transform the pool to a box that determines the system perimeter. The system name will be the concatenation of the pool name and the word "System". Then, add an actor corresponding to each business workers; apply Rule 3.1 to rename it.

*Figure 4. R4 illustration.*

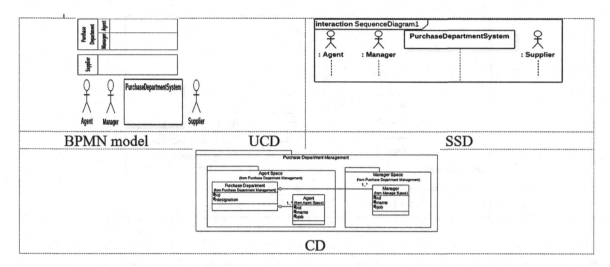

2. *SSD:* add lifelines and activation zones representing the system as well as all actors, whichare generated by Rule 4.1.a.

**R4.2.** If the pool contains only business actors then transform each business actor to:

1. UC: a secondary actor. Apply Rule 3.1.b to rename the actor.
2. SSD: a lifeline and an activation zone for the instance of the secondary actor generated by Rule 4.2.a.

In both cases, transform the business actors and workers of each pool to a package and class, which are generated by Rule 3.2. We note that the pool containing only business actors is addressed in neither UCD nor SSD. That has been tied to the fact that the pool represents another business, which is out of the system scope.

**R5.** For each service task performed in the lane, we apply **R1** and **R2**. In addition, if the service task label respects the renaming pattern:

**R5.1.** « Action verb + BusinessObject » then:

1. *SSD:*
   a. add a new synchronous message from the actor corresponding to the lane, which is already generated by R4.2, to the system. The message name is *ActionVerb()*.
   b. add a response message from the system pointing back to the original lifeline. The response label is a concatenation between the *BusinessObject*and the passive voice of the *ActionVerb*. Furthermore, the business context of the activity or its associated data object will indicate more details about the method signature. In fact, we add all extendedattributes as parameters of the method *ActionVerb()* (See Figure 5).
2. *CD:* add a class with a name *BusinessObject,* and a new method with a name *ActionVerb()* (See Figure 5).

*Figure 5. Rule 5.1 illustration*

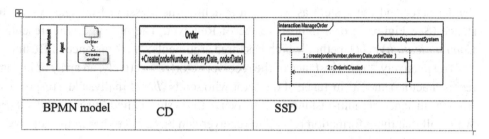

**R5.2.** « Action verb + NominalGroup», then

1. If the pre/post-modifier is a noun that merely represents a pure value:
   a. *SSD:* Apply Rule 5.1.1. onthe *HeadWord* of the *NomnialGroup*,and add parameters to the identified method A*ctionVerb()* as follows: since the pre/post-modifier represents a pure value, add it as a parameter (See Figure 6).
   b. *CD:* Apply R5.1.2 on the *Headword* and add an attribute to the class corresponding to the *HeadWord*. The attribute has the same name of pre/post-modifier. The attribute is also considered as a parameter of the method *ActionVerb()* (See Figure 6);
2. If the pre/post-modifier is a complex noun (an entity) then:
   a. SSD: Add the extended attributes of the entity, as parameters of the method *ActionVerb()* and apply Rule 5.1.1.
   b. CD: Apply R5.1.2 on the *Headword* and add a new class with the name pre/post-modifier, and an association between the two generated classes (*HeadWord* and pre/post-modifier).

**R6.** For each script/send/receive task, we apply R1 and R2. In addition, when the task name follows this pattern:

*Figure 6. R5.2 illustration (pure value)*

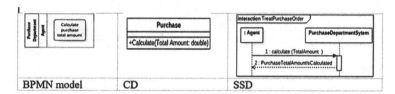

**R6.1.** «CommunicationVerb+ BusinessObject + [[to ReceiverName] | [from SenderName]]»:

1. SSD:
   a. Add two lifelines representing respectively an instance of the system, and the sender, if they are not already created. If the receiver noun is singular (respectively plural), also add a lifeline representing an instance of the receiver (respectively, a multi-instance of the receiver).

b.  If the task type is *"send task"* then, add a asynchronous message between the instance of Sender actor and the system as well as a synchronous message from the system to an instance (See Figure 7) or a multi-instance of Receiver. The message is represented by the *CommunicationVerb()* method which has three arguments: *"bo"* instance of BusinessObject, *"r"* (respectively, *"r[]"*) instance of the receiver actor(respectively, an array of instance of all receiver actors) and *"s"* instance of the actor who sends *"bo"*. Finally, add a response message from the instance or multi-instance of Receiver to the system called *BusinessObjectIsReceived*. We recall that the information related to receiver can be found either in the activity business context or label.

c.  If the task type is *"receive task"* then add an asynchronous message called *send()* from the sender to the system and a synchronous message called *send()* from the system to the instance of Receiver. The method has three arguments: *"bo"* instance of *BusinessObject,* *"r"* instance of the receiver actor, and *"s"* instance of the sender actor. Add a response message from the instance of Receiver to the system called *BusinessObjectIsReceived*.

2. *CD:*

a.  New Classes with name *BusinessObject, senderName and ReceiverName,* if they were not yet created;

b.  New attribute *email* or *phoneNumber* in the Class with a name *SenderName and ReceiverName*;

c.  Method with a name *CommunicationVerb()* to the class corresponding to the business object.

    i.  In the case of Send Task, add three parameters to *CommunicationVerb()* method: *"bo"* instance of *BusinessObject* and *"r"* instance of class which receives *"bo"* and *"s"* instance of class which sends *"bo"*.

    ii.  In the case of receive Task, substitute the *CommunicationVerb()* method with a boolean method *"isReceived()"*.

    iii.  In both cases, add a dependency between the *BusinessObject* class and *Sender* and *Receiver* classes, when there is not an association between them.

*Figure 7. R6.1 illustration (case of send task, one receiver)*

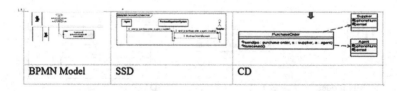

**R6.2.** « CommunicationVerb+ NominalGroup+ [[to ReceiverName] | [from SenderName]]»

1.  If the pre/post-modifier is a noun that simply represents a pure value

a.  *SSD:* add parameters to the identified method *ComminucationVerb()*

b.  *CD:* apply R6.1.2 on the *HeadWord* and add an attribute to the class corresponding to the *HeadWord*. The attribute has the same name of pre/post-modifier.

2.  If the pre/post-modifier is a complex noun (an entity) then:

a. *SSD:* Add the extended attributes of the entity as parameters of the method *ComminucationVerb( ).*

b. *CD:* apply R6.1.2 on the *HeadWord,* add a new class with the name *pre/post-modifier,* and an association between the two generated classes (*HeadWord* and *pre/post-modifier).*

We note when this expression [[to ReceiverName] | [from SenderName] ] is omitted, then we can extract this semantic information from the description field of the activity element according to **R1.**

**R7.** Transform to a class each data store/object, identified by a name, if it is not already generated. The class name has the same data object name. Then, apply **R1** and **R2.**

**R8.** For each gateway in the BPMN model *P,* add

1. SSD:

   a. An interaction operator *Par* with a combined frame if the gateway is parallel. Each *Par* frame has as many operands to the outgoing flows of the parallel gateway.

   b. An *Alt* frame if the gateway is an exclusive or inclusive one. Each *Alt* frame has as many operands to the outgoing flows of the exclusive/inclusive gateway. We note that when an outgoing flow contains only an end node, it will not be calculated. If the number of operands is equal one, then change *Alt* frame to *Opt* frame. In all cases, the outgoing message label is used to define the guard of each operand.

2. CD: If the exclusive gateway label refers to an existing business object or a new one, then apply the *State* design pattern on it with: the *Context* class name corresponds to the business object name; the *StateAbstract* class name is a concatenation of the "*Business object*" name and "*State*" Word; and the super class has as many sub classes as the number of outgoing gateway alternatives.

**R9.** For each fragment *F* in the BPMN model *P:*

**R9.1.** If the fragment is composed of a set of activities that belong to the same lane, then: 1) create a use case *UC_F* with the name of the first activity *SA* of *F,* and 2) add a two-way association between the actor whose Lane contains the activity *SA* and *UC_F*

**R9.2.** If one of these activities (A) is defined in another lane and its name *is* "receive x" (or any synonyms of receive), then add a one-way from *UC_F* to the Actor (as a secondary actor) whose Lane contains the activity A, else, add a two-way association between *UC_F* and the Actor (as a secondary actor) whose Lane includes the activity *A* (see Figure 8).

**R10.** Each fragment *F* composed of only one activity labeled with:

**R10.1.** "Send x" or "Send x to y", its corresponding use case *UC_F* will be named "Generate x";

*Figure 8. Rule 9.2 illustration*

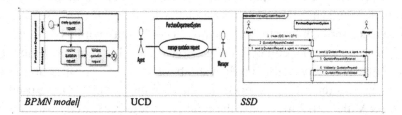

**R10.2.** "Receive x" or "Receive x from y",its corresponding use case *UC_F* will be named "Manage x"; add Y as a primary actor, and transform the lane including the activity into secondary actor. The association between the use case and the secondary actor is unidirectional. We note that the information related to the sender can be found in the business context of the activity.

**R11.** If the first activity *SA* of a fragment *F* is labeled "Create x" then the corresponding use case *UC_F* will be named "Manage x".

**R12.**For each gateway between two fragments *PF* (entry) and *NF* (exit) such that the activities of both fragments are in the same lane, add an <<extend>> relationship from the use case *UC_NF* to the use case *UC_ PF*; and add an extension named as the first activity's name of the second fragment (NF. SA) in the use case of the entry fragment PF (Figure 9).

*Figure 9. Rule 12 illustration*

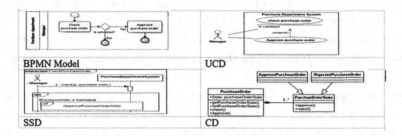

**R13.** For each gateway between two fragments,*PF* (entry) and *NF* (exit), such that the activities of both fragments are in different lanes and:

**R13.1:** if the name of the first activity of *NF* is *"send X to Y"* and *Y* is not transformed yet into an actor, then: *1)* create a secondary actor *Y*; *2)* apply **R10.1** to rename the use case *UC_NF*; *3)* add one-way association from *UC_NF* to the secondary actor.

**R13.2:** if *NF* contains just one activity that is named *"receive X"* or *"send X"*, then delete the use case *UC_NF* as well as its associations, and its corresponding *SSD*. Add a two-way association between *UC_PF* and the actor corresponding to *NF*.

Rules R9, R10, R11, R12, and R13 call and apply R5, R6 and/or R7 on each activity of the fragment F to generate the SSD and UC.The succession between those activities determines the message order.

## Quality Evaluation of the Generated Diagram

As aforementioned, the construction of high quality use cases model has an impact on the development of the IS. We evaluated the syntactic and semantic quality of the generated use case model. The syntactic quality is evaluated through the study of the model conformity with its meta-model: Because our transformation process is meta-model-based, the generated model is conforming to the UML use case meta-model. The semantic quality deals with the validity of use cases' construction and composition as well as the completeness of the use cases regarding the domain. To this end, we used the anti-patterns defined by (El-Attar & Miller, 2012)to evaluate the validity of the use cases' construction and composition. These anti-patterns require the examination of the use case diagram and its textual description in order to look for any inconsistency or redundancy. In terms of the completeness of the set of transformations, our preliminary syntax-based investigation of the possible structures of the fragment patterns shows that the proposed set is complete. For more rigor, we are formalizing the completeness proof.

In addition, we examined the performance of the transformations experimentally through the calculation of recall and precision rates as well as the F-measure. These measures aim to compare the performance of our method to the human performance by analyzing the results given by our method to those supplied by the expert. We recall that the precision is the ratio of real elements generated by our transformation that were identiðed by the expert. It indicates how accurate the transformation rules are in the generation of UCD (usecase, actor, etc) (See. Formula 1). The recall is the ratio that indicates the capacity of our transformations to return all elements speciðed by the expert. High scores for both ratios show that the transformations return both an accurate UCD (high precision), and the majority of all relevant accurate UCD elements (high recall). It means that the generated UCD covers the whole domain precisely in accordance to the experts' perspective (See. Formula 2). To have the harmonic mean of recall and precision, we have used the F-measure. F-measure has a parameter that sets the trade off between recall and precision. The standard F-measure is F1, which gives equal importance to recall and precision (See. Formula 3). We calculate these rates according the following equations:

$$\text{Precision} = TP/(TP+FP) \tag{1}$$

$$\text{Recall} = TP/(TP+FN) \tag{2}$$

$$F1 = (2*recall*precision)/(recall + precision) \tag{3}$$

Where:

- True positive (TP) is the number of existing real elements generated by our transformation;
- False Positive (FP) is the number of not existing real elements generated by our transformation;
- False Negative (FN) is the number of existing real elements not generated by our transformation.

## CASE STUDY

To illustrate the application of our transformation rules, we use an example of the "Purchase department process" model as shown in Figure 10.

First, we annotated the BPMN model according to the renaming linguistic patterns and we tagged each pool/lane with the stereotypes: business actor and business worker. The *"Manager"* and *"Agent"* are considered as business worker, while the supplier and customer are business actors. So that, the activities of Supplier pool are out of the system scope and are ignored in the generation of the UCD.

Secondly, we decomposed the BPM on fragments: F1, F2, F3, F4 and F5 (Figure 10). F1 is decomposed into three sub-Fragments: F1.1, F1.2 and F1.3. The first one F1.1 *"Receive purchase request"*, the second one F1.2 contains the sub-process *"Quotations",* and the third one F1.3 contains two activities which are *"Create purchase order"* and *"Approve purchase order"*. F2, F3 and F4 are expressed respectively by "*Send purchase order*", "*Receive invoice*" and "*Receive item*" activities. F5 includes "*Process payment*" and "*Notify payment*" activities.

Figure 11 shows the use case diagram which is generated as follows: First, by applying **R4.1.a** we transform the pool "*Purchase Department*" that contains the business workers to a box "*PurchaseDepartmentSystem*"; Each pool's lane that represents the business workers "*Agent*" and "*Manager*" is transformed into an actor. The business actor "*Supplier*" and "customer" are transformed into a secondary actor by applying **R4.2.a.** For each generated business (respectively actor) worker, a lifeline and an activation zone is added based on **R4.1.b** (respectively **R4.2.b).**

Second, by applying **R3.2**, we generate "*Purchase Department*", "*Agent*", "*Manager*", "*Supplier*" and "*Customer*"classes. Since **R3.2** uses R1, we createan aggregation with multiplicity between the "*Purchase Department*" and "*Agent*" (respectively, "*Manager*") classes. The rule **R3.2** calls **R2**, which adds the attributes to all classes (Figure11).

The use cases are derived from the fragments. The fragment F1.1 includes only one activity which is "*ReceivePurchaseRequest*". By applying **R10.2**, we generate a "*ManagePurchaseRequest*" use case and we add an association stereotyped "*secondary*" between the use case and the actor "*Agent*". The business context of the "*ReceivePurchaseRequest*" reveals that the customer is its performer. So that, **R10.2** generates also a primary actor "*Customer*" and adds an association between the generated use case and the actor "*Customer*". To describe the behaviour of this use case (See Figure10), we first apply **R4.1.b** that creates a lifeline representing the system "*PurchaseDepartment System*". Then, we call **R4** to generate respectively a lifeline for the actor and the corresponding class. Finally, we invoke **R6.1.1.c** that transforms the task "*Receive purchase request*" to an asynchronous message called *send( )* from the "*customer*" to the "*PurchaseDepartmentSystem*" as well as a synchronous message with the same name from the "*PurchaseDepartmentSystem*" to the "*Agent*" which represents the receiver instance. The method has three arguments: "*pr*" instance of the business object "*purchaseRequest*", "*a*" instance of the agent who receives "*pr*" and "*c*" instance of the customer who sends "*pr*". Then, the rule adds a response message *PurchaseRequestIsReceived* from the instance of Receiver "*Agent*" to the system. The application of **R6.1.2** adds new classes with names "*PurchaseOrderRequest*", "*Customer*" representing the sender and "*Agent*" expressing the "*Receiver*",a new attribute *email* or *phoneNumber* in the Sender and Receiver classes; and a new method with a name "*IsReceive*" to the "*PurchaseOrderRequest*" class.

The fragment F1.2 includes the "*Quotation*" sub process whichis composed of a set of sequential tasks "*Request quotations*", "*Receive quotations*" and "*Select supplier*". By using **R9.1**, we create the use case "*Request Quotations*" that encapsulates the fragment behaviour and adds a two-way association between the actor "*Agent*" whose lane contains the activity and the use case. Then, we generate two lifelines by applying **R4.1.b** corresponding to the actor "Agent" and the system (See Figure11).

By applying **R5** and **R6** on each activity of the fragment, we first generate a synchronous message from the agent to the system, called "*request()*" that has as parameters the extended attributes of the quotation. Then, the activity "*Receive quotations*" introduces a new lifeline which is a multi-instance of suppliers. This is inferred from the business context of the activity. This leads to update the generated use case by adding a secondary "*Supplier*" and an association between the use case "*Request Quotations*" and the "*Supplier*".By applying **R6.1.1.c**, we add an asynchronous message *send( )* from the multi-instance supplier lifeline to the system and a synchronous message called *send( )* from the system to the receiver instance: "*agent*". Both of them have the same arguments: "*q*" instance of the business object "*quotation*", "*a*" instance of the agent who receives "*q*", and "*s*" instance of the supplier who sends "*q*". We add a response message from the "*Agent*" to the system called *QuotationIsReceived*. Finally, the transformation of the activity *"Select supplier"* adds a new lifeline *"s"* instance of *"Supplier"* and a message called *"select(s: Supplier)"* from the agent to the system. The business context of the activity reveals that the supplier must be notified by the agent decision. This leads to add another asynchronous message from the system to the supplier.

Third, we apply **R5.1** on the following service tasks: *"Request quotations"*, and *"Select supplier"*.

This rule generates one class *"Quotation"*. The *"Supplier"* class is already generated by **R4**.*request()* to *"Quotation"* class; and *select()* to *"Supplier"* class.

The fragment F1.3 includes two activities, which are *"Create purchase order"* and *"Approve purchase order"*.**R11**generates the corresponding use case *"ManagePurchaseOrder"*. The fragment F2 (respectively F3 and F4) includes just one send activity (respectively, receive activity), which is transformed into a use case by applying **R10.1** (respectively **R10.2**).However, each fragment is preceded by a gateway, which calls to apply **R13.2.** The latter deletes the generated use cases and includes their behaviour to the use case corresponding to the previous fragment F1.3. The system sequence diagram that describes the behaviour of the use case *"Manage Purchase Order"*is obtained by applying **R5,R6** and **R8**. The first activities of the fragment generate two synchronous messages that are *"create (orderNumber, de-liveryDate, orderDate)"* and *"approve(p:purchaseOrder)"*. We note that the parameters are extracted from the business context ofthe corresponding activities. The exclusive gateway calls to apply **R8.1.b.** The latter generates an Opt frame called *"PurchaseOrderApproval"* that contains 1) a sequence of messages derived by applying R5.1 on the activity "Send Purchase Order", 2) a *Par frame* that contains two operands. Each one of them models the behaviour of *"Receive Invoice"* and *"Receive Item"*. This is obtained by applying **R8.1.a** and **R6.1.**

We apply **R5.1** and weadd the methods:*create()*, *approve()*to *"Purchase order"* class.By applying**R7**, the transformation of all data objects enhances the existing classes by calling **R1** and**R2**, which add at-tributes, classes and associations. For example, we have added the attributes *deliveryDate, orderDate, orderNumber* to *"Purchase order"* class because these extended attributes are pure values. Furthermore, the extended attribute *"orderLine"*is a complex entity. According to **R2,** we extract a new class *"order-Line"*, and a composition relation between the latter and *"Purchase order"*.

The fragment F5 generates the use case *"Process Payment"* based on **R9.1**. Its SSD and the corre-sponding class are obtained by applying **R5.1.**

We examined the performance of the transformations experimentally through the calculation of re-call and precision rates. These measures aim to compare the performance of our method to the human performance by analyzing the results given by our method to those supplied by the expert.

For each element type of the class diagram CD (class, attribute, association, etc), UCD (use case, actor, etc) and SSD (object, message, parameters, etc), the recall and precision rates are calculated (See Table 2).

The class diagram is experimentally evaluated as follows:

$$\text{Precision(CD)} = 57/(57+10)=0.85 \qquad (4)$$

$$\text{Recall(CD)}= 57/(57+8) =0.87 \qquad (5)$$

We evaluate then the use case diagram:

*Figure 10. Purchase order Business Process in BPMN*

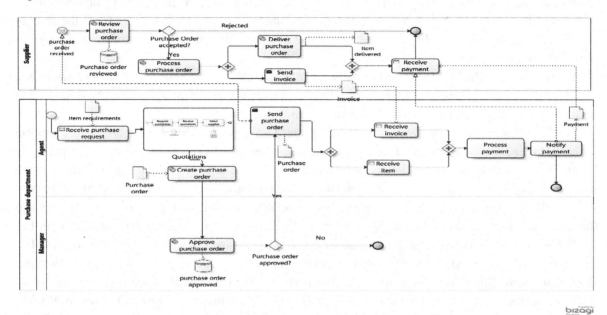

$$Precision(UC) = 16/18=0.89 \tag{6}$$

$$Recall(UC)=16/17=0.94 \tag{7}$$

For the system sequence diagrams, we calculate the average ($AVG_{SSDs}$) of recall and precision rates.

$$AVG_{SSDs}(Precision)=0.75 \tag{8}$$

$$AVG_{SSDs}(Recall)=0.79 \tag{9}$$

The high scores for both ratios mean that the generated class diagram, use case diagram and sequence diagrams cover the whole domain precisely in accordance with the experts' perspective (See Figure 12). We can deduce that the performance of our method approaches the human performance.

## CONCLUSION

This paper proposed a transformation-based approach to generate use case, system sequence and class diagrams from business process models. It provides for the generation of IS entities and their relations that are aligned to the business logic. Compared to existing works, our approach has the merit of accounting for both the semantic and structural aspects of the business process model. To do so, we proposed to define the business process context expressing the relation semantics and type.

*Figure 11. The generated analysis model for the purchase order business process model.*

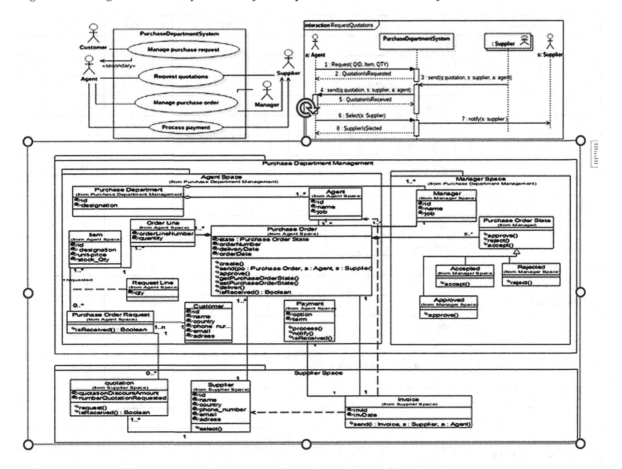

We have illustrated the application of the proposed approach by using a "Purchase Order Business Process" case study. Despite the encouraging results identified by the recall and precision ratio, the ambiguous nature of the activity names (being written in natural language) may produce incorrect similarities particularly when reasoning word by word. To mitigate this threat, we will use machine learning concepts in future work. In the other hand, when the requirements are unclear and/or incomplete e.g. *missing activity, missing output data group, missing control structures,* the quality of the derived IS model is not guaranteed in terms of dependencies between elements.

Ongoing work focuses on 1) conducting an experimental evaluation to assess the coverage and precision of all generated use case, class and system sequence diagrams; and 2) enhancing the transformations in order to cover interaction in the design sequence diagram and component diagram.

*Table 2. Recall & Precision Calculation.*

| Diagram | Elements | TP | FP | FN |
|---|---|---|---|---|
| Class Diagram | Package | 0 | 3 | 0 |
| | Class | 12 | 1 | 1 |
| | Attributes and methods | 31 | 0 | 3 |
| | Association | 10 | 2 | 3 |
| | Composition | 2 | 0 | 0 |
| | Aggregation | 1 | 1 | 0 |
| | G/S | 1 | 1 | 0 |
| | Dependency | 0 | 2 | 1 |
| Total | | 57 | 10 | 8 |
| Use Case Diagram | System perimeter | 1 | 0 | 0 |
| | Use case | 4 | 0 | 0 |
| | Primary Actor | 2 | 0 | 0 |
| | Secondary Actor | 2 | 0 | 0 |
| | Extend | 0 | 0 | 0 |
| | Include | 0 | 0 | 1 |
| | G/S | 0 | 0 | 0 |
| | Association between actors and use cases | 7 | 2 | 0 |
| Total | | 16 | 2 | 1 |
| System Sequence Diagram of Use case Request Quotation | Participants | 3 | 0 | 0 |
| | System | 1 | 0 | 0 |
| | Messages | 4 | 1 | 2 |
| | Parameters | 0 | 10 | 0 |
| Total | | 8 | 11 | 2 |

*Figure 12. The elaborated analysis model*

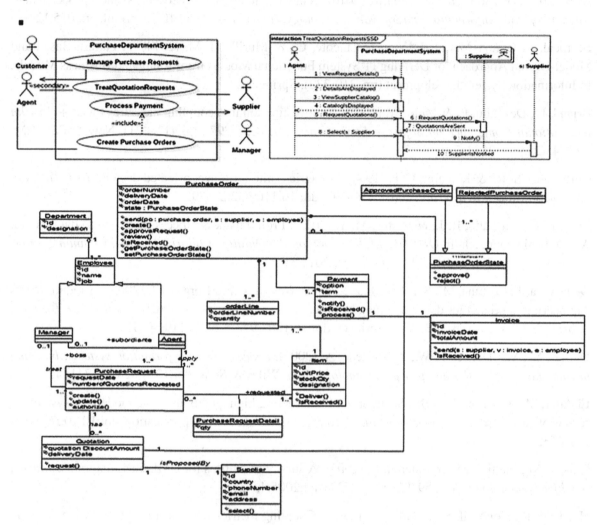

# REFERENCES

Abrahão, S., Gravino, C., Insfrán, E., Scanniello, G., & Tortora, G. (2013). Assessing the effectiveness of sequence diagrams in the comprehension of functional requirements. *IEEE Transactions on Software Engineering*, *39*(3), 327–342. doi:10.1109/TSE.2012.27

Abreu, F. B., & Melo, W. (1996). Evaluating the impact of object-oriented design on software quality. *3rd International Symposium on Software Metrics: From Measurement to Empirical Results*. 10.1109/METRIC.1996.492446

Amstel, M. F., F.J., L. C., & Chaudron, M. R. (2007). Four Automated Approaches to Analyze the Quality of UML Sequence Diagrams. *31st Annual International Computer Software and Applications Conference (COMPSAC 2007)*. 10.1109/COMPSAC.2007.119

Aversano, L., Grasso, C., & Tortorella, M. (2016). Managing the alignment between business processes and software systems. *Information and Software Technology, 7*(3), 171–188. doi:10.1016/j.infsof.2015.12.009

Berrocal, J., Garcıa-Alonso, J., Vicente-Chicote, C., & Murillo, J. M. (2014). A Pattern-Based and Model-Driven Approach for Deriving IT System Functional Models from Annotated Business Models. In Information System Development (pp. 319-332). Springer.

Briand, L., Devanbu, P., & Melo, W. (1997). An investigation into coupling measures for c++. In *19th International Conference on Software Engineering, ser. ICSE '97* (pp. 412–421). New York: ACM. 10.1145/253228.253367

Chidamber, S. R., & Kemerer, C. F. (1994). A metrics suite for object oriented design. *IEEE Transactions on Software Engineering, 20*(6), 476–493. doi:10.1109/32.295895

Cruz, E. F., Machado, R. J., & Santos, M. Y. (2012). From business process modeling to data model: A systematic approach. In *QUATIC'12, 8th Conf. on the Quality of Information and Communications Technology*, (pp. 205-210). 10.1109/QUATIC.2012.31

De la Vara, J., Fortuna, M., Sanchez Diaz, J., Lima Werner, C., & Borges, M. (2009). A requirements engineering approach for data modelling of process-aware information systems. In *BIIS'09, Business Information Systems* (pp. 133–144). Springer. doi:10.1007/978-3-642-01190-0_12

Dumas, M., Van Der Aalst, W., & Hofstede, A. (2005). *Process-aware information systems: bridging people and software through process technology.* John Wiley & Sons. doi:10.1002/0471741442

El-Attar, M., & Miller, J. (2012, September). Constructing high quality use case models: A systematic review of current practices. *Requirements Engineering.* Advance online publication. doi:10.100700766-011-0135-y

Genero, M., Piattini, M., & Caleron, C. (2005). A survey of metrics for UML class diagrams. *Journal of Object Technology, 4*(9), 59–92. doi:10.5381/jot.2005.4.9.a1

Harrison, R., Counsell, S., & Nithi, R. (1998). Coupling metrics for object oriented design. In *Fifth International Software Metrics Symposium. Metrics (Cat. No.98TB100262)*, (pp. 150-157). 10.1109/METRIC.1998.731240

Kardoš, M., & Drozdová, M. (2010). Analytical Method of CIM to PIM Transformation in Model Driven Architecture (MDA). *JIOS*, 89-99.

Kriouile, A., Addamssiri, N., & Gadi, T. (2015). An MDA Method for Automatic Transformation of Models from CIM to PIM. *American Journal of Software Engineering and Applications*, 1-14.

Lorenz, M., & Kidd, J. (1994). *Object-oriented Software Metrics: A Practical Guide.* Prentice-Hall, Inc.

Meyer, A., Pufahl, L., Fahland, D., & Weske, M. (2013). Modeling and Enacting Complex Data Dependencies in Business Processes. In *PM'13, 11th proceedings of Inter Conference* (pp. 171-186). Lecture Notes in Computer Science.

OMG. (2011). *BPMN. Business Process Model and Notation (BPMN). formal/2011-01-03.* Object Management Group.

OMG. (2014). *Model Driven Architecture (MDA)-MDA Guide rev. 2.0*. Object Management Group.

OMG. (2015). *OMG Meta Object Facility (MOF)*. Core Specification.

OMG. (2015). *OMG Unified Modeling Language (OMG UML). formal/2015-03-01*. OMG.

Przybyłek, A. (2014). A Business-Oriented Approach to Requirements Elicitation. *9th Inter. Conf. on Evaluation of Novel Approaches to Software Engineering (ENASE 2104)*.

Qazi, A., Rehman, M., & Saif Kazmi, M. S., N., R., & R., M. (2011). Enhanced model driven architecture software development life cycle with synchronized and consistent mapping. In *International Conference on Computer Communication and Management (ICCCM 2011)* (pp. 395-399). Singapore: IACSIT Press.

Reichert, M., & Weber, B. (2012). *Enabling flexibility in process-aware information systems: Challenges, methods, technologies*. Springer. doi:10.1007/978-3-642-30409-5

Rhazali, Y., Hadi, Y., & Mouloudi, A. (2016). A Based-Rule Method to Transform CIM to PIM into MDA. *International Journal of Cloud Applications and Computing, 6*(2), 11–24. doi:10.4018/IJCAC.2016040102

Siqueira, F. L., & Silva, P. S. (2014). Transforming an entreprise model into a use case model in business process systems. *Journal of Systems and Software, 96*, 152–171. doi:10.1016/j.jss.2014.06.007

Suchenia, A., Kluza, K., Jobczyk, K., Wisniewski, P., Wypych, M., & Ligeza, A. (2017). *Supporting BPMN Process Models with UML Sequence Diagrams for Representing Time Issues and Testing Models*. ICAISC. doi:10.1007/978-3-319-59060-8_53

Vachharajani, V., Vasant, S., & Jyoti, P. (2016). Feasibility Study of Proposed Architecture for Automatic Assessment of Use-Case Diagram. In *Proceedings of International Conference on ICT for Sustainable Development. Advances in Intelligent Systems and Computing* (pp. 97-104). Singapore: Springer.

# Chapter 12
# A Disciplined Method to Generate UML2 Communication Diagrams Automatically From the Business Value Model

**Nassim Kharmoum**

https://orcid.org/0000-0001-9105-1062

*Faculty of Sciences, Mohammed V University in Rabat, Morocco*

**Sara Retal**

*Faculty of Sciences, Mohammed V University in Rabat, Morocco*

**Yassine Rhazali**

https://orcid.org/0000-0003-1488-0216

*ISIC Research Team of ESTM, LMMI Laboratory of ENSAM, Moulay Ismail University of Meknes, Morocco*

**Soumia Ziti**

https://orcid.org/0000-0002-5357-9170

*Faculty of Sciences, Mohammed V University in Rabat, Morocco*

**Fouzia Omary**

*Faculty of Sciences, Mohammed V University in Rabat, Morocco*

## ABSTRACT

*One of the most crucial objectives of enterprises is bridging the gap between its businesses and information systems. In this vein, many approaches have emerged among them: the Model-Driven Architecture (MDA). This approach is an initiative of the Object Management Group (OMG) and considers the model as the central entity in the software systems development process offering many techniques allowing transformation between models. In addition, the OMG introduces for the MDA three abstraction levels,*

DOI: 10.4018/978-1-7998-3661-2.ch012

*namely Computation Independent Model (CIM), Platform Independent Model (PIM), and Platform-Specific Model (PSM). This contribution proposes a disciplined method that ensures an automatic alignment between businesses and information system models at CIM and PIM levels. The source model consists of E3value model, which is the Business Value model, whereas, the generated model represents UML2 Communication diagrams, that are the UML's behavior and interaction models. The transformation is achieved automatically using meta-models and ATLAS Transformation Language and proved to be effective.*

## INTRODUCTION

Currently, the majority of enterprises of different sizes are seeking to align their business with the information system (Doumi et al., 2013). For that reason, new approaches appear, in the midst of them, the Model-Driven Architecture (MDA), which is introduced by the Object Management Group (OMG). This approach is proposed at the beginning of the 21st century (OMG-MDA, 2014) and focuses on the models in the development process of any software system (Bézivin and Briot, 2004). These models aim to facilitate the development process (Maatouguiet al., 2016) based on a variety of means; among them, the models' transformation task. Therefore, theOMG offers three abstraction levels for the MDA approach, namely Computation Independent Model (CIM), PlatformIndependent Model (PIM), and Platform Specific Model (PSM).

Figure 1 illustrates the main model generations between the different MDA approach levels; the CIM level isregarded as the higher abstraction level. Models at this level do not provide any technical consideration or systemimplementation. The PIM level presents the average abstraction level and also displays some models not containingany implementation and technical specifications. However, the PSM level is considered as the lowest abstraction levelbecause it is related to the platform execution. The Code is not considered a level in MDA approach; it is just a purposeand a goal expected from the different transformations, and it is just a translation of the PSM in a textual formalism(Rhazali et al., 2015).

Most researchers put much focus on the PIM to PSM transformation because these levels have multiple common features (Kharmoum et al., 2016). Still, the transformation from CIM to PIM is rarely considered because of the nature of these two distinct levels representing higher abstraction models, such as requirements models (dos Santos Soareset al., 2011; Rhazali et al., 2018). In this paper, the authors emphasize on the models' construction and the transformation from the CIM level to the PIM level. The CIM level is represented by the E3value model, while the generated PIM level model is rendered by UML2 (i.e., Unified Modeling Language 2) Communication diagrams (OMG-UML, 2017), which are called UML Collaboration diagrams in the UML1.x. Consequently, The E3value source model presents the Business Value Model which is the value-based requirements engineering (Gordijn and Akkermans, 2003; GARRIGO'S et al.,2012); it unifies the e-business models notations from a value aspect, by revealing how the economic value is created, exchanged and consumed within a network of actors (Gordijn and Akkermans, 2001). Thus, the Business Value Model makes models more comprehensible by «Business Executives» and «Business Value Analysts». The UML's behavior and interaction model that is automatically generated will be represented by the second version of the UML Communication diagrams. The

*Figure 1. Overview of the MDA transformation*
*(Blanc and Salvatori, 2011).*

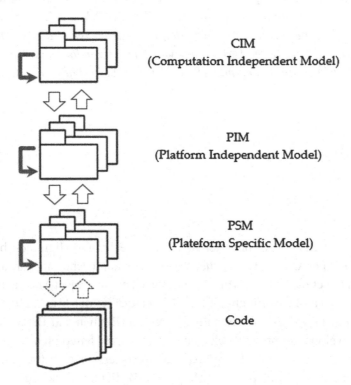

authors choose the UML model, as it is the modeling standard of OMG (OMG-UML, 2017; Skersys et al., 2018), where, the diagrams are usually created by «Developers» and «Systems Engineer» to describe and understand the system behavior. This model designs in a standard way the messages' interaction between different objects and system actors, taking into consideration the order of various messages. Hence, this method will allow stakeholders who do not know about UML2 conception to generate their UML2 Communication diagrams.

Furthermore, models are generated automatically using ATLAS Transformation Language (ATL) (Jouault et al.,2006). This latter uses OMG standards; such as Object Constraint Language (OCL)(OMG-OCL, 2014), Meta-Object Facility (MOF) (OMG-QVT, 2016) and XML Metadata Interchange (XMI) (OMG-XMI, 2015), which allow the development acceleration of the e-business information system process by reducing effort and time; and in consequence, decreasing the cost to guarantee competitiveness in the software industry.

The remainder of this paper is organized as follows. Section 2 shows the related work that generates UML2 Communication diagrams. Section 3 explains the proposal, reveals the source and the target meta-models, and describes all transformation rules used in this method. A case study illustrates this work, which is shown in Section 4. Section 5 provides analysis and discussion of all the obtained results. In the last section, the authors conclude this contribution and introduce their future work.

## RELATED WORK

This section highlights the different research conducted over the last decade that generates the PIM level models from CIM level models following the MDA approach, particularly the studies generating the UML's diagrams in the PIM level. Until now, few methods focus on this generation, but the authors succeeded in detecting some work proposed in this regard.

First, De Castro et al. (2011) apply a semi-automatic CIM-to-PIM model transformation for the service-oriented development of information systems. They build their CIM level, using the Business Process Model and Notation(BPMN) (OMG-BPMN, 2011) and the E3value model to display the business view. Whereas, the generated PIM level is structured by the UML Use Case diagrams (i.e., Use Case diagram & extended Use Case diagram) and the Activity diagrams (i.e., Process model Service & Service composition model) using ATL.

Schuster and Motal (2009) propose an enhancement of the Business Modeling Ontology (BMO) (Osterwalder and Pigneur, 2002), by employing their own mapping rules to transform the E3value notation into an REA-stereotyped (McCarthy, 1982) UML Class diagram.

Besides, Bouzidi et al. (2017) suggest a semi-automatic approach to resolve the problem of the alignment in the MDA approach between Business Process Model at the CIM level and UML2 Use Case diagrams and notations at the PIM level. The proposed approach uses the ATL to specify the transformations rules. Additionally, they generate textual descriptions for each complicated Use Case by using the Acceleo template principle (Brambilla et al., 2012).

Rhazali et al. (2015) design the business process in the CIM level through BPMN using the model of collaboration diagram and the model of the business process. PIM level models are obtained via a semi-automatic transformation using ATL and containing the three types of view. The Use Case diagram presents the functional view; the dynamic view is given by the State diagram, whereas the Class and package diagrams show the static view.

In Bousetta et al. (2013), the researchers deliver the CIM level with the functional, behavioral, and static views of the system based on the BPM. They start by defining the BPM high level, and then, they detail them to have the BPM low level. Moreover, they generate the UML models, namely the Class diagram, the Domain diagram, and the Sequence diagram of external systems behavior developing their PIM level.

Kherraf et al. (2008) construct their CIM level based on the business process and requirements using patterns and archetypes. The business process is presented by the Activity and the Use Case diagrams, while the detailed Activity diagram shows the system requirement. Moreover, the PIM level consists of the Class and Components diagrams.

Furthermore, Zhou et al. (2017) apply an affinity analysis based on the transformation from UML Use Case diagram which is considered in this study in the CIM level to the PIM level models, which are the UML state chart diagram, the UML class diagram as well as the UML Sequence diagram. The researchers implement their algorithm with Natural Language Processing (NLP).

Finally, a Domain Specific Language (DSL) (Hoyos et al., 2013) is used by Miranda et al. (2017) for automating the generation of UML's Use Case diagrams, Class diagrams, and Sequence diagrams, from textual Use Cases, based on LUCAM tool.

After studying the above work, the authors notice, on the one hand, that in the source model creation method, most of the research is based on one or more models in a graphical representation in the CIM level. On the other hand, to generate the UML diagrams in the PIM level, they execute several transformation stages, which are based on a non-automatic way using human language. However, in other studies, the researchers automatically generate the models using their algorithm or a transformation language.

Therefore, unlike the mentioned studies approaches, in this paper, the authors propose a new method that automatically generates UML2's Communication diagrams from a value-based requirements model with a graphical representation. Thus, the approach proposed in this article is considered as a new contribution to the automatic transformations from the CIM level to the PIM level and is a part of the enhancements of the related studies. The following section will take a closer look at the proposed method.

## PROPOSAL METHOD

## Approach Overview and Methodology

In this section, the authors will shed more light on their disciplined proposed method. The purpose is to construct and transform the CIM level automatically to the PIM level for an e-business information system, according to the MDA approach. They stress the fact that this proposal is the continuation of their work: (Kharmoum et al., 2018, 2019a,b,c,d).

In this method, the authors generate the UML2 Communication diagrams from the E3value model respecting the MDA approach (See Figure 2). The source E3value model shows the business value model in the CIM level, while the target diagram presents the behavior and interaction model at the PIM level. The transformation is executed automatically via ATL; the objective is to produce an e-business system containing the correct E3value model and UML2 Communication diagrams. This method's models are used as the backbone of the system's understanding, and facilitating communication between technical and e-business stakeholders such as «*Developers*», «*Systems Engineer*», «*Business executives*» and «*Business Analysts*». Furthermore, the authors intend to complete the development process of their e-business information system by generating other models in the lower abstraction level PSM.

*Figure 2. Proposed method.*

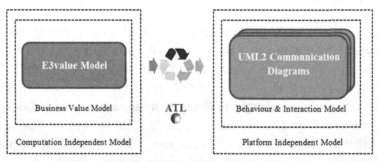

Model Driven Architecture approach

To develop this method according to the MDA approach, the authors follow the steps depicted in Figure 3 that illustrates the transformation process. The first step is the definition of the meta-models; the purpose is to create and generate correct models and to offer automated model transformations (Rodríguez

*Figure 3. Transformation process of our proposed method*

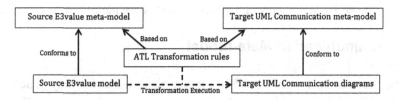

et al., 2010). Therefore, the source meta-model is the E3value meta-model, describing the structure of the Business Value Model on the higher abstraction level. After that stage, the authors determine the target UML2 Communication meta-model describing the structure of the generated UML's behavior and interaction model in the average abstraction level. They specify the constraints during the source model construction. Then, they explain the set of mapping rules implemented via ATL to generate their target models automatically from the source model.

## Source E3value Meta-model

This part describes the structure of the E3value source meta-model that any created E3value model must conformto it. The objective is to build a correct model explaining the way with which the economic value is created, exchanged, and consumed in a network of several actors. The E3value meta-model presents a novel meta-model (See Figure 4(a)) consists of the following elements, which are mostly inspired since Gordijn et al. (2006); Gordijn and Akkermans(2018):

- «*Actor*»: is an independent economic entity that can be a consumer or a producer of the economic value. Two types of actors are distinguished, «*Elementary Actor*» that represents an individual actor and «*Market Segment*»that represents a set of actors that have common properties;
- «*Value Object*»: is the economic value exchanged by the «*Actors*», it can be a service, a good, an experience, or money;
- «*Value Port*»: is an «*Actor*» that provides «*Value Objects*» via «*Port Out*» or requests them via «*Port In*». The «*Port Out*» and «*Port In*» are used to extend «*Value Port*»;
- «*Value interface*»: assembles several «*Value Ports*» and shows economic reciprocity;
- «*Value Exchange*»: connects two «*Value Ports*» to exchange potential «*Value Objects*». For the meta-model, the «*Value Exchange*» can have type «*request*» or «*response*»;
- «*Value Activity*»: presents one or more operational activities that an «*Actor*» can process to yield a profit;
- «*Value Transaction*»: groups a set of «*Value Exchanges*» that participate in the same economic transaction;
- «*Dependency Element*»: various kinds exist, «*Element AND*» and «*Element OR*»; these two elements acceptas behavior: «*Join*», «*Fork*» or both «*Fork_Join*». The authors define «*Stimulus Element*» that can be «*StimulusStart*» or «*Stimulus End*»;
- «*Connect Element*»: connects all «*Dependency Elements*» between them or with «*Value interface*» by specifyingthe source and target for each «*Connect Element*»;
- «*Comment*»: is used to add a comment or a note for all the elements mentioned above;

- Finally, to rearrange the E3value meta-model, all elements are grouped in *«E3valueModel»* which are all of the type *«E3valueObject»* and all its instances are identified by the *«Name»* attribute.

## Target UML2 Communication Meta-model

This part describesthe construction of the UML2 target meta-model that any generated diagram must conform to it. The UML2 Communication diagrams are generated automatically from the E3value source model and explain the system behavior, by designing in a standard way the messages' interaction between different objects and system actors, taking into consideration the order of different messages. The UML2 Communication meta-model (See Figure 4(b)) elements are extracted from (OMG-UML, 2017) and are proposed by OMG:

- *«Actor»*: it represents a participant in a communication diagram, in this case, it represents an independent economic entity that maybe the producer or consumer of the proposed economic values;
- *«Lifeline»*: represents an interacting entity in a communication diagram; in this case, it can be a subsystem or aservice that can exchange *«Messages»*;
- *«Message»*: defines a particular communication between *«Actors»* or *«Lifeline»*. It can have *«MessageParameter»*and/or *«MessageReturn»*. And every *«Message»* has a type that expresses its behavior. It can be recursive ornot, and has the attribute *«sequenceNumber»* to take into consideration the order of different messages;
- *«CommunicationLink»*: represents the elements which link other UML2 Communication diagram elementsmore precisely *«Actors»* or *«Lifelines»*;
- *«Frame»*: groups UML2 Communication diagram elements belonging the same sub-function system;
- Finally, to rearrange the UML2 Communication meta-model, all elements are grouped in *«UMLCommunicationModel»*, which are all of the type *«CommunicationObject»*, and all its instances are identified by the *«Name»* attribute.

## Source E3value Model Construction Rules

Regarding the source model creation, the only considered constraint is to respect the meta-model that is previously explained and illustrated in Figure 4(a) to create a correct source E3value model.

## Transformation Rules From E3value Model to UML2 Communication Diagrams

To transform the Business Value Model automatically to the UML's behavior and interaction model, and after presenting all E3value and UML2 Communication meta-models elements, this part lists the E3value model transformation rules toward the UML2 Communication diagrams based on their meta-models.

To produce a well-detailed e-business information system, the authors will not generate all communications in a single diagram. However, they will generate different communication diagrams based on the sub-functions system. In this proposal, the *«Value Activity»* element is considered as a sub-function for each e-business system. Therefore, this part details the transformation rules proposed in this method for each generated UML2 Communication diagram via simple diagrams. Table 1 generally lists the set

*Figure 4. Proposed Meta-models: (a)E3value meta-model, (b) UML2 Communication diagrams meta-model.*

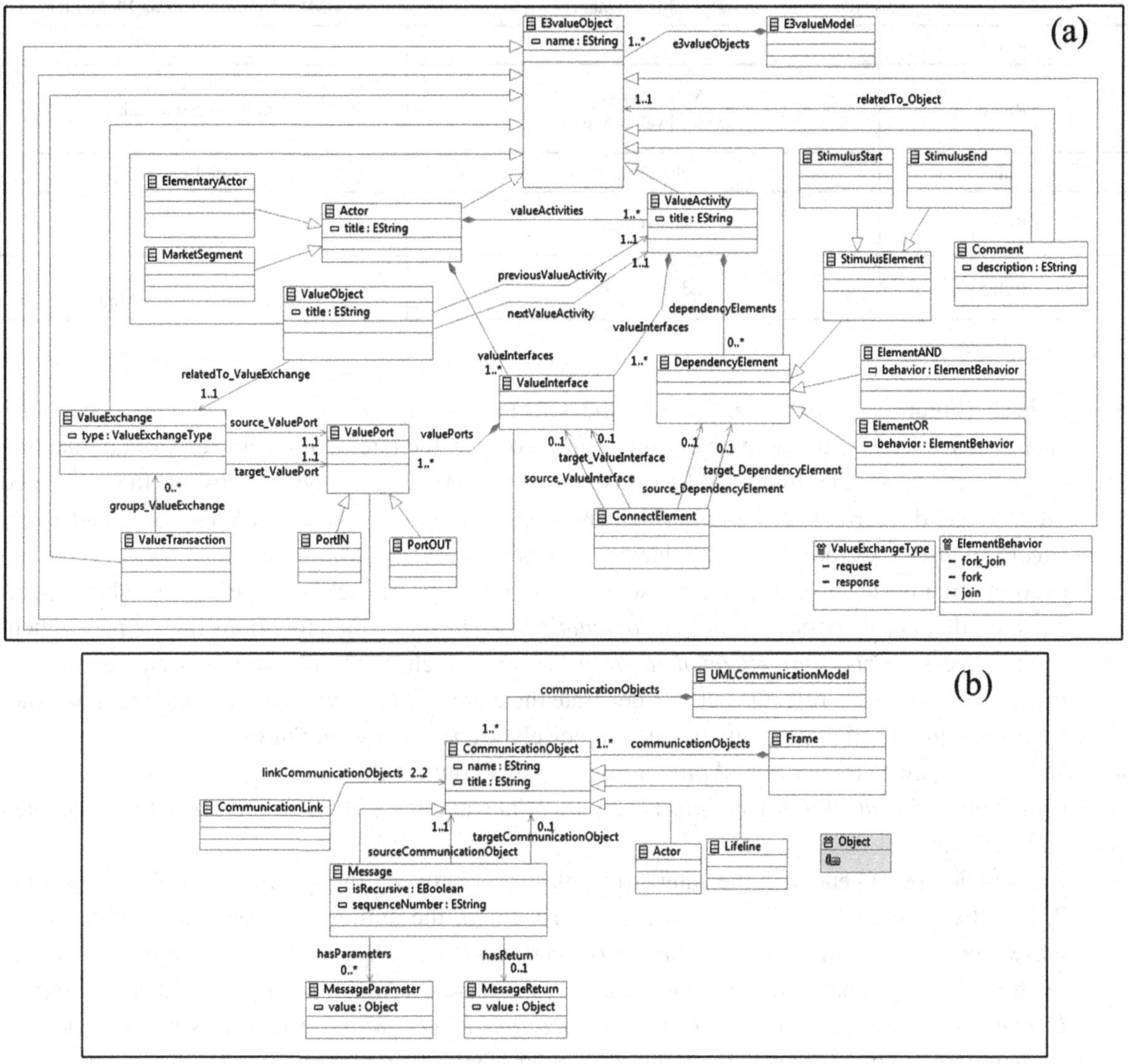

of transformation rules proposed in this method, while Figure 5 details graphically Table 1 via a simple diagram. Then Figure 6 and Figure 7 present those transformation rules via ATL.

As depicted in Figure 6, the authors start by initializing the name of E3value «*Value Activity*» to be generated to the UML2 Communication diagram using the variable «*selectedValueActivity*».

- Rule 1: (Figure 6) presents the transformation from E3value «*Actor*» (i.e., it can be «*Elementary Actor*» or «*Market Segments*») to the UML2 Communication diagram «*Actor*». Regarding this transformation, the authors select justthe «*Actor*» who performs the selected «*Value Activity*»; via the helper «*isActorInclude()*». Thus, the source«*Actor*» has the same «*name*» and «*title*» as the target one.

*Table 1. E3value model to UML2 Communication diagram transformation rules*

| Rule | Source Model (E3value Element) | Target Model (UML2 Communication Element) |
|---|---|---|
| Rule1 | Actor | Actor |
| Rule2 | Value Activity (Selected value Activity) | LifeLine CommunicationLink Message |
| Rule3 | Value Activity | Life Line |
| Rule4 | Value Object | CommunicationLink Message |
| Rule5 | E3valueModel | Frame UML Communication Model |

- Rule 2: (Figure 6) allows transforming the selected «*Value Activity*» to «*Lifeline*». The suffix «*subsystem*» is added to the «*name*» and «*title*». To show the interaction between Communication diagram elements, the authorsadd to this rule three «*Messages*» types between the generated «*Actor*» and the current «*Lifeline*», which are«*messageRequest*», «*messageRecursive*», and «*messageResponse*». All these messages have as attributes«*sequenceNumber*» which specifies the execution order of the message, «*name*» which gives the name of eachmessage, «*title*» which specifies the title of each message, «*sourceCommunicationObject*» which mentions the source element of each message and «*targetCommunicationObject*» which mentions the target elementof each message. Also, in this rule, the authors generate the element «*CommunicationLink*» that link other UML2Communication diagram elements precisely «*Actors*» or «*Lifelines*»;

- Rule 3: (Figure 6) transforms «*Value Activities*» that connect the selected «*Value Activity*» (i. e., using helper«*isValueActivityInclude( )*»), to «*Lifeline*» and we add suffix «*service*» to the «*name*» and «*title*»;

- Rule4: (Figure 7) generates the interaction messages between the generated «*Lifeline*» in Rule 2, and the generated«*Lifeline*» in «*Rule 3*». To do so, the authors also generate for that three «*Messages*» which are «*messageRequest*»,«*messageRecursive*», and «*messageResponse*»; all of these messages have the following attributes; «*sequenceNumber*»,«*name*», «*title*», «*sourceCommunicationObject*» and «*targetCommunicationObject*». Moreover, in thisrule, the element «*CommunicationLink*» is generated that link other UML2 Communication diagram elementsprecisely «*Actors*» or «*Lifelines*»;

- Rule 5: (Figure 7) generates the «*Frame*» that groups all generated Figure 6 and Figure 7 «*UMLCommunicationModel*» elements belonging to the selected sub-function system based on the initialed E3value «*Value Activity*»in Initiation part.

## CASE STUDY

In this section, the authors show the University Library Management case study transformation through the ATL plugin in the Eclipse Integrated Development Environment (IDE). Figure 8 illustrates the proposed practical case study in three mainfolders; the first contains meta-models (has extensions

*Table 2. Case study files and their corresponding figures*

| File | Explanation | Corresponding Figures |
|------|-------------|----------------------|
| E3value_metaModel.ecore<br>E3value_metaModel.ecore_diagram | Illustrate the E3value source meta-model. | Figure 4(a) |
| UMLCommunication_metaModel.ecore<br>UMLCommunication_metaModel.ecore_diagram | Illustrate the UML2 Communication target meta-model. | Figure 4(b) |
| E3value_model.xmi | Represents the proposed E3value-source model in XMI format (OMG-XMI, 2015). | XMI: Figure 9(a)<br>Graphical: Figure 10(a) |
| UMLCommunication_model.xmi | Represents the generated UML2 Communication diagram in XMI format. | XMI: Figure 9(b)<br>Graphical: Figure 10(b) |
| E3valueToUMLCommunication TransformationRules.atl<br>E3valueToUMLCommunication TransformationRules.asm | Represent the transformation rules from the E3value model to UML2 Communication diagram. | Figure 5<br>Figure 6<br>and Figure 7 |

*Figure 5. Transformation rules from E3value model to UML2 Communication diagram*

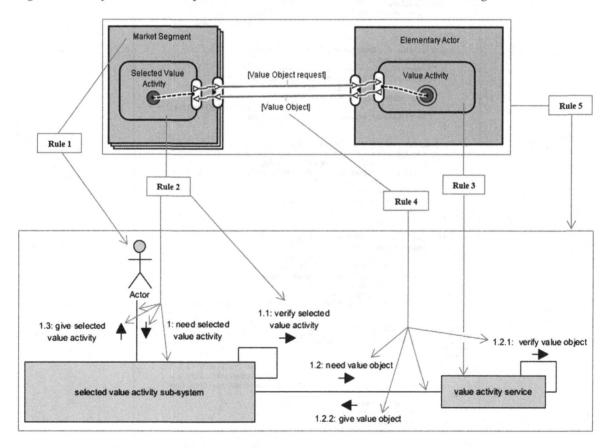

*Figure 6. ATL Transformation rules from E3value model to UML2 Communication diagram -part1.*

```
Initialization: We select the name of the generated «Value
Activity»
helper def : selectedValueActivity : String = 'accessing_library_resources';
```

```
ATL Rule1: From [Actor] To [Actor]
rule Rule1 {
    from
        actor : MME3value!Actor(actor.oclIsKindOf(MME3value!Actor) and
                                            actor.isActorInclude())
    to
        UMLActor : MMUMLCommunication!Actor (
            name <- actor.name,
            title <- actor.title
        )
}
```

```
ATL Rule2: From [Value Activity] To
                        • [Lifeline]
                        • [Communication Link]
                        • And [Messages]
rule Rule2 {
    from
        valueActivity : MME3value!ValueActivity(valueActivity.name =
                                    thisModule.selectedValueActivity)
    to
        lifeline : MMUMLCommunication!Lifeline (
            name <- valueActivity.name + '_sub-system',
            title <- valueActivity.title + ' sub-system'
        ),

        communicationLink : MMUMLCommunication!CommunicationLink (
            linkCommunicationObjects <- Sequence{valueActivity,
                            valueActivity.refImmediateComposite()}
        ),

        messageRequest : MMUMLCommunication!Message (
            sequenceNumber <- '1',
            name <-'need_' + valueActivity.name,
            title <-  messageRequest.sequenceNumber + ': need ' +
                    valueActivity.title,
            sourceCommunicationObject <-
                            valueActivity.refImmediateComposite(),
            targetCommunicationObject <- valueActivity
        ),

        messageRecursive : MMUMLCommunication!Message (
            sequenceNumber <- '1.1',
            name <- 'verify_' + valueActivity.name,
            title <- messageRecursive.sequenceNumber + ': verify ' +
                    valueActivity.title,
            sourceCommunicationObject <- valueActivity,
            targetCommunicationObject <- valueActivity,
            isRecursive <- true
        ),

        messageResponse : MMUMLCommunication!Message (
            sequenceNumber <- '1.' +
                        valueActivity.getCounterForLastMessages(),
            name <- 'give_' + valueActivity.name,
            title <- messageResponse.sequenceNumber + ': give ' +
                    valueActivity.title,
            sourceCommunicationObject <- valueActivity,
            targetCommunicationObject <- valueActivity.refImmediateComposite()
        )
}
```

```
ATL Rule3: From [Value Activity] To [Lifeline]
rule Rule3 {
    from
        valueActivity : MME3value!ValueActivity(valueActivity.name <>
                            thisModule.selectedValueActivity and
                            valueActivity.isValueActivityInclude())
    to
        lifeline : MMUMLCommunication!Lifeline (
            name <- valueActivity.name + '_service',
            title <- valueActivity.title + ' service'
        )
}
```

*Figure 7. ATL Transformation rules from E3value model to UML2 Communication diagram -part2*

```
ATL Rule4: From [Value Object] To
                          • [Communication Link]
                          • And [Messages]
rule Rule4 {
   from
      valueObject : MME3value!ValueObject(
                     valueObject.relatedTo_ValueExchange.type = #response and
                     valueObject.nextValueActivity.name =
                     thisModule.selectedValueActivity )
   to
      communicationLink : MMUMLCommunication!CommunicationLink (
            linkCommunicationObjects <- Sequence{
            valueObject.previousValueActivity, valueObject.nextValueActivity}
      ),

      messageRequest : MMUMLCommunication!Message (
            sequenceNumber <- '1.' + thisModule.getCounter(),
            name <- 'need_' + valueObject.name,
            title <- messageRequest.sequenceNumber + ': need ' +
                     valueObject.title,
            sourceCommunicationObject <- valueObject.nextValueActivity,
            targetCommunicationObject <- valueObject.previousValueActivity
      ),

      messageRecursive : MMUMLCommunication!Message (
            sequenceNumber <- messageRequest.sequenceNumber + '.1',
            name <- 'verify_' + valueObject.name,
            title <- messageRecursive.sequenceNumber + ': verify ' +
                     valueObject.title,
            sourceCommunicationObject <- valueObject.previousValueActivity,
            targetCommunicationObject <- valueObject.previousValueActivity,
            isRecursive <- true
      ),

      messageResponse : MMUMLCommunication!Message (
            sequenceNumber <- messageRequest.sequenceNumber + '.2',
            name <- 'give_' + valueObject.name,
            title <- messageResponse.sequenceNumber + ': give ' +
                     valueObject.title,
            sourceCommunicationObject <- valueObject.previousValueActivity,
            targetCommunicationObject <- valueObject.nextValueActivity
      )
}
```

```
ATL Rule5: From [E3value Model] To
                          • [Frame]
                          • And [UMLCommunicationModel]
rule Rule5 {
   from
      e3valueModel : MME3value!E3valueModel
   to
      frame : MMUMLCommunication!Frame (
            name <- 'com_' + thisModule.selectedValueActivity,
            title <- 'Com : ' + thisModule.selectedValueActivity,
            communicationObjects <- MMUMLCommunication!Actor.allInstances()
                  -> union(MMUMLCommunication!Lifeline.allInstances())
                  -> union(MMUMLCommunication!CommunicationLink.allInstances())
                  -> union(MMUMLCommunication!Message.allInstances())
      ),

      UMLCommunicationModel : MMUMLCommunication!UMLCommunicationModel (
            communicationObjects <- MMUMLCommunication!Frame.allInstances()
      )
}
```

«*.ecore*» and «*.ecore_diagram*»), the second contains models(with «*.xmi*» extensions) while the third folder covers the transformation rules (with extensions «*.asm*» and «*.atl*»).For the sake of simplicity, each folder contains two subfolders; one for the source (i.e., E3value), while the other is fortargets (i.e., UML2 Communication diagrams). To better position the Figure 8 in the current method, Table 2 links each file in Figure 8 with the created and generated figures.

In this case, the authors suggest the following «*Actors*»: «*Patrons*», «*Library*», «*Publishing Companies*» and «*ResearchDatabases*». They assume that every «*Patrons*» can access «*Library*» resources. For instance, the access to«*Books*» and «*Online Research Articles*» by paying fees for the chosen access. From its part, the «*Library*» isalways concentrating on the «*Patron's*» requests; it lends «*Books*», browses «*Research Articles*» if the requested need exists, if not, it manages its needs by communicating them to suppliers who are «*Publishing Companies*» and «*Research Databases*». These latter offer the requested «*Books*» and «*Access to Research Databases*». The purchase of each «*Book*» or «*Access to Research Databases*» automatically requires fees.

*Figure 8. Our practical case structure*

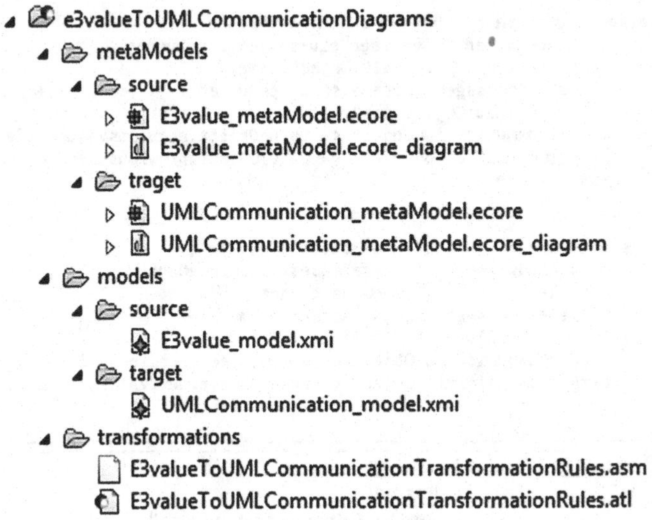

The rest of the section illustrates the «*University Library Management*» case study source and target models.

## E3value Model Proposal

The authors focus, in the source model, on the E3value model offering the business value model of the case study in XMIformat (see Figure 9(a)). They based on the XMI (XML Metadata Interchange) format because it is a standard and trademark from the OMG. Also, it allows defining, interchanging, manipulating, and integration XML data and objects. To doso, the XMI modelis symbolizedgraphically as illustrated in Figure 10(a).

The «*Actors*» can be «*Elementary Actors*» such as «*library*» or can be «*Market Segments*» like «*patrons*»,«*publishing companies*» or «*research databases*». Each «*Actor*» can have at least one «*Value Activity*». In thismodel, the «*patrons*» can «*access library resources*». The «*library*» has as an option «*lending books*», «*browsing research articles*» and «*managing library needs*». The «*publishing companies*» can «*sell books*», whereas the «*research databases*» can «*sell access to research databases*». The «*Value Objects*» can be a request like «*access to books registration fees*», «*online access to research articles registration fees*», «*collected books registration fees*», «*collected research articles registration fees*», «*purchasing books fees*» and «*research databases subscription fees*». Moreover, «*Value Objects*» can be a response such as «*access to books*», «*online access to research articles*»,«*access to available books*», «*access to available research articles*», «*books*», and «*access to research databases*».

In this case, the E3value model exploits «*Value Exchange*» to explain the dependency path direction. These dependency paths connect E3value dependency elements, which can be «*Start Stimulus*», «*End Stimulus*», «*And-Join*», «*And-Fork*», «*Or-Join*» or «*Or-Fork*».

## Generated UML2 Communication Diagram

In this section, the authors describe the generated model, based on the set of defined elements that constitute the source model, the target meta-model, and the set of previously explained transformations.

*Figure 9. Case study XMI models format: (a) E3value-source XMI model format. (b) UML2 CommunicationGenerated XMI model format*

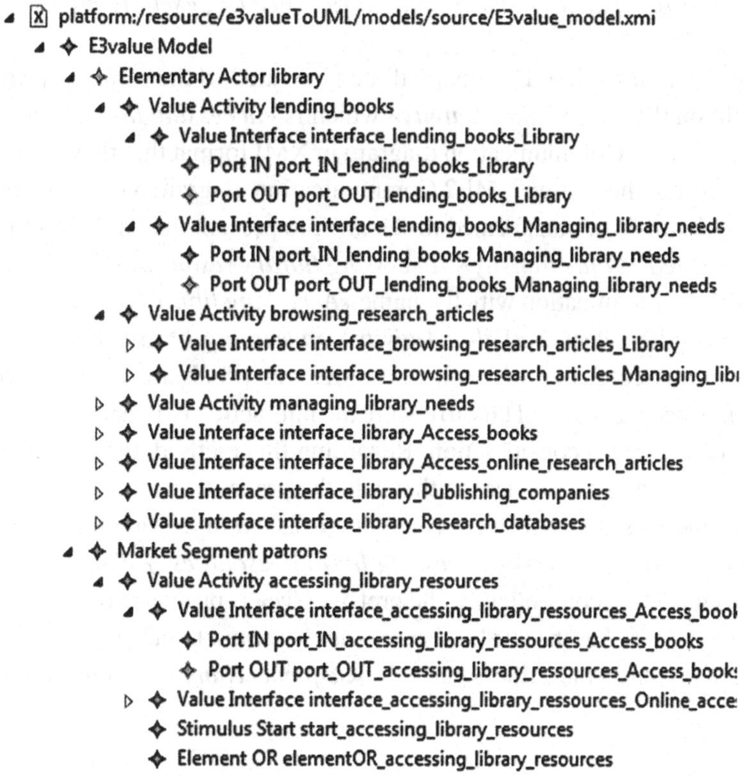

*Figure 10. Case study graphical format: (a) E3value-source model. (b) Generated UML2 Communication diagram for «accessing library resources».*

> ◢ [X] platform:/resource/e3valueToUML/models/target/UMLCommunication_model.x
>   ◢ ◆ UML Communication Model
>     ◢ ◆ Frame com_accessing_library_resources
>         ◆ Actor patrons
>         ◆ Lifeline accessing_library_resources_sub-system
>         ◆ Lifeline lending_books_service
>         ◆ Lifeline browsing_research_articles_service
>         ◆ Communication Link
>         ◆ Communication Link
>         ◆ Communication Link
>         ◆ Message need_accessing_library_resources
>         ◆ Message verify_accessing_library_resources
>         ◆ Message give_accessing_library_resources
>         ◆ Message need_access_books
>         ◆ Message verify_access_books
>         ◆ Message give_access_books
>         ◆ Message need_online_access_research_articles
>         ◆ Message verify_online_access_research_articles

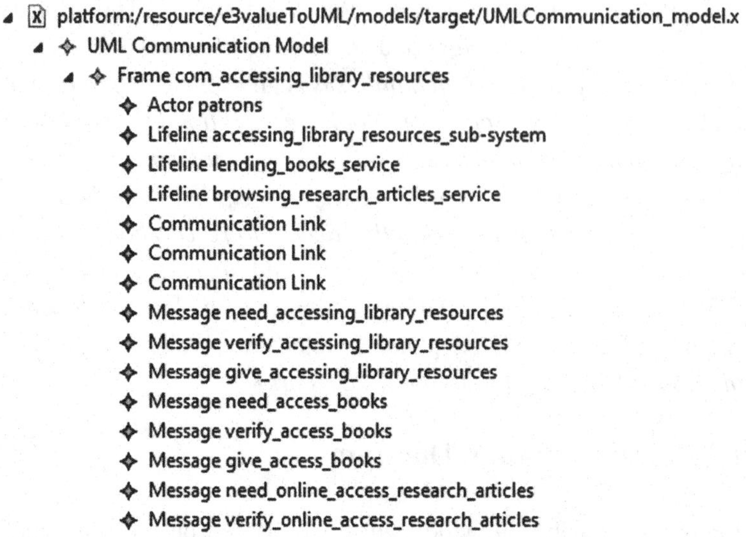

As mentioned before and to accurately obtain detailed UML2 Communication diagrams. These diagrams are generated according to their system sub-functions. In this case, the authors will generate a communication diagram per E3value «*Value Activity*», so they can produce six UML2 Communication diagrams, which correspond to the following «*Value Activities*»: «*accessing library resources*», «*lending books*», «*browsing research articles*», «*managing library needs*», «*selling books*» and «*selling access to research databases*».

Seen that all the communication diagrams will be generated in the same way, in this study, the authors shed more light on the first «*Value Activity*» which is «*accessing library resources*». Figure 9(b) represents the chosen UML2 Communication diagram in XMI format that they symbolize it graphically in Figure 10(b). As a result, the chosen UML2 Communication diagram will be generated as follows; the «*Market Segments*» «*library*» is transformed to «*Actor*», to present the participant in a communication diagram. Then the selected «*Value Activity*» «*accessing library resources*» will be transformed into the main «*Lifeline*» in this communication with the name «*Accessing library resources sub-system*». «*Value Activities*» that connect the selected «*Value Activity*» «*accessing library resources*» are transformed to «*Lifelines*», and in this case, two «*Lifelines*» are treated, which are «*Lending books service*» and «*Browsing research articles service*». Thus, to ensure the interaction between the generated elements, the message elements are taken into consideration. Regarding this method, the authors propose three message types, the first is to request a service, so they add the prefix «*need*» (e.g., «*need accessing library resources*»). The second message is for verifying what is asked in the previous message; therefore, the prefix «*verify*» is proposed (e.g., «*verify accessing library resources*»). The third is for giving what is asked in the previous message; consequently, the prefix «*give*» is proposed (e.g., «*give accessing library resources*». Every «*Message*» has the attribute «*sequenceNumber*» to take into consideration the order of different messages. In this case, the authors place the «*sequenceNumber*» value before every «*Message*».

## ANALYSIS AND DISCUSSION

This section analyzes and discussesthe proposed method based on an analytical survey of all the studied related work. For that purpose, the authors focus on the OMG recommendations (OMG-MDA, 2014) and the following work (Rhazaliet al., 2015; Kriouile et al., 2013; Yue et al., 2011; Mokhtar et al., 2017) to deduce their evaluation criteria.

Therefore, the deduced criteria are grouped according to the model level construction, the model transformation, and the use of assessment methodology. These latter are explained as follows:

- Model construction criteria: present the coverage of the graphical representation for each model. And the participation in one of the MDA approach levels;
- Transformation criteria: Verify the transformation automation, the meta-models based transformation, and the existence of the mapping rules definition; to ensure the correctness of the transformation, which are one of the essential concepts in MDA (OMG-MDA, 2014; Cetinkaya and Verbraeck, 2011).
- Evaluation approach criteria: Present the occurrence of the assessment methodology (Fogli and Guida, 2015).

The rest of this section analyses the studied related work and compares these searches with the proposed method through an analytical survey based on the concluded criteria.

*Figure 11. Studied papers comparison based on the evaluation criteria*

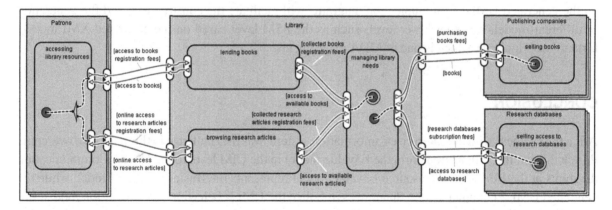

Figure 11 presents the result of the evaluation criteria analysis. The figure columns display the deduced criteria, whereas the figure lines show the studied papers.

First, in model construction criteria; on the one hand, most of the methods achieve the transformation from CIM to PIM to generate the UML diagrams, except the proposed methods in Schuster and Motal (2009) and Miranda et al. (2017) where the researchers did not place their models in the MDA approach. On the other hand, most researchers prefer the use of a graphical representation for their source and destination models, except in both methods in Bouzidi et al. (2017) and Miranda et al. (2017), where the researchers use a textual representation for the UML Use Case diagram.

Regarding the transformation criteria, just five methods are distinguished that are based on the meta-models which are in the studies in De Castro et al. (2011), Schuster and Motal (2009), Bouzidi et al. (2017) and Rhazali et al. (2015) as well as the proposed method. Thus, for the transformation automation, some researchers use their algorithm like in Zhou et al. (2017) and Miranda et al. (2017) while other researchers transform their models relying on a transformation language; for instance, ATL in De Castro et al. (2011), Bouzidi et al. (2017), Rhazali et al. (2015) and the proposed method. However, in some methods, the models' transformation is performed manually, relying on a human language like in Schuster and Motal (2009), Bousetta et al. (2013), and Kherraf et al. (2008). Furthermore, for the mapping rules definition, all the studied work explain clearly the transformation rules. Finally, regarding the evaluation approaches criteria, all methods use a case study in the assessment methodology.

After analyzing all the studied methods, most of the methods do not validate all the proposed criteria in this study, except for the work in De Castro et al. (2011), Rhazali et al. (2015), and the proposed method. These last three methods generate a graphically represented UML diagram in the PIM level from proposed models in the CIM level. Moreover, the execution of the transformation rules is meta-model based, and the target diagrams are generated automatically using ATL. Besides, the authors of these papers deal with a case study in the assessment methodology. It is worth stressing out that the proposed method is considered as a unique method that generates the second version of the UML communication diagram in the PIM level from an essential model in the CIM level, which is the E3value model.

Finally, the use of the proposed method in e-business systems will allow generating correct behavior and interaction models in the PIM level based on a simple method which can be created by non-technical stakeholders who do not know about computer modeling. On the one hand, it will reduce the effort, the time. Consequently, the development cost of e-business projects as all transformations is automated by increasing the chance of being more competitive in the software industry. On the other hand, relying on the generated UML2 Communication diagrams will facilitate the construction, and the generation of different models for other lower levels such as the PSM level based on the generated XMI models format (see Figure 9), which is one of MDA experiments.

## CONCLUSION

Align the business with the enterprises' information system, was the challenge in this paper. To overcome this challenge, the authors transform the E3value model in the CIM level to the UML2 Communication diagrams at the PIM level. The source E3value model represents the Business Value Model, while the generated UML2 Communication diagrams symbolize the UML's behavior and interaction model. For that purpose, the authors started by the definition of source and target meta-models, and they specified the constraints during the source model construction. Then, they explained the set of transformation rules implemented via ATL. Besides, a case study is presented to illustrate the proposed method. The obtained results are analyzed and discussed and give a satisfactory conclusion compared to the related work.

In the ongoing research, the authors propose to complete the e-business information system construction, emphasizing on their generated UML2 Communication diagrams. They aim to offer a new disciplined method that produces models in the PSM level, that will eventually be models throw the OMG standard.

## REFERENCES

Bézivin, J., & Briot, J.-P. (2004). Sur les principes de base de l'ingénierie des modèles. *L'OBJET*, *10*(4), 145–157. doi:10.3166/objet.10.4.145-157

Blanc, X., & Salvatori, O. (2011). *MDA en action: Ingénierie logicielle guidée par les modèles*. Editions Eyrolles.

Bousetta, B., El Beggar, O., & Gadi, T. (2013). A methodology for cim modelling and its transformation to pim. *Journal of Information Engineering and Applications*, *3*(2), 1–21.

Bouzidi, A., Haddar, N., Abdallah, M. B., & Haddar, K. 2017. Deriving use case models from bpmn models. In *2017IEEE/ACS 14th International Conference on Computer Systems and Applications (AICCSA)*. IEEE. 10.1109/AICCSA.2017.49

Brambilla, M., Cabot, J., & Wimmer, M. (2012). Model-driven software engineering in practice. *Synthesis Lectures on Software Engineering*, *1*(1), 1–182.

Cetinkaya, D., & Verbraeck, A. (2011). Metamodeling and model transformations in modeling and simulation. *Proceedings of the Winter Simulation Conference. Winter Simulation Conference*, 3048–3058. 10.1109/WSC.2011.6148005

De Castro, V., Marcos, E., & Vara, J. M. (2011). Applying cim-to-pim model transformations for the service-oriented development of information systems. *Information and Software Technology*, *53*(1), 87–105. doi:10.1016/j.infsof.2010.09.002

dos Santos Soares, M., Vrancken, J., & Verbraeck, A. (2011). User requirements modeling and analysis of software intensive systems. *Journal of Systems and Software*, *84*(2), 328–339. doi:10.1016/j.jss.2010.10.020

Doumi, K., Baina, S., & Baina, K. (2013). Strategic business and it alignment: Representation and evaluation. *Journal of Theoretical & Applied Information Technology*, *47*(1).

Fogli, D., & Guida, G. (2015). A practical approach to the assessment of quality in use of corporate web sites. *Journal of Systems and Software*, *99*, 52–65.

Garrigós, I., Mazón, J.-N., Koch, N., & Escalona, M. J. (2012). Web and requirements engineering. *IET Software*, *6*(2), 83–84. doi:10.1049/iet-sen.2012.0044

Gordijn, J., & Akkermans, H. (2001). Designing and evaluating e-business models. *IEEE Intelligent Systems*, *16*(4), 11–17. doi:10.1109/5254.941353

Gordijn, J., & Akkermans, H. (2018). *Value Webs: Understanding e-Business Innovation*. The Value Engineers.

Gordijn, J., & Akkermans, J. (2003). Value-based requirements engineering: Exploring innovative e-commerce ideas. *Requirements Engineering*, *8*(2), 114–134. doi:10.100700766-003-0169-x

Gordijn, J., Yu, E., & Van Der Raadt, B. (2006). E-service design using i* and e/sup 3/value modeling. *IEEE Software*, *23*(3), 26–33. doi:10.1109/MS.2006.71

Hoyos, J. R., García-Molina, J., & Botía, J. A. (2013). A domain-specific language for context modeling in context-awaresystems. *Journal of Systems and Software, 86*(11), 2890–2905. doi:10.1016/j.jss.2013.07.008

Jouault, F., Allilaire, F., Bézivin, J., Kurtev, I., & Valduriez, P. (2006). Atl: a qvt-like transformation language. In *Companion to the 21st ACM SIGPLAN symposium on Object-oriented programming systems, languages, and applications*. ACM.

Kharmoum, N., Ziti, S., & Omary, F. (2016). An analytical study of the cim to pim transformation in mda. International Workshop on Computing Sciences (WCOS'16), 14–19.

Kharmoum, N., Ziti, S., & Omary, F. (2019a). A novel automatic transformation method from the business value modelto the uml use case diagram. *2nd Edition of the International Conference on Advanced Intelligent Systems for Sustainable Development.*

Kharmoum, N., Ziti, S., Rhazali, Y., & Omary, F. (2018). Automatic transformation method from e3value model to the dataflow diagram: An mda approach. *International Conference on Modern Intelligent Systems Concepts MISC'2018.*

Kharmoum, N., Ziti, S., Rhazali, Y., & Omary, F. (2019b). An automatic transformation method from the e3value modelto ifml model: An mda approach. *Journal of Computational Science, 15*(6), 800–813. doi:10.3844/jcssp.2019.800.813

Kharmoum, N., Ziti, S., Rhazali, Y., & Omary, F. (2019c). A method of model transformation in MDA approach from E3value model to BPMN2 diagrams in CIM level. *IAENG International Journal of Computer Science, 46*(4), 1–17.

Kharmoum, N., Ziti, S., Rhazali, Y., & Omary, F. (2019d). An automatic transformation method from the E3value model to UML2 sequence diagrams: An MDA approach. *International Journal of Computing, 18*(3), 316–330.

Kherraf, S., Lefebvre, É., & Suryn, W. (2008). Transformation from cim to pim using patterns and archetypes. *19th Australian Conference on Software Engineering (ASWEC 2008), 338–346.* 10.1109/ASWEC.2008.4483222

Kriouile, A., Gadi, T., & Balouki, Y. (2013). Cim to pim transformation: A criteria based evaluation. *International Journalof Computer Technology and Applications, 4*(4), 616.

Maatougui, E., Bouanaka, C., & Zeghib, N. (2016). Towards a meta-model for quality-aware self-adaptive systems design. ModComp@ MoDELS, 12–18.

McCarthy, W. E. (1982). The rea accounting model: A generalized framework for accounting systems in a shared data environment. *The Accounting Review*, 554–578.

Miranda, M. A., Ribeiro, M. G., Marques-Neto, H. T., & Song, M. A. J. (2017). Domain-specific language for automaticgeneration of uml models. *IET Software, 12*(2), 129–135. doi:10.1049/iet-sen.2016.0279

Mokhtar, R., Rahman, A. A., & Othman, S. H. (2017). Towards model driven architecture in academic quality assurance information system development. *Journal of Telecommunication Electronic and Computer Engineering, 9*(1-3), 95–100.

OMG-BPMN. (2011). *Business Process Model and Notation version 2.0*. OMG.

OMG-MDA. (2014). *MDA Guide version 2.0*. OMG.

OMG-OCL. (2014). *Object Constraint Language version 2.4*. OMG.

OMG-QVT. (2016). *Meta Object Facility (MOF) 2.0 Query/View/Transformation Specification, OMG Adopted SpecificationVersion 1.3*. OMG.

OMG-UML. (2017). *Unified Modeling Language version 2.5.1*. OMG.

OMG-XMI. (2015). *XML Metadata Interchange version 2.5.1*. OMG.

Osterwalder, A., & Pigneur, Y. (2002). An ebusiness model ontology for modeling ebusiness. *BLED 2002 Proceedings, 2*.

Rhazali, Y., Hadi, Y., Chana, I., Lahmer, M., & Rhattoy, A. (2018). A model transformation in model driven architecturefrom business model to web model. *IAENG International Journal of Computer Science, 45*(1).

Rhazali, Y., Hadi, Y., & Mouloudi, A. (2015). A methodology of model transformation in mda: From cim to pim. *InternationalReview on Computers and Software, 10*(12), 1186–1201. doi:10.15866/irecos.v10i12.8088

Rodríguez, A., de Guzmán, I. G.-R., Fernández-Medina, E., & Piattini, M. (2010). Semi-formal transformation of securebusiness processes into analysis class and use case models: An mda approach. *Information and Software Technology, 52*(9), 945–971. doi:10.1016/j.infsof.2010.03.015

Schuster, R., & Motal, T. (2009). *From e3-value to rea: Modeling multi-party e-business collaborations. In 2009 IEEE Conference on Commerce and Enterprise Computing*. IEEE.

Skersys, T., Danenas, P., & Butleris, R. (2018). Extracting sbvr business vocabularies and business rules from uml use casediagrams. *Journal of Systems and Software, 141*, 111–130. doi:10.1016/j.jss.2018.03.061

Yue, T., Briand, L. C., & Labiche, Y. (2011). A systematic review of transformation approaches between user requirementsand analysis models. *Requirements Engineering, 16*(2), 75–99. doi:10.100700766-010-0111-y

Zhou, D., Chen, X., Jin, Q., Kuang, Z., & Yang, H. (2017). An affinity analysis based cim-to-pim transformation. *Multiagent and Grid Systems, 13*(3), 269–286. doi:10.3233/MGS-170271

# Chapter 13
# SERIES:
## A Software Risk Estimator Tool Support for Requirement Risk Assessment

**Chetna Gupta**
*Jaypee Institute of Information Technology, India*

**Priyanka Chandani**
*Jaypee Institute of Information Technology, India*

## ABSTRACT

*Requirement defects are one of the major sources of failure in any software development process, and the main objective of this chapter is to make requirement analysis phase exhaustive by estimating risk at requirement level by analyzing requirement defect and requirement inter-relationships as early as possible to using domain modeling to inhibit them from being incorporated in design and implementation. To achieve this objective, this chapter proposes a tool to assist software developers in assessing risk at requirement level. The proposed tool, software risk estimator, SERIES in short, helps in early identification of potential risk where preventive actions can be undertaken to mitigate risk and corrective actions to avoid project failure in collaborative manner. The entire process has been supported by a software case study. The results of the proposed work are promising and will help software engineers in ensuring that all business requirements are captured correctly with clear vision and scope.*

## INTRODUCTION

Every software system exhibit uniqueness and contains significant numbers of uncertainties in terms of key objectives, specific features, preferences and user expectations. This makes software structurally complex and versatile which progressively evolves over time to accommodate changing customer requirements, latest market demand, new sophisticated technologies, imprecise estimation of budget, schedules, product deployment and maintenance (Mens, 2012). These factors have strong impact on software development and strongly support the need of proactive assessment measures to control these uncertainties. If failing to do so, it raises the possibility of potential risk throughout the project lifecycle

DOI: 10.4018/978-1-7998-3661-2.ch013

ranging from delays to economic losses to customer dissatisfaction. According to PMBOK reports (2017), the global software market which is at US\$333 billion in 2016 estimated to grow by 7.2% and global software projects (US and Europe) success in 2015 is 29% only (CHAOS, 2015) while 71% of projects have failed, due to diverse reasons and risks (Vahidnia, Tanriöver&Askerzade, 2016). Therefore, it is desirable to follow software risk analysis and management practices to understand, identify, and manage underlying risks to prevent the loss further in expenditure (Samantra, Datta, Mahapatra, &Debata, 2016). In software engineering domain, risk is considered as a potential problem or unwanted outcome that might have positive or negative consequences on a project PMBOK (2017). However, according to to(Hijazi, Alqrainy, Muaidi, &Khdour, 2014) risks in software development do appear due to items (usually called software risk factors) that present a threat to software project success. According to (Chen & Huang, 2009) problems in requirement are considered as one of the major sources of project failure constituting nearly 32.65%. These problems include analyzing imperfection that compromises requirement correctness, completeness, stability and meeting the objectives/ project goals and such imperfections are categorized as defects within requirements. These requirement defects are most expensive problems that persist throughout the software life cycle (Hamill & Katerina, 2009) and can be generated from different perspectives of users, practitioners, project execution or knowledge. The cost to fix a defect varies according to how far along you are in the software life cycle. The cost of fixing requirements defects is 3 times higher in the course of design, 10 times higher during development, 50 times higher at the time of testing and up to 100 times higher after the release (Boehm &Basili, 2001; Pressman, 2014). Hence, it is desirable to include risk management practices in every software project as early as possible, in particular, within Requirements Engineering (RE) phase. A project without risk management admits severe problems such as reworks of project artifacts and cost/schedule overrun.

In the past, literature has explored various issues concerning risk factors in software projects (Hijazi, Alqrainy, Muaidi, &Khdour, 2014; Islam &Houmb, 2010; Christiansen, Wuttidittachotti, Prakancharoen, &Vallipakorn, 2015) but the research is general in nature, not concentrating on perspectives including risk assessment and estimation practices in requirement engineering phase itself, uncovering requirement defects. Risk management is one such influential approaches acknowledged by all the project management and software engineering guidebooks (PMBOK, 2017; Pressman, 2014, CMMI, 2010; Thayer &Dorfman, 2013; SWEBOK, 2014). Risk can arise in any phase of the software development lifecycle and can be detrimental to the project causing huge losses. In the study conducted by (Hijazi, Alqrainy, Muaidi, &Khdour, 2014), key risk factors that threaten each phase of Software Development Life Cycle (SDLC) are presented which according their study claimed that every phase of SDLC is vulnerable to several types of risks. Many such risk factors are discussed that are common to most software development projects. With a successful risk management practices employed particularly in RE phase and by identification/analysis of risk factors related to requirements, a project manager can prevent potential risks and deter project failures. However, a comprehensive risk management plan is not possible due to paucity of resources and more onus is on saving time and budget and due to that the benefit of risk management practices cannot be reaped.

This paper proposes a tool to assist software developers in assessing risk at requirement level. The proposed tool, **S**oftwar**ERi**sk**Es**timator, SERIES in short, helps in early identification of potential risk where preventive actions can be undertaken to mitigate risk and corrective actions to avoid project failure in collaborative manner. The business objective to mitigate risk is fulfilled through the proposed tool, though it is separated from the technology implementation alike the MDA (model driven architecture) approach(Rhazali et al., 2020; Rhazali, Hadi&Mouloudi, 2016). Here, the requirements are listed down and analyzed further, the stakeholder and developer viewpoint is ascertained to deepen the understanding on the business models (CIM) created. The interaction diagram and uses cases are created based on the clear understanding from business models.The risk identification and mitigation at the forefront eases the stages of Platform Independent Model (PIM) and Platform Specific Model (PSM)of the application development when MDA approach is followed.

## RELATED WORK

This section discusses literature on various techniques and approaches presented in the past related to requirements defects, defect classification, risk assessment and management and its impact on success of any software project. Requirements defects have an impact throughout the project lifecycle, detecting and correcting those defects is the most expensive activities in software development (Kumaresh, Ramachandran, 2012).It is essential to identify and analyze various requirement defects before a decision of inclusion of a requirement is taken in software development. These defect identification and analysis techniques or models are essential in order to be sure that all the requirements are captured correctly which focus on delivering value to the customer and are selected by taking right decision using risk estimation. Many software development organizations have successfully applied various defect analysis and prevention techniques showing significant reductions in errors (Mays, 1990; Suma &Gopalakrishnan, 2008; Kumaresh&Baskaran, 2010). Using a proper defects classification and taxonomy for requirements is essential to analyze the problems and their root causes which further reduce the risks associated with requirements. Some of the popular approaches for defect classification are Beizer taxonomy (Beizer, 1990), Orthogonal Defect Classification (ODC) approach (Chillarege et al., 1992), HP approach (Grady, 1992), IEEE taxonomies (1998), Margarido (Margarido, Faria, Vidal & Vieira, 2011), Walia (Walia& Carver, 2009) and Huffman Hayes (Hayes, 2003).

Risks in software projects can occur in any of phase of software development life cycle (SDLC) and should be handled there and then using strategies planned for individual phases of SDLC. Risk assessment and management is recognized as an essential practice which helps in identifying, analyzing, and mitigating risks and risk factors before they materialize into problems (PMBOK, 2017; Pressman, 2014; SWEBOK, 2014).Various approaches in the past have focused on assessing risks in all phases of software life cycle, by integrating risk management practices at every phase. However, several attempts have been made to integrate risk analysis in the initial phases of the software lifecycle process, which contribute towards increasing the software project success by fixing risk at the earliest (Vahidnia, Özgür&Askerzade, 2017; Bhukya&Pabboju, 2018; Cornford, Feather, Heron & Jenkins, 2006).

In the past, a few studies have ascertained systematic models of risk assessment using Analytic Hierarchy Process, Bayesian belief network, machine learning, risk metrics, fuzzy entropy, goal-oriented methodologies, decision trees, UML etc. (Hsieh, Hsu & Lin, 2016; Ghane, 2017; Meng, 2017; Zhi, Zhang, Liu &Shen, 2017; Kamila &Sutikno, 2016; Cailliau&Lamsweerde, 2015; Sipayung&Sembiring, 2015; Anthony, Noraini, Nor &Jusoh, 2015; Asnar, Giorgini&Mylopoulos, 2011; Amber, Shawoo& Begum, 2012; Li, & Liu,2009; Kumar &Yadav, 2015), they cumulatively conclude that assessment of risk can effectively give consistent software quality by reducing the exposure to software risk.Additionally, some research work(Amber, Shawoo& Begum, 2012; Lobato et al., 2012; Gallardo, 2012) also deals with specific cases like risk management in requirement engineering, risk-based testing, project risk dependencies, etc.The existing models of risk management have minimal focus towards considering software risks in early stage of SDLC. Adoption of early risk discovery and the corresponding mitigation strategy helps in minimizing the loss in software project.

## SERIES: PROPOSED SOFTWARE RISK ESTIMATOR TOOL

The analysis in the risk assessment approach is often an interactive and iterative procedure, which requires elaborate discussions within/with the project teams and stakeholders. The calculations are monotonic and it is essential for the researchers and project teams to concentrate on the data with the stakeholders. Based on the quantative data it is easier for taking the decision on the validity of a risk. This paper aims to develop a risk management tool to identify, access and manage risk in requirements engineering and reduce chances of failure and disagreement between the project teams and stakeholders along with varied other business or technical challenges to develop a quality product. An attempt is made to keep the overhead specific to risk estimation activity as low as possible and developed tool to support labor-intensive aspects of the process to reduce the effort and time. This tool is built using VBA macros on Microsoft Excel 2017. The implementation of software tool supports the execution of the risk estimation process, as well as the capturing of the information inferred during this process. Final risk values are computed using viewpoints of both stakeholder and developer for enhancing effective communication between both the parties.

### Elicitation of Stakeholder's Value ($S_v$)

The process starts with capturing the stakeholder's value (preference) for each requirement based on three main parameters namely, urgency, necessity, and business importance/value. These preferences are captured using interactive GUI provided by SERIES tool. Stakeholder's can select one out of five categories. Table 1 presents the description of each category and its corresponding value.

*Table 1. Requirement Categorization*

| Type | Remarks | Weight |
|------|---------|--------|
| Mandatory | Essential to have with primary importance | 5 |
| Major | Good to Have with secondary importance | 4 |
| Moderate | OK to Have with tertiary importance | 3 |
| Minor | Can Have but can do without | 2 |
| Malformed | Should not Have, good to be without | 1 |

Figure 1 provides a snapshot of initial preferences provided by stakeholder's for an example set of 12 requirements selected from a sub module of an example project, which assists clients to provide bays for customer parking through mobile application on android and IOS platforms is selected to carry out results analysis. The project has 12 high-level requirements (refer Table 2) consisting of 20 sub-modules with 112 sub- requirements in total. A high level architecture is shown in Figure 2 and its corresponding interaction diagram detailing out the high level of abstraction and flow of control between the

*Figure 1. Snapshot of Elicitation of stakeholder's preference (S$_v$)*

| Enter Requirements | | 12 | Submit |
|---|---|---|---|

| Requirment | Stakeholder Requirement Type Selection | Stakeholder Value (S$_v$) | Next |
|---|---|---|---|
| R1 | Major | 4 | |
| R2 | Mandatory | 5 | |
| R3 | Mandatory | 5 | |
| R4 | Moderate | 3 | |
| R5 | Moderate | 3 | |
| R6 | Major | 4 | |
| R7 | Major | 4 | |
| R8 | Minor | 2 | |
| R9 | Minor | 2 | |
| R10 | Major | 4 | |
| R11 | Major | 4 | |
| R12 | Malformed | 1 | |

objects and messagesis shown in Figure 3. It shows the behavior of the system and helps in identifying the events which define the execution flow in the application. The interaction diagram shows the main modules which are login, location management, rate management system, profiling, notifications and commission. The rate management system module encloses the audit log, rate tester and publishing as well. The execution flow of all the possible paths corresponding to all the requirements can be defined and analyzed from the diagram.

## Elicitation of Developer's Value (D$_v$)

Developers follow a twofold process in which first of all requirements are analyzed for presence of any defects and later a relationships among requirements (dependency) are studied using domain modeling to understand the potential impact of requirements on one another. Requirement defects refer to analysis conducted on each independent requirement to check whether it meets intended purpose and satisfies business value to the stakeholder. Requirements defects have a considerable impact on whole software lifecycle and specific defects classification is essential for root cause analysis of the problems, in order to understand risks associated with requirements problems. Using this approach, developers will be able to gain key information to support risk estimation using defects and dependency analysis.

### Defect Analysis

Having a specific defects classification for requirements is important to analyze the root causes of problems to access risk associated with it. Literature lists following defect taxonomies which are available for classifying the defects namely, Orthogonal Defect Classification (ODC) approach (Chillarege et al., 1992), HP approach (Grady, 1992),Beizertaxonomy (Beizer, 1990), IEEE taxonomies (1998) and Huffman Hayes (Hayes, 2003). For this work, Hayes (Hayes, 2003) taxonomy is used because it is most relevant to this research as their approach emphasized on requirements rather than on design and code to classify defects and is summarized in Table 3.

Each requirement is validated with respect to (w.r.t.) presence of type of defect(s) listed in Table 2. This mapping will help in addressing defects related to requirements enabling project managers to vi-

*Table 2. Requirement Set of industrial project data*

| Requirement Number | Requirements Details |
|---|---|
| R1 | **User Management**: The super admin's, admin's (suppliers) and their employee's should be able to login to Self Service Portal to manage the units, suppliers and their existing rates |
| R2 | **Recurring Rate Management**: The Supplier should be able to view (week and day) the recurring rates through a concerned week. The rates can be edited, deleted or created, the rates shall be flat or incremental, draft rates can be created |
| R3 | **Event Rate Management**: The Supplier should be able to view (week and day) the event rates through a concerned week. The rates can be edited, deleted or created, the rates shall be flat or incremental, draft rates cannot be created |
| R4 | **Audit Log**: The events or behaviors by the user can be Audit checked. The whole length of check has to be 90 days |
| R5 | **Rate Tester**: The rates (recurring and event) can be modified by the supplier, there should be a rate tester component which can metric the rate on filtered clauses for the supplier to view |
| R6 | **Rate Publishing Service**: the published rates should have an option to become live to the market based upon the desire of the supplier |
| R7 | **Types**: The application should take care of On Demand and Reservation rates for super admin users |
| R8 | **Profiling**: The supplier admin can modify the profile assigned. The admin should have a privilege to create, delete sub users, it should work on Siri and Google Assistant, the super admin can create users |
| R9 | **Notification Service**: Upon Configuration of an Email Address, the supplier should get notifications for all behaviors |
| R10 | **Locations Management**: The locations viewed to a supplier should be geo located. The MAPs should be visible to view the exact location with address. The supplier should on view it's company locations, the super admins can view/ update all locations |
| R11 | **Commission Service**: The admin's should have a functionality to modify the commission earned by XXX company from Suppliers, the commission service should sent weekly emails (configurable) to BOD only if good total commission is earned |
| R12 | **Access Management**: The super admin user can revoke rights of normal user |

*Figure 2. High Level Architecture*

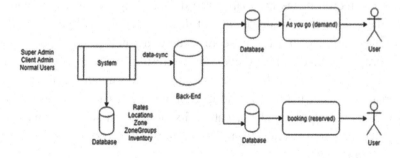

sualize and access potential benefit or risk between the needs and expectations of stakeholders for both individual and as well as set of requirements depicting whole project.

*Table 3. Defect Types*

| Type of Defect | Remarks |
|---|---|
| Incomplete | Fails to fully describe all the requirements of a function |
| Missing | Fails to specify lower level of abstraction of higher level or specification of missing value in a requirement |
| In-Correct | Fails to fully describe system with respect to input or output value or specification of incorrect value in requirement |
| Ambiguous | Difficult to understand or having lack of clarity |
| Infeasible | Impossible or not feasible to implement with respect to factors like speed, cost |
| Inconsistent | Incompatible having internal or external conflicts |
| Over Specification | Having excessive detail for operational need leading to additional system cost |
| Non-Traceable | Requirement which cannot be traced to other phases |
| Unachievable | Requirement which is specified but not achievable in the product lifetime |
| Non verifiable | Failure to verify and validate the requirement by any testing method |
| Misplaced | Information that is marked in different segment of requirement document |
| Intentional Deviation | Specified at the higher level but deviated from the purpose at the lower level from specifications |
| Redundant | Requirement already specified elsewhere in the specification |

(Hayes, 2003)

After mapping of requirement with each defect type, percentage score of each defect type is computed. This score is defined as the percentage of total number of requirements in a particular defect category with the total number of requirements as calculated using equation (1)

*Percentage of defect by category= Rd/Rt* (1)

where,

Rd = Number of requirements in a particular defect category
Rt = Total number of requirements

For instance, if two requirements are mapped to defect category "missing" and there are 8 total requirements then the score value for percentage of defect category will be 2/8 = 25%. These defect categories are assigned weights w.r.t. to the score value computed in equation (1). These values are relative to specific project at hand and is purely based on results and mapping of requirement defects.

Next, weights are assigned to define the level of risk by considering the score of defect category. This will help project managers to visualize risk and its root cause to assist management decision making. Table 4 presents various levels of this classification, its description and corresponding weight. These weights are represented as a set of values from 0 to 5 representing very low, low, moderate, high, very high and extreme values respectively.

Lastly, a defect score of each individual requirement will be computed to access risk and its consequences throughout the whole project. This requirement defect weight score is defined as summation of weights corresponding to each defect category computed in Table 4, w.r.t. of each requirement belonging

*Figure 3. Interaction Diagram*

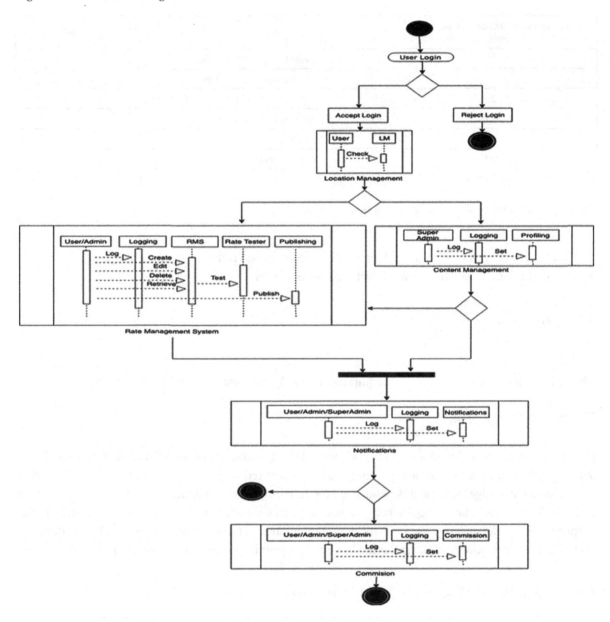

to different defect categories and is summarized in equation (2). For instance, if a requirement has two defects namely, ambiguous and incomplete then the requirement defect weight (Dw) will be summation of defect weight of ambiguous and defect weight of incomplete category computed in Table4.

$$Requirement\ defect\ value\left(Dw\right) = \sum_{i=1}^{n}\left(Rdwi\right) \qquad (2)$$

*Table 4. Level classification of percentage of defect score*

| Percentage of Defects by Category Score | Description | Weight |
|---|---|---|
| > 25% | Extreme high chances of defect | 5 |
| 20-25% | Very high chances of defect | 4 |
| 15-20% | High chances of defect | 3 |
| 10-15% | Nominal chances of defect | 2 |
| 5-10% | Low chances of defect | 1 |
| < 5% | Very Low chances of defect | 0 |

*Rdwi − weight of each defect category in a requirement*

Finally, defect density is computed for each requirement and is defined as percentage of requirement defect weight with summation of all defect weights equation 3.

$$Defect\ Density\ D_d\left(\%\right) = \frac{D_w}{D_{size}} \qquad (3)$$

where, $D_w$ is the defect weight of the requirement and $D_{size}$ is summation of all defect weights

## Dependency Analysis

Each requirement is assigned a weight score according to influence of a node connection in a dependency graph. In a dependence flow graph, nodes represent requirements which are dependent on other requirements and edges represent dependence among them. Often dependency is represented over time and it indicates that a latter requirement cannot be processed until its dependencies are fulfilled. The purpose of using dependency graphs is to capture interactions among requirements which help developers to (i) analyze requirements for counting in-stream (incoming edges) and out-stream (outgoing edges)

*Figure 4. Snapshot of Computation of Defect Analysis*

| Requirment | Defect Type | Requirement Defect Weight | Defect Density ($D_d$) | Next |
|---|---|---|---|---|
| R1 | Incomplete, Ambiguous | 5 | 9.6 | |
| R2 | Over Specification | 2 | 3.8 | |
| R3 | Over Specification | 2 | 3.8 | |
| R4 | Incomplete | 3 | 5.8 | |
| R5 | Missing | 4 | 7.7 | |
| R6 | Missing, Non-Traceable | 5 | 9.6 | |
| R7 | Incomplete, Ambiguous | 5 | 9.6 | |
| R8 | In-Correct, Infeasible | 5 | 9.6 | |
| R9 | Missing | 4 | 7.7 | |
| R10 | Missing, In-Correct | 8 | 15.4 | |
| R11 | In-Correct, Inconsistent | 5 | 9.6 | |
| R12 | In-Correct | 4 | 7.7 | |

*Figure 5. Adjacency matrix, Eigenvector values*

| Requirements | Eigen score |
|:---:|:---:|
| R1 | 3.3663 |
| R2 | 1.3348 |
| R3 | 1.3348 |
| R4 | 0.6355 |
| R5 | 0.6355 |
| R6 | 1.2443 |
| R7 | 0.00059 |
| R8 | 1 |
| R9 | 0.576 |
| R10 | 0.576 |
| R11 | 1.2348 |
| R12 | 0.435 |

dependencies for a given node (ii) find an implementation order such that the dependencies are satisfied by the time we get there (iii) draw inferences among indirect dependent (transitive) requirements (iv) highlight and expedite non linear branching situations while prioritization. Non linear branching refers to situations when at a given point there are more than one requirement available for implementation and the decision of assigning higher rank is based on the fact that, their dependencies are satisfied.

For this purpose we use the concept of Eigen centrality measure (Eigenvector) to analyze nodes of a dependency graph to identify the influence of node connection in a graph. Given the adjacency matrix in the form of dependency graph, an automated procedure selects the values corresponding to requirements to compute eigenvector score for each node in a dependency graph. For the example project discussed in section 3, Eigen centrality measure score are as follows:

A high score measure depicts more importance as it is less dependent in terms of inter -connections with other nodes. Now the relative dependency score value for each requirement will be computed by summing up the eigenvector score of each dependent requirement as shown in Figure 6.

## RELATIVE RISK SCORE

Finally, relative risk score value is computed which is defined as the multiplicative factor of stakeholder's value (Sv) and developer's analysis of summation of defect density score and dependency score for each requirement and given in equation 4:

$$Relative\ Risk = S_v \times D_v \qquad (4)$$

*Figure 6. Snapshot of Dependency Score calculation*

| Requirment | Depedent On | Dependency Score (Dep$_i$) | |
|---|---|---|---|
| R1 | R5 - R8 | 4.3663 | Next |
| R2 | R1 - R9 | 3.9423 | |
| R3 | R1 - R4 | 4.0018 | |
| R4 | R1 - R5 - R8 | 5.0018 | |
| R5 | R1 - R2 - R9 - R10 | 5.8531 | |
| R6 | R1 - R3 - R4 | 5.3366 | |
| R7 | R1 - R2 - R3 - R4 - R5 - R6 - R9 - R10 | 9.7032 | |
| R8 | R1 - R2 - R3 - R4 - R5 - R6 - R7 - R9 - R10 | 9.70379 | |
| R9 | R2 - R6 - R10 | 3.1551 | |
| R10 | R1 - R5 - R9 | 4.5778 | |
| R11 | R5 - R8 | 1.6355 | |
| R12 | R1 - R9 | 3.9423 | |

where, $D_v$ is summation of defect density and dependency score

Relative risk score for example scenario taken as case study is given in Figure 7.

*Figure 7. Snapshot of Final Risk Score Computation*

| Requirement | Stakeholder Value (Sv) | Developers Value (Dv) | Relative Risk Score |
|---|---|---|---|
| R1 | 4 | 14.0 | 55.9 |
| R2 | 5 | 7.7 | 38.7 |
| R3 | 5 | 7.8 | 39.0 |
| R4 | 3 | 10.8 | 32.4 |
| R5 | 3 | 13.6 | 40.7 |
| R6 | 4 | 14.9 | 59.7 |
| R7 | 4 | 19.3 | 77.2 |
| R8 | 2 | 19.3 | 38.6 |
| R9 | 2 | 10.9 | 21.7 |
| R10 | 4 | 20.0 | 79.9 |
| R11 | 4 | 11.2 | 44.9 |
| R12 | 1 | 11.6 | 11.6 |

A high score measure depicts more risk which implies the relative impact and urgency of a risk as compared to another one in that project. It can vary between different kind of projects and portfolio the company is aligned with. The comparison helps in fixing the risk with the highest relative score affecting the overall success of the project.

## VALIDATION

A survey through a series of meetings with the project practitioners was done to understand their general experience of including such tool particularly in requirement engineering phase. The brainstorming sessions were included before the risk estimation tool was presented and later their view was taken on effectiveness of approach in risk management and was formally done with the people involved. The results of feedback in general conclude that risk estimation indeed has a positive effect on the software project when integrated with the early phase. It is effective in terms of finding requirements which have high risk based on the understanding of the defects and the interactions among the requirements. The actual project estimation on real project data was compared with the estimation results of risk estimation approach and concluded that the proposed tool lead to saving of considerable project time. This process helps in reduction of system testing time period desired by the testers and stakeholders. As per the feedback from the survey participants, it was also found out that the activities of the approach did not incur any extra burden to requirement engineering.

## CONCLUSION

This chapter presents a software risk assessment model which computes risk of implementing requirements at the very first stage of software development life cycle. Through this work, it is shown that how categorization of requirements and their defects as well as requirement dependency can be used to understand the requirements and know the risk level. Requirement understanding and classification helps in identifying specific information on defects which can improve the validation process. The viewpoints of both stakeholder and developer help in computing the final risk values using both defect score and dependency score. Through the computed risk values, the tool identifies risky requirements which are communicated further to the stakeholders to fix the defects in them by explaining the modalities of the process. It will help in decreasing the chances of failure, risk, and conflicts between stakeholder and developer and other challenges involved to develop the project.

## REFERENCES

Amber, S., Shawoo, N., & Begum, S. (2012). Determination of Risk During Requirement Engineering Process. *International Journal of Emerging Trends in Computing and Information Sciences, 3*(3), 358–364.

Anthony, B., Noraini, C. P., Nor, R. N. H., & Jusoh, Y. Y. (2015). A risk assessment model for collaborative support in software management. *9th Malaysian Software Engineering Conference (MySEC)*, 217-223. 10.1109/MySEC.2015.7475224

Asnar, Y., Giorgini, P., & Mylopoulos, J. (2011). Goal-driven risk assessment in requirements engineering. *Requirements Engineering Journal, 16*(2), 101–116. doi:10.100700766-010-0112-x

Beizer, B. (1990). Software testing techniques (2nd ed.). New York, NY: Van Nostrand Reinhold.

Bhukya, S. N., & Pabboju, S. (2018). Software engineering: Risk features in requirement engineering. *Cluster Computing*, 1–13.

Boehm, B., & Basili, V. (2001). Software Defect Reduction Top 10 List. *IEEE Computer, 34*(1), 135–137. doi:10.1109/2.962984

Cailliau, A., & Lamsweerde, A. (2015). Handling knowledge uncertainty in risk-based requirements engineering. *IEEE 23rd International Requirements Engineering Conference (RE)*.

Chen, J. C., & Huang, S. J. (2009). An empirical analysis of the impact of software development problem factors on software maintainability. *Journal of Systems and Software*, *82*(6), 981–992. doi:10.1016/j.jss.2008.12.036

Chillarege, R., Bhandari, I. S., Chaar, J. K., Halliday, M. J., Moebus, D. S., Ray, B. K., & Wong, M. Y. (1992). Orthogonal Defect Classification-A Concept for In-Process Measurements. *IEEE Transactions on Software Engineering*, *18*(11), 943–956. doi:10.1109/32.177364

Christiansen, T., Wuttidittachotti, P., Prakancharoen, S., & Vallipakorn, S. (2015). Prediction of Risk Factors of Software Development Project by using Multiple Logistic Regression. *Journal of Engineering and Applied Sciences (Asian Research Publishing Network)*, *10*(3).

Cornford, S. L., Feather, M. S., Heron, V. A., & Jenkins, J. S. (2006). Fusing quantitative requirements analysis with model-based systems engineering. *Proceedings of the 14th IEEE international requirements engineering conference,* 279–284. https://en.wikipedia.org/wiki/Eigenvector_centrality

Gallardo, E. (2012). Using Configuration Management and Product Line Software Paradigms to Support the Experimentation Process in Software Engineering. *Proceedings of International Conference on Research Challenges in Information Science RCIS-2012*, 1-6. 10.1109/RCIS.2012.6240454

Ghane, K. (2017). *Quantitative planning and risk management of Agile Software Development. In IEEE Technology & Engineering Management Conference*. TEMSCON.

Grady, R. B. (1992). *Practical Software Metrics for Project Management and Process Improvement*. Prentice-Hall.

Hamill, M., & Katerina, G. P. (2009). Common Trends in Software Fault and Failure Data. *IEEE Transactions on Software Engineering*, *35*(4), 484–496. doi:10.1109/TSE.2009.3

Hayes, J. H. (2003). Building a Requirement Fault Taxonomy: Experiences from a NASA Verification and Validation Research Project. In *Proceedings of the 14thInternational Symposium on Software Reliability Engineering (ISSRE'03)*. Denver, CO: IEEE Computer Society. 10.1109/ISSRE.2003.1251030

Hijazi, H., Alqrainy, S., Muaidi, H., & Khdour, T. (2014). A Framework for Integrating Risk Management into the Software Development Process. *Research Journal of Applied Sciences, Engineering and Technology*, *8*(8), 919–928. doi:10.19026/rjaset.8.1054

Hsieh, M. Y., Hsu, Y. C., & Lin, C. T. (2016). Risk assessment in new software development projects at the front end: A fuzzy logic approach. *Journal of Ambient Intelligence and Humanized Computing*, *9*(2), 295–305. doi:10.100712652-016-0372-5

IEEE. (1998). *IEEE Standard for Software Reviews*. IEEE Std 1028– 1997, 1–37.

IEEE Computer Society Professional Practices Committee. (2014). *Guide to the Software Engineering Body of Knowledge (SWEBOK® Guide), Version 3.0*. IEEE.

Islam, S., & Houmb, S. H. (2010). Integrating Risk Management Activities into Requirements Engineering. *2010 Fourth International Conference on Research Challenges in Information Science RCIS-2010*, 299-310. 10.1109/RCIS.2010.5507389

Kamila, A. R., & Sutikno, S. (2016). Analysis of cause and effect relationship risk using fishbone diagram in SDLC SPASI *v. 4.0* business process. *International Conference on Information Technology Systems and Innovation (ICITSI)*, 1-5.

Kumar, C., & Yadav, D. (2015). A Probabilistic Software Risk Assessment and Estimation Model for Software Projects. *Procedia Computer Science*, *54*, 353–361. doi:10.1016/j.procs.2015.06.041

Kumaresh, S., & Baskaran, R. (2010). Defect Analysis and Prevention for Software Process Quality Improvement. *International Journal of Computers and Applications*, *8*(7), 42–47. doi:10.5120/1218-1759

Kumaresh, S., & Ramachandran, B. (2012). Defect Prevention based on 5 dimensions of Defect Origin. *International Journal of Software Engineering and Its Applications*, *3*(4).

Li, X., & Liu, Q. (2009). Requirement Risk Assessment Focused-on Stakeholder Risk Analysis. *Proceedings of 33rd Annual IEEE International Computer Software and Applications Conference, COMPSAC '09*, *1*, 640-641. 10.1109/COMPSAC.2009.199

Lobato, L. L. (2012). Risk Management in Software Product Lines: An Industrial Case Study. *Proceedings of International Conference on Software and System Process ICSSP*, 180-189. 10.1109/ICSSP.2012.6225963

Margarido, I. L., Faria, J. P., Vidal, R. M., & Vieira, M. (2011).*Classification of defect types in requirements specifications: Literature review, proposal and assessment*. Paper Presented at *6th Iberian Conference on Information Systems and Technologies (CISTI)*, Chaves, Portugal.

Mays, R. G. (1990). Applications of Defect Prevention in Software Development. *IEEE Journal on Selected Areas in Communications*, *8*(2), 164–168. doi:10.1109/49.46867

Meng, Y. (2017). Study on software project risk assessment based on fuzzy analytic hierarchy process. *IEEE 3rd Information Technology and Mechatronics Engineering Conference (ITOEC)*, 853-857.

Mens, T. (2012). On the complexity of software systems. *IEEE Computer*, *45*(8), 79–81. doi:10.1109/MC.2012.273

Pressman, R. S. (2014). Software Engineering: A Practitioner's Approach (8th ed.). Academic Press.

Project Management Institute. (2017). A guide to the project management body of knowledge (PMBOK ® guide), Sixth Edition. PMI.

Rhazali, Y., Hachimi, A., Chana, I., & Lahmer, M. (2020). *Automate Model Transformation From CIM to PIM up to PSM in Model-Driven Architecture. In Modern Principles, Practices, and Algorithms for Cloud Security*. IGI-Global.

Rhazali, Y., Hadi, Y., & Mouloudi, A. (2016). CIM to PIM Transformation in MDA: From Service-Oriented Business Models to Web-Based Design Models. *International Journal of Software Engineering and Its Applications*, *10*(4), 125–142. doi:10.14257/ijseia.2016.10.4.13

Samantra, C., Datta, S., Mahapatra, S., & Debata, B. (2016). Interpretive structural modelling of critical risk factors in software engineering project. *Benchmarking*, *23*(1), 2–24. doi:10.1108/BIJ-07-2013-0071

Sipayung, J. J. P., & Sembiring, J. (2015). Risk assessment model of application development using Bayesian Network and Boehm's Software Risk Principles. *International Conference on Information Technology Systems and Innovation (ICITSI)*, 1-5. 10.1109/ICITSI.2015.7437722

Software Engineering Institute. (2010). CMMI for Systems Engineering/Software Engineering/Integrated Product and Process Development, V1.3. Pittsburgh, PA: Author.

Suma, V., & Gopalakrishnan Nair, T. R. G. (2008). Effective Defect Prevention Approach in Software Process for Achieving Better Quality Levels. Proceedings of World Academy of Science, Engineering and Technology, 32.

Thayer, R. H., & Dorfman, M. (2013). Software Engineering Essentials: Vol. 3. *The Engineering Fundamentals* (4th ed.). Software Management Training Press Carmichael.

Vahidnia, S., Özgür, Ö., & Askerzade, I. (2017). An Early Phase Software Project Risk Assessment Support Method for Emergent Software Organizations. *International Journal of Advanced Computer Science and Applications*, 8(5), 2017. doi:10.14569/IJACSA.2017.080514

Vahidnia, S., Tanriöver, O., & Askerzade, I. (2016). An Evaluation Study of General Software Project Risk Based on Software Practitioners Experiences. *International Journal of Computer Science and Information Technology*, 8(6), 01–13. doi:10.5121/ijcsit.2016.8601

Walia, G. S., & Carver, J. C. (2009). A systematic literature review to identify and classify software requirement errors. *Information and Software Technology*, 51(7), 1087–1109. doi:10.1016/j.infsof.2009.01.004

Zhi, H., Zhang, G., Liu, Y., & Shen, Y. (2017). A novel risk assessment model on software system combining modified fuzzy entropy-weight and AHP. *IEEE 8th Conference on Software Engineering and Service Science*, 451-454.

# Compilation of References

A Linux Foundation Collaborative Project. (2016). *Ovsdb : description*. Consulté à l'adresse http://docs.openvswitch.org/en/latest/ref/ovsdb.7/

Abdelzad, V., & Lethbridge, T. C. (2015). Promoting Traits into Model-Driven Development. *Software & Systems Modeling*, *16*(4), 997–1017. doi:10.100710270-015-0505-x

Abrahão, S., Gravino, C., Insfrán, E., Scanniello, G., & Tortora, G. (2013). Assessing the effectiveness of sequence diagrams in the comprehension of functional requirements. *IEEE Transactions on Software Engineering*, *39*(3), 327–342. doi:10.1109/TSE.2012.27

Abreu, F. B., & Melo, W. (1996). Evaluating the impact of object-oriented design on software quality. *3rd International Symposium on Software Metrics: From Measurement to Empirical Results*. 10.1109/METRIC.1996.492446

Abstratt. (2020). *TextUML*. Retrieved from http://abstratt.github.io/textuml/readme.html

Acceleo. (2006). https://www.eclipse.org/acceleo/

Adesina, O., Lethbridge, T. C., Somé, S., Abdelzad, V., & Boaye Belle, A. (2018). Improving Formal Analysis of State Machines with Particular Emphasis on And-Cross Transitions. *Computer Languages, Systems & Structures*, *54*, 544–585. doi:10.1016/j.cl.2017.12.001

Agborubere, B., & Sanchez-Velazquez, E. (2017).OpenFlow Communications and TLS Security in Software-Defined Networks. *2017 IEEE International Conference on Internet of Things (iThings) and IEEE Green Computing and Communications (GreenCom) and IEEE Cyber, Physical and Social Computing (CPSCom) and IEEE Smart Data (SmartData)*. 10.1109/iThings-GreenCom-CPSCom-SmartData.2017.88

Agner, L. T. W., & Lethbridge, T. C. (2017). A Survey of Tool Use in Modeling Education. In *20th International Conference on Model Driven Engineering Languages and Systems* (MODELS) (pp. 303-311). IEEE. 10.1109/MODELS.2017.1

Agner, L. T. W., Lethbridge, T. C., & Soares, I. W. (2019). Student Experience with Software Modeling Tools. *Software & Systems Modeling*, *18*(5), 3025–3047. doi:10.100710270-018-00709-6

Alencar, F. (n.d.). *Felipealencar/mdn*. Consulté le 10 décembre 2019, à l'adresse https://github.com/felipealencar/mdn

Alfraihi, H. (2016). Towards improving agility in model-driven development. *Joint Proceedings of the Doctoral Symposium and Projects Showcase Held as Part of STAF 2016 co-located with Software Technologies: Applications and Foundations (STAF 2016)*, 2-10.

Al-Saqqar, F., Bentahar, J., & Sultan, K. (2016). On the soundness, completeness and applicability of the logic of knowledge and communicative commitments in multi-agent systems. *Expert Systems with Applications*, *43*, 223–236. doi:10.1016/j.eswa.2015.08.019

Alshnta, A. M., Abdollah, M. F., & Al-Haiqi, A. (2018). SDN in the home: A survey of home network solutions using Software Defined Networking. *Cogent Engineering, 5*(1). Advance online publication. doi:10.1080/23311916.2018.1469949

Amber, S., Shawoo, N., & Begum, S. (2012). Determination of Risk During Requirement Engineering Process. *International Journal of Emerging Trends in Computing and Information Sciences, 3*(3), 358–364.

Amstel, M. F., F.J., L. C., & Chaudron, M. R. (2007). Four Automated Approaches to Analyze the Quality of UML Sequence Diagrams. *31st Annual International Computer Software and Applications Conference (COMPSAC 2007)*. 10.1109/COMPSAC.2007.119

Anthony, B., Noraini, C. P., Nor, R. N. H., & Jusoh, Y. Y. (2015). A risk assessment model for collaborative support in software management. *9th Malaysian Software Engineering Conference (MySEC)*, 217-223. 10.1109/MySEC.2015.7475224

Asnar, Y., Giorgini, P., & Mylopoulos, J. (2011). Goal-driven risk assessment in requirements engineering. *Requirements Engineering Journal, 16*(2), 101–116. doi:10.100700766-010-0112-x

Assmann, U., Zschaler, S., & Wagner, G. (2006). Ontologies, meta-models, and the model-driven paradigm. In *Ontologies for software engineering and software technology* (pp. 249–273). Springer.

Asturias, D. (2017, mars 21). *9 Types of Software Defined Network attacks and how to protect from them.* Consulté à l'adresse https://www.routerfreak.com/9-types-software-defined-network-attacks-protect/

Atkinson, C., & Kuhne, T. (2001). The essence of multilevel metamodling. In UML 2001 - The Unified Modeling Language. Modeling Languages, Concepts and Tools (Vol. 2185, pp. 19-33). Berlin: Springer.

Aversano, L., Grasso, C., & Tortorella, M. (2016). Managing the alignment between business processes and software systems. *Information and Software Technology, 7*(3), 171–188. doi:10.1016/j.infsof.2015.12.009

Azab, M., & Fortes, J. A. B. (2017). Towards proactive SDN-controller attack and failure resilience. *2017 International Conference on Computing, Networking and Communications (ICNC)*. 10.1109/ICCNC.2017.7876169

Baclawski, K., Kokar, M. K., Kogut, P. A., Hart, L., Smith, J., Letkowski, J., & Emery, P. (2002). Extending the Unified Modeling Language for ontology development. *Software & Systems Modeling, 1*(2), 142–156. doi:10.100710270-002-0008-4

Badreddin, O., Lethbridge, T. C., & Forward, A. (2014). A Novel Approach to Versioning and Merging Model and Code Uniformly. In *2nd International Conference on Model-Driven Engineering and Software Development (MODELSWARD)*, (pp. 254-263). INSTICC and IEEE.

Badreddin, O., Forward, A., & Lethbridge, T. C. (2012). *Model Oriented Programming: An Empirical Study of Comprehension. In Conference of the Center for Advanced Studies on Collaborative Research.* IBM Corp and ACM.

Badreddin, O., Forward, A., & Lethbridge, T. C. (2013a). *Exploring a Model-Oriented and Executable Syntax for UML Attributes. In Software Engineering Research, Management and Applications.* Springer.

Badreddin, O., Forward, A., & Lethbridge, T. C. (2013b). *Improving Code Generation for Associations: Enforcing Multiplicity Constraints and Ensuring Referential Integrity. In Software Engineering Research, Management and Applications.* Springer.

Badreddin, O., & Lethbridge, T. C. (2012). Combining Experiments and Grounded Theory to Evaluate a Research Prototype: Lessons from the Umple Model-Oriented Programming Technology. In *First International Workshop on User Evaluation for Software Engineering Researchers* (USER) (pp. 1-4). IEEE. 10.1109/USER.2012.6226575

Bahaj, M., & Bakkas, J. (2013). Automatic conversion method of class diagrams to ontologies maintaining their semantic features. *Int. J. Soft Comput. Eng., 2*.

Balasubramanian, D., Levendovszky, T., Dubey, A., & Karsai, G. (2014). Taming Multi-Paradigm Integration in a Software Architecture Description Language. In D. Balasubramanian, C. Jacquet, P. Van Gorp, S. Kokaly, & T. Meszaros (Ed.), *8th Workshop on Multi-Paradigm Modeling (MPM@MODELS 2014)* (vol. 1237, pp. 67-76). RWTH Aachen University: Sun SITE Central Europe. Retrieved from http://ceur-ws.org/Vol-1237/paper7.pdf

Balci, O. (2012, July). A Life Cycle for Modeling and Simulation. *Simulation, 88*(7), 870–883. doi:10.1177/0037549712438469

Beingmeta. (2005). *FramerD*. Retrieved December 4, 2019, from http://www.framerd.org

Beizer, B. (1990). Software testing techniques (2nd ed.). New York, NY: Van Nostrand Reinhold.

Belghiat, A., & Bourahla, M. (2012). Automatic generation of OWL ontologies from UML class diagrams based on meta-modelling and graph grammars. *World Academy of Science, Engineering and Technology, 6*(8), 380–385.

Beltrán-Ferruz, P. J., González-Calero, P. A., & Gervás, P. (2004). Converting Mikrokosmos frames into description logics. In *Proceedings of the Workshop on NLP and XML (NLPXML-2004): RDF/RDFS and OWL in Language Technology* (pp. 35–42). Association for Computational Linguistics.

Bendix, L., & Emanuelsson, P. (2008). Diff and Merge Support for Model Based Development. In *International workshop on Comparison and Versioning of Software Models (CVSM '08)* (pp. 31–34). ACM. 10.1145/1370152.1370161

Berners-Lee, T., Hendler, J., & Lassila, O. (2001). The semantic web. *Scientific American, 284*(5), 28–37. doi:10.1038 cientificamerican0501-34 PMID:11341160

Bernon, C., Cossentino, M., Gleizes, M.-P., Turci, P., & Zambonelli, F. (2004). Article In J. Odell, P. Giorgini, & J. P. Muller (Eds.), Agent Oriented Software Engineering V (Vol. 3382, pp. 62-77). Berlin: Springer. doi:10.1007/978-3-540-30578-1_5

Berrocal, J., Garcıa-Alonso, J., Vicente-Chicote, C., & Murillo, J. M. (2014). A Pattern-Based and Model-Driven Approach for Deriving IT System Functional Models from Annotated Business Models. In Information System Development (pp. 319-332). Springer.

Bézivin, J., & Briot, J.-P. (2004). Sur les principes de base de l'ingénierie des modèles. *L'OBJET, 10*(4), 145–157. doi:10.3166/objet.10.4.145-157

Bhukya, S. N., & Pabboju, S. (2018). Software engineering: Risk features in requirement engineering. *Cluster Computing*, 1–13.

Bimba, A. T., Idris, N., Al-Hunaiyyan, A., Mahmud, R. B., Abdelaziz, A., Khan, S., & Chang, V. (2016). Towards knowledge modeling and manipulation technologies: A survey. *International Journal of Information Management, 36*(6), 857–871. doi:10.1016/j.ijinfomgt.2016.05.022

Bjorklund, M. (2010). *YANG - A Data Modeling Language for the Network Configuration Protocol (NETCONF)*. IETF., doi:10.17487/rfc6020

Blanc, X. (2005). *MDA en action*. Ed. Eyrolles.

Blanc, X., & Salvatori, O. (2011). *MDA en action : Ingénierie logicielle guidée par les modèles*. Editions Eyrolles.

Blanc, X., & Salvatori, O. (2011). *MDA en action: Ingénierie logicielle guidée par les modèles*. Editions Eyrolles.

Boehm, B. W. (1988, May). A Spiral Model of Software Development and Enhancement. *IEEE Computer, 21*(5), 61–72. doi:10.1109/2.59

Boehm, B., & Basili, V. (2001). Software Defect Reduction Top 10 List. *IEEE Computer, 34*(1), 135–137. doi:10.1109/2.962984

Bousetta, B., El Beggar, O., & Gadi, T. (2013). A methodology for CIM modeling and its transformation to PIM. *Journal of Information Engineering and Applications, 2*(3), 1–21.

Bousetta, B., El Beggar, O., & Gadi, T. (2013). A methodology for cim modelling and its transformation to pim. *Journal of Information Engineering and Applications, 3*(2), 1–21.

Bouzidi, A., Haddar, N., Abdallah, M. B., & Haddar, K. 2017. Deriving use case models from bpmn models. In *2017 IEEE/ ACS 14th International Conference on Computer Systems and Applications (AICCSA).* IEEE. 10.1109/AICCSA.2017.49

Brambilla, M. (2014). *The IFML book – OMG's Interaction Flow Modeling Language explained* (1 edition). Morgan Kaufmann. https://marco-brambilla.com/2015/02/10/the-ifml-book-omgs-interaction-flow-modeling-language-explained/

Brambilla, M., Cabot, J., & Wimmer, M. (2012). Model-driven software engineering in practice. *Synthesis Lectures on Software Engineering, 1*(1), 1–182.

Brambilla, M., Cabot, J., & Wimmer, M. (2017). Model-driven software engineering in practice. *Synthesis Lectures on Software Engineering, 3*(1), 1–207. doi:10.2200/S00751ED2V01Y201701SWE004

Briand, L., Devanbu, P., & Melo, W. (1997). An investigation into coupling measures for c++. In *19th International Conference on Software Engineering, ser. ICSE '97* (pp. 412–421). New York: ACM. 10.1145/253228.253367

Brinkkemper, S., Saeki, M., & Harmsen, F. (1999). Meta-Modelling Based Assembly Techniques for Situational Method Engineering. *Information Systems, 24*(3), 209–228. doi:10.1016/S0306-4379(99)00016-2

Brockmans, S., Colomb, R. M., Haase, P., Kendall, E. F., Wallace, E. K., Welty, C., & Xie, G. T. (2006). A model driven approach for building OWL DL and OWL full ontologies. *International Semantic Web Conference,* 187–200. 10.1007/11926078_14

Brooks, F. P. (1987, April). No Silver Bullet Essence and Accidents of Software Engineering. *IEEE Computer, 20*(4), 10–19. doi:10.1109/MC.1987.1663532

Brunet, G., Chechik, M., Easterbrook, S., Nejati, S., Niu, N., & Sabetzadeh, M. (2006). A Manifesto for Model Merging. In *International Workshop on Global Integrated Model Management (GaMMa '06)* (pp. 5-12), ACM.

Bryl, V., Giorgini, P., & Mylopoulos, J. (2009, February). Designing Socio-Technical Systems: From Stakeholder Goals to Social Networks. *Requirements Engineering, 14*(1), 47–70. doi:10.100700766-008-0073-5

Cailliau, A., & Lamsweerde, A. (2015). Handling knowledge uncertainty in risk-based requirements engineering. *IEEE 23rd International Requirements Engineering Conference (RE).*

Cernuzzi, L., Cossentino, M., & Zambonelli, F. (2005, March). rocess Models for Agent-Based Development. *Engineering Applications of Artificial Intelligence, 18*(2), 205–222. doi:10.1016/j.engappai.2004.11.015

Cetinkaya, D., & Verbraeck, A. (2011). Metamodeling and model transformations in modeling and simulation. *Proceedings of the Winter Simulation Conference. Winter Simulation Conference,* 3048–3058. 10.1109/WSC.2011.6148005

Chen, J. C., & Huang, S. J. (2009). An empirical analysis of the impact of software development problem factors on software maintainability. *Journal of Systems and Software, 82*(6), 981–992. doi:10.1016/j.jss.2008.12.036

Chen, M., Mao, S., & Liu, Y. (2014). Big data : A survey. *Mobile Networks and Applications, 19*(2), 171–209. doi:10.100711036-013-0489-0

Chidamber, S. R., & Kemerer, C. F. (1994). A metrics suite for object oriented design. *IEEE Transactions on Software Engineering, 20*(6), 476–493. doi:10.1109/32.295895

Chikofsky, E. J., & Cross, J. H. (1990, January). Reverse engineering and design recovery: A taxonomy. *IEEE Software.* https://ieeexplore.ieee.org/document/43044

Chillarege, R., Bhandari, I. S., Chaar, J. K., Halliday, M. J., Moebus, D. S., Ray, B. K., & Wong, M. Y. (1992). Orthogonal Defect Classification-A Concept for In-Process Measurements. *IEEE Transactions on Software Engineering, 18*(11), 943–956. doi:10.1109/32.177364

Christiansen, T., Wuttidittachotti, P., Prakancharoen, S., & Vallipakorn, S. (2015). Prediction of Risk Factors of Software Development Project by using Multiple Logistic Regression. *Journal of Engineering and Applied Sciences (Asian Research Publishing Network), 10*(3).

Ciccozzi, F. a., Vangheluwe, H., & Weyns, D. (2019). Blended Modelling – What, why and how. *First International Workshop on Multi-Paradigm Modelling for Cyber-Physical Systems.* Retrieved from https://msdl.uantwerpen.be/conferences/MPM4CPS/2019/wp-content/uploads/2019/09/mpm4cps2019_Blended.pdf

Coad, P., Lefebvre, E., & De Luca, J. (1999). Java Modeling. In *Color With UML: Enterprise Components and Process.* Prentice Hall PTR Upper Saddle River.

Connolly, D., van Harmelen, F., Horrocks, I., McGuinness, D. L., Stein, L. A., & Lucent Technologies Inc. (2001). *Annotated DAML+OIL Ontology Markup.* Retrieved January26, 2020, from https://www.w3.org/TR/daml+oil-walkthru/

Corcoglioniti, F., Aprosio, A. P., & Rospocher, M. (2015). Demonstrating the Power of Streaming and Sorting for Non-distributed RDF Processing: RDFpro. *International Semantic Web Conference.*

Corcoglioniti, F., Rospocher, M., & Aprosio, A. P. (2016). A 2-phase frame-based knowledge extraction framework. In *Proceedings of the 31st Annual ACM Symposium on Applied Computing - SAC '16* (pp. 354–361). New York: ACM Press. 10.1145/2851613.2851845

Cornford, S. L., Feather, M. S., Heron, V. A., & Jenkins, J. S. (2006). Fusing quantitative requirements analysis with model-based systems engineering. *Proceedings of the 14th IEEE international requirements engineering conference,* 279–284. https://en.wikipedia.org/wiki/Eigenvector_centrality

Cossentino, M., Seidita, V., Hilaire, V., & Molesini, A. (2014). *FIPA Design Process Documentation and Fragmentation Working Group.* Retrieved from FIPA Design Process Documentation and Fragmentation Working Group: http://www.pa.icar.cnr.it/cossentino/fipa-dpdf-wg/

Cossentino, M., Gaglio, S., Garro, A., & Seidita, V. (2007). Method fragments for agent design methodologies: From standardisation to research. *International Journal of Agent Oriented Software Engineering, 1*(1), 91–121. doi:10.1504/IJAOSE.2007.013266

Cruz, E. F., Machado, R. J., & Santos, M. Y. (2012). From business process modeling to data model: A systematic approach. In *QUATIC'12, 8th Conf. on the Quality of Information and Communications Technology,* (pp. 205-210). 10.1109/QUATIC.2012.31

CTAN. (n.d.). Consulté le 11 décembre 2019, à l'adresse http://www.ctan.org/tex-archive/macros/latex/contrib./supported/IEEEtran/

Dalibor, M., Jansen, N., Rumpe, B., Wachtmeister, L., & Wortmann, A. (2019). Model-Driven Systems Engineering for Virtual Product Design. *MPM4CPS 2019: First International Workshop on Multi-Paradigm Modelling for Cyber-Physical Systems.* Retrieved from https://msdl.uantwerpen.be/conferences/MPM4CPS/2019/wp-content/uploads/2019/09/Paper_MDSE4VirtualProductDesign.pdf

DAML.org. (2006). *The DARPA Agent Markup Language Homepage.* Retrieved January26, 2020, from http://www.daml.org/

Davies, P. (1992). *The mind of God: the scientific basis for a rational world.* Simon & Schuster.

De Castro, V., Marcos, E., & Vara, J. M. (2011). Applying CIM-to-PIM model transformations for the service-oriented development of information systems. *Journal of Information and Software Technology, 53*(1), 87–105. doi:10.1016/j.infsof.2010.09.002

De Giacomo, G., Lembo, D., Lenzerini, M., Poggi, A., & Rosati, R. (2018). Using ontologies for semantic data integration. In *A Comprehensive Guide Through the Italian Database Research Over the Last 25 Years* (pp. 187–202). Springer. doi:10.1007/978-3-319-61893-7_11

De la Vara, J., Fortuna, M., Sanchez Diaz, J., Lima Werner, C., & Borges, M. (2009). A requirements engineering approach for data modelling of process-aware information systems. In *BIIS'09, Business Information Systems* (pp. 133–144). Springer. doi:10.1007/978-3-642-01190-0_12

De Lara, J., & Vangheluwe, H. (2002). AToM 3 : A Tool for Multi-formalism and Meta-modelling. *International Conference on Fundamental Approaches to Software Engineering,* 174–188. 10.1007/3-540-45923-5_12

De Paepe, D., Thijs, G., Verborgh, R., Mannens, E., & Buyle, R. (2017). Automated UML-Based Ontology Generation in OSLO2. In E. Blomqvist, K. Hose, H. Paulheim, A. Ławrynowicz, F. Ciravegna, & O. Hartig (Eds.), *Proceedings of the 14th ESWC: Posters and Demos (Lecture Notes in Computer Science)* (pp. 93–97). Springer.

Deeptimahanti, D. K., & Babar, M. A. (2009). An automated tool for generating UML models from natural language requirements. *ASE2009 - 24th IEEE/ACM International Conference on Automated Software Engineering.* 10.1109/ASE.2009.48

Demuth, B., & Hussmann, H. (1999). Using OCL Constraints for Relational Database Design. In *Proceedings, The Unified Modeling Language, Second Int. Conference* (pp. 598-613). 10.1007/3-540-46852-8_42

Denil, J., Vangheluwe, H., De Meulenaere, P., & Demeyer, S. (2012). *Calibration of Deployment Simulation Models: A Multi-Paradigm Modelling Approach. In 2012 Symposium on Theory of Modeling and Simulation — DEVS Integrative M&S Symposium (TMS/DEVS '12).* Society for Computer Simulation International. Retrieved from https://dl.acm.org/citation.cfm?id=2346629

Detwiler, L. T., Mejino, J. L. V., & Brinkley, J. F. (2016). From frames to OWL2: Converting the Foundational Model of Anatomy. *Artificial Intelligence in Medicine, 69,* 12–21. doi:10.1016/j.artmed.2016.04.003 PMID:27235801

Dévai, G., Kovács, G. F., & An, A. (2014).Textual, Executable, Translatable UML. OCL@ MoDELS, 3-12.

Di Marzo Serugendo, G., Gleizes, M.-P., & Karageorgos, A. (2006, January). Self-Organization in Multi-Agent Systems. *The Knowledge Engineering Review, 20*(2), 165–189. doi:10.1017/S0269888905000494

Diallo, S., Andreas Tolk, A., Gore, R., & Padilla, J. (2005). Modeling and simulation framework for systems engineering. In D. Gianni, A. D'Ambrogio, & A. Tolk (Eds.), Modeling and Simulation-Based Systems Engineering Handbook (pp. 377-401). Boca Raton, FL: CRC Press. doi:10.1201/b17902

Dieste, Juristo, & Danilo. (2013). Software industry experiments: a systematic literature review. *Proceedings of the 1ˢᵗ International Workshop on Conducting Empirical Studies in Industry*, 2–8.

DKM. (2016). *rdfpro - Home*. Retrieved January26, 2020, from https://dkm.fbk.eu/technologies/rdfpro

dos Santos Soares, M., Vrancken, J., & Verbraeck, A. (2011). User requirements modeling and analysis of softwarein-tensivesystems. *Journal of Systems and Software, 84*(2), 328–339. doi:10.1016/j.jss.2010.10.020

Doumi, K., Baina, S., & Baina, K. (2013). Strategic business and it alignment: Representation and evaluation. *Journal of Theoretical & Applied Information Technology, 47*(1).

Dumas, M., Van Der Aalst, W., & Hofstede, A. (2005). *Process-aware information systems: bridging people and software through process technology.* John Wiley & Sons. doi:10.1002/0471741442

Durak, U. (2015). *Extending the Knowledge Discovery Metamodel for architecture-driven simulation modernization.* Academic Press.

Durand, J. (2015). *SDN pour les nuls.* Consulté à l'adresse https://hepia.infolibre.ch/Virtualisation-Reseaux-2018-2019/Le_SDN_pour_Les_Nuls_Jerome_Durand_JRES_2015.pdf

Dyba, T., & Dingsoyr, T. (2009). *What do we know about agile software development?* doi:10.1109/MS.2009.145

Eclipse, J. D. T. J. (n.d.). *Eclipse Java development tools (JDT) | The Eclipse Foundation.* Retrieved March 19, 2019, from https://www.eclipse.org/jdt/

Ehrig, H., Engels, G., Kreowski, H.-J., & Rozenberg, G. (1999). *Handbook of Graph Grammars and Computing by Graph Transformation.* World Scientific. doi:10.1142/4180

El Khalfi, C., El Qadi, A., & Bennis, H. (2017). A Comparative Study of Software Defined Networks Controllers. *Proceedings of the 2nd International Conference on Computing and Wireless Communication Systems - ICCW-CS'17.* 10.1145/3167486.3167509

Elallaoui, M., Nafil, K., & Touahni, R. (2018). Automatic Transformation of User Stories into UML Use Case Diagrams using NLP Techniques. *Procedia Computer Science, 130*, 42–49. doi:10.1016/j.procs.2018.04.010

El-Attar, M., & Miller, J. (2012, September). Constructing high quality use case models: A systematic review of current practices. *Requirements Engineering.* Advance online publication. doi:10.100700766-011-0135-y

Elbendak, M., Vickers, P., & Rossiter, N. (2011). Parsed use case descriptions as a basis for object-oriented class model generation. *Journal of Systems and Software, 84*(7), 1209–1223. Advance online publication. doi:10.1016/j.jss.2011.02.025

Elsayed, E. K., & El-Sharawy, E. E. (2018). Detecting Design Level Anti-patterns; Structure and Semantics in UML Class Diagrams. *Journal of Computers, 13*(6), 638–655. doi:10.17706/jcp.13.6.638-654

Esbai, R., Erramdani, M., Elotmani, F., & Atounti, M. (2017). Model-to-Model Transformation in Approach by Modeling to Generate a RIA Model with GWT. *International Conference on Information Technology and Communication Systems*, 82–94.

Escalona & Aragon. (2008). A model-driven approach for web requirements. *IEEE Trans. Software Eng., 34*(3), 377–390.

Escalona, M. J., Gutierrez, J. J., Villadiego, D., & Le'on, A. (2007). *Practical Experiences in Web Engineering.* Springer, US.

Essebaa, I., & Chantit, S. (2016). Toward an automatic approach to get PIM level from CIM level using QVT rules. In *11th International Conference on Intelligent Systems: Theories and Applications (SITA)2016*(pp. 1–6). IEEE. 10.1109/SITA.2016.7772271

Essebaa, I., & Chantit, S. (2018). 2018c Scrum and V Lifecycle Combined with Model-Based Testing and Model Driven Architecture to Deal with Evolutionary System Issues. In E. Abdelwahed, L. Bellatreche, M. Golfarelli, D. Méry, & C. Ordonez (Eds.), *Model and Data Engineering*. MEDI. doi:10.1007/978-3-030-00856-7_5

Essebaa, I., & Chantit, S. (2018). Model Driven Architecture and Agile Methodologies: Reflexion and discussion of their combination. In *Federated Conference on Computer Science and Information Systems* (FedCSIS) (pp. 939-948). IEEE. 10.15439/2018F358

Essebaa, I., & Chantit, S. (2018a). A combination of v development life cycle and model-based testing to deal with software system evolution issues. *Proceedings of the 6th International Conference on Model-Driven Engineering and Software Development*, 528-535. 10.5220/0006657805280535

Essebaa, I., & Chantit, S. (2018b). Tool support to automate transformations from SBVR to UML use case diagram. *Proceedings of the 13th International Conference on Evaluation of Novel Approaches to Software Engineering*, 525-532. 10.5220/0006817705250532

Evermann, J. (2007). A meta-level specification and profile for AspectJ in UML. *Proceedings of the 10th International Workshop on Aspect-Oriented Modeling*, 21–27. 10.1145/1229375.1229379

Extensible Markup Language (XML). (2017). https://www.w3.org/XML/

Falquet, G., Métral, C., Teller, J., & Tweed, C. (2011). *Ontologies in urban development projects*. Springer Science & Business Media. doi:10.1007/978-0-85729-724-2

Fatolahi, A., Somé, S. S., & Lethbridge, T. C. (2008). Towards a semi-automated model-driven method for the generation of web-based applications from use cases. In *Proceedings, 4th Model Driven Web Engineering Workshop* (pp 31-45). Toulouse, France: Academic Press.

Feamster, N., Rexford, J., & Zegura, E. (2014). The road to SDN: An Intellectual History of Programmable Networks. *Computer Communication Review*, *44*(2), 87–98. doi:10.1145/2602204.2602219

Floodlight OpenFlow Controller. (n.d.). Consulté le 10 décembre 2019, à l'adresse http://www.projectfloodlight.org/floodlight/

Fogli, D., & Guida, G. (2015). A practical approach to the assessment of quality in use of corporate web sites. *Journal of Systems and Software, 99*, 52–65.

Fondement, F., & Silaghi, R. (2004). Defining Model Driven Engineering Processes. In M. Gogolla, P. Sammut, & J. Whittle (Eds.), *3rd UML Workshop in Software Model Engineering (WiSME 2004)* (pp. 1-11). Lisbon, Portugal: Universidade Nova de Lisboa. Retrieved from http://ctp.di.fct.unl.pt/UML2004/workshop.html#ws5

Forward, A. (2010). *The Convergence of Modeling and Programming: Facilitating the Representation of Attributes and Associations in the Umple Model-Oriented Programming Language* (Doctoral Dissertation). University of Ottawa, Canada.

Forward, A., & Lethbridge, T. C. (2008). Problems and Opportunities for Model-Centric Versus Code-Centric Software Development: A Survey of Software Professionals. In *International Workshop on Models in Software Engineering*, (pp. 27-32). ACM. 10.1145/1370731.1370738

Foster, J., & Juell, P. (2006). A visualization of the frame representation language. In *Companion to the 21st ACM SIGPLAN conference on Object-oriented programming systems, languages, and applications - OOPSLA '06* (p. 708). New York: ACM Press. 10.1145/1176617.1176685

Friedman-Hill, E. J. (2008). *Jess, The Rule Engine for the Java Platform*. Retrieved January26, 2020, from https://jessrules.com/jess/docs/71/index.html

Fuggetta, A. (2000). Software Process: A Roadmap. In *ICSE '00: Proceedings of the Conference on The Future of Software Engineering* (pp. 25-34). Limerick, Ireland: ACM Press. 10.1145/336512.336521

Gallardo, E. (2012). Using Configuration Management and Product Line Software Paradigms to Support the Experimentation Process in Software Engineering. *Proceedings of International Conference on Research Challenges in Information Science RCIS-2012*, 1-6. 10.1109/RCIS.2012.6240454

Garc'ıa-Garc'ıa. Alba, Garc'ıa-Borgon~'on, & Escalona. (2012). Ndt-suite: A model-based suite for the application of NDT. *Web Engineering-12th International Conference, ICWE2012 Proceedings*, 469–472.

Garousi, V., Petersen, K., & Ozkan, B. (2016). Challenges and best practices in industry-academia collaborations in software engineering: A systematic literature review. *Information and Software Technology*, *79*, 106–127. doi:10.1016/j.infsof.2016.07.006

Garrigós, I., Mazón, J.-N., Koch, N., & Escalona, M. J. (2012). Web and requirements engineering. *IET Software*, *6*(2), 83–84. doi:10.1049/iet-sen.2012.0044

Garzon, M., & Lethbridge, T. C. (2012).Exploring how to Develop Transformations and Tools for Automated Umplification. In *Working Conference on Reverse Engineering (WCRE)*, (pp. 491-494). IEEE. 10.1109/WCRE.2012.58

Gašević, D., Djurić, D., & Devedžić, V. (2007). MDA-based automatic OWL ontology development. *International Journal of Software Tools for Technology Transfer*, *9*(2), 103–117. doi:10.100710009-006-0002-1

Genero, M., Piattini, M., & Caleron, C. (2005). A survey of metrics for UML class diagrams. *Journal of Object Technology*, *4*(9), 59–92. doi:10.5381/jot.2005.4.9.a1

Gennari, J. H., Mork, P., & Li, H. (2005). Knowledge transformations between frame systems and RDB systems. In *Proceedings of the 3rd international conference on Knowledge capture - K-CAP '05* (p. 197). New York: ACM Press. 10.1145/1088622.1088666

Ghane, K. (2017). *Quantitative planning and risk management of Agile Software Development. In IEEE Technology & Engineering Management Conference*. TEMSCON.

Gibbs, W. W. (1994). Software's chronic crisis. *Scientific American*, *271*(3), 72–81. doi:10.1038cientificamerican0994-86 PMID:8091191

Giese, H., & Levendovszky, T. (Eds.). (2006). Proceedings of the Workshop on Multi-Paradigm Modeling: Concepts and Tools 2006. In *Proceedings of the Workshop on Multi-Paradigm Modeling: Concepts and Tools.2006/1*. BME-DAAI Technical Report Series. Retrieved from http://avalon.aut.bme.hu/\~mesztam/conferences/mpm06/mpm06\_proc.pdf

Github. (2020a). *Umple*. Retrieved from http://code.umple.org

Github. (2020b). *UmpleOnline Module to Allow Running Experiments*. Retrieved from https://github.com/umple/umple/issues/1490

Gogolla, M., Büttner, F., & Richters, M. (2007). USE: A UML-based specification environment for validating UML and OCL. *Science of Computer Programming*, *69*(1-3), 27–34. doi:10.1016/j.scico.2007.01.013

Gómez-Pérez, A., Fernández-López, M., & Corcho, O. (2006). *Ontological engineering: with examples from the areas of knowledge management, e-commerce and the Semantic Web* (1st ed.). Springer.

Gonzalez-Perez, C., McBride, T., & Henderson-Sellers, B. (2005). A Metamodel for Assessable Software Development Methodologies. *Software Quality Journal*, *13*(2), 195–214. doi:10.100711219-005-6217-7

Gordijn, J., & Akkermans, H. (2001). Designing and evaluating e-business models. *IEEE Intelligent Systems*, *16*(4), 11–17. doi:10.1109/5254.941353

Gordijn, J., & Akkermans, H. (2018). *Value Webs: Understanding e-Business Innovation*. The Value Engineers.

Gordijn, J., & Akkermans, J. M. (2003). Value based requirements engineering: Exploring innovative e-commerce idea. *Requirements Engineering Journal*, *8*(2), 114–134. doi:10.100700766-003-0169-x

Gordijn, J., Yu, E., & Van Der Raadt, B. (2006). E-service design using i* and e/sup 3/value modeling. *IEEE Software*, *23*(3), 26–33. doi:10.1109/MS.2006.71

Gotti, Z., & Mbarki, S. (2016). *Java Swing Modernization Approach—Complete Abstract Representation based on Static and Dynamic Analysis*. ICSOFT-EA. doi:10.5220/0005986002100219

Gotti, Z., Mbarki, S., Gotti, S., & Laaz, N. (2018). Nooj Graphical User Interfaces Modernization. In S. Mbarki, M. Mourchid, & M. Silberztein (Eds.), *Formalizing Natural Languages with NooJ and Its Natural Language Processing Applications* (pp. 227–239). Springer International Publishing. doi:10.1007/978-3-319-73420-0_19

Grady, R. B. (1992). *Practical Software Metrics for Project Management and Process Improvement*. Prentice-Hall.

Grigorova, D., & Nikolov, N. (2007). Knowledge representation in systems with natural language interface. In *Proceedings of the 2007 international conference on Computer systems and technologies - CompSysTech '07* (p. 1). New York: ACM Press. 10.1145/1330598.1330670

Group, O. (2008). *SPEM 2.0*. Tratto da Software & Systems Process Engineering Metamodel Specification. Version 2.0: https://www.omg.org/spec/SPEM/2.0/

Group, O. M. (2003). *Meta Object Facility (MOF) 2.0 Core Specification*.

Group, O. M. (n.d.). *Unified Model Language V2.5*. http://www.omg.org/ spec/UML/2.5/

Gude, N., Koponen, T., Pettit, J., Pfaff, B., Casado, M., McKeown, N., & Shenker, S. (2008). NOX: Towards an Operating System for Networks. *Computer Communication Review*, *38*(3), 105–110. doi:10.1145/1384609.1384625

GuideM. R. (2015). *2.0, OMG*.

Guskov, G., Namestnikov, A., & Yarushkina, N. (2017). Approach to the Search for Similar Software Projects Based on the UML Ontology. *International Conference on Intelligent Information Technologies for Industry*, 3–10.

Guti'errez, J. J., Escalona, M. J., & Mejías, M. (2015). A model-driven approach for functional test case generation. *Journal of Systems and Software*, *109*, 214–228. doi:10.1016/j.jss.2015.08.001

Gutiérrez, J. J., Nebut, C., Escalona, M. J., Mejías, M., & Ramos, I. M. (2008). Visualization of use cases through automatically generated activity diagrams. In *Proceedings, 11th International Conference MoDELS'08*. (pp83-96). Toulouse, France. 10.1007/978-3-540-87875-9_6

H¨ofer & Tichy. (2006). Status of empirical research in software engineering. *Empirical Software Engineering Issues. Critical Assessment and Future Directions, International Workshop*.

Hafeez, A., Mussavi, S. H. A., Rehman, A.-U., & Shaikh, A. (2018). Ontology-Based Finite Satisfiability of UML Class Model. *IEEE Access: Practical Innovations, Open Solutions*, *6*, 3040–3050. doi:10.1109/ACCESS.2017.2786781

Hahn, C., Dmytro, P., & Fischer, K. (2010). A model-driven approach to close the gap between business requirements and agent-based execution. In *Proceedings, 4th Workshop on Agent-based Technologies and applications for enterprise interoperability* (pp. 13–24). Toronto, Canada: Academic Press.

Hamill, M., & Katerina, G. P. (2009). Common Trends in Software Fault and Failure Data. *IEEE Transactions on Software Engineering, 35*(4), 484–496. doi:10.1109/TSE.2009.3

Hardebolle, C., & Boulanger, F. (2009, November). Exploring Multi-Paradigm Modeling Techniques. *Simulation, 85*(11-12), 688–708. doi:10.1177/0037549709105240

Harman, M., & Hierons, R. (2001). An overview of program slicing. *Software Focus, 2*(3), 85–92. doi:10.1002wf.41

Harrison, R., Counsell, S., & Nithi, R. (1998). Coupling metrics for object oriented design. In *Fifth International Software Metrics Symposium. Metrics (Cat. No.98TB100262)*, (pp. 150-157). 10.1109/METRIC.1998.731240

Hayes, J. H. (2003). Building a Requirement Fault Taxonomy: Experiences from a NASA Verification and Validation Research Project. In *Proceedings of the 14thInternational Symposium on Software Reliability Engineering (ISSRE'03)*. Denver, CO: IEEE Computer Society. 10.1109/ISSRE.2003.1251030

Hazboun, E. (2015). The Interface to the Routing System. *Innovative Internet Technologies and Mobile Communications, WS2015*, 25–31. doi:10.2313/NET-2016-07-1

Henderson-Sellers, B. (2002). Process Metamodelling and Process Construction: Examples Using the OPEN Process Framework OPF. *Annals of Software Engineering, 14*(1), 341–362. doi:10.1023/A:1020570027891

Henderson-Sellers, B., & Gonzalez-Perez, C. (2005, January). A Comparison of Four Process Metamodels and the Creation of a New Generic Standard. *Information and Software Technology, 47*(1), 49–65. doi:10.1016/j.infsof.2004.06.001

Herchi, H., & Ben Abdessalem, W. (2013). *From user requirements to UML class diagram.* https://gate.ac.uk/

Hernández, J. Z., & Serrano, J. M. (2001). Knowledge-based models for emergency management systems. *Expert Systems with Applications, 20*(2), 173–186. doi:10.1016/S0957-4174(00)00057-9

Hijazi, H., Alqrainy, S., Muaidi, H., & Khdour, T. (2014). A Framework for Integrating Risk Management into the Software Development Process. *Research Journal of Applied Sciences, Engineering and Technology, 8*(8), 919–928. doi:10.19026/rjaset.8.1054

Hillairet, G. (2007). *ATL Use Case-ODM Implementation (Bridging UML and OWL).* http://www. eclipse. org/m2m/atl/usecases/ODMImplementation

Hoffer, J. A., & George, J. J. A. (2004). Valacich, Modern System Analysis and Design. Prentice Hall.

Home. (n.d.). Consulté le 10 décembre 2019, à l'adresse https://www.opendaylight.org/

Horrocks, I., Patel-Schneider, P. F., & van Harmelen, F. (2003). From SHIQ and RDF to OWL: The making of a Web Ontology Language. *Journal of Web Semantics, 1*(1), 7–26. doi:10.1016/j.websem.2003.07.001

Hoyos, J. R., García-Molina, J., & Botía, J. A. (2013). A domain-specific language for context modeling in context-awaresystems. *Journal of Systems and Software, 86*(11), 2890–2905. doi:10.1016/j.jss.2013.07.008

Hsieh, M. Y., Hsu, Y. C., & Lin, C. T. (2016). Risk assessment in new software development projects at the front end: A fuzzy logic approach. *Journal of Ambient Intelligence and Humanized Computing, 9*(2), 295–305. doi:10.100712652-016-0372-5

Husseini Orabi, M., Husseini Orabi, A., & Lethbridge, T.C. (2020). Umple-TL: A Model-Oriented, Dependency-Free Text Emission Tool. *Communications in Computer and Information Science, 1161*, 127-155.

I&K Group. (2006). *Knowledge Structure Manager.* Retrieved January26, 2020,http://www.dia.fi.upm.es/grupos/I&K/KSM-home.htm

IEEE Computer Society Professional Practices Committee. (2014). *Guide to the Software Engineering Body of Knowledge (SWEBOK® Guide), Version 3.0.* IEEE.

IEEE. (1998). *IEEE Standard for Software Reviews.* IEEE Std 1028– 1997, 1–37.

IN2. (n.d.). *Opina.* http://opinahq.com

Islam, S., & Houmb, S. H. (2010). Integrating Risk Management Activities into Requirements Engineering. *2010 Fourth International Conference on Research Challenges in Information Science RCIS-2010,* 299-310. 10.1109/RCIS.2010.5507389

Javed, M., & Lin, Y. (2018). Iterative process for generating ER diagram from unrestricted requirements. *ENASE 2018 - Proceedings of the 13th International Conference on Evaluation of Novel Approaches to Software Engineering,* 192–204. 10.5220/0006778701920204

Jayaraman, P., Whittle, J., Elkhodary, A. M., & Gomaa, H. (2007). *Model Composition in Product Lines and Feature Interaction Detection Using Critical Pair Analysis. In Model Driven Engineering Languages and Systems. MODELS 2007* (Vol. 4735). Springer.

Jedlitschka, A., Juristo, N., & Rombach, D. (2014). andH.D.Rombach.Reportingexperiments to satisfy professionals' information needs. *Empirical Software Engineering, 19*(6), 1921–1955. doi:10.100710664-013-9268-6

Jensen, K., & Kristensen, L. M. (2009). *Coloured Petri Nets. Modelling and Validation of Concurrent Systems.* Springer. doi:10.1007/b95112

Jouault, F., Allilaire, F., Bézivin, J., Kurtev, I., & Valduriez, P. (2006). Atl: a qvt-like transformation language. In *Companion to the 21st ACM SIGPLAN symposium on Object-oriented programming systems, languages, and applications.* ACM.

Jouault, F., Allilaire, F., Bézivin, J., Kurtev, I., & Valduriez, P. (2006). ATL: a QVT-like transformation language. *Proceedings of the 21st ACM SIGPLAN symposium on Object-oriented programming systems, languages, and applications.* 10.1145/1176617.1176691

Juba, Y., Huang, H.-H., & Kawagoe, K. (2013). Dynamic Isolation of Network Devices Using OpenFlow for Keeping LAN Secure from Intra-LAN Attack. *Procedia Computer Science, 22,* 810–819. doi:10.1016/j.procs.2013.09.163

Juristo & Gomez. (2010). *Replication of software engineering experiments. In Empirical Software Engineering and Verification-International Summer Schools, LASER 2008-2010.* Revised Tutorial Lectures.

Juristo & Moreno. (2001). Basics of software engineering experimentation. Kluwer.

Juristo, N. (2016). Experiences conducting experiments in industry: the ESEIL fidipro project. Proceedings of the 4th International Workshop on Conducting Empirical Studies in Industry, 1–3.

Kamila, A. R., & Sutikno, S. (2016). Analysis of cause and effect relationship risk using fishbone diagram in SDLC SPASI *v. 4.0* business process. *International Conference on Information Technology Systems and Innovation (ICITSI),* 1-5.

Kardoš, M., & Drozdová, M. (2010). Analytical Method of CIM to PIM Transformation in Model Driven Architecture (MDA). *JIOS,* 89-99.

Kardoš, M., & Drozdová, M. (2010). Analytical method of CIM to PIM transformation in model driven architecture (MDA). *Journal of Information and Organizational Sciences, 34*(1), 89–99.

Kardoš, M., & Drozdová, M. (2010). Analytical method of CIM to PIM transformation in Model Driven Architecture (MDA). *Journal of Information and Organizational Sciences, 34*(1), 89–99.

Kaur, K., Singh, J., & Singh Ghumman, N. (2014).Mininet as Software Defined Networking Testing Platform. *International Conference on Communication, Computing & Systems (ICCCS–2014).*

Keti, F., & Askar, S. (2015). Emulation of Software Defined Networks Using Mininet in Different Simulation Environments. *2015 6th International Conference on Intelligent Systems, Modelling and Simulation.*10.1109/isms.2015.46

Kharmoum, N., Ziti, S., & Omary, F. (2016). An analytical study of the cim to pim transformation in mda. International Workshop on Computing Sciences (WCOS'16), 14–19.

Kharmoum, N., Ziti, S., & Omary, F. (2019a). A novel automatic transformation method from the business value modelto the uml use case diagram. *2nd Edition of the International Conference on Advanced Intelligent Systems for Sustainable Development.*

Kharmoum, N., Ziti, S., Rhazali, Y., & Omary, F. (2018). Automatic transformation method from e3value model to the dataflow diagram: An mda approach. *International Conference on Modern Intelligent Systems Concepts MISC'2018.*

Kharmoum, N., Ziti, S., Rhazali, Y., & Omary, F. (2019b). An automatic transformation method from the e3value modelto ifml model: An mda approach. *Journal of Computational Science, 15*(6), 800–813. doi:10.3844/jcssp.2019.800.813

Kharmoum, N., Ziti, S., Rhazali, Y., & Omary, F. (2019c). A method of model transformation in MDA approach from E3value model to BPMN2 diagrams in CIM level. *IAENG International Journal of Computer Science, 46*(4), 1–17.

Kharmoum, N., Ziti, S., Rhazali, Y., & Omary, F. (2019d). An automatic transformation method from the E3value model to UML2 sequence diagrams: An MDA approach. *International Journal of Computing, 18*(3), 316–330.

Kherraf, S., Lefebvre, É., & Suryn, W. (2008). Transformation from CIM to PIM using patterns and Archetypes. In *Proceedings, 19th Australian Software Engineering Conference* (pp. 338 – 346). 10.1109/ASWEC.2008.4483222

Kim, K., Lee, C., Jung, S., & Lee, G. G. (2008). A frame-based probabilistic framework for spoken dialog management using dialog examples. In *Proceedings of the 9th SIGdial Workshop on Discourse and Dialogue* (pp. 120–127). Columbus, OH: Association for Computational Linguistics. 10.3115/1622064.1622088

Kleppe, A., Warmer, G. J., & Bast, W. (2003). *MDA Explained: The Model Driven Architecture: Practice and Promise.* Addison-Wesley.

Konys, A. (2016). Ontology-Based Approaches to Big Data Analytics. *International Multi-Conference on Advanced Computer Systems,* 355–365.

Kornienko, A. A., Kornienko, A. V., Fofanov, O. B., & Chubik, M. P. (2015). Knowledge in Artificial Intelligence Systems: Searching the Strategies for Application. *Procedia: Social and Behavioral Sciences, 166,* 589–594. doi:10.1016/j.sbspro.2014.12.578

Kozaki. (n.d.). *Ontology Engineering for Big Data* [Technologie]. https://fr.slideshare.net/KoujiKozaki/ontology-engineering-for-big-data

Kramer, S., & Kaindl, H. (2004). Coupling and cohesion metrics for knowledge-based systems using frames and rules. *ACM Transactions on Software Engineering and Methodology, 13*(3), 332–358. doi:10.1145/1027092.1027094

Kriouile, A., Addamssiri, N., & Gadi, T. (2015). An MDA Method for Automatic Transformation of Models from CIM to PIM. *American Journal of Software Engineering and Applications,* 1-14.

Kriouile, A., Gadi, T., & Balouki, Y. (2013). Cim to pim transformation: A criteria based evaluation. *International Journalof Computer Technology and Applications, 4*(4), 616.

Kuhn, T. S. (2012). The Structure of Scientific Revolutions (50th Anniversary ed.). Chicago: University of Chicago Press.

Kulkarni, V., Barat, S., & Ramteerthkar, U. (2011). Early experience with agile methodology in a modeldriven approach. *Model Driven Engineering Languages and Systems, 14th International Conference, MODELS 2011 Proceedings*, 578-590.

Kumar, C., & Yadav, D. (2015). A Probabilistic Software Risk Assessment and Estimation Model for Software Projects. *Procedia Computer Science, 54*, 353–361. doi:10.1016/j.procs.2015.06.041

Kumaresh, S., & Baskaran, R. (2010). Defect Analysis and Prevention for Software Process Quality Improvement. *International Journal of Computers and Applications, 8*(7), 42–47. doi:10.5120/1218-1759

Kumaresh, S., & Ramachandran, B. (2012). Defect Prevention based on 5 dimensions of Defect Origin. *International Journal of Software Engineering and Its Applications, 3*(4).

Kumar, V. N., Kumar, A. P., & Abhishek, K. (2011). A Comprehensive Comparative study of SPARQL and SQL. *(IJCSIT). International Journal of Computer Science and Information Technologies, 2*(4), 1706–1710.

Laaz, Naziha, & Mbarki. (2016). Integrating IFML models and owl ontologies to derive UIs web-Apps. *Information Technology for Organizations Development (IT4OD), 2016 International Conference on*, 1–6.

Laaz, N., & Mbarki, S. (2019). *OntoifML : Automatic generation of annotated web pages from IFML and ontologies using the MDA approach: A case study of an EMR management application*. Scopus.

Laaz, N., Wakil, K., Mbarki, S., & Jawawi, D. N. A. (2018). Comparative Analysis of Interaction Flow Modeling Language Tools. *Journal of Computational Science, 14*(9), 1267–1278. doi:10.3844/jcssp.2018.1267.1278

Lantz, B., Heller, B., & McKeown, N. (2010a). A network in a laptop. *Proceedings of the Ninth ACM SIGCOMM Workshop on Hot Topics in Networks - Hotnets '10*.10.1145/1868447.1868466

Lara, J. d., & Vangheluwe, H. (2002). Computer Aided Multi-paradigm Modelling to Process Petri-Nets and Statecharts. In A. Corradini, H. Ehrig, H. -J. Kreowski, & G. Rozenberg (Eds.), Graph Transformation (Vol. 2505, pp. 239-253). Berlin: Springer. doi:10.1007/3-540-45832-8

Larman, C., & Basili, V. R. (2003, June). Iterative and Incremental Development: A Brief History. *IEEE Computer, 36*(6), 47–56. doi:10.1109/MC.2003.1204375

Lefebvre, E. (2005). Building Platform-Independent Models with Business Archetypes and Patterns. *Proceedings of the Montreal Conference on eTechnologies*, 127.

Lethbridge, T. C. (2019). UmpleOnline as a Testbed for Modeling Empirical Studies: A Position Paper. In *Fourth International Workshop on Human Factors in Modeling (HuFaMo)*, (pp. 412-413). IEEE 10.1109/MODELS-C.2019.00064

Lethbridge, T. C., & Algablan, A. (2018). Using Umple to Synergistically Process Features, Variants, UML Models and Classic Code. In *International Symposium on Leveraging Applications of Formal Methods*, (pp. 69-88). Springer. 10.1007/978-3-030-03418-4_5

Lethbridge, T. C., Mussbacher, G., Forward, A., & Badreddin, O. (2011). *Teaching UML using Umple: Applying Model-Oriented Programming in the Classroom. In Software Engineering Education and Training (CSEE&T)*. IEEE.

Li, Q., & Chen, Y.-L. (2009). *Modeling and Analysis of Enterprise and Information Systems*. Springer Berlin Heidelberg. doi:10.1007/978-3-540-89556-5

Liu, J., Pacitti, E., & Valduriez, P. (2018). A Survey of Scheduling Frameworks in Big Data Systems. *International Journal of Cloud Computing*, 1–27.

Li, X., Lei, Y., Wang, W., Wang, W., & Zhu, Y. (2013). *A DSM-based Multi-Paradigm Simulation Modeling Approach for Complex Systems. In 2013 Winter Simulation Conference: Simulation: Making Decisions in a Complex World (WSC '13).* IEEE Press. Retrieved from https://dl.acm.org/citation.cfm?id=2675983.2676133

Li, X., & Liu, Q. (2009). Requirement Risk Assessment Focused-on Stakeholder Risk Analysis. *Proceedings of 33rd Annual IEEE International Computer Software and Applications Conference, COMPSAC '09, 1,* 640-641. 10.1109/COMPSAC.2009.199

Lobato, L. L. (2012). Risk Management in Software Product Lines: An Industrial Case Study. *Proceedings of International Conference on Software and System Process ICSSP*, 180-189. 10.1109/ICSSP.2012.6225963

Lopes, F. A., Lima, L., Santos, M., Fidalgo, R., & Fernandes, S. (2016). High-level modeling and application validation for SDN. *NOMS 2016 - 2016 IEEE/IFIP Network Operations and Management Symposium.* 10.1109/noms.2016.7502813

Lopes, F., Bauer, R., Stenio, F., & Fernandes, L. (2016). Capability-Aware SDN Application Models: Dealing with Network Heterogeneity. *IEEE Computer.*

Lopes, F. A., Santos, M., Fidalgo, R., & Fernandes, S. (2015). Model-driven networking: A novel approach for SDN applications development. *2015 IFIP/IEEE International Symposium on Integrated Network Management (IM).* 10.1109/INM.2015.7140372

Lorenz, T., & Jost, A. (2006). Towards an Orientation Framework in Multi-Paradigm Modeling: Aligning Purpose, Object and Methodology in System Dynamics, AGent-Based Modeling and DIscrete-EVent-Simulation. In A. Grosler, E. A. Rouwette, R. S. Langer, J. I. Rowe, & J. M. Yanni (Eds.), *24th International Conference of the System Dynamics Society* (pp. 2134-2151). Albany, NY: System Dynamics Society. Retrieved from https://www.systemdynamics.org/conferences/2006/proceed/papers/LOREN178.pdf

Lorenz, M., & Kidd, J. (1994). *Object-oriented Software Metrics: A Practical Guide.* Prentice-Hall, Inc.

Lucassen, G., Robeer, M., Dalpiaz, F., van der Werf, J. M. E. M., & Brinkkemper, S. (2017). Extracting conceptual models from user stories with Visual Narrator. *Requirements Engineering, 22*(3), 339–358. Advance online publication. doi:10.100700766-017-0270-1

Lundell, B., Lings, B., Persson, A., & Mattsson, A. (2006). *UML Model Interchange in Heterogeneous Tool Environments: An Analysis of Adoptions of XMI 2. In Model Driven Engineering Languages and Systems (MODELS)* (Vol. 4199). Springer.

Lynch, C., Padilla, J., Diallo, S., Sokolowski, J., & Banks, C. (2014). A multi-paradigm modeling framework for modeling and simulating problem situations. In *Proceedings of the Winter Simulation Conference 2014* (p. 1688-1699). Savanah, GA: IEEE. 10.1109/WSC.2014.7020019

Maatougui, E., Bouanaka, C., & Zeghib, N. (2016). Towards a meta-model for quality-aware self-adaptive systems design. ModComp@ MoDELS, 12–18.

Mahe, V., Combemale, B., & Cadavid, J. (2010). *Crossing model driven engineering and agility – preliminary thoughts on benefits and challenges.* Academic Press.

Margarido, I. L., Faria, J. P., Vidal, R. M., & Vieira, M. (2011).*Classification of defect types in requirements specifications: Literature review, proposal and assessment.* Paper Presented at *6th Iberian Conference on Information Systems and Technologies (CISTI)*, Chaves, Portugal.

Mariani, S., & Omicini, A. (2013). Molecules of Knowledge: Self-Organisation in Knowledge-Intensive Environments. In *G. Fortino, C. Badica, M. Malgeri, & R. Unland (Eds.), Intelligent Distributed Computing VI.446* (pp. 17–22). Springer. doi:10.1007/978-3-642-32524-3_4

Marinov, M. (2004). Using XML to represent knowledge by frames. In *Proceedings of the 5th international conference on Computer systems and technologies - CompSysTech '04* (pp. 1-6). New York: ACM Press. 10.1145/1050330.1050350

Marinov, M. (2008). Using frames for knowledge representation in a CORBA-based distributed environment. *Knowledge-Based Systems, 21*(5), 391–397. doi:10.1016/j.knosys.2008.02.003

Martinez-Cruz, C., Blanco, I. J., & Vila, M. A. (2012). Ontologies versus relational databases: Are they so different? A comparison. *Artificial Intelligence Review, 38*(4), 271–290. doi:10.100710462-011-9251-9

Mays, R. G. (1990). Applications of Defect Prevention in Software Development. *IEEE Journal on Selected Areas in Communications, 8*(2), 164–168. doi:10.1109/49.46867

Mazón, J., Pardillo, J., & Trujillo, J. (2007), A model-driven goal-oriented requirement engineering approach for data warehouses. In *Proceedings, Conference on Advances in Conceptual Modeling: Foundations and Applications, ER Workshops* (pp. 255–264). 10.1007/978-3-540-76292-8_31

McCarthy, W. E. (1982). The rea accounting model: A generalized framework for accounting systems in a shared data environment. *The Accounting Review*, 554–578.

McKeown, N., Anderson, T., Balakrishnan, H., Parulkar, G., Peterson, L., Rexford, J., Shenker, S., & Turner, J. (2008). OpenFlow: Enabling Innovation in Campus Networks. *Computer Communication Review, 38*(2), 69–74. doi:10.1145/1355734.1355746

Medved, J., Varga, R., Tkacik, A., & Gray, K. (2014).OpenDaylight: Towards a Model-Driven SDN Controller architecture. *Proceeding of IEEE International Symposium on a World of Wireless, Mobile and Multimedia Networks 2014*. 10.1109/WoWMoM.2014.6918985

Medvidovic, N., Egyed, A., & Rosenblum, D. S. (1999).Round-trip Software Engineering Using UML: From Architecture to Design and Back. *Second International Workshop on Object-Oriented Reengineering(WOOR'99)*, 1-8.

Mellor, S. J., & Balcer, M. (2002). *Executable UML: A Foundation for Model-Driven Architectures*. Addison-Wesley Longman.

Meng, Y. (2017). Study on software project risk assessment based on fuzzy analytic hierarchy process. *IEEE 3rd Information Technology and Mechatronics Engineering Conference (ITOEC)*, 853-857.

Mens, T. (2012). On the complexity of software systems. *IEEE Computer, 45*(8), 79–81. doi:10.1109/MC.2012.273

Meservy, T. O., & Fenstermacher, K. D. (2005). Transforming software development: An MDA road map. *Computer, 38*(9), 52–58. doi:10.1109/MC.2005.316

Meyer, A., Pufahl, L., Fahland, D., & Weske, M. (2013). Modeling and Enacting Complex Data Dependencies in Business Processes. In *PM'13, 11th proceedings of Inter Conference* (pp. 171-186). Lecture Notes in Computer Science.

Mich, L. (1996). NL-OOPS: From natural language to object oriented requirements using the natural language processing system LOLITA. *Natural Language Engineering, 2*(2), 161–187. Advance online publication. doi:10.1017/S1351324996001337

Mich, L., & Garigliano, R. (2002). *NL-OOPS: A requirements analysis tool based on natural language processing*. Management Information Systems.

Miles, R., & Hamilton, K. (2006). *Learning UML 2.0*. O'Reilly Media.

Miller, J., & Mukerji, J. (2001). *Model Driven Architecture (MDA)*. Architecture Board ORMSC. Retrieved January 26, 2020, from https://www.omg.org/mda/

Miller, J., Mukerji, J., & Belaunde, M. (2003). *MDA guide*. Object Management Group.

Mininet. (n.d.). *Mininet/mininet*. Consulté le 10 décembre 2019, à l'adresse https://github.com/mininet/mininet/wiki/Introduction-to-Mininet

MininetOverview. (2018). Consulté à l'adresse http://mininet.org/overview/

Minsky, M. (1974). A Framework for Representing Knowledge. *MIT-AI Laboratory Memo 306*. Retrieved January 20, 2020 from https://courses.media.mit.edu/2004spring/mas966/readings.htm

Miranda, M. A., Ribeiro, M. G., Marques-Neto, H. T., & Song, M. A. J. (2017). Domain-specific language for automaticgeneration of uml models. *IET Software*, *12*(2), 129–135. doi:10.1049/iet-sen.2016.0279

Mirshams Shahshahani, P. (2011). *Extending the Knowledge Discovery Metamodel to Support Aspect- Oriented Programming* [Masters, Concordia University]. https://spectrum.library.concordia.ca/7329/

MOF. (2009). *Omg, meta object facility (mof)2.0query/view/transformation specification*. https://www.omg.org/spec/QVT/1.0/PDF

Mokhtar, R., Rahman, A. A., & Othman, S. H. (2017). Towards model driven architecture in academic quality assurance information system development. *Journal of Telecommunication Electronic and Computer Engineering*, *9*(1-3), 95–100.

Mokrys, M. (2012). Possible transformation from Process Model to IS Design Model. In *Proceedings, 1th International Virtual Conference* (pp. 71–74). Academic Press.

Molesini, A. (2008). *Meta-Models, Environment and Layers: Agent-Oriented Engineering of Complex Systems* (Ph.D Thesis). Alma Mater Studiorum - Università di Bologna, Dipartimento di Elettronica, Informatica e Sistemistica, Bologna.

Mosterman, P. J., & Vangheluwe, H. (2002, October). Guest Editorial: Special Issue on Computer Automated Multi-Paradigm Modeling. *ACM Transactions on Modeling and Computer Simulation*, *12*(4), 249–255. doi:10.1145/643120.643121

Mosterman, P. J., & Vangheluwe, H. (2004). Computer Automated Multi-Paradigm Modeling: An Introduction. *Simulation*, *80*(9), 433–450. doi:10.1177/0037549704050532

Musen, M. A. (2015). The Protégé Project: A Look Back and a Look Forward. *AI Matters*, *1*(4), 4–12. doi:10.1145/2757001.2757003 PMID:27239556

Musset, J., Juliot, É., Lacrampe, S., Piers, W., Brun, C., Goubet, L., Lussaud, Y., & Allilaire, F. (2006). *Acceleo user guide*. See also http://acceleo. org/doc/obeo/en/acceleo-2.6-user-guide. pdf

Mustafiz, S., Denil, J., Lucio, L., & Vangheluwe, H. (2012). The FTG+PM Framework for Multi-paradigm Modelling: An Automotive Case Study. In *6th International Workshop on Multi-Paradigm Modeling (MPM '12)* (pp. 13-18). New York, NY: ACM. 10.1145/2508443.2508446

Musumbu, K. (2013). Towards a Model Driven Semantics Web using the Ontology. *The 2013 International Conference on Advanced ICT for Business and Management (ICAICTBM2013), 700*.

Nadal, S., Romero, O., Abelló, A., Vassiliadis, P., & Vansummeren, S. (2018). *An integration-oriented ontology to govern evolution in big data ecosystems*. arXiv preprint arXiv:1801.05161

Nakamura, Y., Tatsubori, M., Imamura, T., & Ono, K. (2005). Model-driven security based on a Web services security architecture. *2005 IEEE International Conference on Services Computing (SCC'05) Vol-1*. 10.1109/SCC.2005.66

Nazaruks, V., & Osis, J. (2017a). A Survey on Domain Knowledge Representation with Frames. In *Proceedings of the 12th International Conference on Evaluation of Novel Approaches to Software Engineering (ENASE 2017)* (pp. 346–354). Porto, Portugal: SCITEPRESS - Science and Technology Publications. 10.5220/0006388303460354

Nazaruks, V., & Osis, J. (2017b). Joint Usage of Frames and the Topological Functioning Model for Domain Knowledge Presentation and Analysis. In *Proceedings of the 12th International Conference on Evaluation of Novel Approaches to Software Engineering (ENASE 2017)* (pp. 379–390). Porto: SciTePress. 10.5220/0006388903790390

Nielsen, C. B., Fitzgerald, J., Woodcock, J., & Peleska, J. (2015). Systems of Systems Engineering: Basic Concepts, Model-Based Techniques, and Research Directions. *ACM Computing Surveys*, *48*(2), 1–41. doi:10.1145/2794381

NoMagic. (2019). *MagicDraw Home Page*. Retrieved 11 20, 2019, from NoMagic: https://www.nomagic.com/products/magicdraw

Number of connected devices reached 22 billion, where is the revenue? (2019, mai 23). [Post de blog]. Consulté à l'adresse https://www.helpnetsecurity.com/2019/05/23/connected-devices-growth/

ODM. (2007). *Ontology Definition Metamodel–OMG Adopted Specification*. Object Management Group. http://www.omg. org/spec/ODM/1.0/Beta2/PDF/

Oliveira, B. C., & Loh, A. (2013). Abstract Syntax Graphs for Domain Specific Languages. In *ACM SIGPLAN 2013 Workshop on Partial Evaluation and Program Manipulation (PEPM '13)* (pp. 87-96). New York, NY: ACM. doi:10.1145/2426890.2426909

OMG. (1997). *UML Home Page*. Retrieved from UML: http://www.uml.org

OMG. (2000). *Metadata Interchange (XMI) Specification*. http://www. omg. org/docs/formal/05-05-01. pdf

OMG. (2001). *MDA Home Page*. Retrieved from MDA: https://www.omg.org/mda/

OMG. (2002). *MOF Home Page*. Retrieved from MOF: https://www.omg.org/mof/

OMG. (2003). *ADM Platform Task Force | Object Management Group*. https://www.omg.org/adm/

OMG. (2008). *Software & Systems Process Engineering Metamodel Specification. Version 2.0*. Retrieved from SPEM: https://www.omg.org/spec/SPEM/2.0/

OMG. (2010). The MDA Foundation Model. *SparxSystems*, 1–9. Retrieved January 20, 2020, from http://www.omg. org/cgi-bin/doc?ormsc/10-09-06.pdf

OMG. (2010). *Unified modeling language (OMG UML), superstructure, version 2.3*. Object Management Group.

OMG. (2011). *BPMN. Business Process Model and Notation (BPMN). formal/2011-01-03*. Object Management Group.

OMG. (2011). *Meta Object Facility 2.0, Query/View/Transformation Specification*.

OMG. (2014). *Model Driven Architecture (MDA)-MDA Guide rev. 2.0*. Object Management Group.

OMG. (2015). *OMG Meta Object Facility (MOF)*. Core Specification.

OMG. (2015). *OMG Unified Modeling Language (OMG UML). formal/2015-03-01*. OMG.

OMG. (2016a). *About the Knowledge Discovery Metamodel Specification Version 1.4*. https://www.omg.org/spec/KDM/

OMG. (2016b). *About the MOF Query/View/Transformation Specification Version 1.3*. https://www.omg.org/spec/QVT/About-QVT

OMG-BPMN. (2011). *Business Process Model and Notation (BPMN)-Version 2.0*. OMG.

OMG-BPMN. (2011). *Business Process Model and Notation version 2.0*. OMG.

OMG-MDA. (2014). *MDA Guide version 2.0*. OMG.

OMG-MDA. (2015). *Object Management Group Model Driven Architecture (MDA)MDA Guide rev. 2.0*. OMG.

OMG-OCL. (2014). *Object Constraint Language version 2.4*. OMG.

OMG-QVT. (2015). *Meta Object Facility (MOF) 2.0 Query/View/Transformation Specification, V1.2*. OMG.

OMG-QVT. (2016). *Meta Object Facility (MOF) 2.0 Query/View/Transformation Specification, OMG Adopted SpecificationVersion 1.3*. OMG.

OMG-SoaML. (2012). *Service Oriented Architecture Modeling Language (SoaML) – Specification for the UML Profile and Metamodel for Services (UPMS)*. OMG.

OMG-UML. (2017). *Unified Modeling Language version 2.5.1*. OMG.

OMG-XMI. (2015). *XML Metadata Interchange version 2.5.1*. OMG.

Omicini, A. (2015). Event-Based vs. Multi-Agent Systems: Towards a Unified Conceptual Framework. In G. Fortino, W. Shen, J.-P. Barthès, J. Luo, W. Li, S. Ochoa, . . . M. Ramos (Eds.), *2015 19th IEEE International Conference on Computer Supported Cooperative Work in Design (CSCWD2015)* (pp. 1-6). Los Alamitos, CA: IEEE Computer Society. doi:10.1109/CSCWD.2015.7230924

Open Networking Foundation. (2015). *OpenFlow Switch Specification*. Consulté à l'adresse https://www.opennetworking.org/wp-content/uploads/2014/10/openflow-spec-v1.3.0.pdf

OpFlex. Opflex Architecture. (n.d.). Consulté à l'adresse https://wiki.opendaylight.org/view/OpFlex:Opflex_Architecture

Organization, S. (2003). *SysML Open Source Project Home Page*. Retrieved from SysML Open Source Project: https://sysml.org/

Osis, J. (1969). Topological Model of System Functioning (in Russian). *Automatics and Computer Science, J. of Academia of Sciences*, (6), 44–50.

Osis, J., & Beghi, L. (1997). Topological Modelling of Biological Systems. In D. A. Linkens & E. R. Carson (Eds.), *Proceedings of the third IFAC Symposium on Modelling and Control in Biomedical Systems (Including Biological Systems)* (pp. 337–342). Pergamon-Elsevier Science Publishing.

Osis, J., & Asnina, E. (2014). Is modeling a treatment for the weakness of software engineering? In *Handbook of Research on Innovations in Systems and Software Engineering* (pp. 411–427). IGI Global.

Osis, J., & Donins, U. (2017). *Topological UML Modeling: An Improved Approach for Domain Modeling and Software Development*. Elsevier. doi:10.1016/B978-0-12-805476-5.00005-8

Osis, J., Gelfandbain, J., Markovich, Z., & Novozilova, N. (1991). *Diagnostics on Graph Models (on the Examples of Aviation and Automobile Technology)*. Transport. (in Russian)

Osterwalder, A., & Pigneur, Y. (2002). An ebusiness model ontology for modeling ebusiness. *BLED 2002 Proceedings, 2*.

Papadopoulos, G. A., Stavrou, A., & Papapetrou, O. (2006, March). An Implementation Framework for {S}oftware {A}rchitectures Based on the Coordination Paradigm. *Science of Computer Programming, 60*(1), 27–67. doi:10.1016/j.scico.2005.06.002

Papyrus. (2010). https://eclipse.org/papyrus/

Parallel Understanding Systems Group. (2001). *SHOE: Simple HTML Ontology Extensions*. Retrieved January 20, 2020, from http://www.cs.umd.edu/projects/plus/SHOE/

Pereira Júnior, J. E., de Oliveira Silva, F., de Souza Pereira, J. H., & Rosa, P. F. (2019). Interfacer: A Model-Driven Development Method for SDN Applications. *Advanced Information Networking and Applications*, 643-654. doi:10.1007/978-3-030-15032-7_54

Pérez-Castillo, R., de Guzmán, I. G.-R., Piattini, M., & Places, Á. S. (2012). A case study on business process recovery using an e-government system. *Software, Practice & Experience, 42*(2), 159–189. doi:10.1002pe.1057

Pérez-Castillo, R., de Guzmán, I. G.-R., Piattini, M., & Weber, B. (2012). Integrating event logs into KDM repositories. *Proceedings of the 27th Annual ACM Symposium on Applied Computing*, 1095–1102. 10.1145/2245276.2231949

Petre, M. (2013). UML In Practice. In *35th International Conference on Software Engineering (ICSE)* (pp. 722-731). IEEE.

Pfleeger, S. L. (1999). Albert Einstein and empirical software engineering. *IEEE Computer, 32*(10), 32–37. doi:10.1109/2.796106

Pinheiro, B., Chaves, R., Cerqueira, E., & Abelem, A. (2013). *CIM-SDN: A Common Information Model extension for Software-Defined Networking. In 2013 IEEE Globecom Workshops*. GC Wkshps. doi:10.1109/glocomw.2013.6825093

Pressman, R. S. (2014). Software Engineering: A Practitioner's Approach (8th ed.). Academic Press.

Project Management Institute. (2017). A guide to the project management body of knowledge (PMBOK ® guide), Sixth Edition. PMI.

Przybyłek, A. (2014). A Business-Oriented Approach to Requirements Elicitation. *9th Inter. Conf. on Evaluation of Novel Approaches to Software Engineering (ENASE 2104).*

Psyché, V., Mendes, O., & Bourdeau, J. (2003). Apport de l'ingénierie ontologique aux environnements de formation à distance. *Sciences et Technologies de l'Information et de la Communication pour l'Éducation et la Formation, 10*(1), 89–126. doi:10.3406tice.2003.858

Qazi, A., Rehman, M., & Saif Kazmi, M. S., N., R., & R., M. (2011). Enhanced model driven architecture software development life cycle with synchronized and consistent mapping. In *International Conference on Computer Communication and Management (ICCCM 2011)* (pp. 395-399). Singapore: IACSIT Press.

Raibulet, C., Fontana, F. A., & Zanoni, M. (2017). Model-Driven Reverse Engineering Approaches : A Systematic Literature Review. *IEEE Access: Practical Innovations, Open Solutions, 5*, 14516–14542. doi:10.1109/ACCESS.2017.2733518

RDF - Semantic Web Standards. (n.d.). Consulté 18 février 2018, à l'adresse https://www.w3.org/RDF/

Rector, A. (2013). Axioms and templates: distinctions and transformations amongst ontologies, frames, and information models. In *Proceedings of the seventh international conference on Knowledge capture - K-CAP '13* (p. 73). New York: ACM Press.

Reichert, M., & Weber, B. (2012). *Enabling flexibility in process-aware information systems: Challenges, methods, technologies*. Springer. doi:10.1007/978-3-642-30409-5

Rhazali, Y., Hadi, Y., & Mouloudi, A. (2015). A Methodology of Model Transformation in MDA: from CIM to PIM. *International Review on Computers and Software, 10*(12), 1186-1201.

Rhazali, Y., Hadi, Y., & Mouloudi, A. (2017a). A model transformation in MDA from CIM to PIM represented by web models through SoaML and IFML. In *Colloquium in Information Science and Technology, CIST* (pp. 116-121). DOI: 10.1109/CIST.2016.7805027

Rhazali, Y., Hadi, Y., Chana, I., Lahmer, M., & Rhattoy, A. (2018). A model transformation in model driven architecturefrom business model to web model. *IAENG International Journal of Computer Science, 45*(1).

Rhazali, Y., El Hachimi, A., Chana, I., Lahmer, M., & Rhattoy, A. (2019). Automate Model Transformation From CIM to PIM up to PSM in Model-Driven Architecture. In *Modern Principles, Practices, and Algorithms for Cloud Security*. doi:10.4018/978-1-7998-1082-7.ch013

Rhazali, Y., El Hachimi, A., Chana, I., Lahmer, M., & Rhattoy, A. (2020). *Automate Model Transformation From CIM to PIM up to PSM in Model-Driven Architecture. In Modern Principles, Practices, and Algorithms for Cloud Security.* IGI Global.

Rhazali, Y., Hadi, Y., Chana, I., Lahmer, M., & Rhattoy, A. (2018). A model transformation in model driven architecture from business model to web model. *IAENG International Journal of Computer Science, 45*(1), 104–117.

Rhazali, Y., Hadi, Y., Chana, I., Lahmer, M., & Rhattoy, A. (2018). A Model Transformation in Model Driven Architecture from Business Model to Web Model. *IAENG International Journal of Computer Science, 45*(1), 14.

Rhazali, Y., Hadi, Y., & Mouloudi, A. (2014). Transformation Method CIM to PIM: From Business Processes Models Defined in BPMN to Use Case and Class Models Defined in UML, International Journal of Computer, Electrical, Automation. *Control and Information Engineering, 8*(8), 1453–1457.

Rhazali, Y., Hadi, Y., & Mouloudi, A. (2015a). A Methodology of Model Transformation in MDA: From CIM to PIM. *International Review on Computers and Software, 10*(11), 1186. Advance online publication. doi:10.15866/irecos.v10i12.8088

Rhazali, Y., Hadi, Y., & Mouloudi, A. (2015b). A Methodology for Transforming CIM to PIM through UML: From Business View to Information System View. *Proceedings, Third World Conference on Complex Systems.* 10.1109/ICoCS.2015.7483318

Rhazali, Y., Hadi, Y., & Mouloudi, A. (2015c). Disciplined Approach for Transformation CIM to PIM in MDA. In *Proceedings, 3rd International Conference on Model-Driven Engineering and Software Development* (pp. 312 – 320). DOI: 10.5220/0005245903120320

Rhazali, Y., Hadi, Y., & Mouloudi, A. (2015d). Transformation Approach CIM to PIM: From Business Processes Models to State Machine and Package Models. *Proceedings, the 1st International Conference on Open Source Software Computing.* 10.1109/OSSCOM.2015.7372686

Rhazali, Y., Hadi, Y., & Mouloudi, A. (2016). CIM to PIM Transformation in MDA: From Service-Oriented Business Models to Web-Based Design Models. *International Journal of Software Engineering and Its Applications, 10*(4), 125–142. doi:10.14257/ijseia.2016.10.4.13

Rhazali, Y., Hadi, Y., & Mouloudi, A. (2016b). Model Transformation with ATL into MDA from CIM to PIM Structured through MVC. *Procedia Computer Science, 83*, 1096–1101. doi:10.1016/j.procs.2016.04.229

Rhazali, Y., Hadi, Y., & Mouloudi, A. (2016c). A Based-Rule Method to Transform CIM to PIM into MDA. *International Journal of Cloud Applications and Computing, 6*(2), 11–24. doi:10.4018/IJCAC.2016040102

Rhazali, Y., Hadi, Y., & Mouloudi, A. (2016d). A new methodology CIM to PIM transformation resulting from an analytical survey. In *Proceedings, 4th International Conference on Model-Driven Engineering and Software Development (MODELSWARD)* (pp. 266-273). 10.5220/0005690102660273

Rhazali, Y., Hadi, Y., & Mouloudi, A. (2017b). *Transformation des modeles depuis CIM vers PIM dans MDA*. Noor Publishing.

Roche, C. (2005). Terminologie et ontologie. *Langages*, *1*(1), 48–62. doi:10.3917/lang.157.0048

Rockstrom, A., & Saracco, R. (1982). SDL-CCITT specification and description language. *IEEE Transactions on Communications*, *30*(6), 1310–1318. doi:10.1109/TCOM.1982.1095599

Rodríguez, A., García-Rodríguez de Guzmán, I., Fernández Medina, E., & Piattini, M. (2007a). Towards CIM to PIM transformation: from Secure Business Processes defined in BPMN to Use-Cases, Business Process Management. *Proceedings of the 5th International Conference on Business Process Management*. 10.1007/978-3-540-75183-0_30

Rodríguez, A., García-Rodríguez de Guzmán, I., Fernández Medina, E., & Piattini, M. (2007b). CIM to PIM Transformation: A Reality. In IFIP International Federation for Information Processing, Volume 255, Research and Practical Issues of Enterprise Information Systems II. Boston: Springer.

Rodríguez, A., & García-Rodríguez de Guzmán, I. (2010). Semi-formal transformation of secure business processes into analysis class and use case models: An MDA approach. *Journal of Information and Software Technology*, *52*(9), 945–971. doi:10.1016/j.infsof.2010.03.015

Roques, P. (2004). *UML in Practice: The Art of Modeling Software Systems Demonstrated through Worked Examples and Solutions*. Wiley.

Ross, W., Ulieru, M., & Gorod, A. (2014). A Multi-Paradigm Modelling & Simulation Approach for System of Systems Engineering: A Case Study. In *9th International Conference on System of Systems Engineering (SoSE 2014)* (pp. 183-188). Piscataway, NJ: IEEE. 10.1109/SYSOSE.2014.6892485

Roux, C. (2013). *Can "Made Up" Languages Help Computers Translate Real Ones?* Retrieved January 20, 2020, from https://europe.naverlabs.com/Blog/Can-made-up-languages-help-computers-translate-real-ones/

Runeson & Host. (2009). Guidelines for conducting and reporting case study research in software engineering. *Empirical Software Engineering*, *14*(2), 131–164.

Ryu S. D. N. Framework. (n.d.). Consulté le 10 décembre 2019, à l'adresse https://osrg.github.io/ryu/index.html

Saber, A., Al-Zoghby, A. M., & Elmougy, S. (2018). Big-Data Aggregating, Linking, *Integrating and Representing Using Semantic Web Technologies. International Conference on Advanced Machine Learning Technologies and Applications*, 331–342.

Sadowska, M. (2018). A Prototype Tool for Semantic Validation of UML Class Diagrams with the Use of Domain Ontologies Expressed in OWL 2. In *Towards a Synergistic Combination of Research and Practice in Software Engineering* (pp. 49–62). Springer. doi:10.1007/978-3-319-65208-5_4

Salman, I., & Tosun, A. (2015). Are students representativesof professionals in software engineering experiments? *37th IEEE/ACM International Conference on Software Engineering, ICSE 2015*, 666–676.

Samantra, C., Datta, S., Mahapatra, S., & Debata, B. (2016). Interpretive structural modelling of critical risk factors in software engineering project. *Benchmarking*, *23*(1), 2–24. doi:10.1108/BIJ-07-2013-0071

Samociuk, D. (2015). Secure Communication Between OpenFlow Switches and Controllers. *The Seventh International Conference on Advances in Future Internet*, 32-37.

Santos, B. M., Landi, A. de S., Santibáñez, D. S., Durelli, R. S., & de Camargo, V. V. (2019). Evaluating the extension mechanisms of the knowledge discovery metamodel for aspect-oriented modernizations. *Journal of Systems and Software*, *149*, 285–304. doi:10.1016/j.jss.2018.12.011

Saripalle, R. K., Demurjian, S. A., De la Rosa Algarín, A., & Blechner, M. (2013). A software modeling approach to ontology design via extensions to ODM and OWL. *International Journal on Semantic Web and Information Systems*, *9*(2), 62–97. doi:10.4018/jswis.2013040103

Satyanarayanan, M. (2001). Pervasive Computing: Vision and Challenges. *IEEE Personal Communications*, *8*(4), 10–17. doi:10.1109/98.943998

Schmidt, D. (2007). Cover Feature Model-Driven Engineering. *IEEE Computer*, 25-31.

Schmidt, D. C. (2006). Guest Editor's Introduction: Model-Driven Engineering. *IEEE Computer*, *39*(2), 25–31.

Schuster, R., & Motal, T. (2009). *From e3-value to rea: Modeling multi-party e-business collaborations. In 2009 IEEE Conference on Commerce and Enterprise Computing*. IEEE.

Shaikh, A., & Wiil, U. K. (2018). Overview of Slicing and Feedback Techniques for Efficient Verification of UML/OCL Class Diagrams. *IEEE Access: Practical Innovations, Open Solutions*, *6*, 23864–23882. doi:10.1109/ACCESS.2018.2797695

Shaw, M. (1990). Prospects for an engineering discipline of software. *IEEE Software*, *7*(6), 15–24. doi:10.1109/52.60586

Shin, M. E., & Ahn, G. J. (2000). UML-based representation of role-based access control. *Proceedings of the 9th IEEE International Workshops on Enabling Technologies: Infrastructure for Collaborative Enterprises*. 10.1109/ENABL.2000.883728

Shiue, W., Li, S.-T., & Chen, K.-J. (2008). A frame knowledge system for managing financial decision knowledge. *Expert Systems with Applications*, *35*(3), 1068–1079. doi:10.1016/j.eswa.2007.08.035

Sim, W. W., & Brouse, P. (2014). Towards an Ontology-based Persona-driven Requirements and Knowledge Engineering. *Procedia Computer Science*, *36*, 314–321. doi:10.1016/j.procs.2014.09.099

Sipayung, J. J. P., & Sembiring, J. (2015). Risk assessment model of application development using Bayesian Network and Boehm's Software Risk Principles. *International Conference on Information Technology Systems and Innovation (ICITSI)*, 1-5. 10.1109/ICITSI.2015.7437722

Siqueira, F. L., & Silva, P. S. (2014). Transforming an entreprise model into a use case model in business process systems. *Journal of Systems and Software*, *96*, 152–171. doi:10.1016/j.jss.2014.06.007

Sjøberg, D. I. K., Hannay, J. E., Hansen, O., Kampenes, V. B., Karahasanovic, A., & Liborg, N. (2005). A survey of controlled experiments in software engineering. *IEEE Trans. Software Eng.*, *31*(9), 733–753.

Skersys, T., Danenas, P., & Butleris, R. (2018). Extracting sbvr business vocabularies and business rules from uml use casediagrams. *Journal of Systems and Software*, *141*, 111–130. doi:10.1016/j.jss.2018.03.061

Skuce, D., & Lethbridge, T. (2001). *CODE4 - Conceptually Oriented Description Environment*. Retrieved January 20, 2020, from http://www.csi.uottawa.ca/kaml/CODE4.html

Skuce, D. (2000). Integrating Web-Based Documents, Shared Knowledge Bases, and Information Retrieval for User Help. *Computational Intelligence*, *16*(1), 95–113. doi:10.1111/0824-7935.00107

Software Engineering Institute. (2010). CMMI for Systems Engineering/Software Engineering/Integrated Product and Process Development, V1.3. Pittsburgh, PA: Author.

Software-Defined Networking (SDN) Definition. (2019a). Consulté à l'adresse https://www.opennetworking.org/sdn-definition/

Software-Defined Networking (SDN) Definition. (2019b, mars 18). Consulté le 29 janvier 2020, à l'adresse https://www.opennetworking.org/sdn-definition/

Soley, R. (2000). *Model driven architecture (mda)*. http://www.omg.org/cgibin/doc?omg/00-11-05

Sommerville, I. (2007). *Software Engineering* (8th ed.). Edinburgh, UK: Addison-Wesley.

SparxSystems. (n.d.). *Enterprise Architect*. http://www.sparxsystems.com

Storey, V. C., & Song, I.-Y. (2017). Big data technologies and Management : What conceptual modeling can do. *Data & Knowledge Engineering*, *108*, 50–67. doi:10.1016/j.datak.2017.01.001

Suchenia, A., Kluza, K., Jobczyk, K., Wisniewski, P., Wypych, M., & Ligeza, A. (2017). *Supporting BPMN Process Models with UML Sequence Diagrams for Representing Time Issues and Testing Models*. ICAISC. doi:10.1007/978-3-319-59060-8_53

Suma, V., & Gopalakrishnan Nair, T. R. G. (2008). Effective Defect Prevention Approach in Software Process for Achieving Better Quality Levels. Proceedings of World Academy of Science, Engineering and Technology, 32.

Syriani, E. (2011). A Multi-Paradigm Foundation for Model Transformation Language Engineering. McGill University.

Syriani, E., & Vangheluwe, H. (2012). *AToMPM Home Page*. Retrieved from AToMPM: http://www-ens.iro.umontreal.ca/$%5Csim$syriani/atompm/atompm.htm

Taneja, R., & Gaur, D. (2018). Robust Fuzzy Neuro system for Big Data Analytics. In *Big Data Analytics* (pp. 543–552). Springer. doi:10.1007/978-981-10-6620-7_52

Tan, H., Kaliyaperumal, R., & Benis, N. (2007). Building frame-based corpus on the basis of ontological domain knowledge. In *Proceedings of BioNLP 2011 Workshop* (pp. 74–82). Portland, OR: Association for Computational Linguistics.

Team, M. (n.d.). *Mininet: An Instant Virtual Network on your Laptop (or other PC) - Mininet*. Consulté le 10 décembre 2019, à l'adresse http://mininet.org

Tettamanzi, A. G. B. (2006). A Fuzzy Frame-Based Knowledge Representation Formalism. In V. Di Gesú, F. Masulli, & A. Petrosino (Eds.), Lecture Notes in Computer Science: Vol. 2955. *Fuzzy Logic and Applications. WILF 2003* (pp. 55–62). Springer Berlin Heidelberg.

Thakur, J. S., & Gupta, A. (2017). *Automatic generation of analysis class diagrams from use case specifications*. https://arxiv.org/abs/1708.01796

Thayer, R. H., & Dorfman, M. (2013). Software Engineering Essentials: Vol. 3. *The Engineering Fundamentals* (4th ed.). Software Management Training Press Carmichael.

The Apache Software Foundation. (2019). *Apache Jena*. Retrieved January 20, 2020, from https://jena.apache.org/

The University of Manchester. (2018). *List of Reasoners | OWL research at the University of Manchester*. Retrieved January 20, 2020, from http://owl.cs.manchester.ac.uk/tools/list-of-reasoners/

Tong, A. (2016, décembre 13). *Why Model-Driven Templating Matters with SDN and NFV networks - Ciena*. Consulté le 29 janvier 2020, à l'adresse https://www.ciena.com/insights/articles/Why-Model-Driven-Templating-Matters-with-SDN-and-NFV-networks.html

Top¸cu, O., Durak, U., & Oguztu¨zu¨n, H. (2016). Distributed Simulation - A Model Driven Engineering Approach. In Simulation Foundations, Methods and Applications. Springer.

Turi, D. (2004). *DIG 1.1 Reasoners API*. Retrieved January 20, 2020, from http://dig.sourceforge.net/javadoc-reasoners/1.1/

UML Designer Documentation. (2018). http://www.umldesigner.org/

Umple. (2020a). *Umple User Manual*. Retrieved from http://manual.umple.org

Umple. (2020b). *Class Diagram of the Umple Compiler Generated by Umple*. Retrieved from http://metamodel.umple.org

Umple. (2020c). *Umple Compiler API of Generated Java Files*. Retrieved from http://javadoc.umple.org

UmpleOnline. (2020). Retrieved From http://try.umple.org

Utting, M., & Legeard, B. (2007). *Practical Model-Based Testing: A Tools Approach*. Morgan KaufmannPublishers Inc.

Vachharajani, V., Vasant, S., & Jyoti, P. (2016). Feasibility Study of Proposed Architecture for Automatic Assessment of Use-Case Diagram. In *Proceedings of International Conference on ICT for Sustainable Development. Advances in Intelligent Systems and Computing* (pp. 97-104). Singapore: Springer.

Vahidnia, S., Özgür, Ö., & Askerzade, I. (2017). An Early Phase Software Project Risk Assessment Support Method for Emergent Software Organizations. *International Journal of Advanced Computer Science and Applications*, 8(5), 2017. doi:10.14569/IJACSA.2017.080514

Vahidnia, S., Tanriöver, O., & Askerzade, I. (2016). An Evaluation Study of General Software Project Risk Based on Software Practitioners Experiences. *International Journal of Computer Science and Information Technology*, 8(6), 01–13. doi:10.5121/ijcsit.2016.8601

Van Tendeloo, Y., Van Mierlo, S., & Vangheluwe, H. (2018). *Modelverse Home Page*. Retrieved from Modelverse: https://msdl.uantwerpen.be/git/yentl/modelverse

Van Tendeloo, Y., Van Mierlo, S., & Vangheluwe, H. (2019, October). A Multi-Paradigm Modelling approach to live modelling. *Software & Systems Modeling*, 18(5), 2821–2842. doi:10.100710270-018-0700-7

Vangheluwe, H. (2002). An Introduction to Multiparadigm Modelling and Simulation. In AI, Simulation & Planning in High Autonomy Systems (AIS 2002) (pp. 9-20). Lisbon, Portugal: Society for Modeling & Simulation International (SCS).

Vegas, Dieste, & Juristo. (2015). Difficulties in running experiments in the software industry: Experiences from the trenches. *3rd IEEE/ACM International Workshop on Conducting Empirical Studies in Industry*, 3–9.

Vickoff, J. P. (2001). *Agile why not?* www.entreprise-agile.com

Vidya Sagar, V. B. R., & Abirami, S. (2014). Conceptual modeling of natural language functional requirements. *Journal of Systems and Software*, 88, 25–41. Advance online publication. doi:10.1016/j.jss.2013.08.036

Vranic, V. (2005, June). Multi-Paradigm Design with Feature Modeling. *Computer Science and Information Systems*, 2(1), 79–102. doi:10.2298/CSIS0501079V

Walia, G. S., & Carver, J. C. (2009). A systematic literature review to identify and classify software requirement errors. *Information and Software Technology*, 51(7), 1087–1109. doi:10.1016/j.infsof.2009.01.004

Wang, S.-Y., Chou, C.-L., & Yang, C.-M. (2013). EstiNetopenflow network simulator and emulator. *IEEE Communications Magazine, 51*(9), 110–117. doi:10.1109/MCOM.2013.6588659

Wegener, H. (2002). Agility in model-driven software development? implications for organization, process, and architecture. *OOPSLA 2002 Workshop on Generative Techniques in the Context of Model Driven Architecture.*

What is SDN controller (software-defined networking controller)? - Definition from WhatIs.com. (n.d.). Consulté le 10 décembre 2019, à l'adresse: https://searchnetworking.techtarget.com/definition/SDN-controller-software-defined-networking-controller

Wohlin, C., Runeson, P., Ho"st, M., & Ohlsson, M. C. (2012). Experimentation in Software Engineering. Springer.

Wu, J. H., Shin, S. S., Chien, J. L., Chao, W. S., & Hsieh, M. C. (2007). An Extended MDA Method for User Interface Modeling and Transformation. *Proceedings of the 15th European Conference on Information Systems*, 1632.

Xia, W., Wen, Y., Foh, C. H., Niyato, D., & Xie, H. (2015). A Survey on Software-Defined Networking. *IEEE Communications Surveys and Tutorials, 17*(1), 27–51. doi:10.1109/COMST.2014.2330903

Xue, Y., Ghenniwa, H. H., & Shen, W. (2010). A Frame-based Ontological view Specification Language. In *The 14th International Conference on Computer Supported Cooperative Work in Design* (pp. 228–233). IEEE. 10.1109/CSCWD.2010.5471972

Xue, Y., Ghenniwa, H. H., & Shen, W. (2012). Frame-based ontological view for semantic integration. *Journal of Network and Computer Applications, 35*(1), 121–131. doi:10.1016/j.jnca.2011.02.010

Yu, E. (1997). Towards modeling and reasoning support for early-phase requirements engineering. *Proceedings of the 3rd IEEE International Symposium on Requirements Engineering.* 10.1109/ISRE.1997.566873

Yue, T., Briand, L. C., & Labiche, Y. (2011). A systematic review of transformation approaches between user requirementsand analysis models. *Requirements Engineering, 16*(2), 75–99. doi:10.100700766-010-0111-y

Zambonelli, F., & Parunak, H. V. (2003). Towards a Paradigm Change in Computer Science and Software Engineering: A Synthesis. *The Knowledge Engineering Review, 18*(4), 329–342. doi:10.1017/S0269888904000104

Zedlitz, J., Jörke, J., & Luttenberger, N. (2012). From UML to OWL 2. In Knowledge Technology (pp. 154–163). Springer.

Zhang, F., Ma, Z. M., & Li, W. (2015). Storing OWL ontologies in object-oriented databases. *Knowledge-Based Systems, 76*, 240–255. doi:10.1016/j.knosys.2014.12.020

Zhang, W., Mei, H., Zhao, H., & Yang, J. (2005). Transformation from CIM to PIM: A Feature-Oriented Component-Based approach. In *Proceedings, MoDELS* (pp. 248-263). 10.1007/11557432_18

Zhi, H., Zhang, G., Liu, Y., & Shen, Y. (2017). A novel risk assessment model on software system combining modified fuzzy entropy-weight and AHP. *IEEE 8th Conference on Software Engineering and Service Science*, 451-454.

Zhou, D., Chen, X., Jin, Q., Kuang, Z., & Yang, H. (2017). An affinity analysis based cim-to-pim transformation. *Multiagent and Grid Systems, 13*(3), 269–286. doi:10.3233/MGS-170271

Zhou, N., & Zhou, X. (2004). Automatic Acquisition of Linguistic Patterns for Conceptual Modeling. *INFO 629. Artificial Intelligence*, 1–19. http://daviszhou.net/Research/INFO629Prj.pdf

Zhu, L., Karim, M., Sharif, K., Du, X., & Guizani, M. (sous presse). SDN Controllers: Benchmarking & Performance-Evaluation. *IEEE JSAC.*

Zopounidis, C., Doumpos, M., & Matsatsinis, N. F. (1997). On the use of knowledge-based decision support systems in financial management: A survey. *Decision Support Systems*, *20*(3), 259–277. doi:10.1016/S0167-9236(97)00002-X

# About the Contributors

**Yassine Rhazali** is a Moroccan professor. He obtained his doctorate in computer science and more specifically in software engineering, his specialty is the engineering of models, he proposed several approaches in model engineering, his approaches are validated in dozens of published scientific articles, international scientific conferences and international scientific journals. He obtained his Ph.D. in Ibn Tofail University, Kenitra, Morocco. He is now a professor-researcher, reviewer, editorial board member and scientific committee member in several international scientific journals and in several international scientific conferences. He has taught computer science in several universities and institutes such as: the faculty of science and the faculty of letters of the Ibn Tofail University of Kenitra, the faculty of sciences and techniques (FST) of the Hassan I University of Settat, Higher School of Technology at Moulay Ismail University of Meknes, the OFPPT Institute of Applied Technology (ISTA) in Kenitra and several higher private institutes in Kenitra and Rabat.

\* \* \*

**Abdulaziz Algablan** is a PhD student at the University of Ottawa focusing on mixsets and product-line development in Umple.

**Priyanka Chandani** has completed her Ph.D from Jaypee Institute of Information Technology. She also holds a Masters of Technology and a Bachelors of Technology degree in Information Technology. Her work experience has been in Infosys Technologies, TechMahindra and JSS Academy of Technical Education. Her research interest includes Requirement Engineering, Software Quality and Software Testing.

**Salim Chantit** is a Professor at Hassan II University of Casablanca and researcher at LIM Laboratory, Computer Science department, Faculty of Sciences and Technology of Mohammedia (FSTM).

**María-José Escalona** is a full professor at the University of Seville in the department of Computer Languages and Systems. She is also the director of the Web Engineering and Early Testing Research Group. Her main research lines are related with Software Engineering, specifically with Software Requirements, Software Early Quality assurance and Early Software Testing. In these areas, she has directed several Ph-Thesis and published a high number of papers in journals and congresses. She is also a member of the editorial board of JWE and IEEE IT Professional and she collaborates as a regular reviewer of several conferences and journals. Besides, she has managed and participated in a high number of transference projects with companies and have important relations with software industry.

**Imane Essebaa** is a PhD Candidate at Hassan 2 University of Casablanca.

**Laura García-Borgoñón** received her engineering degree in Computer Science by University of Zaragoza (Spain) in 2001 and her Ph.D. in Software Engineering by the University of Seville (Spain) in 2016. Since 2003, she has been a R&D researcher at Aragon Institute of Technology. She is member of the Web Engineering and Early Testing group (IWT2) at the University of Seville. Her main research interests focus on model-driven engineering, requirements engineering, software quality and software process improvement. She also is involved in initiatives about computational thinking for kids and women in ICT. Besides, she participates as a member committee in several international congresses and journals in the Software Engineering area.

**Sara Gotti** got her Doctorate of High Graduate Studies degrees in Computer Sciences from Ibn Tofail University, Morocco, in 2019. She is a researcher in executing UML and IFML models. Her main research interests are related to the establishment of a virtual machine for direct models' execution by ignoring source code generation.

**Zineb Gotti** received her master degree in software quality in 2013 from ibn tofail University, Morocco, and Doctorat of High Graduate Studies degrees in Computer Sciences from IBN TOFAIL University, Morocco, 2019. Her activities of research focusing on Interactive systems evolution based on Architecture-Driven Modernization approach.

**Chetna Gupta** is Associate Professor in Jaypee Institute of Information Technology, Noida, India. She holds Ph.D, M.Tech and a Bachelor of Engineering degree in Computer Science and Engineering. Her area of research is software engineering - requirement engineering, software testing, software project management and data mining, with emphasis on software testing, software re-usability and analysis. Her research to date has involved program analysis to compute and provide the kinds of analysis information about a program, such as data-flow, change impact sets, classification of data using software engineering concepts and data mining, predicting software components for reuse - needed for software engineering tasks for estimating impact analysis, regression testing.

**Adra Hammoud** was born in Meknès, Morocco, in 1988. She received the Bachelor's degree in Computer Sciences from Moulay Ismail University, Meknès in 2009 and the Master degree in software development "software quality" from Mohammed V university, Rabat, in 2011. Her research interests include Software Defined Network and Model Driven Architecture.

**Natalia Juristo** has been full professor of software engineering with the School of Computer Engineering at the Technical University of Madrid, Spain, since 1997. She was awarded a FiDiPro (Finland Distinguished Professor Program) professorship at the University of Oulu, from January 2013 until June 2018. Natalia belongs to the editorial board of EMSE and STVR. In 2009, Natalia was awarded an honorary doctorate by Blekinge Institute of Technology in Sweden.

**Nassim Kharmoum** received his Master Degree in Engineering Information Systems from the Cadi Ayyad University Marrakech, Morocco in 2010. Currently, he is a Software Engineering and Development Officer at the National Center for Scientific and Technical Research in Morocco. He is a member of the

IPPS (Intelligent Processing Systems & Security) team, and he prepares his Ph.D. degree at the Faculty of Sciences, Mohammed V University in Rabat, Morocco. His research interest focuses on analysis and conceptual modeling, software requirements, and modernization of legacy systems.

**Wiem Khlif** is an Assistant professor in computer science, with the Institute of the High Commercial Studies, Sfax, Tunisia. His research interests include various topics in the area of business process management, enterprise architecture and information systems. He has published several research papers and articles, among others in Business Process Management journal, Business Information Systems, Software Technologies, Evaluation of Novel Approaches to Software Engineering. His Ph.D. thesis was on the elaboration of a new method to evaluate and improve the quality of business process models.

**Naziha Laaz** holds a Master Degree in software quality, from the faculty of science, Ibn Tofail University, Morocco, Received her Doctorat of High Graduate Studies degrees in Computer Sciences from IBN TOFAIL University, Morocco, 2019. Her main research interests are related to the model driven engineering using ontologies

**Mohammed Lahmer** is an associate professor at the High School of Technology, Moulay Ismail University. He received his Ph.D. degree in computer science from the ENSIAS Mohammed V University in 2008. He received his engineering degree in computer science from ENSIAS in 1996. He has over twenty years of teaching experience and several scientific publications in top IEEE conferences and journals. His research interests lie with the field of codes, security, and software engineering.

**Timothy Lethbridge** obtained his BSc and MSc from the University of New Brunswick in 1985 and 1987 respectively, and then his PhD from the University of Ottawa in 1994. He has taught software engineering and computer science at the University of Ottawa full time since 1994. His research has focused on program comprehension and usable software engineering tools. He leads the Umple project. He has published over 150 scientific papers and two editions of a software engineering textbook. He has worked for Bell-Northern Research and has collaborated with companies such as Mitel, IBM and General Motors.

**Guillermo López-Nicolás** received his industrial engineering degree by University of Zaragoza (Spain) in 1995. He has completed courses of the 3rd cycle in the department of computer systems and languages of the School of Engineering and Architecture Center of Zaragoza (EINA). He works since 1999 at Aragon Institute of Technology (ITAINNOVA) as a R&D researcher. He has experience in developing AIDC systems (Automatic Identification and Data Capture) and multidisciplinary research and development projects. He has participated in projects to improve the quality of software development carrying out consultancy work involved in assessing organizations of Aragon. He is member since 2015 of the Web Engineering and Early Testing group (IWT2) at the University of Seville. Currently belongs to the mechatronics department of ITAINNOVA where he participates in system simulation projects.

**Samir Mbarki** received the B.S. degree in applied mathematics from Mohammed V University, Morocco, 1992, and Doctorat of High Graduate Studies degrees in Computer Sciences from Mohammed V University, Morocco, 1997. In 1995 he joined the faculty of science Ibn Tofail University, Morocco where he is currently a Professor in Department of computer science. His research interests include software engineering, model driven architecture, software metrics and software tests. He obtained an HDR in computer Science from Ibn Tofail University in 2010.

**Samia Nasiri** is a PhD student at LMMI Laboratory of ENSAM, Moulay Ismail University of Meknes, Morocco. She is an engineer in computer science, and she is a professor in the computer science department of the higher school of technology of Meknes, Morocco.

**Vladislavs Nazaruks** received a degree of Master of Engineering Science (Mg. sc. ing.) in Computer Systems in 2009 from Riga Technical University (RTU), Latvia. Now he is Researcher at the Institute of Applied Computer Systems, RTU. He also works as Systems Analyst. Fields of his research interests: computer science, mathematics, pedagogy. Special interests: systems analysis and modeling, Topological Functioning Modeling, algorithms, protection of information.

**Fouzia Omary** obtained her first Ph.D. in 1988 in Computer Sciences at Mohammed V University in Rabat and the second in 2006 in Security, namely Cryptography in the same University. Dr. Fouzia Omary is a Professor in the Computer Sciences Department of the Faculty of sciences in Mohammed V University in Rabat since 1984. She is Director of the Computer Sciences Research Laboratory (LRI) from 2012 to 2016. Now she is Director of the Intelligent Processing Systems & Security team since 2016. Her research interests include cryptography, information security, and information system.

**Andrea Omicini** is Full Professor at the DISI, the Department of Computer Science and Engineering of the Alma Mater Studiorum-University of Bologna, from which he received his laurea degree in Electronic Engineering (1991) and his PhD in Computer Engineering (1995). Over the years, he has taught many different courses in the area of Computer Science and Engineering, such as Foundations of Computer Science, Software Engineering, Artificial Intelligence, Programming Languages. Currently, he teaches Distributed Systems and Autonomous Systems. His main research interests range over multi-agent systems, coordination, programming languages, intelligent systems, middleware, simulation, software engineering, self-organisation, pervasive systems & IoT. On those topics he has written over three hundred articles published in international journals, books, conferences, and workshops. He has also edited several international books, guest-edited many special issues of international journals, and held talks and tutorials at international conferences and schools. He has organised and chaired several international conferences and workshops; he has been a member of the Program and Scientific Committees of hundreds of international conferences, workshops, and symposia. He has participated to the coordination of national and international journals. Currently, he is Member of the Editorial Board of: ACM Transactions on Autonomous and Adaptive Systems (TAAS); Intelligenza Artificiale; BioData Mining; PeerJ Computer Science; Applied Sciences. He was the Chair of the SIG on Agents and Multi-Agent Systems (MAS-AIIA) of the Italian Association for Artificial Intelligence (AI*IA), and the ACM Representative in the IFIP Technical Committee 12 "Artificial Intelligence". Currently, he is Emeritus Member of the Board of Director of the European Association for Multi-Agent Systems (EURAMAS).

**Jānis Osis** is Professor at Faculty of Computer Science and Information Technology at Riga Technical University, Latvia. He obtained his Dr.sc.ing. Degree from Kaunas Technological University, Lithuania. After defence of habilitation thesis titled "Diagnostics of Complex systems" he received his Dr.habil. sc.ing. Degree in system analysis from Latvian Academy of Sciences. He was visiting researcher at Department of Electrical Engineering and Computer Science, University of California, Berkeley, USA and Dipartimento di Matematica Pura ed Applicata, Universita' degli Studi di Padova, Italia. His research is about creating a software development paradigm that will overcome the protracted software crisis (low quality and unfinished projects, cost overruns and overdue deadlines, etc.). Paradigm is based on original Topological Model of Functioning (TFM). The TFM holistically describes the system for which the software is developed and is a single diagram model that combines structure and behavior. It is an attempt to create 21st Century appropriate software development paradigm. Since 1998 he is Honorary Member of Latvian Academy of Sciences.

**Mohammed Ramdani** is a Professor at Hassan II University of Casablanca and researcher at LIM Laboratory, Computer Science department, Faculty of Sciences and Technology of Mohammedia (FSTM).

**Sara Retal** received her diploma of doctor degree in Computer Science from the faculty of sciences in Rabat. She participated in the ICT Mosaic Maghreb Technology Platform project co-funded by the European Community's ICT Program under FP7. She also participated in the research projects of Mobile Network Softwarization & Service Customization laboratory in Aalto University funded by Tekes, European Commission, and EIT ICT Labs. Her work focuses on artificial intelligence. Her research interests include Cloud Computing and Constraint Programming.

**Fatima Sifou** received the Bachelor's degree in Mathematics and Computer Sciences in 2009 and the Master degree in software development "software quality" in 2011, from the faculty of sciences. Since 2017 she is a predoctoral researcher in the Department of computer sciences at Mohammed V University where she is pursuing a PhD degree. Her main research interests are Cyber security in IoT, Cloud Computing and their applications.

**Sira Vegas** has been associate professor of software engineering with the School of Computer Engineering at the Technical University of Madrid, Spain, since 2008. Sira belongs to the review board of IEEE Transactions on Software Engineering, and is a regular reviewer of the Empirical Software Engineering Journal. She was program chair for the International Symposium on Empirical Software Engineering and Measurement in 2007.

**Karzan Wakil** is a lecturer in the Department of Computer Science, Institute of Training and Educational Development in Sulaimani, Iraq. He received his BSc degree in Computer Science, College of Science Education from University of Salahaddin. Iraq, 2006. And his MSc degree from the Department of Computer Science in the Faculty of Computing, University Technology Malaysia (UTM). Malaysia, 2013. PhD in the Department of Software Engineering, Faculty of Engineering, University Technology Malaysia,2019. He is a teacher from 2006 till now, and at the same time, he has served as an ICT Director in University of Human Development. In 2016 he became the head of Science Department in the Institute of Training and Educational Development in Sulaimani, Iraq. Later on, He became a member in some international organizations and communities such as, IEEE, IACSIT, IAENG, and SERG. His research interests are in Web Engineering, Software Engineering, Web Development, Software Development, Web and Software Modeling, Artificial Intelligence, and Information Retrieval and Educational Development.

**Soumia Ziti**, Ph.D. in Computer Science, is a habilitated professor in the faculty of sciences in Rabat. Her research domains include Special Classes of Graphs: Structural and Algorithmic Aspects. Her applications cover Information System Engineering, Information System Modeling, Meta-modeling, Big Data, Internet of things, Data, Graphs, metaheuristics, etc. Professor Soumia is an author and a co-author of several papers published in international journals and conferences.

# Index

Ensure Quality Research is Introduced to the Academic Community

# Become an IGI Global Reviewer for Authored Book Projects

Premier Reference Source
Emerging GIS Applications for Emergency and Disaster Management

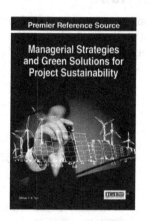
Premier Reference Source
Managerial Strategies and Green Solutions for Project Sustainability

Premier Reference Source
Comparative Approaches to Using R and Python for Statistical Data Analysis

Premier Reference Source
Solutions for High-Touch Communications in a High-Tech World

## The overall success of an authored book project is dependent on quality and timely reviews.

In this competitive age of scholarly publishing, constructive and timely feedback significantly expedites the turnaround time of manuscripts from submission to acceptance, allowing the publication and discovery of forward-thinking research at a much more expeditious rate. Several IGI Global authored book projects are currently seeking highly-qualified experts in the field to fill vacancies on their respective editorial review boards:

## Applications and Inquiries may be sent to:
development@igi-global.com

Applicants must have a doctorate (or an equivalent degree) as well as publishing and reviewing experience. Reviewers are asked to complete the open-ended evaluation questions with as much detail as possible in a timely, collegial, and constructive manner. All reviewers' tenures run for one-year terms on the editorial review boards and are expected to complete at least three reviews per term. Upon successful completion of this term, reviewers can be considered for an additional term.

If you have a colleague that may be interested in this opportunity, we encourage you to share this information with them.

# IGI Global Proudly Partners With eContent Pro International

## Receive a 25% Discount on all Editorial Services

## Editorial Services

IGI Global expects all final manuscripts submitted for publication to be in their final form. This means they must be reviewed, revised, and professionally copy edited prior to their final submission. Not only does this support with accelerating the publication process, but it also ensures that the highest quality scholarly work can be disseminated.

### English Language Copy Editing

Let eContent Pro International's expert copy editors perform edits on your manuscript to resolve spelling, punctuaion, grammar, syntax, flow, formatting issues and more.

### Scientific and Scholarly Editing

Allow colleagues in your research area to examine the content of your manuscript and provide you with valuable feedback and suggestions before submission.

### Figure, Table, Chart & Equation Conversions

Do you have poor quality figures? Do you need visual elements in your manuscript created or converted? A design expert can help!

### Translation

Need your documjent translated into English? eContent Pro International's expert translators are fluent in English and more than 40 different languages.

## Hear What Your Colleagues are Saying About Editorial Services Supported by IGI Global

"The service was very fast, very thorough, and very helpful in ensuring our chapter meets the criteria and requirements of the book's editors. I was quite impressed and happy with your service."

– Prof. Tom Brinthaupt,
Middle Tennessee State University, USA

"I found the work actually spectacular. The editing, formatting, and other checks were very thorough. The turnaround time was great as well. I will definitely use eContent Pro in the future."

– Nickanor Amwata, Lecturer,
University of Kurdistan Hawler, Iraq

"I was impressed that it was done timely, and wherever the content was not clear for the reader, the paper was improved with better readability for the audience."

– Prof. James Chilembwe,
Mzuzu University, Malawi

**Email: customerservice@econtentpro.com**          **www.igi-global.com/editorial-service-partners**